T0375213

The Internationalisation of Asset Ownership in Europe

Financial markets in Europe have become increasingly integrated in recent years, leading to a rise in foreign ownership of domestic equities and other assets. This volume brings together ten expert contributions to provide an authoritative analysis of the evolution and implications of foreign ownership in Europe today.

In addition to providing new data on the extent of foreign ownership in Europe, the authors analyse some of the major challenges it brings for policy-makers at both the European and the national level. Part I looks at the legal framework for foreign ownership and for cross-border mergers and acquisitions. Part II explores important aspects of the economic impact of foreign ownership, including taxation and labour market outcomes, from a European perspective. The volume concludes with four in-depth country studies that focus on the process of asset internationalisation in Sweden, Finland, the United Kingdom and Italy.

HARRY HUIZINGA is Professor of Economics at the University of Tilburg, the Netherlands, and former Economic Adviser to the Directorate General for Economic and Financial Affairs of the European Commission, Brussels (2000–2003). He is editor (with S. Eijffinger) of *Positive Political Economy: Theory and Evidence* (Cambridge 1998).

LARS JONUNG is Professor and Research Adviser to the Directorate General for Economic and Financial Affairs of the European Commission, Brussels. He is former Professor of Economics at the Stockholm School of Economics, Sweden, and Chief Economic Adviser to Prime Minister Carl Bildt (1992–4). He has published numerous books, both as editor and author, including *The Stockholm School of Economics Revisited* (Cambridge 1991) and *Lessons for EMU from the History of Monetary Unions* (with M. D. Bordo, IEA 2000).

The Internationalisation of Asset Ownership in Europe

Edited by

Harry Huizinga and Lars Jonung

CAMBRIDGE
UNIVERSITY PRESS

CAMBRIDGE
UNIVERSITY PRESS

University Printing House, Cambridge CB2 8BS, United Kingdom

Cambridge University Press is part of the University of Cambridge.

It furthers the University's mission by disseminating knowledge in the pursuit of education, learning and research at the highest international levels of excellence.

www.cambridge.org
Information on this title: www.cambridge.org/9780521852951

© European Communities 2005

First published 2005

A catalogue record for this publication is available from the British Library

ISBN 978-0-521-85295-1 Hardback

Contents

Figures

Tables

Contributors

KPATE ADJAOUTÉ HSBC Republik Bank – Switzerland

JYRKI ALI-YRKKÖ Research Institute of the Finnish Economy (ETLA), Helsinki

ERIK BERGLÖF Stockholm School of Economics

MIKE BURKART Stockholm School of Economics

FORREST CAPIE City University, London

JEAN-PIERRE DANTHINE University of Lausanne

CÉCILE DENIS European Commission

MAGNUS HENREKSON Stockholm School of Economics

HARRY HUIZINGA Tilburg University

DUŠAN ISAKOV University of Fribourg

ULF JAKOBSSON Research Institute of Industrial Economics (IUI), Stockholm

SEBNEM KALEMLI-OZCAN University of Houston

SERGIO MARIOTTI Politecnico of Milan

GAËTAN NICODÈME European Commission

MARTTI NYBERG Research Institute of the Finnish Economy (ETLA), Helsinki

FABRIZIO ONIDA Bocconi University, Milan

LUCIA PISCITELLO Politecnico of Milan

JEAN-PIERRE RAES European Commission

KENNETH SCHEVE University of Michigan

FRANK SENSENBRENNER City University, London

MATTHEW J. SLAUGHTER Tuck School of Business at Dartmouth, Hanover, New Hampshire

BENT SØRENSEN University of Houston

GEOFFREY WOOD City University, London

PEKKA YLÄ-ANTILLA Research Institute of the Finnish Economy (ETLA), Helsinki

OVED YOSHA University of Tel Aviv

Preface

As the economies of Europe become ever more integrated, a key dimension of change is the growing cross-border ownership of assets. This internationalisation of ownership brings important economic advantages. As asset portfolios become diversified across borders, incomes are increasingly buffered against shocks to production – and this in turn can help foster greater specialisation and efficiency in the production process. But this ongoing process also poses challenges to European policy-makers, because the integration of financial markets has moved well ahead of adjustments in the policy-making process.

To shed further light on these issues, and also to promote policy discussion, this volume documents recent developments in the foreign ownership of assets across Europe, analyses major drivers of the process and explores some of its implications.

The chapters in this book were originally presented at a conference on 'The Internationalisation of Asset Ownership in Europe', hosted by the Directorate General for Economic and Financial Affairs of the European Commission (DG ECFIN) in Brussels on 27–28 February 2003.

Remarks prepared by the discussants and by outside commentators greatly helped the authors in revising their contributions. At DG ECFIN, we would like to thank Klaus Regling, Director-General, and Jürgen Kröger, Director of Economic Studies and Research, for their generous support for this project. We are also grateful to Michèle Devuyst and Bénédicte Herry for secretarial support.

BRUSSELS, JULY 2004
HARRY HUIZINGA AND LARS JONUNG

Introduction

Harry Huizinga and Lars Jonung

The creation of a single European financial market is an objective that, to a considerable extent and in a formal sense, has already been attained. By 1990 the European Union had abolished most restrictions on international asset holdings. This means that EU member states are obliged to allow residents of other EU countries and of third countries to own national 'domestic' assets. Firms, for instance, have the right of establishment anywhere in the Union. At the same time, restrictions on the national asset composition of private and pension portfolios have been lifted. The Maastricht Treaty, which came into force in 1994, elevated the principle of internal and external capital mobility in the European Union to treaty status.

Financial market liberalisation leads to a more international investment strategy on the part of institutional as well as individual investors. On the institutional side, we expect financial market integration to cause investment funds to allocate a larger share of their overall portfolios to foreign assets, inside as well as outside the euro area. Larger foreign shares in investment portfolios logically lead to larger shares of national assets being owned by foreigners. Hence, foreign ownership of all kinds of assets – including bank assets, government bonds and equities – is expected to increase with growing financial market integration. The logic of international portfolio diversification would imply that the foreign ownership of some assets – and exchange-traded securities in particular – could approach 100 per cent, at least for some of the smaller EU member states. This would be a startling outcome, and also one for which many policy-makers seem not to be fully prepared at present.

De jure financial liberalisation has contributed to financial market integration in Europe in several ways. Figure I.1 shows the evolution of the level of international financial integration for an aggregate of industrial countries and for a sub-aggregate of EU member countries between 1991 and 2001, using an index developed by Lane and Milesi-Ferretti

1

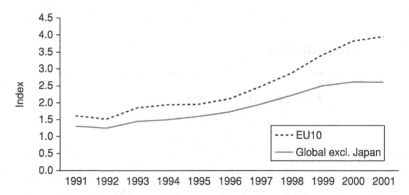

Figure I.1 International financial integration.

Note: The EU10 countries are Austria, Belgium, Denmark, Finland, France, Germany, Italy, the Netherlands, Spain and the United Kingdom. The group referred to as 'global excl. Japan' consists of the EU10 countries plus Australia, Canada, New Zealand, Switzerland and the United States.

(2003).[1] This index measures the sum of foreign assets and foreign liabilities as a ratio of GDP.[2] Figure I.1 demonstrates a strong positive trend, with a marked acceleration from the mid-1990s onwards. EU member states demonstrate above-average levels of international financial integration.

Although it is masked by the aggregate data, there is considerable cross-country variation in the degree of international financial integration and the relative importance of equity versus debt components. Table I.1 displays the country data for the most recent year available (2001, but 2000 for Sweden). The data reflect high foreign ownership rates for several asset classes in Europe. For instance, the foreign ownership shares of the equity of non-listed firms for Western and Eastern Europe are calculated to be 19.2 and 44.2 per cent respectively in 2000, as reported in this volume. In comparison, the foreign ownership shares of the equity of exchange-listed firms in Western and Eastern Europe are calculated at 27.0 and 14.2 per cent respectively in 1997. In contrast, Cai and Warnock (2004) report a foreign ownership share of US-traded equity of only 5.4 per cent in 2000. Especially in recent years the foreign ownership of exchange-traded shares in Europe has increased significantly, with foreign ownership exceeding 70 per cent of exchange-traded shares in Finland in 2000. Price-based measures of financial market

[1] See also chapter 5 in *The EU Economy: 2003 Review* (European Commission, DG ECFIN, 2003).
[2] The membership of these aggregates is determined by data availability.

Table I.1. *Overall cross-border exposure – country data*

	Sum of foreign assets and foreign liabilities as percentage of GDP	Sum of FDI and portfolio equity assets and liabilities as percentage of GDP	Net foreign assets as percentage of GDP
Austria	3.2	0.6	−0.2
Belgium	6.6	2.4	0.6
Denmark	3.1	1.3	−0.2
Finland	3.6	2.0	−0.9
France	3.6	1.7	0.1
Germany	3.0	1.0	0.1
Greece	1.5	0.2	−0.4
Ireland	15.0	6.1	−0.1
Italy	2.0	0.5	0.0
Netherlands	6.7	3.1	−0.1
Portugal	3.3	0.8	−0.4
Spain	2.4	0.9	−0.2
Sweden	3.2	1.6	−0.3
United Kingdom	6.5	2.0	0.0

Note: Figures refer to 2001 for all countries apart from Sweden, for which data refer to 2000.
Source: European Commission, DG ECFIN (2003).

integration also point to increased integration in recent years. Money market and also government bond yield differences in the euro area, for instance, have narrowed since the advent of the common currency, the euro.

Financial market integration is expected to yield a range of economic benefits. Foreign direct investment (FDI) leads to a rationalisation of production as firms aim to exploit their firm-specific technological advantages internationally. The international application of best technologies by multinational firms should enhance labour productivity everywhere and ultimately lead to higher returns to capital and higher wages. Improved international portfolio diversification, in turn, helps individuals – and also countries – to attain higher welfare by smoothing consumption in the face of asymmetric or country-specific productivity shocks.

Financial market integration may already be yielding significant benefits in terms of higher productivity and more effective international risk diversification. Further gains will be realised in the years to come, as economic agents continue to adjust to the reality of international capital mobility. However, policy-makers as well as private agents need to adjust to realise the full potential benefits of financial market integration. In the days before capital mobility, countries determined their tax and legal regimes governing capital ownership more or less in isolation, neglecting open-economy considerations. These policies mostly affected the domestic owners of national assets, thereby limiting the potential for creating international policy externalities. In the last decade or so EU countries have experienced almost complete international capital mobility, which is putting the spotlight on the implications for foreign investors of national regimes towards asset ownership. In fact, some of the shortcomings of national policy autonomy in the tax and legal areas are now becoming apparent.

With increased cross-ownership of assets, part of the incidence of capital income taxation rests on the foreign owners of national assets. In other words, part of the corporate income tax can effectively be exported to non-resident owners. International ownership of assets thus introduces an incentive for countries to increase their corporate income taxes. Some economists predict that foreign ownership will reach high levels for small open economies in the future, and consequently that tax exportation could lead to taxation levels that are 'too' high. On the other hand, increased tax competition among member states may contribute to the opposite outcome — that is, taxation levels that are 'too' low. Recently, several member states have reduced taxes on capital income significantly. At present, it is unclear which of these opposing forces will dominate in the future.

A second policy-related problem stemming from increased financial market integration is that countries may be more inclined to excuse defensive measures against hostile takeovers. The reason is that with capital mobility, a bidder for a national firm is more likely to be a foreigner. Hence, defensive measures that effectively increase the agreed takeover price for foreigners may force foreigners to pay more to acquire domestic assets. Some aspects of corporate law can thus be equivalent to export taxes on the sale of national assets in their impact on asset prices. Such implicit asset export taxation may be rational from a national political economy perspective, but it may prevent efficient international mergers and acquisitions from taking place and hence be undesirable from an EU perspective.

Along similar lines, one may argue that the internationalisation of asset ownership may constitute a barrier to improved investor protection in the form of, say, improved information flows to investors and the guaranteed independence of company boards. The reason is that, for publicly traded companies, the management and controlling sharehold-ers are often domestic, while foreigners are more commonly minority shareholders holding some shares as portfolio investments. In this scen-ario, improved investor protection will prevent domestic parties (i.e. management and controlling shareholders) from taking advantage of foreign parties (i.e. foreign, atomistic investors). In this instance, the gains to be reaped from improved investor protection will, to a large extent, accrue to foreign residents because stock prices will start to reflect the improved investor protection. Thus, the incentives for coun-tries to improve investor protection may be reduced after a significant foreign ownership share of the common stock of exchange-listed firms has been established. On the other hand, there are strong reasons for countries competing for foreign capital to improve and maintain their attractiveness by offering a good corporate governance structure.[3] Thus, we would expect the future to tell us which of these opposing forces will be the stronger one.

It is possible to argue that the problems related to the tax and legal treatment of asset ownership may get worse *after* a substantial foreign ownership share has been established. This suggests that, ideally, coun-tries should get their national tax and legal regimes in order *before* establishing full international capital mobility. However, free capital mobility has now been enshrined in the Maastricht Treaty, and hence policy-makers no longer have the luxury of discussing the optimal ordering of policy moves when considering financial market liberalisa-tion. Rather, policy-makers today face the challenge of establishing a tax and legal regime governing asset holdings that is the proper one for the European Union as a whole in the face of free capital mobility.

In practice, we see considerable variation across EU member states both in terms of capital income taxation and in the areas of the law and corporate governance. This suggests that some countries may be able to institute better policies than others, perhaps by establishing and uphold-ing an international reputation for the proper treatment of international investors. As indicated, tax and legal policies regarding asset holdings potentially have some inherently 'beggar thy neighbour' aspects, in that they may advantage domestic residents (either public or private) at the expense of foreign residents. This suggests that policies that are appro-priate for Europe as a whole cannot be established by reputation build-ing at the national level alone. Policy coordination at the European level will be necessary. Indeed, following the corporate debacles of Enron and

---

[3] This argument is stressed in chapter 5 in *The EU Economy: 2003 Review*, (European Commission, DG ECFIN 2003).

other firms in the United States, the European Union introduced a Corporate Governance Action Plan in 2003 aimed at improving corporate governance by strengthening shareholder rights through improving access to company information and facilitating voting *in absentia*. Also, the roles of independent non-executive directors and the board's accountability for the company's financial statements are to be strengthened. Similarly, coordinated policies to prevent excessive exportation of corporate income tax can be envisaged at some point in the future.

Judging from the above account, much has already happened and much is continuing to happen concerning the internationalisation of asset ownership in Europe. This volume brings together ten expert contributions that shed light on the significance and evolution of foreign ownership in today's Europe. It contains – in addition to this introduction – six 'horizontal' chapters dealing with a particular aspect of foreign ownership for several countries, followed by four country studies that examine a variety of aspects of foreign ownership for individual countries. The book is divided into three parts. Part I deals with the legal framework regarding foreign ownership in the European Union. It outlines the development of restrictions on foreign ownership in the Union and focuses on European aspects of takeover regulation. Part II is concerned with a range of recent developments regarding foreign ownership. These include how foreign ownership affects labour markets and corporate tax policies. Evidence on the extent of international portfolio diversification in the Union is also presented. Its ultimate impact on the smoothing of national consumption aggregates in the face of shocks to GDP is considered as well. Part III contains four country studies for Sweden, Finland, the United Kingdom and Italy. These case studies focus on several aspects of the process of asset internationalisation for the country in question.[4]

Part I The legal framework

A detailed account of the legal framework pertaining to foreign ownership of assets within the European Union is given in the chapter by Raes. His starting point is the Treaty of Rome, which established the free movement of goods, persons, services and capital when it came into force in 1958. However, progress concerning the free flow of capital

---

[4] The focus in this volume is on the internationalisation of asset ownership in Europe. Aspects of the evolution of ownership from a global perspective have recently been examined in the contributions in Mork (2005).

was slow. The full liberalisation of purchases and sales of financial assets and financial services did not become part of EU law until 1990. The Maastricht Treaty instituted full freedom for internal and external capital movements in the Union in 1994.

As described by Raes, the legal framework allows a number of exceptions to free capital movements, thus restricting foreign ownership. These restrictive measures are based on Community laws, on agreements between the Union and individual member states, and on the Organisation for Economic Co-operation and Development (OECD) and General Agreement on Trade in Services (GATS) frameworks. Restrictions on the free flow of capital may, according to Community laws, be based on several grounds, 'general interest' considerations being perhaps the most pertinent to current policy-making. Under this heading we find a set of nationally applied techniques to prevent or reduce foreign ownership, such as 'golden shares', limits on share voting rights, veto rights concerning mergers and acquisitions, etc. Raes also deals with third-country restrictions adopted by the Community, and with international cooperation concerning capital flows. Finally, he notes that the abstract rules of the Maastricht Treaty are being clarified by crucial decisions by the European Court of Justice. Thus, case law is currently in the process of evolving in this field.

Barriers to international takeovers that one member state considers to be in the 'general interest' may stand in the way of the restructuring of corporate Europe – a process that is commonly deemed necessary to improve overall production capacity. The legal barriers to such a restructuring have become more glaring since the introduction of the common currency and the elimination of across-the-board capital controls. The solution appears to be an EU directive on takeovers.

In their chapter, Berglöf and Burkart point out that large differences in corporate governance among EU member states, in particular between the UK system and those of Continental Europe, have made it difficult to establish pan-European takeover directives. Attempts by the European Commission to get legislation passed by the European Parliament failed in 2001.

To get things moving again, the Winter Group, set up by the European Commission, examined these and related issues in a set of reports published in 2002.[5] The Winter Group advocates more contestability of corporate ownership and a more level playing field for takeovers by suggesting a mandatory bid rule and a break-through rule. The latter rule is to enable a bidder who has achieved a qualified majority of equity

---

[5] See European Commission (2002) – 'the Winter Report'.

to overcome statutory defences, including any differentiation of votes. This break-through rule proved controversial and was subsequently dropped from the Commission's draft directive on cross-border mergers. In the final directive the break-through rule and the defensive measure provisions were reinserted, but as optional items.

After describing the prevailing systems of ownership and control in Europe, Berglöf and Burkart make an assessment of the impact of various proposals for pan-European takeover rules, based on a survey of empirical and theoretical work on corporate governance and on takeovers. Here they identify a number of trade-offs and inconsistencies. In short, every step towards a common system will impact differentially across the member states due to differences in initial conditions. In their conclusions, Berglöf and Burkart stress that existing corporate governance structures in Europe have evolved into complex and interdependent systems. We should not expect the search for a common system to be an easy one. They suggest that national as well as EU takeover regulation should aim primarily at improving transparency as a way of fostering corporate governance in Europe.

Part II Recent developments

Firms engaging in FDI combine international technology and product knowledge with local labour. Thus, FDI can be expected to affect national labour markets. Indeed, one major potential benefit of inward FDI is improved labour market opportunities for local workers. Scheve and Slaughter set out to evaluate the impact of inward FDI on European labour markets in their contribution. After reviewing recent trends in US foreign direct investment in Europe, they conclude that it is unclear whether multinationals increase the relative demand for high-skill labour in host countries. There is substantial evidence, however, that multinationals pay higher wages, even after controlling for plant characteristics such as plant size. This wage premium may reflect higher worker productivity due to the superior technology or business practices used by multinationals. Alternatively, multinationals may pay higher wages due to greater job insecurity.

Scheve and Slaughter argue that multinationals that operate in more competitive international markets may display a relatively elastic labour demand that at the same time is subject to shocks in the international market place. As a result, local labour market outcomes at foreign-owned plants may be more variable. Indeed, they find that worker insecurity in the United Kingdom, as perceived by the workers themselves, is positively correlated with the FDI share in their industry of employment.

As evidence of international rent sharing, Scheve and Slaughter further discuss the finding that worker compensation at foreign plants appears to be influenced by a multinational's worldwide profitability.

A second major advantage of FDI is that multinational firms contribute corporate income taxes to national treasuries. In fact, high rates of foreign ownership in local firms may provide countries with an incentive to impose relatively high corporate income taxes, as part of the corporate income tax burden is effectively exported. In their contribution, Denis, Huizinga and Nicodème report some evidence that foreign ownership and effective rates of corporate taxes are indeed positively related across Europe. The positive impact of foreign ownership on taxation may have prevented a 'race to the bottom' in corporate income tax rates in Europe so far. It may turn into a challenge for policy-makers if foreign ownership rates continue to increase in the future. For the year 2000 the average foreign ownership share in Europe is reported to be 26.7 per cent for firms without an exchange listing. There are reasons to expect this number to grow in the future.

Denis, Huizinga and Nicodème also present some evidence on the determinants of the foreign ownership of non-listed equities. Among these determinants are indicators of the quality of a country's corporate governance and of its rule of law. Specifically, foreign ownership rates appear to be higher in countries with weaker investor protection. The reason may be that multinational firms – subject to relatively high-quality home-country investor protection standards – have a comparative advantage when operating in countries with lower standards. The tendency for countries with weak shareholder protection to attract high rates of foreign ownership may provide these countries with an incentive to improve investor protection in order to avoid completely losing control over their private sectors.

The mirror image of the internationalisation of national physical assets is the internationalisation of investment portfolios. Adjaouté, Danthine and Isakov ask whether the investment portfolios of Europeans are now better diversified than they were five or ten years ago, and whether trends towards increased international diversification have been accelerated by the advent of the euro. The evidence they present points towards some favourable, if modest, changes. The elimination of currency-matching requirements within the euro area has certainly led institutional investors to increase their holdings of international securities. This has been accompanied by a strong convergence of yields on EU government securities.

Similarly, there is evidence that equity risk premia across European stock markets are converging. For firms in countries with hitherto high-risk premia, this convergence has brought a reduction in the cost of equity capital. The introduction of the euro is reported to have led to a shift in the investment strategies of European equity investors from focusing on country portfolios to focusing on Europe-wide industry portfolios. Such a paradigm shift makes sense if the introduction of the euro has significantly reduced the country-level risk associated, for instance, with national currencies. The authors do, in fact find some evidence that in recent years a strategy of combining industry portfolios could have performed better than the old method of weighing country portfolios. An exclusive focus on industry risk, however, would leave some opportunities to diversify risk internationally unexploited, even in the current euro area. Changes in investor behaviour and asset price formation have so far not led to a strong correlation of consumption growth rates across European countries. This suggests that significant progress can still be made in asset diversification in Europe.

Kalemli-Ozcan, Sørensen and Yosha examine in detail whether the recent rise in financial integration in Europe, including cross-border holdings of financial claims and cross-border ownership of firms, has contributed to risk sharing and consumption smoothing. They start from the fact that capital markets allow individuals as well as countries to separate production (output) and consumption decisions. Hence, in principle, capital markets can provide a mechanism for risk sharing, or 'macroeconomic insurance'. In line with this, the authors explore empirically the extent of risk sharing within the European Union through net factor income flows – being the difference between GDP (the value of the aggregate production within a country) and GNP (the value of aggregate production owned by residents of a country). Their econometric tests for the EU member states show that, in most recent years, financial integration across member states has buffered asymmetric shocks in a way identical to the pattern reported for the United States. Furthermore, risk sharing is rising in the euro area, although it is far less pronounced than in the United States. They expect this rise to continue in the future.

Finally, turning to policy conclusions, Kalemli-Ozcan, Sørensen and Yosha recommend measures to foster financial integration within the European Union. Such measures will lead to improved risk insurance, thus facilitating adjustment to country-specific shocks in the Union.

Part III Country studies

This part presents case studies of the evolution and impact of foreign ownership in four European countries: Sweden, Finland, the United

Kingdom and Italy. Sweden and Finland have experienced remarkable increases in foreign ownership in the past ten years as a result of financial deregulation and other legal changes affecting foreign investors. Due to this rapid transformation of the distribution of the ownership of firms and financial assets, foreign ownership has received considerable attention in public debate.[6] In contrast, the United Kingdom has traditionally been more open to foreign investments, and foreign ownership of United Kingdom enterprises has not been seen as a concern in political discussion.

For the case of Sweden, Henrekson and Jakobsson provide a broad survey of the forces determining the ownership structure and corporate governance in a small open economy with a strong corporatist political culture where the ownership of capital and the control of firms are strongly separated, as in many other European countries – in contrast to the US corporate governance model. In fact, no other industrial country demonstrates such a large gap between cash-flow rights and control rights as Sweden. Benefiting from access to a wealth of data (generally lacking for most EU member states), they explain the evolution of the Swedish model of corporate governance since World War II. They distinguish between two phases. In the first phase, from the end of World War II to the mid-1980s, when financial markets were strongly regulated and foreigners were barred from the Stockholm Stock Exchange, a small set of domestic owners emerged controlling the equity – that is, the voting rights – of Swedish industry. According to Henrekson and Jakobsson, this pattern was due to a 'paradoxical' but deliberate policy regarding ownership and private wealth creation. Tax policies as well as other policies were designed to discourage private wealth holdings, while corporate policies encouraged the control of ownership with a small private wealth basis through the use of differential voting rights and of private foundations with tax-exempt status.

The second phase began when Swedish financial markets and the market for ownership were deregulated during the 1990s, allowing foreign capital to flow into Sweden and foreign investors to compete with domestic ones for the ownership of Swedish companies. As domestic ownership remained subject to discriminatory taxation compared to foreign ownership, this contributed to a process whereby foreigners rapidly acquired a sizeable share of Swedish firms and equity. Several

---

[6] For example, economic issues pertaining to foreign ownership in Sweden are examined in the contributions in Jonung (2002). They deal with three major questions: the causes of changes in domestic/foreign ownership, the consequences of foreign ownership, and policy responses to foreign ownership. In Finland a similar debate is taking place, as reported in chapter 8.

major companies listed on the Stockholm Stock Exchange, such as Volvo, Saab, Aga and other 'crown jewels', were taken over by foreign companies. The number of employees in foreign-owned firms has expanded rapidly in the past ten years.

At present two different forces are challenging the Swedish corporate control model: first, rising foreign ownership; and, second, the growth of large corporatist pension funds. Henrekson and Jakobsson argue that the present corporate model does not appear to be sustainable. Current owners do not command the financial resources required to maintain their control. Thus, pressure is strong to reduce the gap between cash-flow rights and control rights. In this way the old Swedish model of concentrated private corporate control will be phased out, or, at least, decline in importance. A model is emerging in which the government and a few large corporate and private pension funds will be the dominating domestic owners. At the same time, the share of foreign ownership will increase. It is too early to tell what kind of corporate governance model will evolve from this new ownership situation.

Finland has seen a dramatic increase in the foreign ownership of shares in listed Finnish companies, to over 60 per cent in 2002, as shown by Ylä-Anttila, Ali-Yrkkö and Nyberg. Fundamental changes in the Finnish financial system over the past twenty years – the liberalisation of both domestic and international capital movements – were instrumental in the internationalisation of the ownership of Finnish assets. These changes, incidentally, contributed to a deep economic crisis in the early 1990s. Foreign investors have been attracted to Finland in part by the potential to benefit from its technological edge, but this also raises concerns that advanced technologies will be transferred abroad.

Ylä-Anttila, Ali-Yrkkö and Nyberg argue that the globalisation of Finnish capital markets has occasioned several changes in the corporate governance of Finnish firms, such as greater stress being placed on more independent boards of directors and a shift of emphasis towards creating shareholder value. Empirical evidence using firm-level data shows that foreign-owned firms have performed much better than domestic ones in creating added value and achieving a high return on capital. The large outward flow of FDI is consistent with the view that Finland is attractive as a country for the location of headquarters. Social stability and high-quality data communication links favour setting up headquarters in Finland. Other factors, however, work towards the migration of corporate headquarters out of Finland – such as the Finnish system of taxation with regard to options and personal income.

In the United Kingdom, foreign direct investment and the foreign ownership of domestic companies have failed to attract political reactions – in contrast to the experience in Sweden and Finland. In their contribution on the political economy of foreign investment in the United Kingdom, Capie, Wood and Sensenbrenner argue that foreign ownership has been a political 'non-issue'. They engage in the task of exploring a set of social, political and economic factors determining why this should be so. After describing the evolution of foreign investment in the United Kingdom in a historical perspective, presenting some 'new political economy' hypotheses to explain the British attitudes of benign neglect towards foreign ownership, and surveying previous work on inward investment into the country, they sift through the evidence.

Pulling together their survey of determinants, they conclude that foreign ownership has not been determined by the party in power, the exchange rate regime or the macroeconomic situation. They point to two important factors behind the UK view. First, the United Kingdom has been a major capital exporter for a long time. Thus, when capital started to flow inwards, there was a general belief in the benefits of free cross-border flows of asset ownership. Second, the UK system of corporate governance has played an important role. The United Kingdom's 'outside' corporate governance system, in contrast to the mostly 'inside' corporate governance systems on the Continent, has given management a strong position vis-à-vis the shareholders. In this case, the issue of whether ownership is national or foreign becomes less of an issue.

Finally, Mariotti, Onida and Piscitello present a study of foreign ownership and firm performance in Italy. In recent years Italy appears to have received relatively little inward FDI. Inward FDI represented only 6.3 per cent of gross capital formation in Italy in 2000 – against 42.2 per cent for the European Union as a whole. In 2002, after the bubble had burst, the difference was smaller but still significant: 6.2 per cent in Italy versus 22.5 per cent in the union. The share of employment at foreign-owned companies in Italy, at 17.9 per cent, was also relatively small in a European context. Data from the Reprint database reveals that most FDI is in manufacturing, is majority-owned by the parent company, has Europe as the investing region and is located in the Italian North-West. In addition, recent flows of inward FDI have been mainly directed at smaller companies, although start-ups or greenfield investments play only a minor role.

Mariotti, Onida and Piscitello go on to test how a foreign acquisition of an Italian plant affects employment and labour productivity, compared to plants that are taken over by a domestic firm or not taken over at all. Compared to no takeover, a foreign takeover leads to significant increases in both employment and labour productivity a few years after the acquisition, especially if the target firm is small or if the investor is a

European firm. A domestic acquisition, by contrast, appears to have no significant impact on labour productivity, while employment may even fall. They conclude that FDI in Italy appears to have brought medium-term benefits in terms of job creation and competitiveness. Thus, policies aimed at attracting foreign investors may have beneficial effects on this account.

Together, these four case studies show that the actual and perceived role of foreign ownership has varied considerably across European countries in recent years. Finland has attained a very high share of foreign ownership of listed companies – at more than 60 per cent in 2002. Financial market liberalisation and the logic of portfolio diversification imply that this may be what is in store for the rest of the European Union as well in the foreseeable future. In fact, foreign capital inflows have already played a major role in the transformation of the economies of the new member states that entered the Union in 2004.

A major challenge for European policy-makers now is to agree on minimum coordinated policies towards the ownership of capital and corporate governance in order to make high levels of foreign ownership sustainable in the future. Only then can Europe fully realise the potential benefits of foreign ownership in terms of higher levels of productivity and risk reduction through portfolio diversification.

REFERENCES

Cai, F., and F. E. Warnock (2004), *International Diversification at Home and Abroad*, International Financial Discussion Paper no. 793, Board of Governors of the Federal Reserve, Washington, DC.
European Commission (2002), *Report of the High-level Group of Company Law Experts on a Modern Regulatory Framework for Company Law in Europe*, Brussels ('the Winter Report').
European Commission, Directorate General for Economic and Financial Affairs, (2003), 'Determinants of international capital flows', *The EU Economy: 2003 Review*, Brussels, chap. 5.
Jonung, L. (ed.) (2002), *Vem skall äga Sverige? (Who Will Own Sweden?)*, SNS Förlag, Stockholm.
Lane, P. R., and G. M. Milesi-Ferretti (2003), 'International financial integration', *International Monetary Fund Staff Papers*, 82–113.
Mork, R. (ed.) (2005), *A History of Corporate Governance Around the World*, University of Chicago Press, Chicago.

Part I

The legal framework

1   Legal restrictions on foreign ownership in the European Union

Jean-Pierre Raes

1.   Introduction

This chapter gives a brief description of the rules that currently govern capital movements, and thus foreign ownership, in the European Union.[1] It starts with the developments that led to the establishment of the full freedom of capital movements. Then it presents the main exceptions to this freedom under the provisions of the Maastricht Treaty. Finally, it comments on the impact of such exceptions on the ownership of EU companies by foreign investors.

2.   Negotiating the rules

Since July 1990 the freedom of capital movements and payments has been established within the European Community.[2] From the outset of the negotiations for the Maastricht Treaty, a majority of the member states were of the opinion that the European Community should apply the principle of full freedom of capital movements, not only within the Community but also vis-à-vis third countries. Furthermore, the belief was that this external opening should be unconditional. Third countries would benefit from this capital movements freedom irrespective of their level of liberalisation towards the European Community.[3]

The purpose was to transform the European internal financial market into an outward-looking and open area, which would allow a more efficient allocation of capital. There were several reasons for this liberalisation towards third countries as well.

The views expressed in this chapter are exclusively those of the author. They should not be attributed to the European Commission.

[1] The European Union, which was established by the Maastricht Treaty, is founded on the European Communities, supplemented by several policies and forms of cooperation such as the 'common foreign and security policy' and the 'common defence policy'.

[2] Through the entry into force of Directive 88/361/EEC of 24 June 1988.

[3] See Vigneron and Steinfeld (1996).

(a) Freedom of capital movements was already practised by a number of member states. Therefore, if some member states were to continue applying restrictions towards third countries, these could be easily circumvented via more liberal member states.

(b) In the context of the scheduled Economic and Monetary Union (EMU), there was a fear that restrictions vis-à-vis third countries might influence the exchange rates of national currencies in the run-up to the determination of conversion rates to the single currency.

(c) The threat of capital movement restrictions vis-à-vis third countries would increase uncertainties in financial markets.

(d) Restrictions would hinder the development of the financial services sector of the European Union.

As most member states wished to apply the principle of full freedom of capital movements vis-à-vis third countries as well, the preliminary draft articles for the new regime contained the following provisions.[4]

(a) The full freedom of capital movements and payments (between member states and towards third countries).

(b) The right of member states to take measures against free capital movements for statistical, taxation or supervision purposes.

(c) The right of the Community to adopt safeguard measures when capital movements to or from third countries cause serious difficulties for the operation of the EMU.

(d) The right to impose financial sanctions on third countries (e.g. the freezing of assets and a ban on investment).

When the comprehensive draft treaty text, which would form the basis for political negotiations, was presented in 1991 to the Conference of the Representatives of the Governments of the Member States, the basic principle of the full freedom of capital movements and payments and the above exceptions were included.

Examining these draft provisions, the Commission services expressed a number of concerns. The overriding external liberalisation – a clear political wish from member states – was not questioned. However, the way this external liberalisation was drafted would have given third-country residents unconditional and unlimited treaty rights with respect to all categories of capital movements. This very liberal approach would have had two effects: first, some existing Community or national laws, including restrictions vis-à-vis third countries, would have been

---

[4] See Bakker (1996).

outlawed, and, second, it would have been impossible to have future Community policies providing for such third-country restrictions.

At the time, potential problems were identified, in particular concerning direct investment and establishment (considering existing restrictions in the Community framework governing transport, shipping, the media, etc.), the admission of securities (in view of existing administrative barriers to issues of third-country securities) and the cross-border provision of services (since a reciprocity condition existed in the Second Banking Directive).

The conference acknowledged these concerns by complementing the draft text with a new article allowing the Community and member states to cover existing restrictions vis-à-vis third countries and to adopt future Community restrictions in the above-mentioned areas.

At the same time, a clause on tax differentiation in capital movements was sought by some member states, as they were worried that they would be obliged to extend tax credits to companies located in tax havens. This was granted.

3.   The present EU regime

Since the Maastricht Treaty on European Union entered into force on 1 January 1994, capital movements and payments have been governed by its Articles 56 to 60. These articles are declared 'directly applicable', which means that they do not require any national transposition measures (e.g. directives, regulations) for their implementation by member states.

Articles 56 to 60 of the Treaty have put the capital movements provisions negotiated at Maastricht in concrete form. By default, the full freedom of capital movements and payments within the European Union and towards third countries is established [Art. 56]. However, this absolute freedom may be limited either by member states or the Union (depending on the exceptions invoked) through recourse to a list of specific exceptions.[5]

Thanks to a grandfathering clause, member states and the European Union have the right to maintain restrictions on capital movements that existed as of 31 December 1993 (i.e. the day before the entry into force of the present regime) under, respectively, national and EU law in relation to 'direct investment – including real estate[6] – establishment,

---

[5] See Raes (2002).

[6] The specification that direct investment could include investment in real estate was inserted at the request of Greece during the 'cleaning process' of the texts adopted in Maastricht.

the provision of financial services or the admission of securities to capital markets' [Art. 57.1]. Furthermore, the Union has the right either to liberalise further or restrict these transactions, subject to more stringent decision-making criteria [Art. 57.2].

In the fiscal area, member states have the right to differentiate between taxpayers according to their place of residence (fiscal non-residents benefit from tax exemptions in most member states) or the place where their capital is invested (usually, foreign investments will be discriminated against through a less favourable tax treatment) [Art. 58.1.a]. Member states also have the right to adopt measures necessary to prevent infringements of national legislation in the field of taxation (e.g. declaration procedures for private individuals, reporting requirements for the financial sector) and the prudential supervision of financial institutions (the existing EU financial legislation is the most relevant source of information with respect to national prudential rules compatible with the regime) [Art. 58.1.b]. Moreover, member states also have the right to adopt any measure justified on grounds of 'public policy' or 'public security' [Art. 58.1.b].

Finally, should exceptionally disturbing capital movements with third countries endanger the operation of the EMU, it is possible for the European Union to adopt restrictive measures for a period not exceeding six months [Art. 59]. In the context of the Common Foreign and Security Policy of the European Union, sanctions against specific third countries may also be enforced [Art. 60].

4.   The potential impact on foreign ownership

The various restrictions that may result from the implementation of Articles 57 to 60 of the Treaty are heterogeneous by nature and by purpose.[7] The EMU clause provides for measures of a temporary character. The financial sanctions that can be enforced vis-à-vis third countries are, in spite of their economic relevance, undoubtedly politically inspired. The measures aimed at protecting financial institutions from excessive risk-taking in their activities are motivated by prudential considerations. In the fiscal area, eligible measures aim either at ensuring the enforcement of domestic tax legislation or at allowing different treatment of domestic and foreign taxpayers.

Although some of these measures may also impact on the foreign ownership of EU assets, and in particular on the ownership of EU companies, this is not their primary purpose. In contrast, the remaining

[7] See Mydske (2000).

exceptions provided for by the EU regime aim (formally or de facto) to monitor or limit the possibility for foreign investors to reach full or majority ownership of companies established in the European Union.

(a) The provisions of Article 57 exclusively target specific capital movements between the Community and third countries. On the one hand, the possibility of restricting the admission of securities to capital markets has been made obsolete by the full development of EU capital markets, while restrictions on the provisions of financial services were substantially reduced through the successive EU offers under the General Agreement on Trade in Services. In contrast, restrictions affecting 'direct investment – including real estate – establishment' have often been maintained by either member states or the European Union,[8] and obviously affect the scope for foreign investors to take control of Community companies.

(b) The 'public policy' and 'public security' exceptions[9] laid down in Article 58.1.b may be invoked by member states to justify, in particular, restrictions on foreign investment, and thus the ownership, of EU companies. Furthermore, the European Court of Justice, which is the sole institution entitled to interpret definitively the EU treaty, has developed in various rulings over the past decade the 'general interest' exception.[10] By nature, this open-ended concept appears to be very close to the concepts of 'public policy' and 'public security', but with a potentially broader scope of application. In particular, the Court of Justice considers that the need to protect the 'general interest' allows member states to derogate from treaty obligations, including those governing capital movements and ownership. Therefore, national restrictions[11] adopted in accordance with the above three exceptions may hinder investments by foreign investors in Community companies.

As far as foreign investment is concerned, the scope of application pertaining to Article 57 is well defined and provides, therefore, for

---

[8] While 'establishment' is not a capital movement as such, it is a subset of 'direct investment' under Community legislation. According to the EU definition, 'direct investment' includes in particular the 'establishment and extension of branches or new undertakings belonging solely to the person providing the capital, and the acquisition in full of existing undertakings'.

[9] Since both concepts are undefined, this leaves a certain margin of discretion to member states in invoking these exceptions either to control or prohibit specific capital movements, which gives rise to some legal uncertainties for foreign investors.

[10] Also known as 'general good' or 'mandatory requirements'.

[11] Ultimately, the European Court of Justice decides on the compatibility of member states' restrictions with the 'general interest' exception.

restrictions that are compatible with the present EU regime. In contrast, the fact that the concepts of 'public policy', 'public security' and 'general interest' are not defined in the Treaty implies that the Court of Justice is responsible for the progressive definition of their scope, including in the field of restrictions on foreign investment.

While the latter may essentially be seen as a legal process, its relevance in regulatory and economic terms should not be underestimated. Considering the lack of interpretation of these general exceptions in the EU treaty, each related Court of Justice ruling assesses the compatibility of national restrictions on investment with respect to (a) the nature and scope of the restrictions and (b) the economic sector where these national restrictions are enforced.

The latter aspect results from the fact that 'general interest' considerations, according to the Court of Justice, do not apply to all economic activities. Furthermore, when 'general-interest'-related activities (mainly in the field of services) are regulated at Community level, they are governed by EU directives or regulations that include some provisions aimed at protecting the 'general interest'. National investment restrictions going beyond these Community 'general interest' clauses can be acknowledged as necessary and legitimate by the Court of Justice.

Therefore, the effect of Court of Justice rulings on national restrictions affecting, for instance, foreign investment in a given company is not limited to the compatibility of such restrictions in that particular company. The scope of applicability of these Court of Justice rulings covers all companies active in the same economic sector and established in the European Community. This explains the high economic relevance of the developing Court of Justice case law in the field of investment restrictions.

5.   Restrictions on foreign investment

As explained earlier, the EU regime on capital movements in conjunction with its related Court of Justice case law allow for the adoption of restrictions on foreign investment either at EU or at member state level. Beyond the legal basis provided by the EU treaty, it is useful to identify (a) the economic activities that are subject to foreign investment restrictions in unquestionable conformity with treaty provisions (i.e. those enshrined in Community legislation), and (b) the economic activities where foreign investment restrictions could be justified on the basis of 'general interest' considerations (i.e. those adopted independently by member states) as well as the possible confirmation provided by the Court of Justice with respect to their compatibility with treaty provisions.

5.1   Restrictions in EU legislation

As far as EU regulations and directives are concerned, investment, and thus ownership, by foreign investors in the European Union is subject to certain restrictions only in a small number of economic sectors, as discussed below.[12,13]

5.1.1 *Air transport*   Following the creation of the Single Market in 1992, and considering the need to ensure the defence of Community interests in the field of air transport, the concept of 'Community air carriers' was established by Community legislation, while free market access was reserved for such companies.[14] 'Community air carriers' must have their principal place of business and registered office located in a member state, and must be effectively controlled by member states and/or nationals of member states, either directly or through majority ownership.

While the requirement for majority Community ownership means that third-country ownership in such carriers is limited to 49.9 per cent of the capital (as compared with a 25 per cent limit in the United States), the complementary 'effective control' condition may further limit such investment possibilities.[15] Depending on the circumstances of an individual case, a single third-country stake of almost 50 per cent may actually prevent Community shareholders from controlling the carrier within the meaning of Community legislation.

5.1.2 *Maritime transport*   Against the same background, the freedom to provide maritime transport services within member states was reserved to 'Community shipowners', which are defined by Community legislation as shipping companies established in a member state

---

[12] Restrictions on investment deriving from horizontal Community regimes will not be assessed here. Broadly, these consist of (a) the competition policy (Articles 85 to 90 of the treaty establish the basic principles for competition rules and merger control on a Community-wide basis and apply indifferently on EU and foreign investors), and (b) the taxation policy (the unusual but binding Community provisions in this area are generally reserved for companies established in the Community).

[13] See Raes (2003).

[14] Council Regulation (EEC) no. 2407/92 of 23 July 1992, on the licensing of air carriers.

[15] Regulation no. 2407/92, Article 2(g). 'Effective control means a relationship constituted by rights, contracts or any other means which, either separately or jointly and having regard to the considerations of fact or law involved, confer the possibility of directly or indirectly exercising a decisive influence on an undertaking, in particular by: (a) the right to use all or part of the assets of an undertaking; (b) rights or contracts which confer a decisive influence on the running of the business of the undertaking.'

and with their principal place of business located, and effective control exercised, in a member state.[16]

    5.1.3 Inland waterways transport The provision of transport services of goods and passengers by carriers, within a member state where they are not established, requires Community establishment and ownership of vessels used either by nationals of member states or by legal persons majority-owned by nationals of member states.[17] As to transport services between member states, the conditions under which carriers may supply such services are similar to those imposed within a member state.[18]

    5.1.4 Energy With respect to prospecting for and the exploration and production of hydrocarbons, member states may be granted the right to deny entry to entities from a third country, if the latter does not grant similar treatment to Community residents.[19]

    5.1.5 Audio-visual There are no Community rules restricting either third-country investments in the Community audio-visual sector or a branch or subsidiary of a third-country undertaking from operating in this sector on equal terms with Community-controlled companies. However, the Community framework provides for specific 'performance requirements' (European works get privileged treatment from broadcasters) and 'financial incentives' (Community financial support in some areas is reserved for Community-controlled companies and member states' nationals) that impact indirectly on third-country investment.

    5.1.6 Financial services The Community framework on financial services provides for certain 'reciprocity requirements' vis-à-vis third countries with respect to direct investment in Community financial institutions and establishment in the Community of third-country institutions. When Community credit institutions, insurance companies or securities firms are not granted by a third-country effective market access and national treatment in the carrying on of their respective activities, member states can retaliate against planned direct investments from firms established in that third-country. While the Community directives

---

[16] Council Regulation (EEC) no. 3577/92 of 7 December 1992.
[17] Council Regulation (EEC) no. 3921/91 of 16 December 1991.
[18] Council Regulation (EEC) no. 1356/96 of 8 July 1996.
[19] Directive 94/22/EC of the European Parliament and of the Council of 30 May 1994.

involved are still in force, most third-country restrictions have been waived by the Community under the GATS.

5.2.   *Restrictions in member states' legislation*

Besides the above restrictions provided by Community legislation, member states also have the right to invoke treaty exceptions ('public policy', 'public security') and Court of Justice case law ('general interest') to enforce restrictions on foreign investment. While these do not necessarily target exclusively third-country investors, it is clear that the latter category is systematically covered by existing national restrictions.

5.2.1 A growing recourse to 'general interest' considerations   First, it should be pointed out that the authorities in member states have resorted more frequently to such types of restrictions over the past decade. During this period the Community adopted a set of directives aimed at gradually liberalising various public utilities sectors (e.g. electricity, gas, telecommunications, post) generally managed by state monopolies. This incited most member states to embark on a privatisation process of such companies with a view to enhancing their efficiency. The consequence of the implemented economic reform was a huge increase of investment flows to and within the Community (see figure 1.1). Confronted with this situation, some member states felt it necessary to introduce specific measures in order to monitor, and in certain cases control, this development.

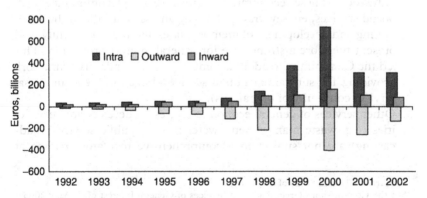

Figure 1.1. EU15 FDI flows.
Source: Eurostat, Newcronos.

Generally, these measures imposed restrictions on investment in the above-mentioned sectors or companies. Depending on their nature, the effect of these restrictions is either direct (e.g. an absolute investment ceiling or an authorisation procedure for the planned acquisition of capital) or indirect (e.g. veto rights on strategic decisions such as mergers and acquisitions, the limitation of voting rights or the privileged representation of national authorities on management boards). In most cases, member states justified such restrictions by the need to protect the 'general interest', arguing that the protective provisions of Community directives were actually insufficient to guarantee the quality and the continuity of service in crisis situations.

5.2.2 *Scope of application*   While the Court of Justice developed the concept of 'general interest' over the 1990s, the relevance of 'services of general economic interest' for the Community was finally recognised in the Treaty of Amsterdam.[20] Although it is not defined in the treaty or in secondary legislation, there is broad agreement that this notion refers to 'services of an economic nature which the member states or the Community subject to specific public service obligations by virtue of a general interest criterion'.[21] By extension, 'services of general interest' have a broader scope and cover both market and non-market services subject to public service obligations.

In spite of the lack of definition, and the evolving character of the concept, the main 'services of general interest' are identified and can be classified in three categories according to the need and intensity of Community action and the role of the member states.[22]

(a) Services of general economic interest provided by large network industries. These economic activities (e.g. telecommunications, postal services, energy, transport) play an essential role in the functioning and development of member states and the Community, and present therefore a strong case for general interest protection. This led the Community to adopt a comprehensive regulatory framework providing for substantial public service obligations (e.g. universal service, continuity of operations).

(b) Other services of general economic interest. These economic activities (e.g. waste management, water supply, public service broadcasting) are not subject to a comprehensive regulatory regime at

---

[20] See Articles 16 and 86(2) of the treaty.

[21] See the Commission's Green Paper on Services of General Interest of 21 May 2003 – COM(2003) 270 final.

[22] See Commission's Green Paper on Services of General Interest.

Community level. Therefore, the need for general interest protection is usually considered at the level of member states and can be subject to diverse interpretations.

(c) Non-economic services and services without effect on trade. Broadly, this category covers activities that constitute prerogatives of public authorities (e.g. justice, foreign relations) as well as those conducted by organisations performing largely social functions (e.g. trade unions, non-profit organisations). In general, these activities are exempted from the basic treaty provisions on Single Market freedoms and competition rules. Consequently, they are usually not governed by harmonised Community rules.

Among these three categories, services of general economic interest provided by large network industries are the most relevant in economic terms. This is the main reason why the European Community gradually developed, since the run-up to the establishment of the Single Market, a Community legal framework governing these specific services. This specific framework (e.g. regulations and directives) aimed at the establishment of a level playing field within the Community by defining common rules for the provision of such services.

In particular, these common rules include a set of public service obligations that aim to protect the 'general interest'. Usually, these public service obligations cover the provision of a 'universal service' (i.e. guaranteed access to all persons in the Community to certain essential services at an affordable price), the continuity of the services concerned (i.e. the uninterrupted provision of some essential services) and minimum quality requirements attached to services offered, as well as the protection of users and consumers.

5.2.3 Implementation of 'general interest' restrictions by member states The EU approach allows that some economic activities carried out in competitive markets must be regulated, among others, by provisions aimed at protecting the 'general interest'. In this context, one of the basic objectives of the EU legislator is to ensure that the nature and scope of public service obligations laid down in the corresponding regulations and directives are such that this protection is effective. Otherwise, member states might consider that the adoption of complementary 'general interest' restrictions is necessary to reach the desired level of protection finally.

Some member states decided to complement the genuine 'general interest' protective measures of the EU framework (and its transposition in national legislation) with several types of measures forming either direct or indirect restrictions on foreign investment and ownership in specific sectors or companies (as mentioned in section 2.2.1). While some of these complementary national restrictions were simply redundant with respect to the existing EU measures in regulations and directives (and therefore unnecessary), others clearly had no direct effect on the protection of the 'general interest' (which implies that these pursued other objectives, sometimes inspired by 'national interest' considerations).

Irrespective of the goal actually pursued by such complementary restrictions, the fact that these are independently designed and enforced by member states weakens the idea of a level playing field established by the Community framework. Furthermore, their frequent discretionary character creates legal certainty for foreign investors trying to take over companies established in the European Community.

Many of these complementary restrictions on investment enforced by the authorities in member states are not justified by 'general interest' (or 'public policy'/'public security') considerations, and are therefore incompatible with the freedom of capital movements guaranteed by the treaty.

Following the European Commission's assessment on the admissibility of these restrictions, in recent years the Court of Justice has ruled a few times on 'general-interest'-related restrictions on investment in EU companies or sectors. In 2000 it condemned Italy for investment restrictions contained in the 1994 Law on Privatisation on ENI and Telecom Italia.[23] In 2002 Portugal was condemned for its framework law on privatisation, which provided for the possibility of restricting foreign participation in several sectors and companies.[24] France was also condemned for holding a 'golden share' in the petroleum company Elf-Aquitaine, which established a system of prior authorisation for all shareholdings exceeding certain voting rights ceilings as well as a veto right to oppose any decision to transfer or use as security the assets of four subsidiaries of the company.[25]

In contrast, the Court of Justice authorised Belgium to maintain its 'golden shares' in Distrigaz SA and Société Nationale de Transport par Canalisations SA (both active in the gas industry), by which Belgium reserved the right to oppose any major strategic company's decision that might 'adversely' affect the country's interest in the energy sector.[26] In

[23] Case C-58/99, judgement of 23 May 2000.
[24] Commission v Portugal (case C-367/98).
[25] Commission v France (case C-483/99).
[26] Commission v Belgium (case C-503/99).

this case, the Court of Justice considered that these special powers were justified, in particular, by the direct link with the public service obligations of both companies.

In 2003 the Court of Justice condemned Spain for its Privatisation Law of 1995, which provided for prior authorisation requirement for the dissolution, sale of assets, change in business aims, and acquisition by any investor of 10 per cent of the capital of privatised companies.[27] At the time of the Court of Justice ruling, special rights were still valid for Endesa (electricity), Telefonica (telecommunication), Repsol (oil) and Indra (banking). At the same time, the 'special share' held by the government of the United Kingdom in BAA (the owner of seven domestic airports) was ruled incompatible with treaty rules.[28] This 'special share' limits all interests in the company to 15 per cent of the voting shares and provides for an authorisation procedure, in particular on the disposal of assets and closing.

These rulings are extremely important, since they clarified significantly which restrictions on capital movements (and in particular on foreign direct investment) could be implemented in sectors of general economic interest. While the Belgian ruling implicitly confirmed that certain (limited and well-defined) indirect restrictions on investment (going beyond the public service obligations laid down in the Community framework) could be justified by 'general interest' considerations, the others revealed that member states sometimes enforce such restrictions for reasons inadmissible in the Single Market context. The respective rulings established a border between the acceptable and the unacceptable.

6.   Summary and future prospects

Two main groups of restrictions concerning the foreign ownership of companies in the European Union exist today in the EU legal framework.

First, specific third-country restrictions laid down in EU legislation are rare. They are found in just six specific sectors: air transport, maritime transport, inland waterways transport, energy, audio-visual and financial services. Furthermore, only the first three are protected from third-country ownership through EU ownership and control requirements. This is also the case on the global level outside the Union in these sectors, where restrictions are similar, or more severe. The other sectors are subject to less stringent indirect restrictions on third-country ownership.

---

[27] Commission v Spain (case C-463/00).
[28] Commission v United Kingdom (case C-98/01).

Second, third-country restrictions adopted by member states have emerged (on the basis of public security, public policy and general interest considerations) in sectors that have undergone privatisation during the past decade. In most cases, these restrictions cover equally potential investors from third countries and from other member states.

In the recent past direct restrictions on ownership have become extremely rare, while indirect restrictions appear to be the preferred control tool of national authorities. Although the latter category of measures may seem to be less constraining for company owners, the wide scope of the special control rights granted to national authorities sometimes prevents the effective control and management of the companies concerned. Furthermore, some authorisation requirements are highly discretionary. Therefore, although the acquisition of capital is not limited, such measures nonetheless constitute strong disincentives for foreign investors.

Most of the identified 'general-interest'-related restrictions have been condemned by the European Court of Justice in recent years, and the member states involved have been forced to ease or remove them. However, the admissible character of similar restrictions in other sectors or companies (such as the 'golden shares' existing in some companies active in telecommunications and postal services) has not been ruled upon yet. Therefore, uncertainty remains with respect to the possibility for member states to adopt restrictions on foreign ownership on the basis of considerations of general interest. Clarification will come over time as the Court of Justice is required to pronounce on these investment restrictions.[29] Once a large range of restrictions has been covered by Court of Justice rulings, the extent of the rights of foreign investors to invest in and own companies established in the European Union will be more clearly defined.

REFERENCES

Bakker, A. F. P. (1996), *The Liberalization of Capital Movements in Europe: The Monetary Committee and Financial Integration, 1958–1994*, Financial and Monetary Policy Studies, Vol. XXIX, Kluwer Academic Publishers, London.

European Commission, Directorate General for Economic and Financial Affairs (2003), *The EU Economy: 2003 Review*, Brussels.

Mydske, T. (2000), 'The free movement of capital and restrictions on direct investments', *European Business Law Review*, November/December.

[29] See European Commission (2003).

Raes, J. P. (2002), *The European Community Regime on the Free Movement of Capital*, The Process of Turkey's Accession to the EU (Book no. 9), Economic Development Foundation, Istanbul.

(2003), 'Restrictions on foreign ownership: European Community and international framework', *European Economy (Economic Papers 2003)*, European Commission, Directorate General for Economic and Financial Affairs, Brussels.

Vigneron, P., and P. Steinfeld (1996), 'La Communauté Européenne et la libre circulation des capitaux: les nouvelles dispositions et leurs implications', *Cahiers de Droit Européen*, 3–4, 401–41.

2   Reforming takeover regulation in Europe

Erik Berglöf and Mike Burkart

1.   Introduction

In its quest for more corporate restructuring and a single market for capital, the European Commission is pushing for Europe-wide takeover regulation. That previous attempts have failed is largely because of differences in corporate governance arrangements across member states. This chapter provides a framework for evaluating the effects of takeover regulation. We apply this framework to some specific proposals in the European debate and show that their impact often depends critically on the structure of ownership and control. In particular, two of the most discussed rules – the strict mandatory bid rule and the break-through rule – have no impact when ownership is dispersed. Also, the proposed break-through rule would affect only firms with dual-class shares – not firms that use other control instruments. Moreover, the two rules would effectively counteract each other, the break-through rule promoting takeovers and the mandatory bid rule impeding them. Introducing a strict mandatory bid rule alone, as the Commission proposed, would slow down restructuring. We argue that, while the increased contestability of control is desirable, hostile takeovers are a rather blunt instrument for achieving this. The market for corporate control is only one of many corporate governance mechanisms to be honed in order to promote corporate restructuring in Europe.

This is a shorter and slightly different version of the article published as Berglöf and Burkart (2003), and it is reprinted here with the permission of the journal *Economic Policy*. The managing editors of the journal, the discussants Tito Boeri and Julian Franks and participants at the 36th Panel Meeting of *Economic Policy* in Copenhagen, 25–26 October 2002, provided very useful comments. We are also grateful to Marco Becht, Rudolfs Bems, Patrick Bolton, and Marco Pagano for their helpful suggestions. Special thanks go to Rolf Skog for his invaluable comments throughout this project. Financial support from Riksbankens Jubileumsfond (for Mike Burkart) is gratefully acknowledged. Part of the work was undertaken while Erik Berglöf was a Visiting Research Fellow at the World Bank. He is grateful to this institution for providing a stimulating environment.

After decades of failed attempts and a stinging defeat in the European Parliament in 2001, the Commission remains committed to the idea of a pan-European takeover directive. The Commission argues that more takeovers will lead to more restructuring, and Europe badly needs more restructuring if it wants to catch up with – and overtake – the United States, as set out in the Lisbon declaration. In 2002 the High-Level Group of Company Law Experts was appointed by the European Commission and, under the leadership of the Dutch Law Professor Jaap Winter, presented two reports: a first report on European takeover regulation (European Commission, 2002a), and a final report on a modern regulatory framework for company law in the European Union (European Commission, 2002c). In the analysis of the Winter Group, the core problems are the entrenched ownership and control structures in most member states and the asymmetry of rules regulating takeovers. Consequently, the Group argues for more contestability in respect of controlling owners and a level playing field in takeover markets.

To achieve contestability and a level playing field the Group proposed a set of measures intended to limit defensive measures after a bid has been made for a company, most of them part of the failed draft directive from 2001. In particular, the proposal required that shareholders, not management, approve any defensive measures once a bid is announced, and that a bidder must pay all shareholders the same price (the mandatory bid rule). But the Group went further in proposing that differentiation of votes, one of the most common methods for separating ownership and control, should be voided in votes on takeover bids. Moreover, a bidder once he had achieved a qualified majority of the equity could undo any statutory defences, including any differentiation of votes (the so-called 'break-through rule'). The break-through rule was later dropped from the draft directive (European Commission, 2002b) after intense criticism from several member states and controlling owners affected by the rule, but – together with the mandatory bid rule – the break-through rule illustrates some fundamental principles in takeover regulation.

Given their far-reaching nature and broad impact (the break-through rule alone, for example, would undermine the controlling position of the leading shareholder in one out of six listed companies with dual-class shares: Bennedsen and Nielsen, 2002), it is remarkable that the proposals from the Winter Group and the Commission are, essentially, devoid of any economic analysis. Moreover, very little reference is made to the extensive empirical and theoretical literature on takeovers and corporate governance in economics. This chapter seeks to provide the missing analysis. We provide a conceptual framework to analyse the interrelationship between the market for corporate control and corporate governance. The framework also allows us to understand how the effects of specific pieces of regulation depend on the context, in particular on existing structures of ownership and control. Ultimately, we ask the question: what type of takeover regulation and corporate governance reform do we need in Europe to achieve more restructuring?

Takeover regulation determines the rules of the game before and after a bid for control over a firm has been placed. These rules influence the distribution of gains from takeovers between the bidding firm and the target firm, and between controlling and minority shareholders in the target firm. The greater the amount of the surplus that is allocated to the bidding firm, the stronger the incentives are to make a bid. And the greater the amount of the surplus the minority shareholders appropriate, the fewer incentives there are to hold controlling blocks. Any body of takeover regulations, such as the Commission's draft directive or the United Kingdom's City Code, contains a substantial number of provisions, most of them generally accepted. In this chapter we focus on three sets of measures where controversy persists: specific defensive measures, mandatory bid rules, and break-through rules. They illustrate the basic economic principles of takeover regulation, and they are central to the debate on takeover regulation and the mobility of corporate control in Europe.

Our analysis shows that the effects of individual pieces of takeover regulation often depend critically on the ownership and control structure in the target firm. For example, neither the mandatory bid rule nor the break-through rule have any impact when a firm's shares are widely dispersed. More importantly, the specific break-through rule proposed by the Winter Group affects only dual-class shares and not other control instruments. Moreover (and this is less well understood), when there is a controlling minority shareholder the mandatory bid rule makes it more costly to take over a firm, and the break-through rule makes it cheaper. In other words, the two rules have opposite effects: one discourages takeover activity while the other encourages such activity.

The Commission's draft directive, without the break-through rule but with a strict mandatory bid rule, further entrenches the existing control structures and reduces contestability, contrary to its intentions. We show that a strict mandatory bid rule does eliminate some value-reducing takeover bids, but at the cost of also getting rid of some value-increasing bids. In other words, this rule *cannot* be used to screen 'bad' bidders from 'good' ones. Rather, the mandatory bid rule effectively shuts down the trade in controlling blocks, the dominant form for control transfer in most of Europe. While the mandatory bid rule in the draft directive is unambiguously detrimental to promoting restructuring, it may or may not be good for minority protection; the rule increases the compensation to minority shareholders in the case of a successful takeover, but it decreases the likelihood of a takeover. Which effect dominates is, ultimately, an empirical issue.

Introducing the break-through rule would effectively undermine the mandatory bid rule, opening up block trades and making possible value-reducing and value-increasing bids previously prevented by the latter rule. The break-through rule alone would unambiguously promote take-over activity and contestability, essentially by lowering the cost of a successful bid. However, since the rule fundamentally alters the initial contracts of the controlling owners, it represents a massive *ex post* government intervention, introducing uncertainty into the fundamental property rights regime with large potential *ex ante* costs for entrepreneurship and the willingness of controlling owners to exercise corporate governance. These costs have to be weighed against potential benefits.

We therefore find that, while increased contestability is a worthwhile goal for European takeover regulation, its exact meaning must be understood in the context of existing ownership and control arrangements in Europe. Contestability is clearly desirable, in that it disciplines controlling owners and managers, and it raises the potential for more efficient owners and managers to take over control. But contestability is neither a sufficient nor a necessary condition for good corporate governance at the level of the individual firm. There are many examples of successful family firms where control is not and has never been contestable. In the system as a whole, contestability must be weighed against any negative effects it might have on incentives for entrepreneurial activity and monitoring by large controlling shareholders, and on the protection of minority investors.

Our analysis suggests that relying solely on hostile takeovers to increase contestability is not recommendable. Hostile takeovers do not guarantee that the existing corporate resources are managed more efficiently. While they can mitigate agency problems between managers and shareholders, hostile takeovers are naturally subject to the same agency problems as any corporate decision. Hostile takeovers are also only one of many mechanisms in the larger corporate governance system. Like other takeovers, these mechanisms have their costs and benefits. And, since the various corporate governance mechanisms are complementary and highly interconnected, changes in one component almost always entail some costs elsewhere. The challenge in corporate governance is to balance the costs and benefits of these different mechanisms in terms of how they affect the larger system.

Creating a level playing field in the market for corporate control is a noble objective. But, as our analysis clearly demonstrates, a level playing field is not the same as the harmonisation of takeover regulation. Specific rules have very different effects in different environments. In particular, the effects of the mandatory bid rule and a break-through rule of the type proposed by the Winter Group depend on the ownership and control structure in the target firm. Given the considerable variation in ownership and control within the European Union (most notably between the United Kingdom and the rest of the Union), the mandatory bid rule, for instance, impedes the takeover of a typical German firm, with its controlling owners, but not that of a typical UK firm, with its dispersed ownership.

The chapter starts by examining the variation in the level and type of takeover activity within Europe, and the various 'barriers' potentially explaining this variation. While there are several contributing factors, we argue that the prevalence of controlling blocks is the single most important 'barrier' limiting hostile takeovers. Using recently accumulated data we provide a more detailed account of the patterns of ownership and control in European firms. In the next section (section 3) we discuss the principles of takeover regulation, and section 4 describes national takeover regulation and attempts to regulate takeovers at the European Union level. Takeover regulation is closely linked to corporate governance, and in section 5 we discuss the interrelationship. Section 6 provides an economic analysis of defensive measures, the mandatory bid rule and the break-through rule. In section 7 we discuss our findings, and we conclude with some policy recommendations in section 8.

2.   Ownership and control in corporate Europe

The overriding concern of the Commission is to promote the restructuring of European industry. Even though there are large fluctuations over time in individual countries, the general perception is that, at least during the 1970s and the 1980s, the United States has been more successful in restructuring its industry (Holmström and Kaplan, 2001). A considerable share of this restructuring was achieved through hostile takeovers, and even when transactions were negotiated the potential for a hostile bid played an important role. Within Europe, hostile takeovers were confined primarily to the United Kingdom. Hostile takeovers – in the sense of tender offers launched in the market – have been very rare in Continental Europe, at least until recently. For instance, in 1989 there were only four hostile takeovers in all the rest of the EU15, compared to thirty-two in the United Kingdom (Becht et al., 2002). The turnover

Table 2.1. *Mergers and acquisitions*

	Australia	Canada	United States	EU15	United Kindom	EU15 excl. United Kindom	Others
Number of announced friendly takeovers							
1989	81	184	1,188	550	316	234	114
1990	69	193	834	597	290	307	188
1991	107	269	790	817	252	565	363
1992	46	194	746	824	181	643	296
1993	100	215	789	803	196	607	456
1994	124	224	1,015	816	221	595	614
1995	162	296	1,106	806	219	587	753
1996	142	277	1,115	676	195	481	745
1997	107	258	1,150	574	201	373	726
1998	103	231	1,203	653	234	419	893
1999	100	289	1,236	801	271	530	1,180
Number of announced hostile takeovers							
1989	3	6	45	36	32	4	10
1990	2	0	12	24	22	2	5
1991	8	1	7	34	31	3	2
1992	10	2	7	20	15	5	4
1993	10	1	11	15	11	4	5
1994	8	11	33	11	8	3	4
1995	18	19	59	22	14	8	7
1996	22	8	45	20	13	7	11
1997	12	17	27	23	11	12	5
1998	12	14	19	14	12	2	5
1999	15	6	19	42	21	21	6

Source: Becht et al. (2002).

of control was also much higher in the United Kingdom, with the number of friendly transactions alone clearly outnumbering those on the European Continent.

During the 1990s the picture changed somewhat, with a large increase in the total number of control transactions, but the number of hostile takeovers remained negligible until the last few years of the 1990s. In fact, in 1999 the number of hostile takeovers was the same in the United Kingdom and the rest of the EU15 (see table 2.1) However, seen in relation to the size of the economy, hostile takeovers played a much more important role in the United Kingdom than in the rest of the European Union (Becht et al., 2002). Nonetheless, there was some variation among the rest of the countries. In particular, Sweden had a total of about 250 takeovers during the period 1990 to 2001, which corresponds to 9 per cent of the number of listed firms, or about the same number of friendly control transactions per listed firm as in the United Kindom (Berglöf et al., 2003). In Germany, with a much larger number of listed firms and an even larger economy, the corresponding figure was about 100.

Interestingly, in the United States overall restructuring activity remained about the same despite a drop in the level of hostile takeovers during the 1990s, with a brief resurgence in the middle of the decade. This decline in hostile control transactions can be attributed largely to the effect of increasingly management-friendly judges in key US states, such as Delaware, where most large companies are incorporated (Holmström and Kaplan, 2001). A series of court decisions came out in favour of managerial defences and of a broad interpretation of the business judgement rule giving management discretion over key strategic decisions.

In interpreting these numbers it is important to remember that 'hostile' and 'friendly' may be harder to differentiate than the names may suggest. The distinction is normally based on whether the board in the target firm supported the bid. But the vote of the board could be influenced by many things, including the prospects of the bid eventually succeeding. In fact, many seemingly friendly transactions have hostile components. Jenkinson and Ljungqvist (2001) document a considerable degree of hostility in a number of control transactions in Germany that fall outside the official classification of hostile takeovers.

Control blocks are also traded without formal takeovers taking place. Köke (2000) examines a larger sample of almost 1,000 German firms (large listed, medium-sized and/or non-listed firms) over the years 1987 to 1994. He finds that there is significant trading in large share blocks, and that the vast majority of these transactions involve controlling blocks. On average, 7 per cent of control changes per year in Germany, compared to 6.3 per cent in Belgium, 6.7 per cent in the United States, and to 9 per cent in the United Kingdom. Such changes in control are typically followed by increased management and board turnover, more asset restructuring and lay-offs.

In addition, there is an active 'private' market for corporate assets and corporate control outside the public exchanges (Wymeersch, 1998). In terms of the number of transactions, about half the number of transactions taking place worldwide involve European companies. These transactions mostly involve privately owned firms, including subsidiaries and divisions of listed corporations. Both in terms of turnover and numbers of transactions, this market exceeds the markets for public takeover bids.

2.1   Barriers to takeover

A number of features of the Continental European (or non-UK) economies have been put forward to explain these differences in the level of
takeover activity. These so-called 'takeover barriers' are functionally
similar to takeover defences, in that they both help to entrench target
management (Ferrarini, forthcoming). Takeover barriers are common in
Continental Europe, while takeover defences are widely used in the
United States. Takeover defences may be divided into pre-bid and
post-bid defences.

Takeover barriers may be further broken down into structural and
technical barriers. Structural barriers are part of the institutional setting,
such as the influence of banks ('Hausbank'), the ownership structure
and the size of the equity market. Technical barriers are part of each
individual firm's governance structure, as laid down in the corporate
charter and allocating the powers among its constituencies (shareholders, management, workers, etc.). Examples of such common technical
barriers that are specifically aimed at frustrating hostile bids are restrictions on the transferability of shares and voting restrictions. Dual-class
shares, pyramidal groups and cross-shareholdings are devices to separate
ownership and control, thereby also providing protection against
unfriendly acquisition attempts.

We will focus our discussion on ownership and control as barriers to
takeovers, but let us first briefly discuss the other suggested structural
barriers. All these barriers are, more or less, associated with Germany,
but not only with that country. The case for co-determination and close
bank–firm relationships as barriers to takeovers rests on the argument
that employees and banks naturally form alliances with the incumbent
management or controlling owners. This, in turn, hinges on the distribution of gains from takeovers, the assumption being that employees
and creditors would somehow lose out (compare the arguments of
Pagano and Volpin, 2001, and Cespa and Cestone, 2002). Empirical
evidence from the United States suggests that wage cuts explain only a
small fraction of the takeover premium (for a survey of the evidence, see
Burkart, 1999). And there is little evidence that creditors would suffer
substantial losses in takeovers.[1]

---

[1] A close relationship to a bank is not always a guarantee against a hostile bid. Franks and
Mayer (1998) show that in all three cases of hostile takeovers in Germany after World
War II the target company's 'house bank' exerted considerable influence over the
outcome through the chairmanship of the supervisory board (this is probably also true
for many of the cases of potential hostile bids that never materialised).

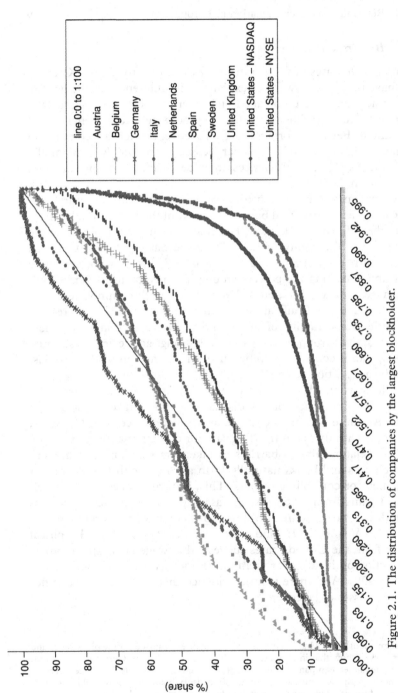

Figure 2.1. The distribution of companies by the largest blockholder.

Note: Listed companies are arranged according to the size of the largest control block. A curve above the 45° line indicates more companies with large control blocks, and a curve far below indicates that most firms have dispersed shareholdings.

Source: Barca and Becht (2002).

As for the size of equity markets as a structural barrier, it is undoubtedly true that only firms listed on exchanges can be subjected to hostile bids. If, as in (for example) Germany and Italy, only a small share of the total number of the country's firms are listed, then this constitutes a limit to the contestability of control in that country's industry. An obvious way to foster contestability is to encourage the public listings of firms. Takeover regulation indirectly affects the incentives to list through its impact on the distribution of gains from a future takeover bid. Obviously, takeover rules that create uncertainty about the fundamental property rights of the controlling owner also discourage listings.

2.2   Ownership and control

Ownership and control in corporate Europe is put forth as a serious obstacle to hostile takeovers and, possibly, to restructuring more generally. Recent comparable data on ownership and control collected within the European Corporate Governance Network (summarised in a recent volume edited by Barca and Becht, 2001) allow us to form a better view of the extent of entrenchment.

Corporate Europe spans a wide range of ownership and control structures, ranging from closely held family firms to firms with widely dispersed shareholdings, but – as in much of the rest of the world – most companies have a large controlling shareholder (Barca and Becht, 2001; La Porta et al., 1999). Corporations in the United Kingdom (and the United States) stand out as having more widely dispersed ownership than those in the rest of the world, but there is also considerable variation in ownership concentration within Continental Europe. In half of the listed non-financial firms in Austria, Belgium, Germany and Italy, a single shareholder controls more than 50 per cent of the votes (compared to 9.9 per cent in the United Kingdom). In Dutch, Spanish and Swedish firms the median blockholder holds 43.5, 34.5 and 34.9 per cent, respectively.

Figure 2.1 shows the distribution of firms by the size of the largest voting block in some selected countries. When the dotted line is far below (above) the diagonal line, there are few (many) firms with large controlling blocks. These distributions suggest a broad spectrum of ownership and control structures with large blockholders on the European Continent. In some cases the owner/manager controls a majority of the votes, and in others the largest blockholder has opted for a blocking minority stake. In addition, the observed clustering at certain levels of voting power illustrates the impact of laws and regulation. For instance, the line for Germany exhibits steps at 25 per cent (blocking minority), 50 per cent (simple majority) and 75 per cent (common qualified majority).

However, the amount of votes controlled by the largest shareholder is but one dimension shaping the governance structure in a firm. Other relevant aspects include how the large shareholder secures control, how the remaining voting and return rights are held, and the relationship between the controlling shareholder and top management. Moreover, it is interesting to know the identity of the controlling owners.

Most countries allow at least one of the three principal mechanisms for separating control from ownership (of cash-flow rights): (1) shares with differentiated voting power; (2) pyramiding, where control is exercised through several layers of companies; and (3) cross-holdings, where a firm directly or indirectly controls its own shares. Pyramiding is the most effective device for separating ownership and control in that it is multiplicative (rather than additive, as for vote differentiation). Assuming that 50 per cent is necessary for controlling a firm, pyramiding by adding one layer allows for control in the firm at the bottom with a mere 25 per cent of the equity (50 per cent $\times$ 50 per cent). The multiplier between capital and votes in the pyramid is $1/(1/2)^n$, where n denotes the number of levels in the pyramid. In other words, the vote multiplier is 4.

These control-enhancing mechanisms are sometimes used together. By combining shares with different voting power and pyramiding, a controlling owner can maintain control over the company at the bottom of the pyramid with even smaller shares of its cash-flow rights. Bennedsen and Nielsen (2002) have calculated that one-fifth of the firms listed on European exchanges make use of differentiated votes, with the practice being particularly widespread in Scandinavia. Faccio and Lang (2002) report that pyramids are used by 19 per cent of listed European firms that have a controlling shareholder at the 20 per cent level. Pyramids are most prevalent in Norway (33.9 per cent) and least prevalent in Finland (7.5 per cent). Cross-holdings are also used in Germany, but they are marginal in other countries. The ownership and control structure where the owner/manager has sold out the majority of shares to dispersed shareholders but retains control is denoted a *controlling minority shareholder*. The possibility of controlling firms with limited equity stakes is at the heart of much of the corporate governance debate in Continental Europe.

The voting and return rights not controlled by the largest shareholder can be held in several ways. The shares may be widely dispersed, but *several* large shareholders with substantial blocks of shares are also common (Barca and Becht, 2001). For a sample of 5,232 European companies, Faccio and Lang (2002) find that 39 per cent of firms have at least two shareholders owning 10 per cent or more of votes, and 16 per cent have three shareholders, each owning at least 10 per cent of the votes. In order to evaluate the role of additional large blockholdings we need to know more about the relationship between the largest blockholder and other blockholders. A controlling minority shareholder could have sold a large block to a friendly investor. Alternatively, an investor could have accumulated a substantial block of previously dispersed shares more or less against the desire of the controlling owner/manager. Whether the other large blockholders are essentially friendly or hostile is going to shape the dynamics of corporate governance in the firm.

The identity of the controlling owner is also likely to shape the nature and dynamics of corporate governance. Recent empirical research has tried to penetrate these complex, often multi-layered, ownership and control arrangements in search of ultimate controlling owners (LaPorta et al., 1999; and Faccio and Lang, 2002). Most publicly traded firms in Europe are either widely held or family-controlled. There is, however, a marked difference in the ranking of these two categories across Europe. In Continental Europe, as in most other countries of the world, family-controlled firms are in the majority. By contrast, widely held firms clearly outnumber family controlled firms in the United Kingdom and Ireland. To understand the predominance of family control we need to establish why, in the first place, founders and investors retain large controlling stakes in firms. After all, abstaining from diversification is costly, and controlling blocks are typically rather illiquid. Individuals and organisations forgo diversification benefits in order to induce those in charge of running the company to take decisions that are in the interests of the suppliers of finance (shareholders). As we will illustrate below, the ownership of large blocks – whether by manager or by outside blockholder – is, however, not unequivocally positive but comes with costs and benefits.

3.   Promoting takeover versus protecting minority interests

Takeover regulation – either implicitly or explicitly – influences how the takeover gains are shared between the bidding and the target firm, and thereby affects the incentives to undertake or accept, respectively, a bid. Since granting one side – the bidder, say – a larger fraction of the takeover gains necessarily implies that target shareholders receive less of the surplus, any takeover regulation has to confront the trade-off between promoting the mobility of corporate control and protecting small (minority) shareholders. To illustrate this general point we briefly review the well-known free-rider problem, identified by Grossman and Hart (1980), which is central to the understanding of both how the tender offer process functions and how regulation affects (the incidence of) takeovers. Thereafter, we turn our attention to the current takeover regulations in Europe. As we will argue the impact, relevance and desirability of a specific takeover rule crucially depend on the corporate governance system to which it is applied.

In their seminal paper, Grossman and Hart (1980) show that managers who are either inefficient or pursue self-serving actions need not be vulnerable to a takeover bid, even though – or, more accurately, precisely because – ownership is widely dispersed. Each small shareholder rightly presumes that his decision to tender has a negligible impact on the tender offer outcome. Accordingly, a shareholder finds it in his interest to tender only if the offered bid price at least matches the post-takeover share value. Otherwise, he prefers to 'free-ride'. By not tendering, he captures the whole value improvement that the bidder can generate. As all small shareholders behave in the same manner the bidder makes zero profit on the shares acquired in the tender offer. Or putting it differently, a success of a value-increasing bid is a public good for the target shareholders, but each individual shareholder has an incentive not to tender in order to free-ride. As a result, there are too few takeover attempts, and if a takeover occurs, most of the gains go to target shareholders.[2] This latter implication of the free-rider result is confirmed by numerous empirical studies (Burkart, 1999).

The literature has suggested two ways to mitigate the free-rider problem, both of relevance in the context of (European) takeover legislation. Grossman and Hart (1980) propose allowing bidders to dilute the value of the post-takeover minority shares. Excluding minority shareholders from part of the takeover gains creates a wedge between the post-takeover share value to the bidder and that to the minority shareholders. This implies that shareholders are willing to tender already at a price at which the bidder still makes a profit.[3] Note also that the bid price does

---

[2] Other (complementary) reasons why a bidder may fail to make a profit are competition by other bidders and defensive actions by the incumbent management.

[3] Another way to overcome the free-rider problem is to grant a successful bidder a squeeze-out right – i.e. the right to compel the remaining minority shareholders to sell their shares (Yarrow, 1985). The squeeze-out right affects the tendering decision in a similar manner to the dilution of minority shareholder rights. When an offer conditional upon acceptance of the freeze-out fraction succeeds, any remaining minority shareholder will be forced to sell his shares on the terms of the original offer. Hence, he may as well accept the original offer. The Commission's latest draft directive (October 2002)

not depend upon whether or not restricted bids are banned. With or without the mandatory bid rule, the bidder simply offers a price equal to the post-takeover minority share value, and the shareholders neither gain nor lose from tendering their shares (given that the takeover succeeds).[4]

The above argument illustrates how (takeover) regulation can affect the distribution of takeover gains and, thereby, the bidder's incentives to undertake a bid, as well as the target shareholders' incentive to accept it. It also makes the conflict between promoting takeovers and protecting minority interests very transparent.[5] Strong (minority) shareholder protection discourages bidders because their profits are eroded by the target shareholders' free-rider behaviour. Hence, a takeover mechanism that fulfils its dual role of creating wealth by exploiting synergies and of disciplining management relies on granting bidders benefits that do not accrue to other shareholders on a prorata basis. Such private benefits conflict with the equal treatment and protection of minority shareholders. Consequently, a functioning market for corporate control cannot be pursued separately from the protection of minority shareholders, but one goal has to be traded-off against the other. To the extent that shareholder protection is tantamount to increasing the target shareholders' share of the takeover gains it diminishes the bidder's private benefits, thereby resulting in a less active market for corporate control.

This trade-off also implies that maximum minority protection is not in the target shareholders' best interest. Less shareholder protection improves the bidder's profit prospect and thereby increases the likelihood that the shareholders collect a takeover premium. In their perspective, the optimal amount of protection maximises the expected takeover premium – i.e. it strikes a balance between a higher bid price in the event of a takeover and a lower probability of a takeover.

introduces the squeeze-out right with a threshold of between 90 and 95 per cent of the equity capital.

[4] The argument implicitly assumes that the takeover is value-increasing, with a post-takeover minority share value that exceeds the current share value under the incumbent management. In a more general single-bidder setting, where the takeover may or may not be value-increasing, the mandatory bid rule can prevent minority shareholders from incurring a loss relative to the current share value. However, the mandatory bid rule never simultaneously secures a bid premium and provides effective protection: either the status quo (current share value) determines the bid price, in which case the takeover premium is zero, or the post-takeover minority share value determines the bid price, in which case the mandatory bid rule has no impact (Burkart, 1999).

[5] Like other takeover regulation, such as the UK City Code and the federal US regulations, both the Winter Report and the various (failed) drafts for a takeover directive endorse the protection of (minority) shareholder interests and a functioning market for corporate control as main regulatory objectives.

A closely related point is that minority protection aimed at restricting the dilution of minority shares does not serve as a screening device.[6] As shown in Berglöf and Burkart (2003), better minority protection does not frustrate those bids where the bidder is the primary recipient of the takeover gains without discouraging even more those bids where the gains are more evenly shared.[7] Due to the free-rider behaviour, better protection raises the bid price for 'good' bidders (who bring large efficiency gains) and 'bad' bidders (who extract large private benefits). Since the profit margin of good bidders is typically smaller than that of bad bidders, better protection is more likely to discourage good bidders.

A second solution to the free-rider problem is the acquisition of a stake prior to the tender offer (Shleifer and Vishny, 1986). If the pre-takeover price of the stake is relatively low, the bidder earns a profit on this stake, making the takeover profitable, even if all tendered shares are acquired at the full post-takeover value. Indeed, pre-takeover holdings are found to have a positive impact on bidder gains and on the success probability of takeovers (Burkart, 1999).

The ease and extent to which a bidder can accumulate an initial stake through secret open-market purchases depend on the market depth and the disclosure requirement. Once a bidder has to disclose his identity (and holdings), further open-market purchases become increasingly less attractive. Thus, by limiting the numbers of shares that a bidder can acquire before submitting a public tender offer, disclosure requirements affect the division of takeover gains. When choosing a disclosure threshold, a regulator faces again the trade-off between promoting takeovers and protecting minority interests. Lax disclosure standards allocate a larger share of the takeover gains to the bidder, thereby promoting an active takeover market. This, however, comes at the expense of those shareholders who sold their shares prior to the bid, thereby forgoing the takeover premium.

Instead of accumulating an initial stake through open-market purchases, the bidder may seek out a large shareholder and negotiate a block sale. Even though the bidder has to surrender part of the subsequent takeover gains on the block to the incumbent blockholder, a block

---

[6] As shown in Berglöf and Burkart (2003), rules that impose a minimum price in a control transaction, such as the mandatory bid rule, can to some extent screen between bidders.

[7] This reasoning implicitly assumes that there is no competition among bidders. When multiple bidders compete for a target, bids and counterbids typically drive the price up beyond the level imposed by minority protection, making the latter a non-binding constraint.

trade may be more profitable than accumulating a stake through secret open-market purchases. Thus, the existence of large shareholdings facilitates takeovers relative to a firm with dispersed ownership. The blockholder's ability to promote a takeover by either selling or tendering his shares also allows him to impede it by retaining his shares. Both increase with the block size – or, more precisely, with the associated number of votes – and an incumbent shareholder with a majority of the votes can unilaterally accept or reject a takeover attempt. This latter possibility has been a main concern in debate on EU takeover regulation in those cases where a majority of the votes are controlled with a much smaller proportion of the equity capital.

4.   Takeover regulation in Europe

This section describes the regulatory framework governing control transfers at the level of member states and provides a brief account of the attempts to regulate takeovers at the level of the Union, including the recommendations of the Winter Group and the Commission's draft directive of October 2002.

4.1   National regulation

Following several highly publicised takeovers the United Kingdom introduced in 1968 its self-regulatory City Code on Takeovers and Mergers, which has since been revised and expanded several times. The purpose of the code is to ensure the fair and equal treatment of all shareholders in connection with corporate takeovers and to provide an orderly framework within which takeovers are conducted. To this end, the code regulates the actions of bidders prior to the announcement of the bid, the content of the information issued to shareholders by bidder and target companies, and the defensive measures available to the target companies.

With respect to the two most debated aspects of takeover regulation, the mandatory bid rule and the scope for defensive actions, the UK City Code adopts strict versions. First, the code obliges a party who reaches, through purchases, the threshold of 30 per cent of the voting rights in a listed company to make an offer to buy the remaining shares. The price in the mandatory offer may be no less than any price paid within the preceding twelve months. Second, the code prohibits managers from taking any defensive action without shareholder consent once an offer is made or seems imminent. It further forbids explicitly the issue of retained shares and options, the sale or acquisition of assets of a material amount, and entering into contracts otherwise than in the ordinary course of business.

Until the 1980s takeover regulation remained essentially a UK (and US) phenomenon. In most Continental European countries takeover bids were still so rare that special regulations were long thought to be unnecessary. Acquisitions traditionally were based on negotiations between the acquirer and the target company's management, and transactions took place outside the public exchanges. During the latter part of the 1980s, however, activity in European stock markets increased dramatically, as did the number of takeover bids targeted directly at the shareholders – in some cases with no prior negotiations at all and in others after negotiations had proved unsuccessful. Cross-border corporate takeovers also increased as wresting control of companies in other countries through public takeover bids became more accepted.

In response to these developments, most member states first adopted some form of self-regulation and later opted for binding legal rules, but some countries have maintained self-regulatory regimes (see table 2.2). These national regulations are strongly influenced by the British example. In fact, the UK City Code has served as the standard in many areas, such as information and disclosure, conduct during the offer, or competing offers (Hopt, 2002). This does, however, not apply to the mandatory bid rule and defensive measures, where some member states opted for different provisions.

Almost all member states have adopted some form of mandatory bid rule, either through self-regulation or by law, but the design of rules differs across jurisdictions. The United Kingdom has the most extreme form of mandatory bid rule, which effectively prevents the acquisition of a controlling block at a premium. Continental European mandatory bid rules are typically less demanding, allowing either for a price discount or restricting the quantity of the outstanding shares that the rival is obliged to acquire (Ferrarini, forthcoming). The level of blockholding triggering a mandatory bid also differs across member states (see table 2.2). Defensive measures by incumbents have also been regulated for in most member states. In general, boards may take such measures only after approval from shareholders. In Germany, however, shareholders can approve measures in advance, in effect giving the supervisory board considerable leeway in responding to takeover bids.

To summarise, national regulations within the European Union have gradually converged to the UK rules, and today variation across member states is limited, although some differences remain as to the mandatory bid rule and the ability of the board to take defensive action, most notably in Germany. Overall investor protection has probably been

Table 2.2. *National takeover regulation*

Area of regulation	Form of regulation	Mandatory bid rule	Rules on defensive measures
Austria	Legislation 1998	Legislation: 'control'	Yes, board may take action only in the interest of all shareholders, holders of other securities, the employees and the public at large
Belgium	Soft law 1964 (rules and guidelines issued by the Banking Commission), legal rules	Soft law 1970s: 'control' legislation 1989: 'control'	Yes, board may in practice not take action without shareholder approval (1990s)
Denmark	Self-regulation 1979, amended 1988, legislation 1995		
Finland	Legislation 1989	67%	
France	Rudimentary self-regulation early 1970s, full takeover regulation by law 1989, amended 1992	Legislation late 1980s: 33% and 50% at certain other occasions	Yes, board may not take action without shareholder approval (1968)
Germany	Voluntary code 1995, legislation (the Takeover Act) 2002	Amendment to the voluntary code 1997: 'control'; legislation 2002: 30%	Yes, board may take action only on the basis of shareholder authorisation, which could, however, be given in advance (1995 and 2002)
Italy	Stock Exchange Code early 1970s, legislation 1992	Legislation 1992: 'control'; later: 30%	Yes, board may not take action without shareholder approval (1992)
Netherlands	Self-regulation (primarily on mergers) early 1970s, takeover legislation 2002		

Table 2.2. (*cont.*)

Area of regulation	Form of regulation	Mandatory bid rule	Rules on defensive measures
Portugal	Legislation 1986	Legislation 1986: 33% and 50%	Yes, board may not take action without shareholder approval (1986)
Spain	Legislation 1984 and 1991	(Very complex)	(Very complex)
Sweden	Self-regulation 1971	Amendment to self-regulation 1999: 40%	Yes, board may not take action without shareholder approval (1971)
UK	Self-regulation 1968 (a role model for the rest of Europe)	In self-regulation 1968: 30%	
Failed Takeover Directive	Binding regulation	Weak mandatory bid rule, allowing national variation	Shareholders must approve defensive measures once a bid has been launched
Winter Proposal	Binding regulation	Strict mandatory bid rule	Shareholders must approve defensive measures once a bid has been launched

Source: National regulations.

strengthened through the introduction of mandatory bid rules, at the expense of mobility in the market for control. But the increasing emphasis on shareholder approval of defensive measures has moderated this shift. Thus, there is little evidence of a 'race-to-the-bottom', in the sense of no regulation.

This picture contrasts sharply with that of the United States, which has a dual regime with both federal and state laws. The principal federal legislation (the Williams Act) is aimed at procedural disclosure rules in the tender offer process. The Williams Act does not interfere with the power of a firm to resist a takeover bid under its corporate charter. But, in contrast to the European Union, the United States has a single, homogeneously defined standard on the accountability of a target firm's board, the so-called 'fiduciary duties', comparable to the well-established business judgement rule for management (Hopt, 2002). It is worthwhile to note that US federal regulation contains no mandatory bid rule. State laws vary considerably across the country. Many states have many anti-takeover statutes;[8] Delaware has only one, but it is the only state that has a well-developed case law on the use of defensive tactics. Mandatory bid rules exist only in Pennsylvania and Maine.

Defensive tactics are within the business discretion of the boards of directors and are widely used.[9] In fact, most Standard and Poor's (S&P) 500 firms and a vast majority of those firms listed on the New York Stock Exchange (NYSE) or Amex are covered by several anti-takeover devices, ranging from poison pills and supermajority amendments to state anti-takeover laws (Burkart, 1999). Court challenges have also become an important defensive weapon in takeover bids, and hostile takeover activity dropped substantially in the United States during the 1990s (Holmström and Kaplan, 2001). States, such as Delaware, that have granted managers broad discretion in implementing takeover defences with reference to the so-called 'business judgement rule,' have been more successful in attracting incorporations.

In one influential view, regulatory competition has generally served the interests of incumbent management (Bebchuk et al., 2002). Despite the variation in treatment across jurisdictions, the extent of regulatory competition should not be exaggerated. For most companies the choice has, in effect, stood between incorporating in Delaware or the company's home state. Moreover, state courts have acted in the shadow of possible federal intervention. The recent reaction in Congress to the spectacular governance failures in companies such as Enron and WorldCom with the passage of the Sarbanes–Oxley Act also illustrates the latent threat of intervention from the legislature. On several occasions – most notably in the aftermath of the Great Depression – the federal authorities, propelled by political populism, asserted their powers to break up corporate governance arrangements. Prior to these interventions ownership and control structures in the United States resembled those of present-day Continental Europe.

---

[8] There are five standard types of anti-takeover statutes: control share acquisition statutes, fair price statutes, business combination statutes, poison pill endorsement statutes and constituency statutes (Bebchuk et al., 2002).
[9] The board can, however, act only as a fiduciary of the shareholders, and these strong fiduciary duties are upheld by the American courts (Hopt, 2002).

4.2   EU takeover regulation

The first attempts to harmonise takeover regulation in the European Union date back to the early 1970s, when the European Commission appointed Professor Robert Pennington to draw up a draft directive for takeover bids.[10] Like later drafts, this draft was strongly influenced by the United Kingdom's City Code. The draft was discussed for a couple of years with representatives of the member states, but interest was limited and eventually the entire project was abandoned. Ten years later the directive plans resurfaced, and towards the end of the 1980s the European Commission presented a proposal for a 13th Company Law Directive. The draft was widely criticised and interest among member states was again limited.

However, the situation changed overnight in January 1988 when the Italian businessman Carlo de Benedetti extended a bid for a controlling stake in the giant Belgian holding company Société Générale de Belgique, thereby starting one of Europe's most controversial takeover fights to date, involving numerous dubious defensive measures and unveiling a considerable void at the core of European takeover regulation. The battle for the company accelerated the Commission's directive plans. At the urging of the European Parliament, the Commission in January 1989 presented a completed proposal for a takeover directive. The proposal triggered an intense debate on the forms a European Takeover Directive should take. Apart from strong objections against individual provisions, many argued that a directive should be limited to certain basic principles for national rules, while leaving the details to member states to decide on. By the end of 1991 the Commission announced its intention to prepare yet another draft proposal, which would take into account the criticism raised.

The new proposal appeared five years later, in 1996, and was amended several times, following comments from the first reading in the European Parliament, intense negotiations within the Council and a protracted conciliation procedure with the European Parliament. The new proposal was a proposal for a 'framework directive', containing general principles that member states would be obliged to follow when drafting their national takeover codes. To silence British opposition, member states would even be permitted to implement the directive through self-regulation if they wished. The Council had also given in to German resistance on several substantive points, but there was one area where the willingness

---

[10] See Skog (2002) for a thorough account of the history of (attempted) takeover regulation at the EU level.

to compromise ran into a wall: the issue of defensive measures. The common position stated that such measures could be enacted only with the approval of the general meeting after a bid has been announced.[11] After extended negotiations the draft was finally rejected by the smallest possible margin – one vote.[12]

Despite this defeat the Commission remained committed to the idea of a single takeover regulation for the Union. In September 2001 the Commission set up the High-Level Group of Company Law Experts under the leadership of Jaap Winter, charged with the task of providing independent advice on issues related to the harmonisation of European corporate law, including rules for takeovers. In January 2002 the Winter Group presented its recommendations on takeover regulation, building on the rejected directive. As guiding principles for the creation of a level playing field the Group advocated shareholder decision-making and proportionality between risk-bearing capital and control. Applying these two principles, the Group made the following main recommendations.

(1) The price in a mandatory bid should be equal to the highest price paid by the bidder during the preceding six to twelve months. The mandatory bid should be made within a short period after the acquisition of control. The exact definition of the 'level of control' would be left for the member states to decide.

(2) The board of the target company must obtain prior shareholder approval before taking any frustrating actions once a takeover bid has been announced.

(3) A bidder who acquires 75 per cent (or more) of the equity capital should be able to override any obstacle, including voting differentiation,[13] that prevents him from taking control over the firm (the

---

[11] German opposition was intense throughout this process, and ultimately Germany no longer backed the common position in the Council; three times Germany was voted down fourteen to one within the Council.

[12] After the conciliation process, it was for the European Parliament in plenary session to vote on the matter. Normally this is little more than a formality, but during the discussion it became evident that differences in opinion split both the conservative and socialist camps and that the vote would therefore be 'free'. In the end, Parliament rejected the conciliation compromise with the smallest possible margin of one vote. The defeat was all the more surprising when it is borne in mind that the proposed directive was based on the UK rules, making the difference between the proposed directive and national regulation much smaller than during previous reform attempts. The directive failed because of the strong (German) opposition to the proposed restrictions on boards' discretion over the use of defensive measures. The resistance was based primarily on a perceived asymmetry vis-à-vis the United States, where most firms are effectively shielded from hostile takeovers.

[13] Company-specific barriers remaining outside the scope of the break-through rule would be provisions restricting the transferability of shares, contractual barriers to takeover bids and pyramid structures.

so-called 'break-through' rule). Furthermore, the bidder would not have to compensate the holder of shares carrying disproportionate voting rights or special control rights.

(4) Dual-class shares, voting caps and other limitations to voting rights would be voided in votes on defensive measures once a takeover bid has been announced.

Recommendations (1) and (2) endorse the controversial provisions of the failed takeover directive, while recommendations (3) and (4) go much further. They aim at removing a controlling minority shareholder's veto power over a takeover bid. In addition, the Group recommended the introduction of the right for a majority shareholder to buy out minority shareholders (the squeeze-out right), and of the right for minority share-holders to compel the majority shareholder to purchase their shares (the sell-out right). As a threshold for triggering both squeeze-out and sell-out rights the Group proposed 90 or 95 per cent of the equity capital.

In October 2002 the Commission presented a new draft directive. This latest proposal had the same scope and principles as its predecessors, but also incorporated some of the recommendations made by the Winter Group. In particular, it introduced a squeeze-out right and a sell-out right,[14] mandated that the bidder pay the same price to controlling and minority shareholders, and retained the principle that shareholders had to approve defensive measures. Because of tremendous opposition and because of legal problems, the Commission did not include the break-through rule (Burkart and Panunzi, 2003). The proposal did, however, void any restrictions on the transferability of shares and restrictions on voting rights against the bidder once a takeover bid had been announced. This new Article 11 removes a target firm's discretion to exclude a bidder from exercising his corresponding voting rights, say through voting caps, or to prevent him from purchasing further shares. In contrast to the break-through rule, the differentiation of votes – i.e. a multi-class security voting structure – is not considered to constitute such a restriction that it is rendered unenforceable by Article 11. The watered-down directive was finally adopted in April 2004.

5.   Corporate governance

The markets for corporate control and corporate governance are strongly interrelated. Corporate governance is concerned with how to

---

[14] Burkart and Panunzi (2003) provide an analysis of the proposed squeeze-out and sell-out provisions.

allocate control over investment decisions and how to ensure that those entrusted with control use the resources efficiently. A critical aspect of any system of corporate governance is the extent to which control can be contested – i.e. what it takes to remove control from an incumbent manager or controlling owner. Contestability is important *ex post* because it allows control to be reallocated, but *ex ante* it also potentially affects the behaviour of those entrusted with control. A number of corporate governance mechanisms have developed for resolving the collective action problem among dispersed investors. Hostile takeovers are one such mechanism, and an important one, promoting contestability. But these mechanisms also include large blockholder monitoring, managerial compensation schemes, shareholder litigation and monitoring by creditors, in particular banks (for surveys, see Shleifer and Vishny, 1997, and Becht et al., 2002). In this section we discuss the role of large (controlling) shareholders in corporate governance and the market for corporate control in contesting their control. For the subsequent assessment it is important to bear in mind that both ownership concentration and the takeover market are interrelated with other economic and legal institutions, and that their effectiveness as governance mechanisms thus depends on the nature of the whole governance system in which they operate.

5.1   Large shareholders

An investor holding a substantial equity stake has the incentives – i.e. cash-flow claims – to engage in information acquisition and the monitoring of management. He also has considerable voting power to put management under pressure. Indeed, several theoretical models show that a large shareholder engages in costly monitoring, thereby partially overcoming the collective action problem among dispersed shareholders (Becht et al., 2002). Starting with Demsetz and Lehn (1985), numerous empirical papers examine the relationship between ownership concentration and firm value/performance for a given country, typically the United States (for a survey, see Holderness, 2003). The recent law and finance literature has broadened this debate by analysing this relationship across different legal regimes (countries). In support of the view that large shareholders play a positive role, large shareholdings are found to be associated with higher turnover rates of CEOs and directors, with lower compensation for top management and with lower levels of discretionary spending, such as advertisement (Denis and McConnell, 2002; Holderness, 2003). However, the empirical evidence on the effectiveness of 'shareholder activism' in the United States finds a negligible impact of large institutional owners (Becht et al., 2002). Overall, the international evidence indicates that ownership most often has a positive impact on firm value and that this relationship varies both by blockholder identity and by country (Denis and McConnell, 2002). As regards the latter, ownership concentration is found to have a stronger positive impact on firm performance in countries with less legal investor protection.[15]

Concentrated ownership also has its costs, however. Indeed, large shareholders can abuse their power to extract more benefits, possibly at the expense of the small shareholders (Shleifer and Vishny, 1997).[16] Not all benefits accruing from controlling a firm can be written into a contract and enforced in a court. These so-called 'private benefits' of control, as distinct from the contractible security benefits, can come from many sources. They may come from making decisions that benefit a particular investor (or management) at the expense of other investors. Alternatively, they may be the power and prestige that is associated with the control over a firm and the influence it may give over social and political events. Demsetz and Lehn (1985) propose the term 'amenity potential' for this latter type of private benefit, which does not dilute the claims of other investors but increases the total utility to investors. Nonetheless, such amenity potential may distort managerial decisions and prevent value-increasing control shifts from taking place.

The size of private benefits and the extent to which they come at the expense of firm value are a source of controversy among researchers. One method to quantify these benefits is to measure the difference between the per share price in the sale of a controlling block and the share price after the announcement of the block trade. Applying this method, Dyck and Zingales (2004) document 412 transactions of a controlling block in thirty-nine countries. In some countries private benefits, by this measure, appear to be very large. For example, eleven Brazilian transactions show an average premium of around 65 per cent, while in the United States and Canada this figure is 2 per cent. In Europe the range of variation is somewhat smaller, but in Italy and Portugal the mean premium is 37 and 20 per cent, respectively, as compared to most other European countries, where mean premia are below 10 per cent.[17]

[15] Burkart et al. (2003) show in a unified model of managerial succession how family control emerges in regimes with weak legal shareholder protection and widely held firms in regimes with good legal protection.

[16] Other costs associated with (partial) ownerhip concentration are reduced risk sharing, reduced market liquidity, excessive risk taking in highly leveraged firms, or the *ex post* expropriation of managerial rents, thereby stifling initiative *ex ante* (Becht et al., 2002).

[17] Measures of private benefits using the control premium should be treated with considerable care, since the size of the premium depends on many things, such as the inequality

The authors' interpretation is that these large valuations of private benefits reflect possibilities to steal assets from companies, but they cannot rule out amenity potential being involved as well. In both interpretations, non-contractible private benefits play an important role for the incentives of (compensation to) managers and possibly large block-holders. The size of these benefits appears to be inversely related to the extent to which a country's legal rules protect (minority) investors (LaPorta et al., 1997, 1998). Closely related, several studies document that the accumulation of control rights in excess of cash-flow rights – whether through dual-class shares, pyramids or cross-holdings – has a negative impact on share value, suggesting that private benefits are extracted at the expense of small shareholders (Denis and McConnell, 2002).

The conflict between the controlling blockholder and minority share-holders may be mitigated by the presence of additional blockholders. A second or third blockholder can provide monitoring or prevent collusion between the controlling blockholder and management. In support of this notion, Lehman and Weigand (2000) find that a second blockholder has a positive impact on the profitability of German listed firms. Volpin (2002) documents that the valuation of Italian firms is higher when a voting syndicate, as compared to a single shareholder, controls the firm. Faccio et al. (2001) report higher levels of dividends in Western Europe when a second blockholder exists, but the reverse in East Asian countries.

To sum up, controlling shareholders can be effective monitors, but they can also extract private benefits at the expense of other investors and stakeholders in the firm. Similarly, large equity ownership by managers also gives rise to two conflicting (alignment and entrenchment) effects. On the one hand, it aligns the interests of the manager with those of the other shareholders, thereby leading to better performance. On the other hand, larger equity stakes let managers pursue their own goals (possibly at the expense of the shareholder) with less risk of reprisal – i.e. they entrench managers. Both sides of the ownership concentration issue are well documented in numerous empirical studies (which often do not distinguish between ownership by managers and outside blockholders). The empirical evidence is inconclusive on whether, on balance, the positive or negative effects of ownership concentration dominate. Furthermore, ownership concentration is found to be much more prevalent

of voting power, the extent of competition in the market for corporate control, the size of the block sold and the distribution of shares in the target firm. The average premium in countries also varies over time, in ways that are hard to explain (Becht et al., 2002).

in countries with weaker legal protection, even though the agency conflict between large and small shareholders is exacerbated in these countries.

5.2   *Contestability and the market for corporate control*

An important aspect of a corporate governance system is the extent to which it allows control transfers. Circumstances may and do arise in the evolution of a firm when a change of control is the optimal course of action, say because the current CEO proves unable or unwilling to adjust to a new environment. The most direct way to achieve contestability is through an active market for corporate control. A functioning (hostile) takeover market subjects firms to a continuous auction process: whenever an outside party is able to improve the value of existing corporate resources, it can bid for the firm's control. Thus, takeovers permit the replacement of incumbent managers who are either less competent or are not acting in the shareholders' best interest. In addition, the mere threat of a takeover affects the behaviour of those entrusted with control – i.e. it disciplines them.

The contestability of control should not, however, be the sole criterion. There are other reasons for, and modes of, changing control. A control transfer can also be efficient simply because the controlling party wishes to sell. In this case, access to a liquid market for control is important for corporate governance. Controlling owners may want to cash out for a number of reasons – e.g. the lack of a family successor, or consumption or liquidity needs. The US venture capital industry illustrates that the ability to exit investments is important for encouraging entrepreneurial activity. Venture capitalists' investments are normally not liquid, and young firms backed by venture capital often do not generate significant returns. Venture capitalists realise the returns on their investments through private sales of the venture to another firm or initial public offerings and subsequent open market sales. The prospect of such exits is crucial for the young firms' ability to attract venture capital in the first place.

The importance of contestability also depends on the nature of the governance system. A controlling investor is much less likely to oppose an efficient control transfer because selling is an attractive option. By contrast, resistance has much lower opportunity costs for a manager of a widely held firm who has nothing to sell. Indeed, managers who gain financially from a successful takeover by owning an equity stake are found to resist takeovers less (Burkart, 1999).

Furthermore, contestability has benefits as well as costs. A takeover offers the possibility of bringing in new management, which can increase firm value, and the threat of a takeover serves as a disciplining device. But takeovers may also be the manifestation of the managers' ability to pursue their own interests at the expense of the shareholders. Indeed, most takeovers are undertaken not by corporate raiders but by firms headed by professional managers (Burkart, 1999). Similarly, the threat of a takeover may exacerbate the agency problem. Rather than disciplining them, the threat may induce managers to undertake manager-specific investments that make them less easily replaceable. Closely related, the prospect of being fired without proper compensation for current private benefits may undermine the manager's willingness to invest long-term human capital in the firm, and shareholders may worry about the possible dilution of their claims in connection with the sale or under new management.

Ultimately, the degree of contestability of controlling owners and managers is a product of the interaction of all the mechanisms of the corporate governance system. Finding the optimal level of contestability is a key problem in corporate governance. The benefits of contestable control rights must be weighed against any loss of incentives to engage in entrepreneurial activities or large shareholder monitoring. As we have argued, contestability may also come at the expense of minority share-holders; the level of minority protection affects the costs of taking over a firm.

6.   Core takeover provisions: an economic analysis

In this section we examine the three regulatory measures that are at the center of the takeover regulation debate. First we briefly review the familiar arguments in favour of the principle that shareholders have to approve defensive measures. Thereafter we analyse the mandatory bid rule and the break-through rule. We show that they interact with each other and how their combined effect depends on the characteristics of both bidder and target firm. This analysis draws on Bebchuk (1994) and Burkart et al. (2000). Bebchuk compares the incidence of majority block transactions in the absence of the mandatory bid with the incidence of such control transfers in a regime with the mandatory bid rule. Burkart et al. analyse a bidder's choice between a negotiated block trade and a tender offer when attempting to gain control over a firm with a dominant minority shareholder. Berglöf and Burkart (2003) also provide a more formal treatment of the arguments.

6.1   Takeover defences

Many commentators consider takeover defences to be an entrenchment device whereby managers protect their private benefits at the expense of the shareholders: by making bids more costly, defensive measures reduce the number of takeovers and hence the disciplinary force of the market for corporate control. Others argue that defensive measures reinforce the bargaining role conferred on management. Since shareholders are too numerous and lack coordination, they need the management to negotiate on their behalf. Providing the management with the power to defend the company benefits shareholders: it prevents coercive bids, and by delaying an initial bid it provides the necessary time to generate competition among bidders, once a company has come into play. Accordingly, the increase in the bid premium due to defensive measures dominates the negative deterrence effect – i.e. the reduction in the probability of a bid. Empirical evidence on takeover defences does not resolve the debate. First, it is not possible to observe how many takeovers have been prevented by defensive measures. Second, the evidence on the deterrence effect is inconclusive (Becht et al., 2002).

When analysing defensive measures it is important to distinguish between the impact of defensive measures and the power to undertake them. Takeovers may potentially be disruptive for the pursuit of long-term profitable strategies, but shareholders should take this into account when accepting or rejecting a particular bid or when voting on defensive measures. The conflict of interests between managers and shareholders is well documented in the empirical literature (Shleifer and Vishny, 1997). This conflict is particularly pronounced in takeovers; the turnover rate for top managers significantly increases following the completion of a tender offer, and those managers who lose their jobs have difficulty finding another senior executive position (for a survey, see Burkart, 1999). If a manager can apply defences without shareholder ratification, he may abuse this discretion in order to secure his position. Although it is difficult to distinguish personal motives from bargaining on behalf of the shareholders, evidence suggests that managers resist to protect their private benefits. For instance, managers seem less inclined to resist when they gain more, financially, from a successful bid. Consequently, shareholders need to supervise the manager's defensive actions closely if they want to ensure that these are indeed being taken in their interest. Shareholder control is surely improved by giving them the authority over takeover defences. Thus, defensive measures should be subject to shareholder approval.

The new Article 11 of the draft directive rules out ceilings on share-holdings (for bidders) and restrictions on the voting rights of already purchased shares. This provision clearly accords with the above reasoning, and with the principle of shareholder decision-making. It removes the discretion of management to veto share purchases by any (potentially) hostile bidder or to limit his voting rights. In fact, the rule goes further. It also deprives management of the ability to try to convince all other shareholders to adopt such restrictions against a bidder. Restrictions on transferability and voting rights are rendered unenforceable.

6.2   Mandatory bid rule

In the absence of the mandatory bid rule, a controlling minority share-holder (henceforth the incumbent) may sell his block at any price that an outside buyer, (henceforth the rival) is willing to pay. Also, the rival has no obligations to let minority shareholders participate in the control transaction. Hence, such a block sale takes place whenever it is mutually beneficial for incumbent and rival. Due to the free-rider behaviour, small shareholders are not willing to sell their shares for less than the value of the share after the block trade. Consequently, the rival does not gain from making a voluntary tender offer and merely acquires the controlling block.[18]

As shown in Bebchuk (1994), such control transfers necessarily benefit both incumbent and rival, but may have a positive or negative impact on the (wealth of the) small shareholders. When the incumbent's private benefits are small compared to the rival's private benefits, a control transfer can be mutually beneficial even if the loss in security benefits exceeds the gains in private benefits. Similarly, when the rival's private benefits are small compared to the incumbent's private benefits, incumbent and rival may not want to trade the block even though a control transfer would be value increasing.

The mandatory bid rule proposed by the Winter Group and the Commission in its latest proposal requires the rival to offer small share-holders the same per share price as he has paid the incumbent in the block trade. In such an environment, a control transfer takes place only if

---

[18] One reason why a rival may nonetheless prefer to acquire all the shares is that it may enable him to transfer losses and profits between firms to minimise his tax obligations. By contrast, with a controlling interest of less than 100 per cent of the shares, taxes must be paid separately on each firm's profit, thereby preventing such tax optimisation (Bergström et al., 1994).

the rival creates sufficient added value to enable him to pay the control premium to the small shareholders as well. Due to the redistribution from rival to small shareholders, the mandatory bid rule has two opposing effects (see Berglöf and Burkart, 2003). On the one hand, it prevents any value-decreasing change of control, and if a control transfer takes place all parties including the minority shareholders gain. The mandatory bid rule forces the rival to internalise any negative externality that a control transfer may have on the shares owned by the small shareholders. Consequently, he is never willing to acquire the firm, unless a control transfer is efficient. On the other hand, the mandatory bid rule increases the likelihood that a value-increasing control transfer fails to take place. Having to pay the control premium to the small shareholders as well can inflate the total purchase price beyond the rival's willingness to pay, even though a control transfer would add value. Thus, the mandatory bid rule can also impose losses – i.e. forgone share value improvements – on the small shareholders.

Which of the effects dominates is an empirical question. For the United States, empirical studies find that trades of large blocks (and block formations) are, on average, associated with abnormal share price increases. While the market appraisal of block transfers is more favourable for trades followed by a full acquisition, cumulative abnormal returns are also positive when no subsequent full takeover occurs (Holderness, 2003). These findings seems to refute the claim that block trades are undertaken with the aim of looting companies at the expense of small shareholders. Even though small shareholders are harmed in some transactions, the average share value increases suggest that improved management is the primary source of gains in block trades.[19] Thus, large as well as small shareholders benefit from the absence of a mandatory bid rule. Only further empirical work can establish whether this holds more generally.

6.3   The break-through rule

From an economist's viewpoint, the novel and interesting contribution of the Commission's Winter Group is the break-through rule. The break-through rule enables an investor who holds a certain fraction (or more) of the equity capital to break through the firm's existing control structure and exercise core control rights, such as replacing top

---

[19] The reported gains to small shareholders do not, however, imply that a control transfer through a block trade is to be preferred to a control transfer through a tender offer (Burkart et al., 2000).

management. With the proposed threshold of 75 per cent, the rule implies that current controlling minority shareholders who own less than 25 per cent of all shares lose their veto power over a control transfer. Bennedsen and Nielsen (2002) identify how many firms in the European Union (except for Greece, Luxembourg and the Netherlands) would be likely to be affected by the proposed break-through rule. In their sample of 5,126 publicly traded European firms, 20 per cent have dual- (or multiple-) class shares. In 3 to 5 per cent, or thirty-three to forty-nine, of the firms with dual-class shares, the (group of) controlling owners would lose their veto power over a control transfer if the break-through rule were to be applied. In addition, a large number of firms with controlling blocks close to the 25 per cent threshold would potentially be affected when issuing equity. These firms are mainly from Denmark, Germany, Italy and Sweden, and twenty to thirty-three belong to the group of the largest European firms.

The formal analysis in Berglöf and Burkart (2003) examines how and when a controlling minority shareholder is ousted by an outside rival in a regime with a break-through rule. While the subsequent discussion presupposes a firm where the proposed break-through rule eliminates the controlling shareholder's veto power over a control transfer, much of the analysis is also applicable to firms with non-controlling minority owners. Control or substantial influence over a firm does not necessarily require a majority of votes. In particular, when the remaining shares are dispersed a minority block may be sufficient. For instance, neither the Ford nor the Wallenberg families own a majority of votes.[20]

By making a firm with a controlling minority shareholder akin to a firm with dispersed ownership for which incumbent and rival compete, the break-through rule indeed facilitates the transfer of control, as intended by the Winter Group. The intuition for this is as follows: the break-through rule gives the rival the option of bypassing the incumbent to take control of the firm, rather than seeking his agreement. Since the negotiated block trade with subsequent mandatory bid is the more expensive mode of gaining control, the rival will always choose to circumvent the incumbent and directly make a tender offer. This leaves the incumbent with no other possibility than to compete if he wants to retain control. Hence, provided that rival and incumbent can finance bids

---

[20] In the sample of Bennedsen and Nielsen (2002), 17 per cent of the firms with dual-class shares have a dominant minority shareholder, who holds (at least) ten times as many voting rights as cash-flow rights without possessing the majority of votes. Among these firms, a significant number are European top-500 firms, such as Fiat and Ericsson. The introduction of the break-through rule would considerably weaken the position of the dominant shareholder.

equal to their valuation of the entire firm, the party with the higher valuation prevails. Thus, in the absence of wealth constraints, the break-through rule ensures an efficient allocation of corporate control. It seems plausible, however, to assume that many – if not all – incumbent controlling minority shareholders are financially constrained. If not, they could regain their veto power over a control transfer by increasing their block above the 25 per cent threshold. Once wealth constraints are taken into account, control allocation need no longer be efficient in a regime with the break-through rule.

When assessing the merits of the break-through rule, it is worthwhile to reflect on the reasons why value-increasing control transfers may fail in the first place. As argued above, the large private benefits of the incumbent can prevent efficient control transfers. The Winter Group seems rather biased towards focusing on this explanation and to viewing controlling minority shareholders as the major obstacle to takeovers and corporate restructuring in Europe. The Group seems to forget that the mandatory bid rule, which is (in the most stringent form) part of the Group's recommendations, is also a reason why value-increasing control transfers can fail. The break-through rule not only allows the rival to bypass the incumbent but also spares him the cost of having to pay all small shareholders a control premium. That is, the break-through rule makes feasible value-increasing control transfers that are frustrated either by the incumbent's opposition or by the mandatory bid rule. Hence, if promoting an active takeover market is a primary objective, one may argue in favour of a regime that combines the break-through rule with no – or a less stringent – mandatory bid rule.

When the incumbent cannot compete with the outside rival for control, the break-through rule also has undesirable effects for the small shareholders, as the analysis in Berglöf and Burkart (2003) establishes. Most notably, the break-through rule can undo the added (minority shareholder) protection that the mandatory bid rule provides. It enables the rival to gain control with a bid equal to the post-takeover (minority) share value, thereby putting small shareholders in the same position as in a regime without the mandatory bid rule. Furthermore, it allows for the possibility that, due to the coordination problems among small shareholders, a bid may succeed even though it is against their collective interests.[21]

---

[21] The same coordination problem can cause the failure of value-increasing takeover bids. All shareholders prefer the bid to succeed, but each wants to free-ride to get the entire value improvement. That is, the failure of value-increasing bids is nothing but the flip side of the success of value-decreasing bids.

The break-through rule is clearly against the interests of the incumbent controlling minority shareholders; it eliminates their veto power over a control transfer and reduces the prospect of getting compensated for the forgone private benefits in a control transaction. As a result, controlling blocks with less than 25 per cent of the equity capital will (drastically) lose in value. This loss will be reflected in smaller (or even zero) price differentials between shares with high voting power and shares with low voting power and lower premium paid in block trades to the extent that such transactions continue to take place (without triggering a mandatory bid). It also seems likely that controlling minority shareholders will respond to the introduction of the break-through rule and try to circumvent it. One way to undermine the break-through rule is the approval of defensive measures in a general shareholder meeting. By virtue of owning a majority of the votes, the controlling minority shareholder can de facto unilaterally decide to frustrate a bid. The Winter Report shuts down this option by prohibiting the use of disproportionate control rights in votes on defence measures.

As already mentioned, raising the block size above the 25 per cent threshold is the most straightforward way to neutralise the break-through rule, provided that the necessary funds are available. According to the estimates of Bennedsen and Nielsen (2002), this strategy is a valid option for only a few firms. The adoption of a pyramidal structure (adding one layer in the pyramid), cross-shareholdings, or other devices for separating ownership and control are alternative means to avoid the risk of becoming a victim of the break-through rule. In fact, the Winter Group explicitly acknowledges that pyramids and dual-class shares serve the purpose of keeping control with little equity capital. Nonetheless, the Group recommends that the break-through rule should not apply to pyramids because it would be too complicated and expensive. Not surprisingly, the report has been criticised for exempting or even promoting pyramids, thereby affecting existing corporate governance arrangements asymmetrically (Bebchuk and Hart, 2002).

Bennedsen and Nielsen (2002) point out that the introduction of the break-through rule may also have an impact on firms in which the controlling minority shareholder currently owns more than 25 per cent of the equity capital. At least some of these firms are likely to be restricted in raising new equity capital without falling under the break-through rule. For such firms, the break-through rule may well either increase the cost of new funds or limit its availability.

Finally, it should be noted that the break-through rule represents a major *ex post* intervention in the property rights of controlling minority shareholders. Such interventions raise, besides fundamental fairness issues, the prospects that there will be more in the future, thus creating uncertainty about the basic property rights. In terms of our analysis, this would undermine the incentives to hold controlling blocks in the first place.

7.   Takeover regulation and corporate governance in Europe

The impact of specific regulation differs fundamentally across countries in Europe, largely due to the differences in the predominant patterns of ownership and control in individual firms. The mandatory bid rule and the break-through rule have no impact when a firm's shares are widely dispersed. When ownership and control are concentrated, or, more precisely, when there are controlling minority shareholders with less equity than the threshold for a break-through rule (and the controlling owner is wealth-constrained), the two rules have opposite effects. If only the mandatory bid rule is binding, it will increase entrenchment. If the controlling owner uses dual-class shares to separate ownership and control, he may well respond by forming the more control-effective pyramids, thus enforcing entrenchment further. We have seen that as many as one-fifth of all listed firms in Europe use shares with differentiated votes (Bennedsen and Nielsen, 2002). In a substantial number of these firms, the controlling owner would incur control losses without receiving any compensation. And an even larger group of firms would be constrained in raising equity because their control block would otherwise fall below the break-through threshold.

More generally, as our analysis has demonstrated, there are also obvious limits to what can be achieved through takeover regulation, in any system. Takeover decisions do themselves suffer from agency problems; in fact, takeovers may be as much manifestations of agency problems as solutions to them. Takeover regulation affects the distribution of the takeover gains among the bidding firm and the target firm, and between a controlling owner and minority shareholders in the target, and thus the incentives to make bids. But it is not possible to screen out bad bids (primarily motivated by control benefits) without also preventing value-enhancing bids. Measures to protect minority investors in takeovers increase the costs of taking over, thus reducing contestability.

Achieving contestability in a corporate governance system such as that of Continental Europe is not trivial. With large controlling stakes the likelihood of a hostile bid succeeding is small. Managerial compensation schemes are unlikely to be as powerful, or as important, when a large controlling shareholder can easily fire management. Similarly, the board of directors cannot be expected to play the same independent function as in a widely held firm, because the members sit there on a mandate from the controlling owner. We will return to what could possible be achieved through other mechanisms such as institutional investor monitoring, litigation and the media.

Moreover, to the extent that takeover regulation discourages monitoring by controlling shareholders, this would increase the discretion of managers. Any evaluation of takeover regulation thus has to compare not only the costs and benefits of controlling shareholders but also the costs and benefits of its alternative – the managerially controlled firm. The evidence on the relative performance of firms with controlling owners and those with dispersed shareholders does not yield conclusive results (Becht et al., 2002). This should not come as a surprise, given the strong interrelationship between competition, the firm's internal organisation and ownership concentration. Moreover, as we have discussed, such comparisons are extremely difficult, since the effects of particular ownership and control structures depend critically on the entire corporate governance system.

Comparisons at the level of systems also fail to yield clear results. The study by Dyck and Zingales (2004) on control benefits using premia in block transactions suggests substantial variations across countries, but the differences are rather small among developed market economies. Examinations of managerial dismissals following shocks to earnings, cash-flows and stock prices suggest no significant differences across countries (Kaplan, 1997). However, the mechanisms through which turnovers of management are achieved differ fundamentally. In Japan, for example, the company's house bank becomes more active, while in the United States board activity increases.

Intervening in corporate governance systems is risky precisely because of the interrelationship between the different mechanisms. If large shareholder monitoring is effectively shut down, it will take time before the other mechanisms adjust. For example, transparency about ownership and control structures and about what owners and managers do is still much poorer in many European countries than in the United States. The tradition of litigation is very different, and the courts have a rather limited role in resolving corporate governance issues in Europe.

8.   A regulatory framework for Europe

There is widespread agreement that the starting point for any regulatory effort in the area of takeover regulation and corporate governance should be contractual freedom. Any intervention must be clearly motivated by externalities stemming from corporate governance failures in individual firms. Even more important, legally signed contracts should be respected. Extraordinary circumstances may require altering contractual rights in existing contracts, such as was done, for example, through the recent Sarbanes-Oxley legislation in the United States strengthening the liability of managers and owners for their financial statements. But these interventions risk creating uncertainty about the basic rules and thus undermine the willingness to engage in entrepreneurial activity and invest in companies.

Even when regulation is warranted, self-regulation has proven effective in many countries, with the United Kingdom's City Code perhaps the most prominent example. However, internationalisation and potential contagion effects from governance failures in individual firms or on individual exchanges suggest that government intervention is warranted. But government intervention can take several forms, and happen at both the national and EU level.

As we have seen, the UK City Code, itself a result of self-regulation, has served as the model for national- and EU-level regulators in Europe. But there are at least two alternative reference points. One model is that of the United States, with its predominance of firms with dispersed shareholdings and considerable variation in corporate laws across states. The potential for competition among jurisdictions plays some role in shaping regulation over time, and Delaware has emerged as the state of preference for large listed corporations. In the EU context the US model would imply an EU-level securities markets regulator and subsidiarity in most aspects of corporate law, but with one or two national jurisdictions emerging as the major attractors for large firms.

A second alternative model is that of Canada, where corporate law also is state-based but considerable coordination takes place at the federal level. The Canadian example combines a regulatory framework requiring a high level of transparency à la United States, with a corporate governance system dominated by concentrated shareholdings and an extensive separation of ownership and control through pyramiding and the differentiation of votes. Minority protection comes primarily from a commonly used general clause against the oppression of minority interests. Interestingly, Canada had the same low level of control premium as the United States in the Dyck and Zingales (2004) study. The Canadian model would also allow variation across EU member states but with extensive coordination at the EU level. For Continental European and Nordic countries reluctant to change their system of corporate governance fundamentally, the Canadian experience offers an interesting alternative to a European framework based on the US and UK experiences.

Our analysis suggests that harmonisation has important downsides, in particular when rules have very different impacts in different countries. For the same reasons, binding EU directives in this area clearly have their drawbacks. At the same time, the ability to buy and sell control freely across member states is an important aspect of the Single Market, and these border-transcending aspects of takeover regulation should be the focus of the European Commission. Much of what is in the current draft directive has this focus, but the strict mandatory bid rule has a broader impact and goes against the objectives of contestability and a level playing field. We would argue in favor of an EU framework for takeover regulation that balances the benefits and costs from harmonisation recognising the differences in corporate governance systems and the different impact of individual pieces of regulation. Such a framework would contain both binding directives and recommendations. But what should the recommendations offer, and what elements should possibly be binding?

In some areas there are already binding rules, in particular when it comes to the disclosure of ownership and control. But careful examination shows that in many countries this regulation is implemented only superficially (Barca and Becht, 2001). It is often very difficult to get access to the relevant information, and even when this information is available the data provided are not sufficient to understand the control structure. The disclosure of ownership and control is critical to the market for corporate control and for monitoring the activities of controlling shareholders. In general, the enforcement of existing regulation might be at least as important as introducing new regulation. Binding disclosure standards should be extended to a much broader range of issues, in particular when it comes to managerial compensation. In fact, the most urgent governance reform at the European level at the moment may be to increase transparency. The combination of the deliberate concealment of relevant information and generally opaque corporate governance environments presents a serious obstacle to cross-border control transactions in many countries in Europe.

The rules that regulate the takeover process and ensure that shareholders have the right to vote on takeover defences once a bid has been made are now largely accepted by most countries, even by Germany. Many of the other rules in the draft directive and the Winter proposals are also uncontroversial. Whether these rules are part of a binding proposal or not seems secondary, since they would presumably be part of any recommendation and be adopted by member states. The provision in the draft directive (Article 11) that renders restrictions on voting rights and on the transferability of shares unenforceable against bidders should probably be part of a binding directive. Regulatory competition from the United States suggests that management or controlling owners may otherwise seek jurisdictions that allow takeover defences such as, for example voting caps.

Our analysis has been critical of the strict mandatory bid rule ruling out any control premium. However, even though the mandatory bid rule reduces control transfers, it does in one important way improve investor protection: the mandatory bid rule prevents control transfers in which the gains for incumbent and new controlling (minority) shareholder do not stem from value creation but are redistribution at the expense of small shareholders. Some form of a mandatory bid rule with a reasonably high threshold for triggering and an allowance for some control premium – i.e. a less strict rule than that advocated by the Winter Group – could also be part of a recommendation, perhaps even of a binding part to a directive (in practice, most member states already have such a rule). For instance, the rule could put an upper limit on the differential between the price paid in the block transaction and the price offered in the subsequent mandatory bid.

Generally, we argue strongly against wholesale changes of corporate governance systems. The strong interrelationship between the different mechanisms suggests great caution in radical reforms. The combined effect of the mandatory bid rule and the break-through rule, as shown in section 6, would have been to reduce drastically the incentives to hold controlling blocks and effectively eliminate controlling shareholders from many companies. Alternatively, the proposal could have triggered new control structures that are hard to foresee, through pyramiding and less transparent arrangements.

In our view, the objective of regulation should not be to intervene in specific control structures or generally discourage controlling blocks. Indeed, we are against discouraging the delegation of control and monitoring to individual large shareholders. Rather, we favour an approach that attempts to improve the general corporate governance environment, in particular by greatly increasing transparency through the stricter enforcement of existing regulation and an extension of these measures to more areas. Controlling shareholders do in most cases perform some positive function in constraining managerial behaviour, and they may be critical to some forms of restructuring (sometimes while appropriating considerable private benefits). The broader objective of regulation should be to make monitoring by large shareholders superfluous, not to get rid of them.

In its quest to increase contestability and corporate governance the Commission should rely less one-sidedly on hostile takeovers and proxy fights. The level of contestability in a particular system stems from the combined effects of all the corporate governance mechanisms. Rather than undermining controlling shareholders, and effectively weakening this critically important mechanism of corporate governance, the Commission should try to exploit the other mechanisms. These mechanisms can constrain controlling shareholders and managers and thus also improve the functioning of the market for corporate control. It is encouraging that the second report from the Winter Group, after its mandate had been extended, is on corporate law reform in the European Union. Many of the proposals in that report are about strengthening these other mechanisms, in particular the recommendations addressing transparency.

We are convinced that improving transparency is key to activating the other mechanisms, especially minority shareholders and the media. More information on what controlling owners and managers do, and how they are compensated, would help curb some of the excesses and put pressure on them to perform. We also believe that making managers, controlling owners and board members more accountable through various measures such as standardised fiduciary duties can help. But we are less optimistic that creditors can play a larger role in corporate governance than they already do. Banks, it seems, are neither capable of nor interested in monitoring management on a daily basis.

The bottom line is that no single mechanism is likely to deliver sufficient corporate governance and restructuring. Large institutional investors with a tradition of portfolio-orientation have been drawn into governance in the United States. In the United Kingdom they have remained more passive. On the Continent some of these institutions are new, but other institutional investors have been deeply involved in corporate governance. The evidence regarding their impact is still weak, but more can be done to entice these institutions to play a more important role. Litigation is another area where European experience is limited. In the United States the exercise of this mechanism has largely benefited lawyers (Romano, 1991), but it could probably be strengthened in Europe, where the risk of abuse appears to be less pronounced due to differences in legal practices. Perhaps some progress could also be made on the independence of directors on boards, forcing controlling owners to accept minority shareholder representatives. The independence of auditors is also desirable.

To conclude, any regulatory exercise, in particular at the EU level, must take into account the fact that a corporate governance system is highly complex and made up of many complementary parts. An intervention in part of the system may have ripple effects that are not immediately obvious, and hard to anticipate fully. The different parts of the system fit together, and changes in one part may undermine the functioning of another, but changes in one mechanism could also reinforce another mechanism. Consequently, the impact of an individual takeover rule need not be uniform but depends on the context. As we have shown, this applies, for example, to the mandatory bid. The strict mandatory bid rule included in the draft takeover directive goes against both objectives set up by the Commission: improved contestability and a level playing field. The rule lowers contestability in firms with controlling shareholders, and, since it has a differential impact depending on the structure of ownership and control, the rule actually makes the playing field less level.

REFERENCES

Barca, F., and M. Becht (eds.) (2001), *Control of Corporate Europe*, Oxford University Press, Oxford.

Bebchuk, L. (1994), 'Efficient and inefficient sales of corporate control', *Quarterly Journal of Economics*, 109, 957–93.

Bebchuk, L., and O. Hart (2002), 'A threat to dual-class shares', *Financial Times*, 31 May.

Bebchuk, L., A. Cohen and A. Ferrell (2002), *Does the Evidence Favor State Competition in Corporate Law?*, John M. Olin Center for Law, Economics, and Business Discussion Paper 352, Harvard University, MA.

Becht, M., P. Bolton and A. Röell (2002), *Corporate Governance and Control*, mimeo, Princeton University, NJ.

Bennedsen, M., and K. Nielsen (2002), *The Impact of a Break-Through Rule on European Firms*, mimeo, Copenhagen Business School.

Berglöf, E., and M. Burkart (2003), 'European takeover regulation', *Economic Policy*, 36, 172–213.

Berglöf, E., B. Holmström, P. Högfeldt, E. Meyersson and H. T. Söderström (2003), *Ägarmakten utmanad*, Center for Business and Policy Studies, Stockholm.

Bergström, C., P. Högfeldt, J. Macey and P. Samuelsson (1994), *The Regulation of Corporate Acquisitions: A Law and Economics Analysis of European Proposals for Reform*, Working Paper No. 62, Department of Finance, Stockholm School of Economics.

Burkart, M. (1999), *Economics of Takeover Regulation*, mimeo, Stockholm School of Economics.

Burkart, M., and F. Panunzi (2003), *Mandatory Bids, Squeeze-Out, Sell-Out and the Dynamics of the Tender Offer Process*, Law Working Paper no. 10/2003, European Corporate Governance Institute, Brussel.

Burkart, M., D. Gromb and F. Panunzi (2000), 'Agency conflicts in public and negotiated transfers of corporate control', *Journal of Finance*, 55, 647–77.

Burkart, M., F. Panunzi and A. Shleifer (2003), 'Family firms', *Journal of Finance*, 58 (5), 2167–201.

Cespa, G., and G. Cestone (2002), *Stakeholder Activism, Managerial Entrenchment, and the Congruence of Interests between Shareholders and Stakeholders*, mimeo, Universitat Pompeu Fabra, Barcelona.

Demsetz, H., and K. Lehn (1985), 'The structure of corporate ownership: causes and consequences', *Journal of Political Economy*, 93, 1155–77.

Denis, D. K., and J. McConnell (2002), *International Corporate Governance*, mimeo, Krannert Graduate School of Management, Purdue University, West Lafayette, IN.

Dyck, A., and L. Zingales (2004) 'Private benefits of control: an international comparison', *Journal of Finance*, 59(2), 533–96.

European Commission (2002a), *Report of the High-level Group of Company Law Experts on Issues related to Takeover Bids*, Brussels ('the first Winter Report').

——— (2002b), *Directive of the European Parliament and of the Council on Takeover Bids*, Brussels.

——— (2002c), *Report of the High-level Group of Company Law Experts on a Modern Regulatory Framework for Company Law in Europe*, Brussels, ('the final Winter Report').

Faccio, M., and L. Lang (2002), 'The ultimate ownership of Western European companies', *Journal of Financial Economics*, 65, 365–95.

Faccio, M., L. Lang and L. Young (2001) 'Dividends and expropriation', *American Economic Review*, 91, 54–78.

Ferrarini, G. (forthcoming), 'Share ownership, takeover law and the contestability of corporate control', in: *Company Law Reform in OECD Countries: A Comparative Outlook of Current Trends* (Conference Proceedings).

Franks, J., and C. Mayer (1998), 'Bank control, takeovers and corporate governance in Germany', *Journal of Banking and Finance*, 22, 1385–403.

Grossman, S. J., and O. D. Hart (1980), 'Takeover bids, the free rider problem, and the theory of the corporation', *Bell Journal of Economics*, 11, 42–64.

Holderness, C. G. (2003) 'A survey of blockholders and corporate control', *Economic Policy Review*, 9 (1), 51–64.

Holmström, B., and S. N. Kaplan (2001), 'Corporate governance and merger activities in the US: making sense of the 1980s and 1990s', *Journal of Economic Perspectives*, 15 (2), 121–44.

Hopt, K. J. (2002) 'Common principles of corporate governance in Europe', in: J. A. McCahery, P. Moerland, T. Raaijmakers and L. Renneboog (eds.) *Corporate Governance Regimes: Convergence and Diversity*, Oxford University Press, Oxford and New York, 175–204.

Jenkinson, T., and A. Ljungqvist (2001), 'The Role of Hostile Stakes in German Corporate Governance', *Journal of Corporate Finance*, 7, 397–446.

Kaplan, S. N. (1997), 'Corporate governance and corporate performance: a comparison of Germany, Japan, and the U.S.', in: *The Bank of America Journal of Applied Corporate Finance*, Winter.

Köke, J. (2000), *The Market for Corporate Control in Germany: Causes and Consequences of Changes in the Ultimate Share Ownership*, mimeo, Centre for European Economic Research (ZEW), Mannheim.

La Porta, R., F. Lopez-de-Silanes and A. Shleifer (1999), 'Corporate ownership around the world', *Journal of Finance*, 54, 471–517.

La Porta, R., F. Lopez-de-Silanes, A. Shleifer and R. W. Vishny (1997), 'Legal determinants of external finance', *Journal of Finance*, 52, 1131–50.

(1998), 'Law and finance', *Journal of Political Economy*, 106, 1113–55.

Lehman, E., and J. Weigand (2000), 'Does the governed corporation perform better? Governance structures and corporate performance in Germany', *European Finance Review*, 4, 157–95.

Pagano, M., and P. Volpin (2001), *Managers, Workers and Corporate Control*, Working Paper no. 352, Institute of Finance and Accounting, London Business School.

Romano, R. (1991), 'The shareholder suit: litigation without foundation?', *Journal of Law, Economics, and Organization*, 7, 55–87.

Shleifer, A., and R. W. Vishny (1986), 'Large shareholders and corporate control', *Journal of Political Economy*, 94, 461–88.

(1997), 'A survey of corporate governance', *Journal of Finance*, 52, 737–83.

Skog, R. (2002), *The Saga of EU Takeover Regulation*, mimeo, Department of Law, Stockholm University.

Volpin, P. (2002) 'Governance with poor investor protection: evidence from top executive turnover', *Journal of Financial Economics*, 64, 61–90.

Wymeersch, E. (1998), 'A status report on corporate governance in some Continental European states', in: Hopt, K. J., H. Kanda, M. J. Roe, E. Wymeersch and S. Prigge, (eds.) *Comparative Corporate Governance: The State of the Art and Emerging Research*, Clarendon Press, Oxford, 1045–199.

Yarrow, G. K. (1985), 'Shareholder protection, compulsory acquisition and the efficiency of the takeover process', *Journal of Industrial Economics*, 34, 3–16.

Part II

Recent developments

3 Foreign direct investment and labour market outcomes

Kenneth Scheve and Matthew J. Slaughter

1. Introduction

The multinationalisation of production is perhaps the most striking and distinguishing characteristic of the process of globalisation over the last two decades. The share of cross-border capital flows accounted for by the foreign direct investment of multinationals has been rising in recent years. In fact, in recent decades cross-border flows of FDI have grown at much faster rates than have flows of goods and services or people. UNCTAD (2001) reports that, from 1986 through to 2000, worldwide cross-border outflows of FDI rose at an annualised rate of 26.2 per cent, versus a rate of just 15.4 per cent for worldwide exports of goods and services. In the second half of the 1990s this difference widened to 37.0 per cent versus just 1.9 per cent.

Given this context, it is not surprising that multinational enterprises are also central to academic and political debates about the consequences of globalisation. The FDI activity of multinationals is claimed to have a host of effects on economic growth and development, the level and incidence of national tax regimes, the labour and environmental regulatory capacities of host countries, and many dimensions of labour market performance. Each of these relationships has important implications for the politics of globalisation and the evolution of economic policy-making around the world. This is especially true in the European Union, for which single-market reforms and the creation of the EMU have dramatically liberalised both intra-EU and external foreign investment policies.

In this chapter we examine the relationship between foreign investment in Europe and labour market outcomes. How is the multinationalisation of production likely to affect the level and distribution of wages and employment? What are its consequences for the volatility of labour market outcomes and the perceptions of risk among workers? Does

We thank Karl Pichelmann for his helpful comments.

foreign ownership make a difference for how firms and workers share profits? Answering these questions is critical for assessing the welfare effects of foreign investment and for beginning to construct a systematic account of the political economy of foreign ownership in Europe.

In this chapter we argue that any assessment of the impact of FDI activity by multinational enterprises requires first an evaluation of the determinants of this activity. Why firms go abroad has important consequences for the effects of their investments on domestic labour markets. We review evidence that there exists substantial heterogeneity, both across countries and over time, in the types of European FDI. Some investment looks horizontal, in that it is motivated primarily by the desire to produce goods and services for consumers in the host country. Some, however, looks vertical, in that investments are designed to take advantage of international factor–price differences and produce goods for export. Other foreign investment in Europe does not fit easily into either of these two standard categories.

Furthermore, we argue that the composition of FDI within a given European country varies significantly, with a set of host-country policies and characteristics. Multinationals appear to tailor their operations, based on considerations such as host-country size, per capita income and policy choices such as EU membership and corporate tax rates. This evidence, along with cross-country and over-time heterogeneity in in-dustry composition, external orientation and factor intensity, belies the conventional view that all FDI into Europe is market-seeking horizontal investment. Moreover, it suggests that government policy may play an important role in shaping the composition of inward FDI flows, above and beyond their overall level. All these patterns have important conse-quences for the host-country labour market impacts of FDI and their variation across Europe.

Having documented this heterogeneity, we turn next to consider the labour market impacts of FDI. Does the nationality of firm ownership matter for the level, distribution and volatility of worker earnings and ownership? More specifically, we consider four dimensions to this ques-tion: the relative demand (and thus earnings and/or employment) be-tween more skilled and less skilled workers economy-wide; the absolute earnings of each worker type; labour demand elasticities and the volatil-ity of worker earnings; and profit-sharing. For all these dimensions, we present both theoretical and empirical evidence that the answer to this question is 'yes'. This all suggests that the impact of multinationals on labour markets is complex, with net impacts on labour market outcomes that can vary in different contexts.

The chapter has three sections. Section 2 examines the patterns of foreign direct investment in Europe by multinational enterprises. Section 3 discusses the labour market consequences of this FDI. Section 4 concludes.

2.   Vertical and horizontal FDI into Europe: evidence and causes[1]

In general, a firm becomes multinational when, through FDI, it establishes in two or more countries business enterprises in which it exercises some minimum level of ownership control. Over the last two decades, in the international-trade literature in economics, there has been substantial progress in modelling multinational firms in general equilibrium. This theoretical literature contains mostly uni-dimensional theories of multinationals, which focus on either *horizontal* or *vertical FDI*.[2]

The vertical FDI view is that multinationals arise to take advantage of international factor–price differences.[3] Suppose that firms engage in two activities: headquarter services (e.g. research and development (R&D) and advertising) and production. Headquarter services use, relatively intensively, physical or human capital; while production uses, relatively intensively, manual labour. If factor prices differ across countries, then firms can become multinational by locating production in countries where manual labour costs are low and headquarters in countries where skilled labour costs are low. Firm-wide production costs are lower with this fragmented structure than they would be if the firm remained integrated in a single country.

The horizontal FDI view is that multinationals arise because trade barriers make exporting costly.[4] Most formalisations of this idea assume that firms have a high-fixed-cost headquarters and one or more production plants. When trade costs are low, a firm produces all output in domestic plants and serves foreign consumers through exports. When

[1] This section (text and tables) draws heavily on the discussion in Slaughter (2003).

[2] This discussion focuses on general-equilibrium trade models of multinational firms. For a discussion of partial-equilibrium treatments, see Caves (1996) and Markusen (1995, 2002).

[3] See Helpman (1984) and Helpman and Krugman (1985). This view is related to models of foreign outsourcing, in which the vertical separation of production occurs *without* multinationals. See, for example, Feenstra and Hanson (1996).

[4] See Markusen and Venables (1998, 2000). Trade models of this variety are similar to older theories of tariff-jumping FDI. See Caves (1996) for a discussion. There have been some attempts to integrate models of horizontal and vertical FDI into a single framework. See an overview in Markusen (2002).

trade costs are high, a firm becomes multinational by building production plants both at home and abroad, each serving just that country's consumers. This type of FDI is called horizontal because the multinational performs the same range of activities (here, production) in all countries.

These two views of multinationals have much in common. Both are typically interpreted as applying to manufacturing. In each case, multinationals arise to avoid duplicating headquarter activities. They also raise world welfare by making global production more efficient. An important dimension along which the two views can differ is in how FDI affects factor incomes within and across countries. If FDI is vertical, then multinationals may reduce absolute wage differences across countries and alter relative wages within countries. If FDI is horizontal, then multinationals may raise income in each country without necessarily changing its distribution. We discuss these issues more in the next section.

Recent academic empirical work tends to conclude that most real-world FDI is horizontal, not vertical. Consider these three findings. First, for decades most FDI flowed from large, rich countries to other large, rich countries (see, e.g., Markusen, 1995; Lipsey, 1999, 2003).[5] That multinationals locate most production in similar, high-wage economies may be consistent with FDI being driven more by market access than by wage differences. Second, sales by foreign affiliates of US multinationals are higher in countries with higher tariffs and transport costs on US goods (Brainard, 1997; Carr et al., 2001). This appears consistent with FDI being motivated by market access. Third, US firms serve foreign markets more through FDI and less through exports the larger the scale of corporate operations relative to the scale of production (Brainard, 1997; Yeaple, 2001). This supports the idea that multinationals arise when scale economies in headquarter activities are strong relative to scale economies in production.[6]

When considering FDI from the United States into Europe, in light of their similarly high levels of development relative to the rest of the world,

---

[5] In a regression setting, Carr et al. (2001) find that sales by affiliates of foreign multinationals in the United States or by foreign affiliates of US multinationals are higher for countries with a GDP more similar to US GDP.

[6] Some representative statements on the predominance of horizontal FDI are Brainard (1997, p. 539) – 'The finding that rising per-worker income differentials reduce affiliate sales . . . [is] inconsistent with explanations of multinational activity that depend on factor-proportion differences [i.e. vertical FDI]' – and Markusen and Maskus (1999, abstract and p. 16) – 'Econometric tests give strong support to the horizontal model and overwhelmingly reject the vertical model. [. . .] The [vertical] model should clearly not be taken seriously as a description of the world.'

one might presume this FDI to be predominantly horizontal in nature. But several recent studies demonstrate that the pattern of European FDI over the 1980s and 1990s has been more complex than one of just horizontal FDI (studies using data on US- as well as European-head-quartered multinationals): see Barba Navaretti et al. (2002), Barrell and Pain (1999), Braconier and Ekholm (2001) and Hanson et al. (2001). As Slaughter (2003) and others emphasise, the 1990s are especially important to examine because some broad European patterns in this decade look quite different from those of the 1980s.

This section will summarise some of the evidence on the nature of European FDI (in particular, the evidence presented in Slaughter, 2003). If horizontal FDI truly characterised the lion's share of multi-national activity, then the data would be dominated by manufacturing affiliates producing and selling into host markets without obvious variation in factor intensities. The main message here is that *there is substantial heterogeneity both across countries and over time in the types of European FDI*. Some looks horizontal, some vertical, and some something else in non-manufacturing activities. The data indicate a richer picture of European FDI than one of just horizontal FDI, of manufacturing activity flowing from one high-income region into another. Manufacturing accounts for less than half of all European FDI; in many countries it is just a minority fraction. Firms clearly do more than make goods; they may sell goods, and/or provide services as well. And, regardless of the composition of industries, different affiliates have different degrees of vertical links to their US parents, through cross-border outsourcing, and also different degrees of external orientation, in terms of exports. All this suggests that government policy may play an important role in shaping the *composition* of inward FDI, above and beyond its overall *level*.

2.1   Vertical and horizontal FDI into Europe: evidence

The tables in this section cover data for majority-owned, non-bank affiliates of US-headquartered corporations, as tracked by the US Bureau of Economic Analysis (BEA). The full data cover affiliate operations in Europe for the four most recent BEA benchmark survey years: 1982, 1989, 1994 and 1999. See Slaughter (2003) for a detailed data discussion.[7]

---

[7] Note that, in the BEA data, each affiliate is measured as a business enterprise, not an establishment (as in other micro-level research, such as work using the US Longitudinal Research Database or the UK Annual Respondents Database). The BEA does not track the number of establishments.

Table 3.1 has a distributional focus: how important high-income countries are for the overall European operations of US multinationals. For three years – 1982, 1989, and 1999 – it reports the share of affiliate activity in Europe (sales or employment in all industries or just manufacturing) accounted for by a set of high-income European countries, defined as countries with a 1982 real per capita GDP of at least $10,000. Thus, for example, in 1982 these high-income countries accounted for 96.0 per cent of the European sales of US affiliates in all industries.

The important message of table 3.1 is that, over the past two decades, high-income countries have accounted for a declining share of total European affiliate activity. All four rows show declining shares from 1982 to 1999, with larger declines in the 1990s versus the 1980s. This intra-European shift is consistent with similar intra-European data for all inward FDI in Barba Navaretti et al. (2002) and Braconier and Ekholm (2001). These falling shares could be consistent with either horizontal FDI (to the extent that it is driven by rising incomes and thus market size outside this group of countries) or vertical FDI (to the extent that it is driven by lower factor costs, even if the differentials were closing, outside this group of countries).

Table 3.2 disaggregates the intra-European focus of table 3.1 for all the individual countries for which various employment aggregates are consistently reported by the BEA. For three years – 1982, 1989 and 1999 – it reports both the level (in thousands of workers) and Europe-wide share of employment, in all industries and manufacturing by itself, for eighteen individual European countries plus a nineteenth 'other'

Table 3.1. *The share of high-income countries in the European activity of affiliates of US multinational firms*

Activity	1982	1989	1999
Sales, all industries	96.0	92.6	87.2
Employment, all industries	91.7	91.1	84.5
Sales, manufacturing	92.1	89.9	83.0
Employment, manufacturing	90.9	89.7	80.5

Note: Cell entries report the share (in percentage terms) of the Europe-wide activity (as measured by that cell's row) of majority-owned affiliates of US multinational firms accounted for by countries with a 1982 real per capita GDP of at least $10,000. (These countries were Austria, Belgium, Denmark, Finland, France, Germany, Iceland, Italy, Luxembourg, the Netherlands, Norway, Sweden, Switzerland and the United Kingdom.)
Source: Bureau of Economic Analysis, US Department of Commerce. This table is taken from Slaughter (2003).

Table 3.2. *The level and share of individual countries in the European employment of affiliates of US multinational firms*

Country	Industry Group	1982 Level	1982 Share	1989 Level	1989 Share	1999 Level	1999 Share
Austria	All industries	23.0	1.0	17.8	0.8	30.0	0.9
	Manufacturing	12.8	0.8	13.0	0.6	18.8	1.0
Belgium	All industries	120.3	5.4	114.3	5.0	113.0	3.3
	Manufacturing	86.8	5.3	80.9	5.4	68.9	3.6
Denmark	All industries	17.4	0.8	16.9	0.7	31.0	0.9
	Manufacturing	7.4	0.5	6.6	0.4	15.5	0.8
Finland	All industries	5.0	0.2	7.1	0.3	14.0	0.4
	Manufacturing	n/a	n/a	1.3	0.1	6.1	0.3
France	All industries	293.2	13.0	333.5	14.5	479.0	14.0
	Manufacturing	208.6	12.8	189.8	12.6	250.2	13.0
Germany	All industries	502.1	22.3	493.7	21.4	632.0	18.5
	Manufacturing	404.2	24.8	383.7	25.4	446.3	23.3
Greece	All industries	11.2	0.5	13.2	0.6	12.0	0.4
	Manufacturing	6.0	0.4	6.1	0.4	6.8	0.4
Ireland	All industries	35.1	1.6	40.8	1.8	81.0	2.4
	Manufacturing	31.7	2.0	37.4	2.5	64.9	3.4
Italy	All industries	173.4	7.7	159.7	6.9	186.0	5.4
	Manufacturing	131.1	8.1	116.9	7.8	122.4	6.4
Luxembourg	All industries	7.1	0.3	7.7	0.3	9.0	0.3
	Manufacturing	7.0	0.4	7.1	0.5	7.7	0.4
Netherlands	All industries	104.0	4.6	115.5	5.0	179.0	5.2
	Manufacturing	69.3	4.3	70.5	4.7	80.1	4.2
Norway	All industries	16.6	0.7	18.5	0.8	27.0	0.8
	Manufacturing	5.2	0.3	2.3	0.2	7.3	0.4
Portugal	All industries	19.7	0.9	21.2	0.9	35.0	1.0
	Manufacturing	14.3	0.9	13.1	0.9	24.6	1.3
Spain	All industries	113.5	5.0	120.0	5.2	164.0	4.8
	Manufacturing	92.3	5.7	93.5	6.2	114.9	6.0
Sweden	All industries	30.8	1.4	26.0	1.1	70.0	2.0
	Manufacturing	15.8	1.0	13.1	0.9	38.7	2.0
Switzerland	All industries	39.8	1.8	40.1	1.7	53.0	1.5
	Manufacturing	14.7	0.9	11.5	0.8	17.0	0.9
Turkey	All industries	5.2	0.2	9.2	0.4	29.0	0.8
	Manufacturing	2.6	0.2	5.0	0.3	14.0	0.7
United Kingdom	All industries	729.3	32.4	749.3	32.5	1,065.0	31.2
	Manufacturing	516.0	31.7	462.2	30.6	465.9	24.3
Other	All industries	1.6	0.1	1.2	0.1	209.0	6.1
	Manufacturing	0.0	0.0	0.1	0.0	149.4	7.8

Note: Cell entries report the level (in thousands) or share (in percentage terms) of the European employment of majority-owned affiliates of US multinational firms accounted for by the country in that cell's row, with two different industry groups reported for each country. The country group 'other' consists of all the other European countries not listed aggregate. This aggregate covers much of Central and Eastern Europe, yet throughout the 1990s nearly 75 per cent of this group's total employment was accounted for by just the three countries mentioned in the table's note.

There are two notable features of table 3.2. One is simply the cross-country variation at each point in time in the absolute level of employment. Each year the three largest countries in terms of absolute affiliate employment are the United Kingdom, Germany and France; together, these three countries account for about two-thirds of total European employment. Belgium, Italy, the Netherlands and Spain are the next largest FDI recipients in terms of absolute employment. All other countries account for less than about 2 per cent of total employment.

A second notable feature of table 3.2 is the evolution over time in country employment shares. For many countries, the shares move little decade by decade. That said, notable increases in all-industry employment shares include France in the 1980s, Sweden in the 1990s and – most dramatically at fully six percentage points – the 'other' group in the 1990s. These were matched by notable declines in all-industry employment shares in the 1990s in Belgium, Germany, Italy and the United Kingdom. There is even more volatility in the manufacturing employment shares during the 1990s. During that decade Ireland's and Sweden's share each rose by about one percentage point, both of which were dwarfed by the dramatic 7.7 percentage point increase for 'other'. These increases were matched by declining shares over the 1990s in the same four countries as above – with the most dramatic fall, of 6.3 percentage points, in the United Kingdom.

These changes in shares, especially for manufacturing employment, appear consistent with shifts from relatively high-wage countries to relatively low-wage countries. Table 3.5 will offer some direct wage evidence for affiliates. Note that the shift was concentrated in the 1990s, coincident with the fall of Communism and the rise of market forces throughout much of Central and Eastern Europe. This coincidence suggests that US firms were responding to these dramatic policy changes.

Notes to table 3.2. (*cont.*)

individually. Throughout the 1990s approximately 75 per cent of this group's activity was accounted for by the Czech Republic, Hungary and Poland. 'N/a' indicates data not available due to confidentiality requirements.
Source: Bureau of Economic Analysis, US Department of Commerce. This table is taken from Slaughter (2003).

A caveat to interpreting these shifting shares, however, is that the direction of change of employment shares need not match the direction of change of employment levels. This matters especially for the 1990s, during which only one country in table 3.2, Belgium, experienced a fall in the absolute number of manufacturing employees. Despite its sizeable drop in manufacturing employment share, even in the United Kingdom absolute employment over this decade actually rose by 3,700. Of course, in many cases share and level changes have the same sign: the dramatic rise in the total employment share of 'other' over the 1990s occurred via an absolute employment rise of 207,800. But an environment in which a country's falling employment share is accounted for by positive employment growth that is slower than in other countries can be very different from one in which its falling share is accounted for by employment contractions.

Table 3.3 shifts the focus from the distribution of affiliate total activity across countries to the industrial distribution of affiliate activity within countries. For two years – 1982 and 1999 – and a large number of countries and country groups, it reports the distribution for each country-year of total affiliate sales across five broad industries: manufacturing; wholesale trade; finance, insurance and real estate (FIRE); other services (e.g. retail trade, legal services, management consulting); and other industries, of which petroleum is typically the main activity. Thus, in the entire world in 1982, 37.1 per cent of all affiliate sales were in manufacturing, and so on.

One important pattern in table 3.3 is the evolution over time in affiliate industry composition common to most countries or country groups. The typical pattern is one of a falling sales share in other industries offsetting a rising sales shares in the other four groups. This cross-industry evolution reflects in part changes in world oil prices, which were relatively high in 1982 and relatively low in 1999. But it probably also reflects forces such as rising incomes, which stimulate demand for many services, including FIRE and retail trade. Seen in this light, the rise over time in sales shares for non-manufacturing, non-oil activities reflects the evolving output compositions of many countries.

A second important pattern in table 3.3 is the cross-country differences in affiliate industry composition, common trends over time aside. The industry mix in Europe is not too dissimilar from that in the rest of the world. But, within Europe, countries show substantial variation. Affiliates are more heavily concentrated in manufacturing in France, Germany, Ireland and Spain. Affiliates in the United Kingdom are more heavily concentrated in FIRE, other services and other industries. Norway also shares this concentration in other industries, consistent

Table 3.3. *The cross-country industry composition in sales of affiliates of US multinational firms*

Country	Year	Manufacturing	Wholesale	FIRE	Services	Other
World	1982	37.1	15.6	3.2	2.4	41.6
	1999	46.2	20.1	7.1	6.7	19.9
Europe	1982	39.7	21.9	1.7	2.9	33.8
	1999	47.1	24.1	6.2	7.4	15.1
Austria	1982	n/a	37.3	0.1	5.5	n/a
	1999	49.9	35.1	1.4	5.8	7.9
Belgium	1982	41.8	23.2	1.0	2.5	31.4
	1999	44.6	37.6	3.1	5.2	9.4
Denmark	1982	15.2	22.2	0.4	2.1	60.2
	1999	31.6	44.2	7.6	8.8	7.9
Finland	1982	5.0	46.2	0.0	n/a	n/a
	1999	38.0	43.3	2.6	4.6	11.5
France	1982	46.7	24.0	0.6	4.2	24.5
	1999	54.0	23.0	2.2	10.7	10.0
Germany	1982	56.6	10.2	0.8	1.5	30.9
	1999	62.7	14.9	5.6	4.6	12.1
Greece	1982	20.8	12.0	0.1	n/a	n/a
	1999	38.8	39.7	4.8	2.8	13.8
Ireland	1982	67.8	6.8	0.6	n/a	n/a
	1999	75.4	7.6	3.8	10.3	2.8
Italy	1982	41.0	20.5	0.6	2.3	35.6
	1999	45.7	26.7	1.7	10.5	15.4
Luxembourg	1982	61.2	2.6	1.5	0.0	34.7
	1999	35.2	48.3	7.0	1.7	7.7
Netherlands	1982	40.2	20.5	1.4	5.0	33.0
	1999	34.0	45.0	4.7	5.8	10.5
Norway	1982	6.4	11.9	0.0	2.1	79.6
	1999	13.7	23.0	1.0	5.4	56.8
Portugal	1982	45.0	23.5	0.0	n/a	n/a
	1999	47.9	33.7	2.6	3.6	12.3
Spain	1982	74.7	11.7	0.5	4.9	8.1
	1999	73.0	16.9	1.9	5.0	3.2
Sweden	1982	31.4	29.4	0.3	3.2	35.8
	1999	54.0	29.8	4.2	4.9	7.1
Switzerland	1982	5.4	54.8	0.6	1.8	37.4
	1999	16.4	72.7	2.6	3.8	4.5
Turkey	1982	19.0	n/a	0.0	n/a	n/a
	1999	53.0	39.4	n/a	2.8	n/a
United Kingdom	1982	37.6	19.8	4.0	3.1	35.5
	1999	39.0	11.1	13.0	10.0	27.0
Other	1982	n/a	n/a	0.6	7.4	n/a
	1999	59.3	20.7	n/a	2.9	n/a

Note: Cell entries report the share (in percentage terms) of that row's country-year sales of majority-owned affiliates of US multinational firms accounted for by that column's with the two countries benefiting from the production of North Sea oil. And several countries have affiliates with sales that are heavily concentrated in wholesale trade relative to Europe overall: Austria, Belgium, Denmark, Finland, Luxembourg, the Netherlands and Switzerland. The magnitude of these cross-country differences is quite large in many cases. In 1999 roughly 75 per cent of Ireland's and Spain's total affiliate sales were in manufacturing, whereas some 75 per cent of Switzerland's total affiliate sales that year were in wholesale trade.

This cross-country variation in affiliate industry composition goes against the idea that all FDI into Europe is driven by the same forces, and thus likely to look the same across countries. The variation is sizeable and, in many cases, growing over time. It suggests that multinationals tailor their industry choices to a set of country characteristics.

Table 3.4 shifts the focus to the external orientation of US affiliates operating in Europe. For three years – 1982, 1989 and 1999 – it reports the share of total affiliate sales that is exported out of the host country. Thus, for example, worldwide in 1982 affiliates sent 34.6 per cent of their total sales to customers outside their respective host countries.[8]

The main message of table 3.4 is the cross-country variation in affiliate export intensity: some countries have high and/or rising export shares, while others have low and/or falling export shares. As the second row of table 3.4 indicates, the export orientation of all European affiliates aggregated together is about that of all affiliates worldwide, at just over one-third. But export shares are well over half – indeed, are approaching 75 per cent – in Belgium, Ireland, Luxembourg, the Netherlands and Switzerland. At the other extreme, export shares are low and/or falling in countries such as Denmark, France, Germany and the United Kingdom.

---

[8] The complement of exports in total sales is same-country or local sales. These local sales are defined by whether or not the entity to which an affiliate sells a good resides in the same country as the affiliate. These entities can, of course, turn around and export their purchased goods to foreign markets. Given that such second-party exports are not captured in the data, the measured ratio of affiliate exports to total sales is a lower bound for the true value.

Notes to table 3.3. (*cont.*)

industry. The country group 'other' consists of all the other European countries not listed individually. Throughout the 1990s approximately 75 per cent of this group's activity was accounted for by the Czech Republic, Hungary and Poland. 'N/a' indicates data not available due to confidentiality requirements.
Source: Bureau of Economic Analysis, US Department of Commerce. This table is taken from Slaughter (2003).

Table 3.4. *Exports as a share of total sales for the affiliates of US multinational firms*

Country	1982	1989	1999
World	34.6	32.3	33.8
Europe	37.3	35.2	36.0
Austria	19.0	22.6	45.6
Belgium	56.4	58.9	56.6
Denmark	23.3	24.7	27.2
Finland	2.4	17.2	22.2
France	27.2	26.6	27.2
Germany	28.4	32.6	27.6
Ireland	60.4	66.0	75.9
Italy	16.3	16.8	20.7
Luxembourg	74.5	72.4	70.4
Netherlands	55.2	56.8	56.0
Norway	n/a	45.2	31.0
Portugal	n/a	n/a	19.1
Spain	19.6	24.5	28.6
Sweden	17.5	17.8	39.1
Switzerland	83.3	72.3	70.4
Turkey	n/a	5.23	24.6
United Kingdom	31.0	25.1	19.8
Other	n/a	56.9	25.5

Note: Cell entries report the share (in percentage terms) of that country-year's total sales of majority-owned affiliates of US multinational firms that were exported out of the host country. The country group 'other' consists of all the other European countries not listed individually. 'N/a' indicates data not available due to confidentiality requirements.
Source: Bureau of Economic Analysis, US Department of Commerce. This table is taken from Slaughter (2003).

In the empirical literature on multinationals, many studies treat all output by foreign affiliates in a country as destined for the local market, and then examine which country and industry characteristics are correlated with affiliate total sales (e.g. Brainard, 1997; Markusen and Maskus, 1999; Yeaple, 2001; Carr et al., 2001). This empirical choice at least partly reflects many standard models, which assume that all affiliate sales are local-market sales. Table 3.4 indicates that multinationals clearly choose their destination of sales.

The last table of this section, table 3.5, presents evidence on labour costs and the factor intensity of affiliates. For a large set of countries in each of two years – 1982 and 1994 – this table reports the level and share of affiliate production worker employment in manufacturing, and also the average affiliate hourly compensation for these production workers.

Table 3.5. *The cross-country skill composition in manufacturing of affiliates of US multinational firms*

Country	Year	Total employment (thousand)	Production worker employment (thousand)	Production worker share (per cent)	Average hourly compensation ($ nominal)
World	1982	3,357.6	1,940.5	57.8	7.27
	1994	3,516.0	2,093.4	59.5	12.57
Europe	1982	1,627.7	886.5	54.5	9.44
	1994	1,590.0	915.0	57.6	18.80
Austria	1982	12.8	7.5	58.6	8.14
	1994	13.0	8.2	63.1	18.86
Belgium	1982	86.8	51.8	59.7	10.66
	1994	62.4	39.6	63.5	23.11
Denmark	1982	7.4	4.5	60.8	8.99
	1994	7.8	4.7	60.3	20.40
Finland	1982	n/a	n/a	n/a	n/a
	1994	3.7	2.4	64.9	19.62
France	1982	208.6	102.7	49.2	10.48
	1994	215.0	110.6	51.4	20.34
Germany	1982	404.2	219.7	54.4	11.50
	1994	394.5	225.0	57.0	27.22
Greece	1982	6.0	3.8	63.3	5.07
	1994	5.5	3.4	61.8	13.73
Ireland	1982	31.7	21.7	68.4	6.15
	1994	44.5	28.7	64.5	13.22
Italy	1982	131.1	69.0	52.6	9.03
	1994	113.2	61.7	54.5	18.06
Luxembourg	1982	7.0	3.7	52.9	13.00
	1994	6.9	4.1	59.4	26.11
Netherlands	1982	69.3	38.8	56.0	10.39
	1994	70.7	41.8	59.1	21.10
Norway	1982	5.2	2.3	44.2	12.82
	1994	4.7	2.8	59.6	18.95
Portugal	1982	14.3	8.6	60.1	3.54
	1994	16.8	11.2	66.7	7.80
Spain	1982	92.3	53.4	57.8	7.27
	1994	90.6	60.5	66.8	15.60
Sweden	1982	15.8	6.8	43.0	10.31
	1994	13.7	7.8	56.9	15.55
Switzerland	1982	14.7	7.4	50.3	11.71
	1994	13.9	7.7	55.4	26.38
Turkey	1982	2.6	1.7	65.4	3.49
	1994	10.5	5.8	55.2	7.01
United Kingdom	1982	516.0	282.0	54.6	8.12
	1994	435.3	244.3	56.1	14.95
Other	1982	n/a	n/a	n/a	n/a
	1994	67.3	44.8	66.6	2.97

In its benchmark-survey years before 1999 the BEA required foreign affiliates in manufacturing to distinguish non-production from production employment. Following a number of studies in the trade and wages literature, one can define the former to be more skilled and the latter to be less skilled.

Compared to the world as a whole, European affiliates employ somewhat more non-production workers. This is consistent with the higher European wages for production workers, and suggests that affiliates choose relative employments in response to the relative wages they face. Many countries within Europe show similar co-variation between relative production employment and production compensation. Ireland, Greece, Portugal, Spain and 'other' are all low-wage countries (or groups) within Europe where affiliates employ a high share of production workers. France, Germany and the United Kingdom are all high-wage countries within Europe where affiliates employ a low share of production workers. Similar evidence on this point was found by Lipsey et al. (1982), who estimated a positive correlation between affiliate capital per worker and affiliate wages.

There is a central conclusion to this subsection: *there exists substantial heterogeneity, both across countries and over time, in the types of European FDI*. Some looks horizontal, some vertical, and some something else. This cross-country and over-time heterogeneity in industry composition, external orientation and factor intensity belies the notion that all FDI into Europe is market-seeking horizontal investment.

2.2   *Vertical and horizontal FDI into Europe: causes*

The heterogeneity seen in tables 3.1 to 3.5 is consistent with the idea that multinationals tailor their European operations to a set of host-country conditions and policies. Regression analysis investigating the role of these conditions and policies appears in studies such as Barba Navaretti et al. (2002), Barrell and Pain (1999), Braconier and Ekholm (2001) and Slaughter (2003).

Notes to table 3.5. (*cont.*)

Note: Cell entries report various manufacturing employment data for the indicated country-years. The country group 'other' consists of all the other European countries not listed individually. 'N/a' indicates data not available due to confidentiality requirements. *Source:* Bureau of Economic Analysis, US Department of Commerce. This table is taken from Slaughter (2003).

These analyses confirm that multinationals seem to tailor their European operations, based on factors such as host-country size, per capita income and policies such as EU membership and corporate tax rates. A representative set of results appear in Slaughter (2003).

A first consideration might be the determinants of the absolute level of affiliate activity in a country – e.g. total affiliate sales. Slaughter (2003) finds that, for five broad industry groups (both manufacturing and non-manufacturing), sales (and also export sales) are rising in per capita GDP and GDP, falling in distance from the United States and in the corporate tax rate. EU membership is significantly positively correlated with manufacturing and FIRE activity. In short, countries that are richer per capita, have larger markets and lower taxes, and are closer to the United States have larger levels of FDI activity in all industries.

This result helps explain the *aggregate level* of US FDI into European countries, but it does not shed light on the forces behind the *industry composition* of FDI documented in section 2. To understand these composition issues better, Slaughter (2003) examines the *share* of total affiliate sales in each country-year accounted for by each of the five industry groups. These specifications capture the differential impact of country variables on particular industries relative to all industries taken together, as the dependent variable implicitly controls for unobserved variables that affect all industries in the same manner.

This framework reveals interesting differences in the effect of various country characteristics on affiliate industry composition. Per capita GDP is significantly negatively correlated with manufacturing activity, but positively correlated with wholesale (significantly) and FIRE activity. GDP is significantly positively correlated with services activity, but negatively so for wholesaling. Distance is significantly negatively correlated with manufacturing and FIRE activity, but significantly positively correlated with wholesaling and other industries. Corporate tax rates are significantly positively correlated with manufacturing activity, but (borderline) significantly negatively correlated with FIRE's share. Finally, EU membership is significantly positively correlated with manufacturing, but significantly negatively correlated with wholesaling. Many of these correlations accord with economic intuition.[9]

---

[9] Consider manufacturing, for example. Countries with lower per capita income and – presumably – lower wages attract a higher mix of manufacturing, an industry for which labour costs are relatively important. And to the extent that many manufactured goods are taxable across borders via tariffs and other non-tariff barriers, US firms contemplating selling to the EU market may prefer producing 'behind the walls' inside an EU country. FIRE activity is concentrated in countries with high per capita GDP, consistent with these services being a luxury good demanded predominantly by high-income

Similar compositional findings are obtained from regressions studying the external orientation of affiliates (i.e. regressions using as regressands the share of exports in affiliate total sales). Affiliates are more export-intensive in host countries that are smaller (measured in terms of GDP), more productive (measured in terms of per capita GDP) and lower-tax (in terms of corporate tax rates).

To conclude subsection 2.2, the overall message from existing research is that the composition of FDI within a given European country varies significantly with a set of host-country policies and characteristics. Multinationals appear to tailor their operations in line with considerations such as host-country size, per capita income and policy choices such as EU membership and corporate tax rates. This evidence, along with the heterogeneity documented in subsection 2.1, presents a richer picture of European FDI than one of just the horizontal FDI of manufacturing activity flowing from one high-income region into another. Manufacturing accounts for less than 50 per cent of all European FDI – in many countries a very low percentage. And, regardless of the composition of industries, different affiliates have different degrees of vertical links to their parents, through cross-border outsourcing, and also different degrees of external orientation, in terms of domestic sales versus exports. All this suggests that government policy may play an important role in shaping the *composition* of inward FDI flows, above and beyond their overall *level*.

This also suggests that the host-country labour market impacts of FDI may be quite different across regions. It is to this next question that we now turn.

3.   The labour market consequences of European FDI

How are European labour markets impacted by FDI activity? There are several dimensions on which labour relations between workers and firms may depend on the nationality of the ownership of those firms. In this section we consider four such dimensions: the relative demand (and thus earnings and/or employment) between more skilled and less skilled workers economy-wide; the absolute earnings of each worker type; labour demand elasticities and the volatility of worker earnings; and profit-sharing. The first three dimensions of labour market outcomes

individuals. And other services being concentrated in high-GDP countries accords with the idea that many of these other services – e.g., retail trade – depend on the overall purchasing power of the host country. For more on the role of taxation, see the evidence in Hines (2001).

are issues arising in perfectly competitive labour markets, while the fourth extends this benchmark framework to important issues of non-competitive interactions as well. In each case, we present both theory and existing empirical evidence. The important message is that *there is both theoretical and empirical evidence that the nationality of ownership does indeed matter for several labour market outcomes.*[10]

3.1   FDI and the relative demand between more and less skilled workers

In many European countries in recent decades, economy-wide labour demand appears to have shifted away from less skilled workers and towards more skilled workers. These shifts have appeared in aggregate labour markets through some mix of higher income inequality across skill groups (e.g. the United Kingdom) and unemployment increases disproportionately falling on less skilled workers (e.g. Germany and France).

There is by now a very large research area investigating the relative contribution to these trends of forces such as technological change, international trade, immigration and FDI. We do not intend to survey this literature, but instead simply to highlight the theory and empirical evidence on the particular role that FDI may be playing.[11] We first address the theory.

Most previous work on the effect of FDI on labour demand has examined the issue from the perspective of vertical FDI. One such example is Feenstra and Hanson (1996), who develop a North–South model to examine the potential effects of FDI inflows on wages in both the host and parent countries. Here, a final good is produced from a continuum of intermediate inputs that vary in the relative amounts of skilled and unskilled labour required. The South has a comparative advantage in unskilled-labour-intensive production. This attracts FDI from the North, which in turn transfers some number of 'marginal' inputs from North production to South production. Interestingly, with greater FDI the relative demand for more skilled labour (and thus the

---

[10] To keep issues manageable, in section 3 our contrast between employment in foreign-owned versus domestically owned firms does not consider possible links between these two types. In particular, we do not consider the important issue of whether foreign-owned firms generate knowledge spillovers for domestic firms in host countries. For evidence on this question, a representative recent study that examines UK evidence is Haskel et al. (2002).

[11] For a representative survey, see Johnson and Slaughter (2001).

skill premium) *rises* in both the North and the South: both regions now produce a more skilled-labour-intensive mix of activities.

The rise in the South is to be noted here. If it is assumed that inward FDI entails new activities that are more skill-intensive than the host country's existing activities, then aggregate host-country demand for skills increases. In contrast, if the inward FDI brings in the opposite kinds of activities (i.e. those that use intensively less skilled labour), then economy-wide demand for skills should fall, not rise. This is the case in Helpman's (1984) vertical FDI framework, where by assumption the assembly activity that multinational enterprises (MNEs) locate in low-wage countries involves only less skilled labour. In general, then, standard models of vertical FDI predict that inward FDI can either raise or lower a host country's demand for skills. It all depends on the skill mix of FDI activities relative to those already performed in the host country.

What about models of horizontal FDI? The same ambiguity exists here, as well, regarding the net impact of inward FDI on relative demand and wages. One representative example is Markusen and Venables (1998), who analyse the influence of horizontal FDI on relative wages in the parent and host countries. They discuss in great detail the ambiguous labour demand effects of various parameter changes, such as endowment growth or trade cost declines. For example, they show that world endowment growth leads to a greater role for multinationals, but also to ambiguous labour demand effects. If initially national firms predominate, then growth triggers a 'regime shift' towards more MNEs. Because multinationals are assumed to be more skilled-labour-intensive than national firms are, demand for skills rises. But, if initially there are relatively few national firms, then growth can lower the skill premium. Here, growth leads to greater firm-scale effects. Since skilled labour makes the firm-specific assets, firm-scale effects arise mainly with multinational assembly operations that use less skilled labour.

In summary, theory suggests that greater MNE activity can either raise or lower the skill mix of activities performed within a host country, and thus help raise or lower wage inequality. These ambiguities highlight the need for empirical work to help inform which equilibrium states of the model seem relevant.

Some empirical studies have found cases where inward FDI appears to raise host-country demand for skills, while others have found no clear link between inward FDI and labour demand. Feenstra and Hanson (1997) find substantial evidence that US FDI into Mexico contributed to rising Mexican demand for more skilled workers across both regions and industries. In contrast, Slaughter (2000) and Blonigen and Slaughter (2001) find no systematic correlation between skill upgrading within US industries and either outward or inward FDI.

3.2   FDI and the absolute level of worker earnings

Distinct from interest in *relative* labour demand and earnings, one may also be interested in the impact of FDI on labour demand and earnings in *absolute* terms. Several studies – of both developed and developing countries – have documented the fact that establishments owned by MNEs pay *higher* wages than domestically owned establishments. This is true even controlling for a wide range of observable worker and/or plant characteristics, such as industry, region and overall size. The magnitudes involved are big. Doms and Jensen (1998) document that, for US manufacturing plants in 1987, worker multinational wages exceeded domestically owned wages by a range of 5 to 15 per cent, with larger differentials for production workers rather than non-production workers.[12]

What accounts for this 'multinational wage premium' remains unknown, largely because the cross-sectional evidence is consistent with several alternative explanations, about which very little is currently known. The premium could be accounted for by higher worker productivity due to superior technology and/or capital at multinationals. This explanation accords with the common thread in models of both vertical and horizontal FDI that multinational firms possess certain 'knowledge assets', such as patents, copyrights and other intellectual property assets, obtained through R&D and related activities. It also accords with existing empirical evidence that MNEs are especially R&D-intensive relative to purely domestic firms.[13]

There are at least two more possible explanations of the multinational wage premium, which are addressed in the next two subsections of this

---

[12] Production workers receive an average of 6.9 per cent less at comparable domestic plants employing more than 500 employees and 15.2 per cent less at comparable domestic plants employing fewer than 500 employees. Non-production workers receive an average of 5.0 per cent less at comparable domestic plants employing more than 500 employees and 9.5 per cent less at comparable domestic plants employing fewer than 500 employees. For additional US evidence, see Howenstine and Zeile (1994). Griffith (1999) presents similar evidence for the United Kingdom; Globerman et al. (1994) for Canada; Aitken et al. (1996) for Mexico and Venezuela; and te Velde and Morrissey (2001) for five African countries.

[13] Slaughter (1998) documents that in recent decades the parents of US-headquartered multinationals have performed 50 per cent to 60 per cent of total US R&D.

chapter. One is that multinationals pay more to compensate workers for the greater labour market volatility associated with MNEs – e.g. for the greater risk of plant shutdowns. If workers for MNEs face a greater risk of job separation because MNEs have more elastic labour demands than purely domestic firms do, then to compensate they may receive higher wages. The other possibility is that multinationals are more profitable and therefore able to share more rents with workers.

Regardless of the cause(s) of the multinational wage premium, its existence is very important for considering how the globalisation of production affects economic insecurity and political economy more generally. All else being equal, this premium is very likely to make multinational employees feel *more* economically secure. The possibly contrasting issues of labour demand elasticities and wage premia suggest that the net impact of MNEs on worker insecurity is *ex ante* unclear. Whether the wage premia are sufficient to compensate workers for increases in risks from higher elasticities is an empirical question. Subsection 3.3 now turns to this issue of worker insecurity; Subsection 3.4 will consider profit-sharing.

3.3   FDI, labour demand elasticities and worker insecurity[14]

3.3.1 *Worker insecurity in labour market equilibrium*   To establish a connection between foreign direct investment and the risks facing workers in the labour market, we start by identifying in general terms those factors that generate employment and wage volatility for workers.[15] In any given labour market, equilibrium prevails where the quantity of labour supplied equals the quantity of labour demanded. In accord with a wide range of empirical evidence, one can introduce volatility into the labour market by assuming that the position of the labour demand schedule is stochastic.

To see what forces drive this volatility, note that each profit-maximising firm hires workers until the wage paid to the last worker hired just equals the value of output – i.e. revenue – generated by that last worker. For each firm, the product prices and the technology it faces are two key determinants of marginal revenue products. Aggregated across all firms, then, the position of the labour demand schedule depends crucially on all relevant product prices and production technologies. Movements in

---

[14] This subsection (text and tables) draws heavily on the discussion in Scheve and Slaughter (2002).
[15] For a formal derivation of key labour market concepts such as elasticities, see Hamermesh (1993). For a discussion of labour demand elasticities in general-equilibrium trade models, see Reddy (2000).

prices and technologies trigger movements in labour demand, and thus in equilibrium wages and/or employment.

For workers, the critical issue at hand is that volatility in labour market outcomes depends not just on the volatility of shifters such as product prices and production technology. It also depends on the magnitudes of the elasticities of labour supply and demand. If the elasticities are assumed fixed, then greater labour market volatility arises if, and only if, there is greater aggregate volatility in prices or technology. But this is not the only way to generate greater labour market volatility. It can also be generated from increasing the elasticity of demand for labour, holding fixed the amount of aggregate risk. Higher labour demand elasticities trigger more volatile labour market responses to price or technology shocks to labour demand.

In sum, this discussion suggests at least two mechanisms by which FDI investment may increase labour market volatility and the risks facing workers: by increasing the variance of firms' marginal revenue products, or by increasing labour demand elasticities.

Although the first mechanism – often referred to as the exposure of domestic labour markets to international shocks – is often discussed, the empirical evidence is mixed. Rodrik (1997) presents evidence that exposure to external risk, measured by the interaction between trade openness and the standard deviation of a country's terms of trade, is positively correlated with growth volatility. Iversen and Cusack (2000) argue that it is not sufficient to show that international price volatility is correlated with growth volatility. Rather, they claim it is necessary either that price volatility in international markets be greater than in domestic markets or that trade concentrates more than it diversifies economic risks. Iversen and Cusack then present evidence that, at least for advanced economies, there is no correlation between trade or capital market openness and volatility in output, earnings or employment. They therefore dismiss the argument that international economic integration increases economic insecurity.

While this line of research has investigated reasonable hypotheses about how integration may increase economic insecurity, the discussion above highlights the fact that it is *not* necessary for integration to increase the magnitude of price and/or technology shocks for it to increase individual economic insecurity in terms of riskier employment and/or wage outcomes. Thus, a lack of correlation between volatility in terms of trade and volatility in employment, wages and output does not necessarily imply that international economic integration generally, and foreign investment specifically, has not contributed to increased economic insecurity. We must evaluate the possibility that integration, and FDI in particular, makes labour demands more elastic and thus increases the risks facing workers in the labour market.

3.3.2 How FDI can make labour demands more elastic: theory and evidence
Standard models in international trade predict that greater FDI by multinationals can make labour demands more elastic. This can happen either by making product markets more competitive, and thus making firms more sensitive to the cost of labour (i.e. the 'scale' effect), or by making workers more substitutable with other factors in production (i.e. the 'substitution' effect). This can boost insecurity via the greater labour market volatility just described. Consider each effect in turn.

Many models predict that FDI and its related international trade make product markets more competitive. Through the scale effect, this should make labour demands more elastic. For example, the liberalisation of FDI policies can force domestic firms to face heightened foreign competition; or developments abroad (e.g. capital accumulation via FDI) can be communicated to domestic producers as more intense foreign competition. In these cases, more competitive product markets mean that a given increase in wages, and thus costs, translates into larger declines in output, and thus demand, for all factors. Different models predict different magnitudes of FDI and/or trade's impact on product market demand.[16]

The second way through which FDI can increase labour demand elasticities is through the substitution effect. Suppose that a firm is vertically integrated with a number of production stages. Stages can move abroad either within firms as multinationals establish foreign affiliates (e.g. Helpman, 1984) or at arm's length by importing the output of those stages from other firms (e.g. Feenstra and Hanson, 1997). The globalisation of production thus gives firms access to foreign factors of production as well as domestic ones, either directly through foreign affiliates or indirectly through intermediate inputs. This expands the set of factors that firms can substitute towards in response to higher domestic wages beyond just domestic non-labour factors, to

---

[16] One example is a monopolistically competitive industry producing for Dixit-Stiglitz consumers who value product variety (e.g. Helpman and Krugman, 1985). Here the representative firm is usually assumed to face a demand elasticity (greater than one) that equals the elasticity of substitution (EOS) among product varieties in consumers' utility function. But the actual demand elasticity is only approximately equal to the EOS. It equals EOS plus a second term, $(1-EOS)/N$, where N is the number of firms in the industry. As N rises – thanks, for example, to FDI by foreign MNEs – so, too, does this elasticity.

include foreign factors as well. Thus, greater FDI raises labour demand elasticities.

In the literature on globalisation and labour markets, there are several recent studies indicating that MNEs and FDI influence labour demand elasticities in the ways just discussed. Using industry-level data for US manufacturing, Slaughter (2001) estimates that demand for production labour became more elastic from 1960 to the early 1990s, and that these increases were correlated with FDI outflows by US-headquartered MNEs. Using industry-level data for all UK manufacturing from 1958 to 1986, Fabbri et al. (2003) estimate increases in labour demand elasticities for both production and non-production labour.

One important margin on which MNEs may affect elasticities is on the extensive margin of plant shutdowns. In response to wage increases, MNEs may be more likely than domestic firms to respond by closing entire plants. Evidence that multinational plants are more likely to close than domestically owned plants has now been documented for the manufacturing sectors in at least three countries. For the United Kingdom, Fabbri et al. (2003) estimate that multinational plants – again, both UK- and foreign-owned – are more likely to shut down than domestic plants are (conditional on a set of operational advantages enjoyed by multinationals that make them less likely to shut down, such as being older and larger). Gorg and Strobl (2003) find that foreign-owned plants in Irish manufacturing are more likely to exit. And, for the United States, Bernard and Jensen (2002) report higher death probabilities for plants owned by firms that hold at least 10 per cent of their assets outside the United States.

To summarise, standard economic models of labour markets suggest that the globalisation of production via MNEs may increase labour demand elasticities. This, in turn, will tend to make labour market outcomes more volatile, and thus workers more insecure. This analysis suggests an empirical test of whether individual self-assessments of economic insecurity are related to FDI exposure in the labour market.

3.3.3 Empirical evidence on the link between FDI and worker insecurity
Scheve and Slaughter (2002) report empirical evidence on the impact of international capital mobility on economic insecurity. They evaluate how individual self-assessments of economic insecurity – understood as an individual's subjective perception of risk (Dominitz and Manski, 1997) – correlate with the presence of highly mobile capital in the form of FDI in the industries in which individuals work.

The individual-level data in their analysis are from the British House-hold Panel Survey (BHPS). This study is a nationally representative sample of more than 5,000 UK households and over 9,000 individuals surveyed annually from 1991 to 1999. It records detailed information about each respondent's perceptions of economic insecurity, employ-ment, wages and many other characteristics. The most important pieces of survey information required for the analysis are a measure of economic insecurity, identification of the respondents' industry of employment and repeated measurement of the same individual over time.

Economic insecurity is measured by responses to the following ques-tion asked in each of the nine years of the panel: 'I'm going to read out a list of various aspects of jobs, and after each one I'd like you to tell me from this card which number best describes how satisfied or dissatis-fied you are with that particular aspect of your own present job – job security.'

The ordered responses are on a seven-point scale ranging from 'not satisfied at all' to 'completely satisfied.' It is important to note that this question measures the anxiety or stress associated with the perception of an economic risk rather than the perception itself. This characteristic of the data means that the analysis assumes that perceptions of economic insecurity generate anxiety or lack of satisfaction, and thus that the BHPS question correlates with individual economic insecurity – albeit mediated by individual characteristics and environmental factors.

Using this BHPS question, the variable 'insecurity' was constructed by coding responses in the reverse order from the original question with a range from 1 for individuals who give the response 'completely satisfied' to 7 for those individuals giving the response 'not satisfied at all'. Higher values of 'insecurity' thus indicate less satisfaction with job security.

Consistent with the theoretical framework above, the primary hypoth-esis to be tested is that high FDI activity in industries may generate economic insecurity among workers in those industries by increasing labour demand elasticities. To test this hypothesis, the variable 'FDI' was constructed as a dichotomous industry-level variable (2-digit SIC80 industries) set equal to 1 if two conditions were met: if the industry had any positive FDI investment, inward or outward; and if the industry's activities did not require producers and consumers to be in the same geographic location. If either of these conditions were not met, 'FDI' was set equal to 0 (see Scheve and Slaughter, 2002, for details).

The logic in defining 'FDI' with these two conditions runs as follows. The first condition for an individual's industry of employment to have positive FDI investment is straightforward. Any inward or outward FDI activity satisfies this. The second condition recognises that FDI activity is less likely to alter labour demand elasticities if business activities cannot be outsourced across countries because the consumer and producer must be in the same geographic location. Consider the examples of wholesale trade, retail trade and personal services (e.g. haircuts). The large majority of business activities in these industries require the co-location of producers and consumers: customers interacting with sales clerks, or sitting in the barber's chair. The notions of economic insecurity related to FDI that we discussed above focus on the ability of MNEs to shift business activities across countries (i.e. on the substitution effect). In reality, in many industries FDI does not have this characteristic; indeed, this FDI arises precisely because foreign customers *cannot* be served at a distance via international trade. Accordingly, the 'FDI' variable identifies not all industries with FDI but, instead, only those industries with FDI in which business activities can be outsourced across countries. So, for industries such as wholesale trade, retail trade and personal services, 'FDI' was coded as 0 regardless of the data on actual FDI.

By matching each BHPS observation with the relevant industry FDI information, Scheve and Slaughter (2002) examine how self-assessments of economic insecurity relate to FDI activity.[17] The starting point for their analysis is to examine cross-sectional variation in economic insecurity for each year of the panel. Table 3.6 reports the results of this cross-sectional analysis. These results are ordinary least squares coefficient estimates of the regression of 'insecurity' on 'FDI' and various demographic control variables. The key finding is that FDI activity is positively correlated with individual economic insecurity. Holding other factors constant, individuals employed in FDI sectors systematically report less satisfaction with their job security. The coefficient estimate for the variable 'FDI' ranges between 0.274 (with a standard error of 0.070) in 1994 to 0.397 (with a standard error of 0.071) in 1993. In every year the estimated parameter is significantly different from 0 at at least the 99 per cent level. Although there is some variation across years in the size of the estimate, in most years it is very close to 0.30 and no trend is evident. These cross-sectional results are strongly consistent with the hypothesis that FDI activity generates economic insecurity among workers.

Despite the robustness of the correlation between 'FDI' and the measure of economic insecurity, there are a number of reasons to be

---

[17] The analyses reported below are based on the BHPS sub-sample of private sector, full-time workers who are not self-employed. It is for this group of workers that our theoretical framework most directly applies. See Scheve and Slaughter (2002) for a discussion of the robustness of the results for larger samples.

Table 3.6. *A cross-sectional analysis of economic insecurity and FDI*

Regressor	Year								
	1991	1992	1993	1994	1995	1996	1997	1998	1999
FDI	0.311	0.322	0.397	0.274	0.315	0.278	0.296	0.371	0.300
	(0.079)	(0.073)	(0.071)	(0.070)	(0.069)	(0.063)	(0.060)	(0.053)	(0.050)
Gender	−0.289	−0.334	−0.285	−0.336	−0.164	−0.158	−0.109	−0.176	−0.106
	(0.081)	(0.074)	(0.071)	(0.070)	(0.071)	(0.064)	(0.063)	(0.054)	(0.052)
Education	0.062	0.113	0.135	0.078	0.189	0.128	0.011	0.047	0.000
	(0.045)	(0.042)	(0.041)	(0.042)	(0.039)	(0.036)	(0.036)	(0.032)	(0.030)
Age	0.009	0.007	0.011	0.012	0.011	0.009	0.011	0.011	0.010
	(0.003)	(0.003)	(0.003)	(0.003)	(0.003)	(0.003)	(0.003)	(0.002)	(0.002)
Income	−0.001	0.000	−0.005	0.001	−0.005	0.000	−0.003	−0.002	−0.003
	(0.003)	(0.002)	(0.003)	(0.002)	(0.002)	(0.002)	(0.002)	(0.001)	(0.001)
Constant	2.519	2.497	2.174	2.230	2.031	2.027	2.232	2.059	2.318
	(0.186)	(0.175)	(0.168)	(0.165)	(0.160)	(0.152)	(0.150)	(0.135)	(0.127)
Standard error of regression.	1.967	1.726	1.636	1.679	1.619	1.548	1.519	1.444	1.566
Observations	2,649	2,385	2,280	2,410	2,377	2,525	2,695	3,060	4,059

Note: These results are ordinary least squares regression coefficient estimates for each year. Each cell reports the coefficient estimate and, in parentheses, its heteroskedastic-consistent standard error. For variable definitions, see the text.
Source: This table is taken from Scheve and Slaughter (2002).

concerned about the validity of these inferences. The period-by-period cross-sectional analysis is inefficient. Further, and more importantly, unmeasured and perhaps unobservable differences among individuals – such as variation in risk aversion – are probably correlated with both perceptions of economic insecurity and the propensity to be employed in an FDI-exposed sector; correlations that would bias cross-sectional parameter estimates.

To address these concerns, Scheve and Slaughter (2002) have pooled the panel data sets and explicitly modelled individual-specific effects using various panel estimators and specifications. The main substantive finding is a continued positive correlation between 'FDI' and the dependent variable 'insecurity'. It is important to contrast the sources of variation in cross-sections versus panels that are generating the main finding of a positive correlation between FDI presence and economic insecurity. The cross-section estimates exploit the variation across individuals in their industry of employment and economic insecurity at a single point in time. In contrast, the panel estimates identify changes in FDI exposure over time. Individuals for whom there is no change in the FDI activity in their industry and who also do not change their industry of employment have their FDI presence measure fully absorbed by their individual fixed effects. Variation across these individuals is used only in the cross-section. Identification in the panel comes from changes over time in individuals' self-assessments of economic insecurity, which occur either with changes over time in FDI activity in individuals' industry of employment and/or with changes over time in individuals' industry of employment.

3.4   FDI and profit-sharing between workers and firms[18]

The preceding discussion of section 3 has been largely from the perspective of competitive labour markets in which workers earn their marginal revenue product. In reality, however, there is ample evidence that workers' earnings depend on firm profitability. Many empirical studies have documented a robustly positive correlation between wages for various micro-units – firms, individuals, union–firm bargaining units – with profits per worker at the level of that micro-unit's firm and/or industry. These industry profits are interpreted as prosperity in the product market enjoyed by firms and available for sharing with workers.

---

[18] This subsection draws heavily on the discussions in and findings of Budd and Slaughter (2004) and Budd et al. (2005).

A common feature of these studies is that they delineate product markets by the same country as that of the micro-units. That is, wages for micro-units located in a specific country are linked with measures of firm or industry profitability constructed using data for operations in that same country. Such profit measures implicitly assume that national borders bound the product markets the prosperity of which is relevant to wages. But is there *international* rent-sharing, with profits shared across borders? And, in particular, might the nationality of firm ownership matter for profit-sharing? These questions have been examined recently by Budd and Slaughter (2004) and Budd et al. (2005). This subsection summarises their approaches and empirical findings.

One way to formalise how the patterns of profit-sharing may differ between multinational and purely domestic firms is to start with the typical closed economy set-up in which risk-neutral workers enjoy some bargaining power for negotiating with their firm over wages. In a Nash bargaining setting, the negotiated wage equals some base 'outside' wage (that workers can earn if negotiations break down) plus some fraction of the relevant profits, where the size of this fraction depends on the degree of worker bargaining power.

There are at least two important ways in which the nature of this generalised wage bargain may differ between multinational and purely domestic firms. One is that workers may enjoy less bargaining power with multinationals than with domestics because MNEs have higher labour demand elasticities. This argument follows directly from the analysis of subsection 3.3, and it has been put forward by Rodrik (1997) and others. All else being equal, this differential bargaining power would suggest that any 'pass-through' of profits to wages will differ across firm types.

The other way is that the relevant scope of profits to negotiate over may differ across firm types. Workers within a multinational may negotiate over not just profits in the host country but also profits within the firm in other countries (and MNEs may agree with such a perspective, based on firm-wide compensation policies). Or, by virtue of having well-established foreign production options, multinational firms may have a different outside option from domestic firms – in particular, a lower threshold at which they will cease wage negotiations.

In general, one can formalise several ways in which patterns of profit-sharing will depend on the nationality of firm ownership. The empirical evidence in Budd and Slaughter (2004) and Budd et al. (2005) confirms the relevance of these channels.

For a sample of 1,014 Canadian manufacturing union contracts from 1980 to 1992, Budd and Slaughter (2004) find that US industry profitability affects Canadian wage outcomes and that the pattern of rent-sharing varies significantly across international linkages, including multinational ownership (as well as union type and trade barriers). Higher Canadian industry profits raise wages for employees of Canadian-owned firms, but higher Canadian industry profits generally have a much smaller (or no) effect on the wages of Canadian employees of US-owned firms. Conversely, higher US profits lower wages for employees of Canadian-owned firms, but higher US profits raise or have zero effect on wages for employees of US-owned firms.

Budd et al. (2005) shift focus to the issue of whether intra-multinational wage bargaining depends on the profitability of both parent and affiliate operations. They use a unique firm-level panel data set of multinational parents and their foreign affiliates that covers the years 1993 to 1998, with a total of 865 parents and 1,919 foreign affiliates in fourteen European countries. Using both fixed-effects and generalised method-of-moments estimators, they estimate that affiliate wage levels depend on both affiliate *and* parent profitability, with many specifications indicating that parents share profits only with majority-owned affiliates, and even more strongly with fully owned affiliates.

The magnitudes of profit-sharing in these multinationals studies are on a par with those found in related closed economy analyses. For example, central estimates in Budd et al. (2005) indicate that a doubling of parent profitability raises affiliate wages by somewhere between 1 and 5 per cent, which can explain over 20 per cent of the observed variation in affiliate wages. This magnitude of cross-border profit-sharing within MNEs appears to be economically important, especially in light of the fact documented in Barba Navaretti et al. (2002) that, in Europe today, nearly 20 per cent of all manufacturing employees work in foreign-owned affiliates.

4.   Conclusions

In this chapter we have examined the relationship between foreign investment in Europe and labour market outcomes. We contend that any assessment of the impact of FDI activity by MNEs requires first an evaluation of the determinants of this activity. Why firms go abroad has important consequences for the effects of their investments on domestic labour markets. We review evidence that there exists substantial heterogeneity, both across countries and over time, in the types of European FDI. Some investment looks horizontal, in that it is motivated primarily by the desire to produce goods and services for consumers in the host country. Some, however, looks vertical, in that investments are designed to take advantage of international factor price differences and produce goods for export. Other foreign investment in Europe does not fit easily into either of these two standard categories.

Furthermore, we argue that the composition of FDI within a given European country varies significantly with a set of host-country policies and characteristics. Multinationals appear to tailor their operations in line with considerations such as host-country size, per capita income and policy choices such as EU membership and corporate tax rates. This evidence, along with cross-country and over-time heterogeneity in industry composition, external orientation and factor intensity, belies the conventional view that all FDI into Europe is market-seeking horizontal investment. Moreover, it suggests that government policy may play an important role in shaping the composition of inward FDI flows, above and beyond their overall level. All these patterns have important consequences for the host-country labour market impacts of FDI and their variation across Europe.

Having documented this heterogeneity, we turn to consider the labour market impacts of FDI. Does the nationality of firm ownership matter for the level, distribution and volatility of worker earnings and ownership? More specifically, we consider four dimensions to this question: the relative demand (and thus earnings and/or employment) between more skilled and less skilled workers economy-wide; the absolute earnings of each worker type; labour demand elasticities and the volatility of worker earnings; and profit-sharing. For all these dimensions, we present both theoretical and empirical evidence that the answer to this question is 'yes'.

All this suggests that the impact of multinationals on labour markets is complex, with net impacts on labour market outcomes that can vary in different contexts. Multinationals tend to pay higher wages – but may also have more elastic labour demands; multinationals can raise or lower the relative demands and wages across skill groups; multinationals appear to share profits with workers differently from domestic firms. In any given instance, different multinationals may have different labour market impacts. In turn, this suggests that how workers perceive multinationals is also variable. Understanding these impacts and perceptions cannot rely on theory alone, but needs empirical evidence as well.

REFERENCES

Aitken, B., A. Harrison and R. E. Lipsey (1996), 'Wages and foreign ownership: a comparative study of Mexico, Venezuela, and the United States', *Journal of International Economics*, 40 (3–4), 345–71.

Barba Navaretti, G., J. I. Haaland and A. Venables (2002), *Multinational Corporations and Global Production Networks: The Implications for Trade Policy*, report prepared for the European Commission Directorate General for Trade, Centre for Economic Policy Reserch, London.

Barrell, R., and N. Pain (1999), 'Domestic institutions, agglomerations and foreign direct investment in Europe', *European Economic Review*, 43, 925–34.

Bernard, A. B., and J. B. Jensen (2002), *The Death of Manufacturing Plants*, Working Paper no. 9026, National Bureau of Economic Research, Cambridge, MA.

Blonigen, B., and M. J. Slaughter (2001), 'Foreign-affiliate activity and US skill upgrading', *Review of Economics and Statistics*, 83 (2), 362–76.

Braconier, H., and K. Ekholm (2001), *Foreign Direct Investment in Central and Eastern Europe: Employment Effects in the EU*, Discussion Paper no. 3052, Centre for Economic Policy Research, London.

Brainard, S. L. (1997), 'An empirical assessment of the proximity-concentration tradeoff between multinational sales and trade', *American Economic Review*, 87, 520–44.

Budd, J. W., J. Konings and M. J. Slaughter (2005), 'International profit sharing in multinational firms', *Review of Economics and Statistics*, 87 (1).

Budd, J. W., and M. J. Slaughter (2004), 'Are profits shared across borders? Evidence on international rent sharing', *Journal of Labor Economics*, 22 (3), 525–52.

Carr, D. L., J. R. Markusen and K. E. Maskus (2001), 'Estimating the knowledge-capital model of the multinational enterprise', *American Economic Review*, 91, 693–708.

Caves, R. E. (1996), *Multinational Enterprise and Economic Analysis*, 2nd edn., Cambridge University Press, Cambridge.

Dominitz, J., and C. F. Manski (1997), 'Perceptions of economic insecurity', *Public Opinion Quarterly*, 61, 261–87.

Doms, M. E., and J. B. Jensen (1998), 'Comparing wages, skills, and productivity between domestically and foreign-owned manufacturing establishments in the United States', in: R. Baldwin, R. E. Lipsey and J. D. Richardson (eds.) *Geography and Ownership as Bases for Economic Accounting*, University of Chicago Press, Chicago, 235–55.

Fabbri, F., J. E. Haskel and M. J. Slaughter (2003), 'Does nationality of ownership matter for labour demands?' *Journal of the European Economics Association*, 1 (2–3), 698–707.

Feenstra, R. C., and G. H. Hanson (1996), 'Foreign investment, outsourcing and relative wages', in: R. C. Feenstra, G. M. Grossman and D. A. Irwin (eds.) *Political Economy of Trade: Policy Essays in Honor of Jagdish Bhagwati*, MIT Press, Cambridge, MA, 89–127.

(1997), 'Foreign direct investment and relative wages: evidence from Mexico's maquiladoras', *Journal of International Economics*, 42 (May), 371–93.

Globerman, S., J. Ries and I. Vertinsky (1994), 'The economic performance of foreign affiliates in Canada', *Canadian Journal of Economics*, 27 (1), 143–56.

Gorg, H., and E. Strobl (2003), 'Footloose multinationals?', *Manchester School*, 71 (1), 1–19.

Griffith, R. (1999), 'Using the ARD establishment level data to look at foreign ownership and productivity in the UK', *Economic Journal*, 109 (June), F416–F442.

Hamermesh, D. S. (1993), *Labour Demand*, Princeton University Press, Princeton, NJ.

Hanson, G. H., R. J. Mataloni, Jr., and M. J. Slaughter (2001), 'Expansion strategies of U. S. multinational firms', in: D. Rodrik and S. Collins (eds.) *Brookings Trade Forum 2001*, 245–94.

Haskel, J. E., S. Pereira and M. J. Slaughter (2002), *Does Inward Foreign Direct Investment Boost the Productivity of Domestic Firms?*, Working Paper no. 8724, National Bureau of Economic Research, Cambridge, MA.

Helpman, E. (1984), 'A simple theory of trade with multinational corporations', *Journal of Political Economy*, 92, 451–71.

Helpman, E., and P. R. Krugman (1985), *Market Structure and Foreign Trade*, MIT Press, Cambridge, MA.

Hines, J. R. (ed.) (2001), *International Taxation and Multinational Activity*, University of Chicago Press, Chicago.

Howenstine, N. G., and W. J. Zeile (1994), 'Characteristics of foreign-owned US manufacturing establishments', *Survey of Current Business*, 74 (1), 34–59.

Iversen, T., and T. Cusack (2000), 'The causes of welfare state expansion', *World Politics*, 52 (April), 313–49.

Johnson, G., and M. J. Slaughter (2001), 'The effects of growing international trade on the U. S. Labour Market', in: R. Solow and A. B. Krueger (eds.) *The Roaring Nineties: Can Full Employment Be Sustained?*, Russell Sage Foundation Publications, New York, 260–306.

Lipsey, R. E. (1999), 'The role of FDI in international capital flows', in: Martin Feldstein (ed.), *International Capital Flows*, University of Chicago Press, Chicago, 307–62.

(2003), 'Foreign direct investment and the operations of multinational firms: concepts, history, and data', in: K. Choi and J. Harrigan (eds.) *Handbook of International Trade*, Basil Blackwell, London, part 3, chap. 1.

Lipsey, R. E., I. B. Kravis and R. A. Roldan (1982), 'Do multinational firms adapt factor proportions to relative factor prices?', in: A. O. Krueger (ed.) *Trade and Employment in Developing Countries: Factor Supply and Substitution*, University of Chicago Press, Chicago 215–55.

Markusen, J. R. (1995), 'The boundaries of multinational firms and the theory of international trade', *Journal of Economic Perspectives*, 9, 169–89.

(2002), *Multinational Firms and the Theory of International Trade*, MIT Press, Cambridge, MA.

Markusen, J. R., and K. Maskus (1999), *Discriminating among Alternative Theories of the Multinational Enterprise*, Working Paper no. 7164, National Bureau of Economic Research, Cambridge, MA.

Markusen, J. R., and A. Venables (1998), 'Multinational firms and the new trade theory', *Journal of International Economics*, 46, 183–203.

(2000), 'The theory of endowment, intra-industry and multinational trade', *Journal of International Economics*, 52, 209–34.

Reddy, S. (2000), *Essays on International Integration and National Regulation*, Ph.D. dissertation, Harvard University, Cambridge, MA.

Rodrik, D. (1997), *Has Globalization Gone Too Far?* Institute for International Economics, Washington, DC.

Scheve, K. F., and M. J. Slaughter (2002), *Economic Insecurity and the Globalization of Production*, Working Paper no. 9339, National Bureau of Economic Research, Cambridge, MA.

Slaughter, M. J. (1998), *American Investments, Global Returns*, Emergency Committee for American Trade, Washington, DC.

——— (2000), 'Production transfer within multinational enterprises and American wages', *Journal of International Economics*, 50 (2), 449–72.

——— (2001), 'International trade and labor-demand elasticities', *Journal of International Economics*, 54 (1): 27–56.

——— (2003), 'Host-country determinants of U. S. foreign direct investment into Europe', in: H. Herrmann and R. E. Lipsey (eds.) *Foreign Direct Investment in the Real and Financial Sector of Industrial Economies*, Springer-Verlag, 7–32.

te Velde, D. W., and O. Morrissey (2001), *Foreign Ownership and Wages: Evidence from Five African Countries*, CREDIT Discussion Paper no. 01/19, Department of Economics, University of Nottingham.

United Nations Conference on Trade and Development (2001), *World Investment Report: Promoting Linkages*, United Nations, New York.

Yeaple, S. R. (2001), *The Determinants of U. S. Outward Foreign Direct Investment: Market Access versus Comparative Advantage*, mimeo, University of Pennsylvania.

4   Foreign ownership in Europe: determinants and taxation consequences

Cécile Denis, Harry Huizinga and Gaëtan Nicodème

1.   Introduction

Europe is largely open to investments from abroad in the form of foreign direct investment and portfolio investment. This openness has not, however, led to an outcome where foreign residents own the lion's share of national assets. Instead, only about a quarter of European equities are currently foreign-owned. This is true both for firms that are listed on an exchange and for firms without such a listing. This relatively small foreign ownership share is the mirror image of the well-known 'home bias' in investment portfolios.

This chapter has three purposes. First, it describes some of the available evidence on the foreign ownership of firms in Europe. Data on the foreign ownership of exchange-listed shares are available from an international survey conducted by the International Monetary Fund (IMF). Indicative foreign ownership shares can be calculated as the ratio of the absolute foreign ownership of shares and the stock market capitalisation. The foreign ownership shares thus obtained display a considerable national variation, with the share exceeding 35 per cent in Ireland, the Netherlands and Finland in 1997. Alternatively, we compute foreign ownership shares for non-traded shares using information from the Amadeus database. This yields an asset-weighted foreign ownership share of 19 per cent in Western Europe in the year 2000, while the foreign ownership share is 44 per cent for Eastern Europe. Foreign ownership of non-traded shares has been fairly stable during the 1996–2000 period in Western Europe, but it is has increased substantially in Eastern Europe.

The second purpose of the chapter is to explain some of the national variation in foreign ownership shares in Europe. Kang and Stulz (1997) and Dahlquist and Robertsson (2001) have previously investigated how

We thank Werner Roeger for many useful discussions and Ramiro Gomez Villalba for technical assistance. The findings, interpretations and conclusions expressed in this chapter are entirely those of the authors. They should not be attributed to the European Commission.

foreign ownership depends on various firm characteristics for the cases of Japan and Sweden, respectively. Extending this research to an international setting, we examine the country characteristics that may affect the foreign ownership of equity. Given that we have firm-level data only for firms without such a listing, our search for cross-country variation in the foreign ownership of shares is limited to firms without such a listing. A particular role is seen for the quality of institutions in the area of investor protection and the rule of law. Somewhat counter-intuitively, foreign ownership of non-traded firms appears to be relatively high in countries with relatively low-quality institutions. To understand this, we note that foreign ownership in the case of shares without an exchange listing tends to involve FDI, where the foreign investor also has control over his investments. FDI may be relatively intense in countries with low-quality legal institutions, as there multinational firms that are subject to the relatively high-quality legal institutions of their home countries may have a comparative advantage to operate.

A third purpose of this chapter is to describe some of the consequences of foreign ownership for corporate income taxation. As documented by Devereux et al. (2002), corporate income taxes as a percentage of GDP have been rather stable at around 2.5 per cent. Hence, a 'race to the bottom' in corporate income taxes due to fierce international tax competition has not occurred in recent decades, despite the increased level of economic integration in Europe. This chapter explores whether the already substantial level of foreign ownership of shares in Europe can provide an explanation for the absence of such a race to the bottom. Several theoretical papers, among them Mintz (1994) and Huizinga and Nielsen (1997), have indicated that higher foreign ownership of equities gives countries an incentive to increase their levels of corporate income taxation, as foreign ownership allows them to export part of this tax. This chapter provides some evidence that European countries with high foreign ownership shares indeed levy relatively high corporate income taxes. Evidence of this is based on a large sample of European firms constructed from the Amadeus database. Empirical estimates indicate that the effect of foreign ownership on the level of corporate taxation is economically significant. An increase in foreign ownership by one percentage point, specifically, is estimated to increase the tax burden as a percentage of assets by 0.028, which is about 1 per cent of the average value of this measure of the tax burden.

Section 2 presents the cross-European evidence on the foreign ownership of shares of firms with and without a stock market listing. Section 3 turns to the available evidence on the determinants of foreign ownership at a national level. Section 4 examines the relationship between foreign ownership and corporate income taxation. Section 5 concludes.

2.   The data

This section reviews data on the foreign ownership of shares in Europe available from two sources.[1] First, the Coordinated Portfolio Investment Survey (CPIS), collected under the auspices of the IMF (1999), provides information on the foreign ownership of equity securities, at market prices, excluding FDI. Second, we use information available from the Amadeus data set to calculate foreign ownership shares for firms that do not have an exchange listing. Firms without an exchange listing typically have a small set of owners, enabling the nationality of all owners, and the foreign ownership share, to be established. Foreign ownership in non-listed firms tends to be direct investment, in that the foreign owners also yield control over the firms they invest in.

2.1   *Foreign ownership of listed equities*

Information on the total foreign ownership of equities excluding FDI is available from the IMF. To see how important foreign ownership is relative to domestic ownership, we need an estimate of the total stock of domestic equities that are available for portfolio investment purposes. For this, we use the capitalisation of the country's stock market. The foreign ownership share of market-traded equities is then calculated as the ratio of total foreign investment and stock market capitalisation.[2] The results for 1997 are reported in table 4.1. The average foreign ownership share in Europe is calculated to be 25.5 per cent (with equal weights for all countries). For the EU15 (minus Luxembourg) the equal-weighted average foreign ownership share is similarly estimated to be 27.1 per cent. Note that foreign ownership shares exceeding 35 per cent are recorded for Ireland, the Netherlands and Finland, and that foreign ownership shares below 15 per cent are shown for Belgium and Greece. Data for two Western European countries outside the

---

[1] We consider the share of a country's equity assets that is foreign-owned. Alternatively, one can consider the share of a country's investments that consists of foreign assets. Adjaouté et al. (2000) and European Commission (2001) report that foreign assets make up a substantial share of European portfolios. Specifically, European Commission (2001, p. 153) documents that foreign financial assets exceed 25 per cent of total financial assets in Belgium, the Netherlands, Spain and the United Kingdom out of the twelve member states for which data are available.

[2] Note that the resulting foreign ownership share is overestimated if some firms traded at a national stock exchange are in fact located or incorporated abroad, and vice versa.

Table 4.1. *Foreign ownership shares of listed firms, 1997*

Country	Foreign securities as percentage of stock market capitalisation
Austria	20.9
Belgium	13.9
Denmark	19.2
Finland	36.7
France	27.4
Germany	19.7
Greece	13.4
Ireland	64.4
Italy	25.6
Netherlands	39.8
Norway	25.2
Poland	23.2
Portugal	29.6
Slovenia	5.2
Spain	26.2
Sweden	26.6
Switzerland	25.0
United Kingdom	17.8
Europe	25.5
EU15	27.1
Western Europe	27.0
Eastern Europe	14.2

Note: 'EU15' excludes Luxembourg. Regional averages weight countries equally.
Source: Data on foreign ownership of equities are from the CPIS. Data on stock market capitalisation are from the International Federation of Stock Exchanges.

European Union, Norway and Switzerland, are in line with those for the Union. Foreign ownership shares in Eastern Europe are, if anything, lower than in Western Europe (23.2 per cent for Poland and just 5.2 per cent for Slovenia).

2.2 Foreign ownership of non-listed equities

Firm-level data for firms used in this study are taken from the Amadeus database, compiled by Van Dijk. This data source provides regular accounting data on European firms as well as information on main shareholders, including their nationality (see appendix 1 for further details on Amadeus). We consider the time period from 1996 to 2000.

From Amadeus, we can obtain full information on the nationality of stock ownership for about 14,000 firms in the year 2000. For each firm, shareholders are divided into domestic and foreign shareholders.

Using this firm-level information we have constructed average national foreign ownership shares, as reported in table 4.2. Specifically, the table provides the asset-weighted national foreign ownership shares for the year 2000, and also yearly averages of these foreign ownership shares for the years 1996 to 2000. In 2000 the foreign ownership share in Europe stands at 26.7 per cent as a whole, while foreign ownership in Western and Eastern Europe separately stood at 19.2 and 44.2 per cent,

Table 4.2. *Foreign ownership shares of non-listed firms, 1996–2000*

Country	Number of firms in 2000	Foreign ownership share (percentage), 2000	Average foreign ownership share (percentage), 1996–2000
Austria	149	21.4	24.1
Belgium	629	29.0	40.3
Bulgaria	419	18.4	7.2
Czech Republic	275	60.5	51.0
Denmark	927	22.5	22.7
Finland	126	7.4	6.5
France	2,489	14.6	15.4
Germany	551	14.2	13.7
Greece	201	23.2	29.0
Hungary	61	86.7	83.2
Italy	1,364	29.7	33.5
Netherlands	487	42.6	40.4
Norway	1,555	24.6	18.2
Poland	120	33.5	17.6
Portugal	111	18.9	18.6
Romania	1,390	31.0	21.3
Slovenia	70	34.8	33.9
Spain	1,005	9.6	22.1
Sweden	1,308	4.1	3.9
United Kingdom	852	7.0	15.6
Europe	14,089	26.7	25.9
Western Europe	11,754	19.2	21.7
Eastern Europe	2,335	44.2	35.7

Note: The foreign ownership share is asset-weighted and based on at least thirty-five observations per year. The average foreign ownership share over 1996–2000 is the average of the annual averages. Regional averages are averages of national averages.

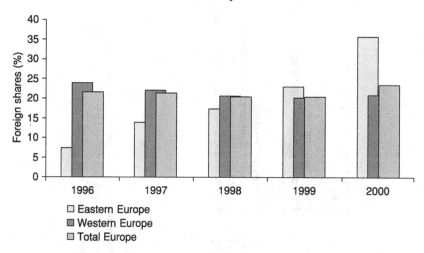

Figure 4.1. The evolution of foreign ownership, 1996–2000.
Note: Data are averages for all firms in the region concerned and year.

respectively.[3] We also see that the average foreign ownership share for the 1996–2000 period is higher (lower) in Western Europe (Eastern Europe) than in 2000. Trends in foreign ownership in Europe during the 1996–2000 period are represented in figure 4.1. We see that foreign ownership in Europe as a whole has increased slightly during the period. This overall increase reflects a slight decline in foreign ownership in Western Europe along with a substantial increase in Eastern Europe.

Foreign ownership varies considerably across economic sectors, as seen in figure 4.2, which shows that foreign ownership exceeds 20 per cent in financial services, manufacturing, and wholesale and retail trade in the whole of Europe. At the same time, agriculture (and hunting and forestry), construction, fishing, and electricity (and gas and water supply) have foreign ownership shares of less than 10 per cent in Europe. Sectoral foreign ownership shares in Eastern and Western Europe differ considerably in several instances, as also seen in figure 4.2. Agriculture, for instance, is far less foreign-owned in Eastern Europe than in Western Europe. This, no doubt, reflects the fact that several Eastern European countries continue to restrict the foreign ownership of land. In contrast,

---

[3] Eurostat (2001) reports on the share of value added produced by foreign-owned firms in 1998 for Denmark, Spain, the Netherlands, Finland, Sweden and the United Kingdom, with an average foreign share of 12.3 per cent for these countries. Eurostat counts only majority-owned foreign enterprises (with a single owner or group of owners having more than 50 per cent of the shares), which explains the rather low figure. Data in the Eurostat study reflect selected services industries only.

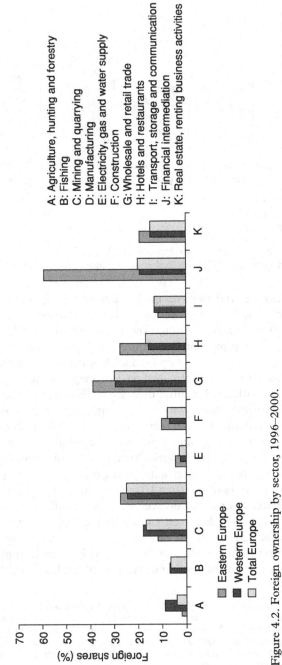

Figure 4.2. Foreign ownership by sector, 1996–2000.

Note: This classification is based on the first two digits of the NACE code. The percentages of foreign-owned shares per sector are simple averages of the data for all firms for which there is full ownership information. 'Western Europe' is EU15 plus Iceland, Norway and Switzerland. The fishing industry in Eastern Europe is represented by six firms (all of which are fully domestically owned).

financial intermediaries in Eastern Europe, with a foreign ownership share of about 60 per cent, are far more highly foreign-owned than in Western Europe. Financial intermediation is an industry where the adequate protection of creditors is crucial, and hence international banks may have a competitive advantage over domestic banks if their foreign origin enables them to 'import' a high level of creditor protection.[4]

Foreign ownership is more likely to enable a firm to import international standards of corporate behaviour if the foreign owners in fact control the company. Foreigners are more likely to be in control if they own 50 per cent or more of the stock.[5] Hence, it is interesting to see the extent to which foreign owners collectively are minority or majority shareholders. To shed light on this, figure 4.3 provides information about the frequency distribution of the firm-level foreign ownership shares for Western Europe and for Eastern Europe separately. The foreign ownership distributions for Western and Eastern Europe in fact look very similar, with more than 70 per cent of firms fully domestically owned in both regions. At the other extreme, in Western and Eastern Europe 20.5 and 15.9 per cent of all firms are fully foreign-owned, respectively. Among firms that are partially foreign-owned, relatively many have a foreign ownership share in the 50–52.5 per cent bracket to guarantee foreign control. Thus, most firms with any foreign ownership are, in fact, 50 per cent or more foreign-owned. For firms without an exchange listing, foreign ownership thus tends to imply foreign control.

3.   Determinants of foreign ownership

It is not straightforward explaining the international variation in the foreign ownership of shares. Foreign ownership serves a range of purposes, such as risk diversification and the facilitation of international trade, and at the same time it entails specific costs. This suggests that a wide range of variables can, in principle, explain foreign ownership patterns. These potential determinants of foreign ownership include macroeconomic variables, proxies for financial market development, tax variables, indices of market access for international investors, and indicators of the quality of institutions, including (foreign) shareholder

---

[4] Foreign banks that are organised as branches tend to fall under the regulation and supervision of the home country. The same may be true for foreign banking subsidiaries that are part of a larger holding company. Alternatively, foreign banks can have a competitive advantage over domestic banks if they use superior banking techniques.

[5] Formal foreign control may require less than 50 per cent of the shares to be foreign-owned if there are shares with multiple voting rights. De facto foreign control may require far less than 50 per cent foreign ownership.

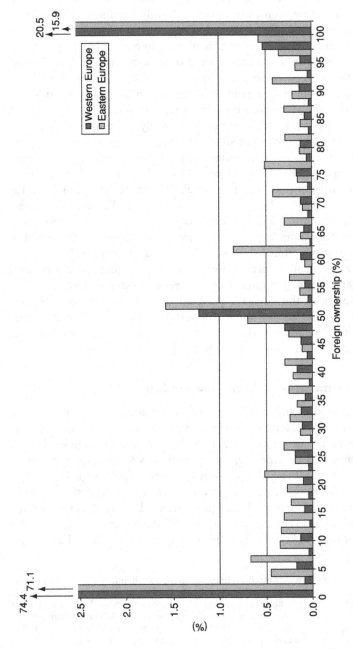

Figure 4.3. The distribution of the foreign ownership percentage, 1996–2000.
Note: The proportion of foreign-owned shares for all firms for which there is full information on share ownership. Europe is EU15 plus Iceland, Norway and Switzerland. Classes are defined as follows: 0–2.5, 2.5–5.0, ... 97.5–100, with the boundaries included in the lower brackets.

protection. The hypotheses that link foreign ownership to these explanatory variables are, in some instances, rather immediate. Wider freedoms for international investors to acquire control of a company, for instance, should lead to broader foreign ownership.

In other instances, the relationship to be expected between foreign ownership and the potential explanatory variables is less clear. This is the case for indicators of the quality and efficacy of legal and other institutions (among these are indices of shareholder protection, the quality of accounting standards and the rule of law). A well-functioning legal system (including effective corporate governance regulation) makes it harder for managers and majority shareholders to disadvantage minority shareholders. This is true for domestically owned and foreign-owned firms. If the main managers and majority shareholders are domestic and the minority shareholders are foreign, good institutions help to protect foreign investors from expropriation by domestic agents, and hence could give rise to a higher national foreign ownership share. Reasoning along these lines underlies the 'natural' hypothesis that international investors are attracted to countries with good institutions.

The opposite, however, may be true, if foreign-owned firms are to some extent able to 'internalise' the good institutions of their home countries. A foreign-owned firm that is part of a larger multinational, for instance, may de facto be subject to some aspects of the law of the home country. This is because the law (including financial market regulations and corporate government codes) can be explicitly or implicitly extraterritorial in a variety of ways. As a result, foreign ownership may enable firms to 'import' good institutions into a country that does not have these itself. This may enable foreign-owned firms to commit, for instance, to treat minority shareholders and creditors fairly, thus lowering their cost of capital. Such a commitment provides foreign-owned firms with a competitive advantage vis-à-vis local firms, and in equilibrium would give rise to a relatively high foreign ownership share in countries with low-quality institutions. Our empirical results indeed suggest that foreign ownership and good institutions are substitutes rather than complements in the case of non-traded firms.

There are a few papers investigating the foreign ownership of equities in particular countries. In the case of Japan, Kang and Stulz (1997) find that foreign holdings of Japanese exchange-traded shares are biased towards large firms, firms with low leverage, firms with low unsystematic risk and firms in manufacturing industries. Controlling for size, these authors further find that firms that export more, have greater share turnover and have issued American Depositary Receipts (ADRs) experience greater foreign ownership. Larger firms with considerable exports may be more highly foreign-owned due to a wider international recognition. With regard to South Korea, Freund and Djankov (2000) similarly find that foreign investors focus on exchange-listed firms that are fast-growing and large, and have low debt and high exports. Finally, Dahlquist and Robertsson (2001) examine the foreign ownership of publicly traded Swedish shares. In part corroborating previous results, these authors find that foreigners prefer to invest in large firms, firms paying low dividends, and firms with large cash positions on their balance sheets. Dahlquist and Robertsson report that foreign investors typically are mutual funds and other institutional investors. The observed investment preferences of foreign investors are attributed to the fact that they are mostly institutional investors. Hence, Dahlquist and Robertsson find that international equity investments are subject to an institutional investor in addition to a foreign investor bias.

Single-country data may yield information about foreign investor biases based on firm characteristics, but multi-country data are needed to uncover any international biases. Based on Huizinga and Denis (2004), we investigate the international ownership of firms in nineteen European countries over the 1996–2000 period using data on firms without an exchange listing taken from the Amadeus database. The foreign ownership of these firms represents foreign direct investment rather than portfolio investment. In this respect, the present chapter differs from previous papers on the foreign ownership of exchange-listed firms in a single country.

A key area of interest for examination is the impact of the legal and regulatory environment on the prevalence of foreign ownership. Specifically, national foreign ownership shares can be related to a variety of indices of the legal environment derived from two sources. Two variables, taken from various issues of the *World Competitiveness Yearbook*, have values that change from year to year. These are IMPROPER (reflecting the propriety of public administration) and INSIDERT (reflecting the scarcity of insider trading); for the definitions of these and other variables, see the appendix. A further five variables – ANTIDR (anti-director rights), ACCSTAN (accounting standards), EFFJS (the efficiency of the judicial system), ROL (the rule of law) and CORRUPT (the scarcity of corruption) – are taken from La Porta et al. (1998). These latter variables do not vary from year to year.

Figure 4.4 provides simple scatter diagrams plotting each of the legal and institutional quality indices against country-level foreign ownership. All data are averaged for the 1996–2000 period. The IMPROPER and INSIDERT measures are available for several Eastern European countries in addition to most Western European countries. The measures

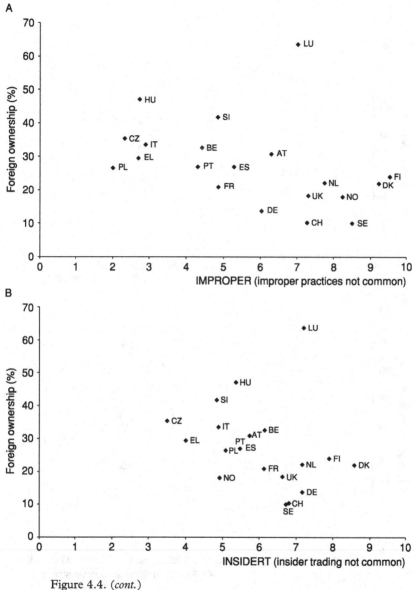

Figure 4.4. (*cont.*)

C

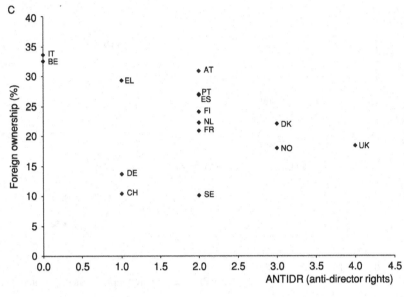

D

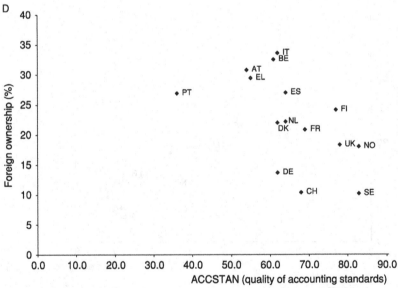

Figure 4.4. (*cont.*)

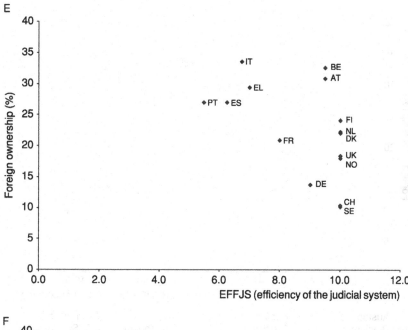

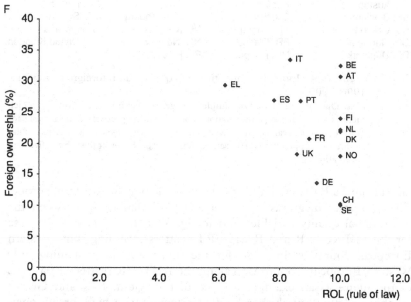

Figure 4.4. (*cont.*)

G

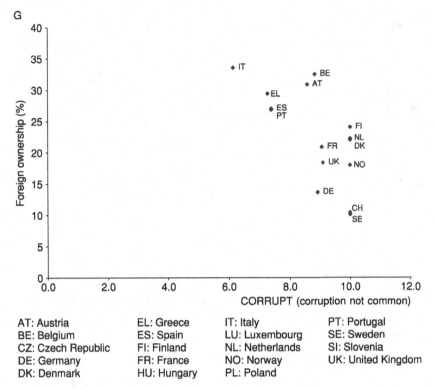

AT: Austria   EL: Greece   IT: Italy   PT: Portugal
BE: Belgium   ES: Spain   LU: Luxembourg   SE: Sweden
CZ: Czech Republic   FI: Finland   NL: Netherlands   SI: Slovenia
DE: Germany   FR: France   NO: Norway   UK: United Kingdom
DK: Denmark   HU: Hungary   PL: Poland

Figure 4.4. Indices of institutional quality and foreign ownership, 1996–2000.

Note: Diagrams are based on simple averages per country of all firms for which there is full ownership information. Data for firms present in the sample for more than one year are first averaged for the years 1996–2000. A particular country is dropped if it is represented in the sample by fewer than thirty-five firm observations.

taken from La Porta et al. (1998) are available only for Western Europe. All the scatter diagrams display a negative relationship between the institutional quality variables and foreign ownership. This is the case for the IMPROPER and INSIDERT scatters including some Eastern European countries, but also for the other scatters containing only Western European countries. Taking the ANTIDR scatter in panel C of the figure as an example, we see that Belgium, Italy and Greece combine relatively weak shareholder protection with high foreign ownership, while the Nordic countries (Denmark, Norway and Sweden) and the United Kingdom display strong shareholder protection and relatively low foreign ownership.

The scatter diagrams suggest that the univariate relationship between institutional quality and foreign ownership is negative. As indicated, firm-level variables, macroeconomic indicators, financial development indices and taxation variables can be expected to affect foreign ownership shares as well. Next, we discuss how some of these variables are hypothesised to affect foreign ownership. Then we discuss the results of a regression linking national foreign ownership shares to a range of possible determinants.

Following Kang and Stulz (1997) and Dahlquist and Robertsson (2001), we will include two firm-level variables in the analysis: assets, as an index of firm size; and solvency, defined as shareholders' equity as a percentage of assets. The expectation, based on the earlier papers, is that both of these variables contribute to higher foreign ownership.

Several potential macroeconomic determinants of foreign ownership are considered as well. GDP is hypothesised to be negatively related to foreign ownership, as larger countries should hold a larger share of their own assets, if international assets are held to diversify risk. Second, GDP per capita is negatively related to inward foreign ownership, if richer countries tend to own the tangible and intangible assets that are the basis of much foreign direct investment.[6] On the other hand, richer countries may specialise more in the production of goods that require the inputs of high-quality human and physical capital from several countries – giving rise to higher FDI and foreign ownership in richer countries. This would also give rise to higher foreign ownership among richer countries. Overall, we do not have a clear prior on how per capita GDP will affect foreign ownership. Third, openness, defined as exports plus imports divided by GDP, is positively related to foreign ownership if foreign asset ownership is a complement to trade, while the relationship is negative if foreign ownership and trade are substitutes.

Next, TURN, defined as stock exchange turnover as a percentage of stock market capitalisation, and SMCAP, defined as stock market capitalisation as a percentage of GDP, are considered as measures of financial development. Well-developed financial markets make any investment, whether foreign-owned or not, more attractive, as they guarantee workable exit options to investors who want to sell their stakes. More related to foreign ownership, a foreign subsidiary of a multinational firm may have privileged access to an internal capital market within the firm. Similarly, foreign owners may have easier direct access to international

---

[6] At least some wealthy countries have strongly positive net foreign asset positions. This could give rise to a negative relationship between GDP per capita and foreign ownership, even if wealthy countries do not disproportionately invest in foreign stocks.

126   *C. Denis, H. Huizinga and G. Nicodème*

financial markets (including international banks) on the basis of their international reputation. All this suggests that foreign-owned firms have relatively easy access to capital in countries with low levels of financial development. This could explain a negative relationship between the financial development variables and foreign ownership.

Next, withholding taxes on dividends accruing to foreign residents can be expected to have a negative impact on foreign ownership. The withholding tax variable we consider, WT, is the minimum of withholding taxes on dividends accruing to American, British, German and Japanese (foreign) residents. Finally, we consider a variable measuring the accessibility to foreign investors of the local markets for control. Specifically, FCONTROL measures the perceived extent to which foreign investors are free to acquire control in a domestic company.

Now we consider the results of a regression relating foreign ownership to the institutional and other variables, as reported in table 4.3. The regression has as the dependent variable the average firm-level foreign ownership share over the period 1996 to 2000. Countries with fewer than thirty-five firms with information on foreign ownership are excluded. Estimation is by weighted least squares, with the weight being the inverse of the number of firms per country. We include the IMPROPER variable as the only variable from the group of institutional quality variables given that variables in this group are highly correlated.

Table 4.3. *Determinants of foreign ownership*

Assets	3.0** (0.38)
Solvency	$7.7\ 10^{-2}$** ($2.7\ 10^{-2}$)
GDP	−5.4 ** (0.84)
GDP per capita	9.2** (1.9)
Openness	4.2 (2.4)
TURN	$-7.2\ 10^{-3}$ ($6.0\ 10^{-3}$)
SMCAP	$4.6\ 10^{-2}$** ($1.5\ 10^{-2}$)
WT	0.36** ($8.9\ 10^{-2}$)
FCONTROL	0.21 (0.61)
IMPROPER	−4.0** (0.47)
Adj. R^2	0.37
Sample size	23,907
Number of countries	17

Notes: The dependent variable is the average foreign ownership share over the period 1996 to 2000 as a percentage. Assets, GDP and GDP per capita are in logs. Unreported industry fixed effects are included. The definitions of the variables, and the data sources, are given in the appendix. Heteroscedasticity consistent errors are given in parenthesis. ** indicates significance at the 1 per cent level.

The regression is based on observations from seventeen countries. We see that foreign ownership is significantly negatively related to the IMPROPER variable, which suggests that foreign ownership is higher in environments characterised by official corruption. As seen in Huizinga and Denis (2004, table 5), the finding that foreign ownership is higher in low-quality institutional environments is robust to several other ways of representing the data and to the replacement of the IMPROPER variable by several of the ones featuring in the scatter diagrams of figure 4.4. Note that, among the controls, it is surprising that foreign ownership is positively related to the WT variable. This result, which potentially indicates that foreign investors are attracted to countries with high tax and spending levels, turns out not to be robust to replacements of IMPROPER by other institutional variables. The results that foreign ownership is positively related to the assets and solvency variables but negatively to GDP, however, are robust to various changes of this kind.

As indicated, foreign-owned firms may be able to function relatively well in low-quality institutional environments, because they are able to import some of the higher-quality institutional standards of their home countries. Our regression analysis, however, does not shed light on how exactly foreign firms may be able to import these relatively high institutional standards. A few potential channels, all the same, can be mentioned. First, foreign-owned firms that are subsidiaries of a multinational firm may be formally subject to the higher-quality accounting standards of the home country. Second, legal standards, including corporate governance codes, may de facto have an extraterritorial reach in the case of multinational firms. Higher-level managers, specifically, may be held accountable in their home country courts for misdeeds committed anywhere. The United States, for instance, forbids bribery by US companies anywhere. Third, international companies may refrain from opportunistic behaviour vis-à-vis local capital providers or other business partners in order to protect their worldwide reputations, even where such opportunism would not be illegal.

As a result of all this, foreign-owned companies may be preferred as business partners in countries with weak institutions. Minority shareholders and creditors, specifically, may stand a better chance of being treated fairly by foreign-owned firms than by local firms. This could lead to a lower cost of capital for foreign-owned firms. Similarly, workers and business partners may believe that foreign firms apply higher standards of corporate behaviour than local firms, which would make international firms the employers and business partners of choice. Wider trust in foreign firms would provide them with a competitive advantage vis-à-vis domestic firms, and could give rise to a larger foreign ownership share at the national level in countries with weak legal institutions.

4.   The taxation consequences of foreign ownership

A considerable literature has investigated how foreign-owned firms may be different from domestically owned firms in terms of productivity, growth and labour market outcomes and how the presence of foreign firms may affect domestic firms in these respects (see Görg and Greenaway, 2002, for a recent survey). In an analogous fashion, foreign-owned firms may be different from domestically owned firms in the amount of corporate income tax they pay, and their presence can – in principle – affect tax policy towards all firms, including domestically owned firms. In fact, more foreign ownership is expected to lead to higher corporate income taxes, if tax authorities are more interested in taxing foreign ownership than domestic ownership. In this section, we first review some of the theoretical work on the relationship between foreign ownership and capital income taxation. We also review some of the previous empirical evidence on foreign ownership and taxation (at both the firm level and the aggregate level). Next, we discuss some new evidence, based on Huizinga and Nicodème (forthcoming), that corporate income taxation in Europe is indeed positively affected by corporate income taxation. Thus, the already high degree of foreign ownership in Europe may be a reason why we have not seen a significant decline, or even a race to the bottom, in corporate income tax levels in recent decades. Finally, we evaluate some of the implications for economic welfare of a positive relationship between foreign ownership and corporate tax burdens.

4.1   Previous literature

A small open economy optimally does not tax internationally mobile capital that just earns its marginal product (see, for instance, Gordon, 1986). The reason is that the incidence of a capital tax will be on immobile factors of production, such as labour. It is then better to tax labour directly, as this leaves the capital input decision undistorted. The corporate income tax in practice taxes mobile capital as well as residual profits. In the absence of a separate profit tax, the corporate income tax can then be rationalised as a crude way of taxing profits. Foreign ownership implies that part of a company's profit stream accrues to foreign residents. The corporate income tax can thus serve to shift some income away from foreign residents to the domestic Treasury or, ultimately, domestic residents (see, for instance, Mintz, 1994). In line with this, Huizinga and Nielsen (1997) show that a higher foreign ownership share will generally rationalise higher source-based capital income taxes (such as the corporate income tax) combined with lower residence-based capital income taxes.

In a multi-country world, foreign ownership will generally increase the level of capital income taxation that materialises in the absence of international tax policy coordination. Foreign ownership therefore affects whether countries can increase their welfare by coordinating their tax policies and if so, whether coordination requires increases or reductions in overall capital income tax levels. Huizinga and Nielsen (2002), for instance, show that a high degree of foreign ownership may obviate the need to increase source-based capital income taxes through coordination in a world where the evasion of residence-based capital income taxes would otherwise justify such coordination.

Sørensen (2000) examines the scope for international tax policy coordination with the aid of a simulation model characterized by partial foreign ownership and an absence of residence-based capital income taxes.[7] The model specifically considers regional capital income tax coordination among EU countries in a model consisting of four European 'regions' and the United States. In the benchmark calibration, the four European regions have a foreign ownership share of 25 per cent. Regional coordination in Europe increases the average capital income tax from 33.8 per cent to 46.5 per cent. Sensitivity analysis reveals that putting the foreign ownership share to zero has the effect of reducing the uncoordinated and coordinated capital income taxes to 23.0 and 41.0 per cent, respectively. Higher foreign ownership shares beyond 25 per cent, conceivably in the 50–60 per cent range, may well imply that tax coordination in Europe implies increasing capital income taxes, although Sørensen does not provide calculations on this.

Empirical work on the relationship between foreign ownership and capital income taxation has so far focused mostly on whether foreign-owned firms pay higher or lower taxes than domestically owned firms, rather than on the impact of macro-level foreign ownership on the overall tax burden. Specifically, Grubert et al. (1993) find that foreign-controlled US corporations pay lower US taxes than purely domestic firms, on the basis of tax return data. About half of the observed difference in taxes paid can be explained by observable factors, such as exchange rate fluctuations, firm size and firm age. The remaining half is attributed to unobservable factors, such as a lower accounting

---

[7] In Sørensen (2000), firms are atomistic. Hence, firms are too small to be able to change the taxes they face by changing their degree of foreign ownership, through, for instance, divestment to domestic owners.

profitability following the manipulation of international transfer prices or lower true profitability due to lower productivity.

Demirgüç-Kunt and Huizinga (2001), further, examine the taxes paid by domestic and foreign banks in eighty countries during the 1988–1995 period using firm-level accounting information. On average, foreign banks pay higher taxes than domestic banks in lower-income countries, while they pay about equal taxes in higher-income countries. Foreign banks, however, are found to pay lower taxes than domestic banks in many individual industrialised countries (among them the United Kingdom and the United States) after controlling for firm characteristics.[8]

In an attempt to shed further light on why foreign firms may pay lower taxes in the United States, Kinney and Lawrence (2000) compare the taxes paid by US firms taken over by foreign firms and other domestic US firms, respectively, during the 1975–1989 period. The firms taken over by foreign firms are shown to pay relatively low taxes. This difference, however, is explained by the fact that foreigners tend to take over US targets that are less profitable than their industry counterparts, and hence it is not attributed to income manipulation by foreign firms.

So far, little evidence exists on the potential relationship between macro-level foreign ownership and the overall corporate tax burden (for foreign and domestic firms alike). Using data for the US states, Eijffinger and Wagner (2001) relate the average corporate tax rate paid to the real productive assets of foreign-owned affiliates (defined to be at least 10 per cent foreign-owned) as a measure of foreign ownership. In the absence of data on aggregate state-level real productive assets, these authors include statewide corporate income or employment as scaling variables in their empirical specification. Also, the authors fail to include firm-level or industry-level controls in their analysis. All the same, they report a positive relationship between the average corporate tax rate and the real productive assets of foreign affiliates in support of the hypothesis that corporate tax levels increase with the level of foreign ownership.

4.2   Cross-country evidence of the impact of foreign ownership on tax burdens

Based on Huizinga and Nicodème (forthcoming), we now present some evidence that foreign ownership and corporate tax burdens are positively

[8] See Demirgüç-Kunt and Huizinga (2001, table 5). These patterns, again, can reflect transfer pricing and differences in underlying productivity. The further finding, that reported profitability rises with the statutory tax rate only for domestic banks, is interpreted as evidence that foreign banks are engaged in international profit shifting.

related across European countries. Our measure of the tax burden is accrued taxes as a percentage of assets, as taken from the Amadeus database.[9] Foreign ownership figures are taken from Amadeus as well, and hence present firms without an exchange listing.[10] In figure 4.5 we plot the average tax burden from 1996 to 2000 per country against the average asset-weighted foreign ownership. Countries in Eastern and Western Europe are markedly different. The figure displays a positive relationship between the tax burden and foreign ownership, at least for Western Europe. Hungary and Bulgaria are distinct outliers, with relatively high and low foreign ownership, respectively.

Regression analysis in Huizinga and Nicodème (forthcoming) confirms a positive cross-country relationship between foreign ownership and taxation, if one controls for a variety of firm-level, industry and macroeconomic effects. Moreover, the empirical results suggest that the relationship between company tax burdens and foreign ownership is economically significant. Specifically, our benchmark results suggest that a doubling of foreign ownership in Europe, from 21.5 to 43 per cent, would increase the average corporate tax rate from about 33 per cent to about 42 per cent. During the 1996–2000 period average foreign ownership in Western Europe appears to have been rather stable, while it increased significantly in Eastern Europe. In the decades to come, foreign ownership can be expected to increase in Western Europe as well, and thus might mitigate any race to the bottom in corporate tax burdens.

4.3   *Evaluation of welfare implications*

Should we be concerned about a positive impact of foreign ownership on corporate tax burdens in Europe? The welfare effects of a positive relationship between foreign ownership and corporate tax burdens appear to be uncertain. Foreign ownership is relatively high in smaller countries. The resulting upward pressure on corporate taxes is therefore also relatively large in smaller countries. This may serve to cancel out, partially or wholly, the relatively strong pressure to reduce taxes in

---

[9] We measure taxes relative to assets rather than some measure of income or profits, as these latter variables are more easily distorted through international profit shifting.

[10] In addition, we exclude firms with a consolidated statement, as these firms may own subsidiaries that pay taxes outside the country of consideration. The focus on firms that are not consolidated by itself implies that we exclude most of the large publicly traded firms. Data on traded firms, even if it were available, would largely be inappropriate to use in this context, as traded firms tend to have consolidated statements that may well represent taxes paid by foreign subsidiaries to tax authorities abroad. Hence, our focus on non-traded firms (which do not have a consolidated statement) is not a limitation in this context.

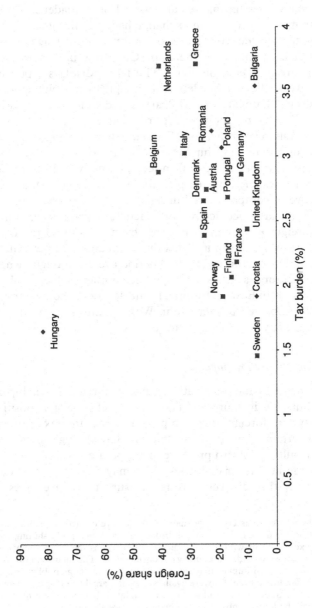

Figure 4.5. Foreign ownership and the tax burden, 1996–2000.

Note: Data for foreign ownership and the tax burden are averages of yearly asset-weighted averages over the 1996–2000 period. Foreign ownership for a given country in a given year is computed only if there are at least thirty-five observations. In that case the corresponding tax burden is computed as well. Detailed variable definitions and data sources are given in appendix 1.

smaller countries in order to attract a larger corporate tax base. The higher foreign ownership in smaller countries therefore, in principle, may help to bring about more equal corporate tax levels across countries. Hence, the foreign ownership effect on taxes could serve to reduce distortions in the international tax system coming from international disparities in corporate tax burdens. In a world of equal-sized, symmetric countries, foreign ownership would simply serve to increase the equal corporate tax burden in the various countries. The welfare effects of such upward pressure on corporate tax levels are unclear. Higher corporate income tax levels could be desirable in a world where tax evasion increasingly erodes residence-based capital income taxes. Higher capital income taxes, however, discourage capital formation, and may ultimately not be welfare-improving.[11]

Whatever its welfare implications, a positive relationship between foreign ownership and taxation affects the attractiveness of and prospects for a concerted European approach to corporate income taxation. The absence of a race to the bottom to date, perhaps on account of the already significant foreign ownership at present, may be the reason that proposals for EU corporate tax coordination have so far not taken hold. In the absence of all-out corporate income tax degradation, EU member states apparently prefer to maintain a high degree of national autonomy over corporate tax policies. This was evident at the Nice EU summit in December 2002, where member states decided to uphold the unanimity requirement regarding EU directives on tax policy.

In the absence of across-the-board tax coordination, EU member states in recent years have focused on identifying elements of 'harmful tax competition'. Peer pressure is applied to convince partner member states to give up tax regimes that are deemed harmful. Examples of these are the low-tax treatments of corporate headquarters in Belgium and the Netherlands and the 10 per cent tax regime in Ireland. Actual tax coordination efforts in the European Union have thus been in the direction of higher corporate income taxes. This suggests that tax policymakers in the Union are of the opinion that corporate tax levels are too low at present. If so, this suggests that they would welcome the foreign ownership effect on corporate tax burdens.

Recent initiatives by the European Commission (see European Commission, 2001) do not call for higher or lower corporate income taxes in the European Union, but, rather, they address the problems associated

---

[11] In one view, optimal income taxes are zero in the long run (see Chamley, 1986), in which case the positive impact of foreign ownership on corporate income taxes appears to be undesirable.

with separate tax accounting in member states. The European Commission at this point favours the introduction of a consolidated corporate tax base in the Union, along with some type of formula apportionment of tax revenues. There is no push for the introduction of a common tax rate, or even a minimum tax rate. A common Union tax base, however, would help to make tax burdens in the Union more transparent, and hence could lead to relatively intense tax competition with a view to altering the apportionment of the tax base among member states. The introduction of a common tax base in the European Union would thus eliminate neither tax competition nor the incentive to levy relatively high corporate income taxes on account of high foreign ownership of domestic firms.

5.   Conclusions

This chapter has presented some cross-country evidence on the foreign ownership of equities in Europe, showing a foreign ownership share of around a quarter in 1997. This is true for shares of firms with an exchange listing (as portfolio investment) and for firms without such a listing (as foreign direct investment). Next, we have presented some evidence, first, on the determinants of foreign ownership and, second, on its consequences, in particular for the level of corporate income taxation.

Our evidence on the determinants of foreign ownership relates to non-traded firms. Hence, it sheds light on the prevalence of foreign direct investment, where the foreign owners exercise control over their investment, rather than on the determinants of foreign portfolio investment. Perhaps surprisingly, foreign ownership and good institutions appear empirically to be substitutes. The likely reason is that foreign-owned firms, which are frequently part of a multinational firm, are able to import some of the good institutions of their home countries. This puts foreign-owned firms at a competitive advantage vis-à-vis domestic firms in countries with weak investor protection.

The negative relationship between institutional quality and foreign ownership may have implications for the prospects for corporate governance reform. Such reform should aim to make it more difficult for managers and majority shareholders to expropriate minority shareholders (and other stakeholders in the firm). The affected managers and majority shareholders can be expected to oppose corporate governance reform in a closed economy setting, and, indeed, they do tend to oppose such reform. This chapter suggests, however, that there may be an international competitive dimension to corporate governance reform. In particular, foreign-owned firms appear to be able to capture a significant share of the assets – and, presumably, of overall economic activity – in countries with weak institutions. Thus, domestic firms in such countries may face the risk either of extinction or of being taken over by a foreign firm, unless domestic corporate governance standards are increased to a higher international level. If so, this could change the political economy of corporate governance reform in favour of the adoption of more stringent standards. Nationalistic sentiments may also help to enact better investor protection, if the alternative is to accept wholesale foreign ownership and control of the domestic economy.

Evidence presented in this chapter on the positive relationship between foreign ownership and corporate tax burdens in Europe relates to non-traded firms as well. The available evidence suggests that company tax burdens are positively related to foreign ownership at the country level. Moreover, the empirical relationship between company tax burdens and foreign ownership appears to be economically significant. The already significant foreign ownership of equities in Europe may have prevented a race to the bottom in corporate income tax levels so far. Higher foreign ownership in the future would, by itself, lead to correspondingly higher corporate tax levels to come. To wit, the estimation results suggest that a doubling of foreign ownership in Europe to 43 per cent would increase the average corporate tax rate from about 33 per cent to about 42 per cent. Foreign ownership therefore is likely to affect the evolution of corporate tax burdens as long as decisions on the level of corporate income taxes are taken by individual EU member states.

Appendix 1: Data sources, sample construction and variable definitions

The Amadeus data set and foreign ownership sample construction

Firm-level data are from the January 2001 and several preceding versions of the Amadeus 'Top 200,000' database compiled by Van Dijk. Firms are included if they meet one of three criteria regarding the magnitude of operating revenues, total assets and the number of employees.[12] Van Dijk states that 95 per cent of the companies in each country that meet at least one of the three criteria are included. As a rule, bankrupt companies are kept in the database for five additional years, so the 2001

---

[12] For the United Kingdom, Germany, France, Italy, Ukraine and the Russian Federation, the inclusion thresholds are € 15 million in operating revenues, € 30 million in assets and 150 employees. For other countries, they are € 10 million in operating revenues, € 20 million in assets and 100 employees.

database includes firms that went bankrupt in the 1996–2000 period. The database provides a NACE rev1 sector code for each firm.

Our ownership variables are based on direct ownership information and they reflect voting rights. Faccio and Lang (2002) conclude for a sample of thirteen European countries that there are significant discrepancies between ownership and control in only a few of the countries in their sample. Sweden, Switzerland, Italy and Finland are countries where a significant proportion of firms have dual-class shares. We exclude entries for firms traded on a stock exchange and firms in primarily public sectors or for which the sector is unknown. We select firms with consolidation code 'U1', which covers firms with an unconsolidated statement without a consolidated companion statement in existence. This is to exclude holding companies with a consolidated statement that may own subsidiaries worldwide. We drop observations with erroneous data in the form of a solvency ratio (ratio of shareholders funds to assets) that is negative or more than one.

Other variable definitions and data sources

Name	Definition	Source
Assets	Value of total assets in thousands of 1990 euros, log transformation	Amadeus database
Solvency	Ratio of shareholders funds to assets, percentage	Amadeus database
GDP	GDP in billions of 1990 euros, log transformation	Ameco database
GDP per capita	GDP per capita in thousands of 1990 euros, log transformation	Ameco database
Openness	(Exports + imports) / GDP	Ameco database
TURN	Ratio of stock exchange turnover to stock market capitalisation, percentage; turnover is computed either under the 'trading system view', which counts only transactions that pass through the stock exchange trading systems (Austria, Finland, Greece, Italy, Luxembourg, Poland, Portugal and Slovenia), or under a reporting system that includes all on- and off-market transactions	International Federation of Stock Exchanges
SMCAP	Ratio of stock market capitalisation to GDP, percentage	International Federation of Stock Exchanges

Table (*cont.*)

Name	Definition	Source
WT	Minimum of the withholding tax on dividends accruing to UK, US, Japanese or German residents, percentage	Publications by PriceWaterhouseCoopers (and its predecessors) and the International Bureau for Fiscal Documentation
FCONTROL	Survey responses to '*Foreign investors are free to acquire control in a domestic company*', scale 0–10, with high marks indicating greater scope for foreign control	*World Competitiveness Yearbook*
LCMARKET	Survey responses to '*Local capital markets are equally accessible to domestic and foreign companies*', scale 0–10, with high marks indicating easier access for foreign companies	*World Competitiveness Yearbook*
CBVENT	Survey responses to '*Cross-border ventures can be negotiated freely*', scale 0–10, with high marks indicating greater freedom of negotiation	*World Competitiveness Yearbook*
IMPROPER	Survey responses to '*Improper practices (such as bribing or corruption) do not prevail in the public sphere*', scale 0–10, with high marks indicating greater scarcity of improper practices.	*World Competitiveness Yearbook*
INSIDERT	Survey responses to '*Insider trading is not common in the stock market*', scale 0–10, with high marks indicating greater scarcity of insider trade	*World Competitiveness Yearbook*
ANTIDR	Anti-director rights, index ranging from 0 to 6, based on the inclusion of six specific shareholder's rights (taken from company law or commercial code)	La Porta et al. (1998)
ACCSTAN	Accountancy standards, measured as number of ninety potentially important items included in the 1990 annual report of surveyed companies. Produced by *International Accounting and Auditing Trends*, Center for International Financial Analysis and Research	La Porta et al. (1998)

Table (cont.)

Name	Definition	Source
EFFJS	Efficiency of judicial system, assessment produced by the Business International Corporation (average 1980–1983), scale 0–10, lower scores indicating lower efficiency levels.	La Porta et al. (1998)
ROL	Rule of law, monthly assessment produced by the International Country Risk agency (average of April and October from 1982 to 1995), scale 0–10 (original scale 0–6), lower scores indicating weaker respect for law and order	La Porta et al. (1998)
CORRUPT	Monthly assessment of the corruption in government, produced by the International Country Risk agency (average of April and October from 1982 to 1995), scale 0–10 (original scale 0–6), lower scores indicating higher levels of corruption	La Porta et al. (1998)

REFERENCES

Adjaouté, K., L. Botazzi, A. Fischer, R. Hamaui, R. Portes and M. Wickens (2000), *EMU and Portfolio Adjustment*, Policy Paper no. 5, Centre for Economic Policy Research, London.

Chamley, C. (1986), 'Optimal taxation of capital in economies with identical private and social discount rates', *Econometrica*, 54, 607–22.

Dahlquist, M., and G. Robertsson (2001), 'Direct foreign ownership, institutional investors, and firm characteristics', *Journal of Financial Economics*, 59, 413–40.

Demirgüç-Kunt, A., and H. Huizinga (2001), 'The taxation of domestic and foreign banking', *Journal of Public Economics*, 79, 429–53.

Devereux, M. P., R. Griffith and A. Klemm (2002), 'Corporate income tax reforms and international tax competition', *Economic Policy*, 35, 451–88.

Eijffinger, S. C., and W. Wagner (2001), *Taxation if capital is not perfectly mobile: tax competition versus tax exportation*, Working Paper no. 3084, Centre for Economic Policy Research, London.

European Commission (2001), 'Financial market integration in the EU', *The EU Economy: 2001 Review*, Brussels, chap. 4.

Eurostat (2001), *Foreign-Owned Enterprises*, Statistics in Focus series, Industry, Trade and Services, no. 20.

Faccio, M., and L. H. Lang (2002), 'The ultimate ownership of Western European corporations', *Journal of Financial Economics*, 65, 365–95.

Freund, C., and S. Djankov (2000), *Which Firms do Foreigners buy?*, Policy Research Working Paper no. 2450, World Bank, Washington, DC.

Gordon, R. H. (1986), 'Taxation of investment and savings in a world economy', *American Economic Review*, 96, 1086–102.

Görg, H., and D. Greenaway (2002), *Much Ado about Nothing? Do Domestic Firms really Benefit from Foreign Investment?* Discussion Paper no. 3485, Centre for Economic Policy Research, London.

Grubert, H., T. Goodspeed and D. Swenson (1993), 'Explaining the low taxable income of foreign-controlled companies in the United States', in: A. Giovannini, R. Hubbard and J. Slemrod (eds.), *Studies in International Taxation*, University of Chicago Press, Chicago, 237–70.

Huizinga, H., and C. Denis (2004), *Are Foreign Ownership and Good Institutions Substitutes? The Case of Non-Traded Equity*, mimeo, European Commission, Brussels.

Huizinga, H., and G. Nicodème (forthcoming), 'Foreign ownership and corporate income taxation: an empirical evaluation', *European Economic Review*.

Huizinga, H., and S. B. Nielsen (1997), 'Capital income and profit taxation with foreign ownership of firms', *Journal of International Economics* 42, 149–65.

(2002), 'The coordination of capital income and profit taxation', *Regional Science and Urban Economics*, 32, 1–26.

International Monetary Fund (1999), *Results of the 1997 Coordinated Portfolio Investment Survey*, Washington, DC.

Kang, J.-K., and R. M. Stulz (1997), 'Why is there a home bias? An analysis of foreign portfolio equity ownership in Japan', *Journal of Financial Economics*, 46, 3–28.

Kinney, M. and J. Lawrence (2000), 'An analysis of the relative U.S. tax burden of U.S. corporations having substantial foreign ownership', *National Tax Journal*, 53, 9–22.

La Porta, R., F. Lopez-de-Silanes, A. Shleifer and R. W. Vishny (1998), 'Law and finance', *Journal of Political Economy*, 106, 1113–55.

Mintz, J. M. (1994), 'Is there a future for capital income taxation?', *Canadian Tax Journal*, 42, 1469–503.

Sørensen, P. B. (2000), 'The case for international tax co-ordination reconsidered', *Economic Policy*, 31, 431–61.

5   Portfolio diversification in Europe

Kpate Adjaouté, Jean-Pierre Danthine and
Dušan Isakov

1.   Introduction

Are Europeans better diversified than five or ten years ago? This is the
question we focus on in this chapter. The importance of this question is
obvious in the face of converging evidence that Europeans have been
insufficiently diversified in the past – across asset classes and on an
international basis – and that this situation has potentially important
welfare consequences. But the home bias in investments also has a
bearing on corporate ownership and industry structure. It means that,
even for publicly traded companies, ownership remains confined to
national borders and that, as a consequence, industrial diversification
pays. At the extreme opposite, in a world of perfectly diversified portfolios, corporate ownership would simply mirror the relative importance
of the international sources of savings. An increase in international
diversification thus has necessary implications for the question: who
owns Europe?

It is not controversial to assert the existence of a long-run trend away
from bank savings and national government bond holdings towards
equity ownership and, within equity holdings, towards more (internationally) diversified portfolios. This trend is evident, for example, in
Massaro and Laakari (2002), who report the changes in European
households' portfolio holdings between 1996 and 2000 (see tables 5.2
and 5.3, in particular). For the entire euro-zone, the shares of 'currency
and deposits', 'securities other than shares' and 'shares and other equity'
went from 37 per cent, 13 per cent and 25 per cent, to 29 per cent, 8 per
cent and 37 per cent, respectively, with 'insurance technical reserves'

We thank Sean Berrigan for his comments. This chapter builds on and extends Adjaouté
and Danthine (2003). Danthine and Isakov's research is carried out as part of the National
Centre of Competence in Research 'Financial Valuation and Risk Management' (NCCR
FINRISK) programme. The NCCR FINRISK is a research programme supported by the
Swiss National Science Foundation.

constituting the remainder.[1] Similarly, the Bank for International Settlements (BIS) Study Group on Fixed Income Markets (2001) reports that

net purchase of equities by euro area households and corporations jumped to nearly 6 per cent of GDP in the 1998–99 period from less than 2 per cent a few years earlier. At the same time, deposit flows, traditionally the savings vehicle of choice in the euro area, halved to 2 per cent. Euro area residents began in the mid-1990s to reduce their holding of debt issued by their own government and to diversify into other assets.

They also note that non-residents were net buyers of euro-area government securities throughout the 1990s, with the result that non-residents' holdings of euro-area government debt rose to 30 per cent of the outstanding stock in 1999 from 21 per cent in 1995.

The question at hand is this: has this trend been accelerated in a discernible manner by the most recent evolution in the euro area, in particular the advent of the euro and accompanying measures of financial integration? That the euro and measures of financial integration are no small matters for this issue is suggested by the general argument that they constitute decreases in the existing obstacles to international investing within Europe. Even a small decrease in the cost of transacting internationally may be significant. This can be inferred from observations made on stock market participation.[2] If even small costs are sufficient to keep investors out of the stock market, presumably because the marginal investor wants to take only limited equity positions, small impediments, a fortiori, are likely to suffice to prevent investors from optimally diversifying abroad.[3] In addition an important fraction of Europeans' investments is intermediated by institutions – pension funds and insurance companies – that were restricted to investing but a small fraction of their wealth in foreign currencies. These currency-matching rules were automatically lifted with the advent of the euro.

There is an alternative view, however, asserting that the main obstacles to international transaction within the euro area had been eliminated before the 1990s and that currency risk was only a minor factor for portfolio investors. De Santis et al. (1999), for example, had predicted that the disappearance of currency risk would have only a limited impact on portfolio investors. They based their view on the observation that, while EMU countries' currency risk was a significant risk factor for portfolio investors in the 1990s and while investors were indeed

---

[1] Of course, the high stock valuations of 2000 make it hard to distinguish behavioural changes from pure valuation changes.
[2] See Guiso et al. (2003) and references cited therein.
[3] Of course, the same argument also suggests that small decreases in cost may matter only if the remaining obstacles themselves are small enough.

compensated for their exposure to this source of risk, its importance had declined in the course of the decade. In addition they estimated that non-EMU currency risk (in particular that associated with the dollar) was quantitatively much larger. While their position can be understood as saying that the *pricing* of European equities, at unchanged fundamentals, would not be significantly altered by the arrival of the euro, it remains the case that the euro and accompanying factors might signify important changes in the fundamentals underlying European equities, with attendant consequences on investors' behaviour.

Be that as it may, the question at hand is ultimately an empirical one, and we attempt to resolve it by exploring four alternative avenues. A first approach is to focus on the final outcome: if European investors are indeed better diversified, their consumption should be increasingly correlated. This is because improved risk-sharing permits the smoothing of idiosyncratic fluctuations in national income and thus leads to increasingly similar consumption patterns. We review the evidence on this score in section 2. A second approach, at the opposite end of the logical spectrum, consists of simply checking the composition of Europeans' portfolios. This approach is not devoid of dangers and difficulties, however. First, data on individual portfolio holdings are hard to come by. We report, in section 3, data on intermediated accounts, which may not tell us much about the final positions held by individuals if the changing circumstances lead to alterations in the relationships between individual investors and their intermediaries. Second, although this problem plagues our entire inquiry, the post-euro sample is at the same time very short and quite extraordinary. Market circumstances since the advent of the euro have been spectacular, on the upside until about mid-2000, on the downside ever since. One would not be surprised if, over the period under review, actual portfolio positions held by private and institutional investors – and changes in them – had been dominated by these circumstances, making it extremely difficult for observers to detect low-frequency structural changes.

Still another perspective is proposed in sections 4 and 5: instead of focusing on quantities, we describe relevant elements in the evolution of returns and prices. The underlying logic is that, if European investors are indeed attempting to exploit new arbitrage opportunities opened up by the euro and European financial integration, then it is likely that these behavioural changes will be matched by significant changes in returns or in the nature of the return-generating process. We look at this hypothesis from a capital asset pricing model (CAPM) perspective, leading us to see equity returns as the sum of a risk-free rate and of an equity premium, in section 4, and then from a multi-factor perspective in section 5. Finally, it is possible that, rather than by focusing on the outcome of the investment process, the answer to our question may be better revealed by examining the changes in the process itself. We pursue this lead in section 6. Section 7 draws conclusions from this investigation.

2.   Consumption

If Europeans are indeed increasingly diversified, their consumption patterns should become increasingly alike. In this section we check whether there is evidence for such a tendency. Note that by taking the viewpoint of aggregate consumption, we are implicitly assuming that, within each country at least, markets are sufficiently complete to permit the assumption that aggregate consumption adequately reflects individual consumption. If this extreme hypothesis is not valid, prudence is called for in concluding from the type of evidence reported here. Evidence on consumption correlations is provided by Adjaouté and Danthine (2003) and Flotho (2002) among others. Looking at the bilateral consumption correlations of a large set of European countries with the EU average, Flotho does not find any tendency for correlations to increase. By contrast, figure 5.1 indicates that the cross-sectional dispersion of country consumption growth rates exhibits a clear downward trend at least until 1996.[4] The equivalent statement is that consumption growth rates are increasingly correlated in the euro area. At first sight, this evidence provides support for the hypothesis of increasing diversification. The case may be overstated, however, because a similar pattern can be found for the growth rates of GDP (also reported in figure 5.1). The observations on consumption may thus simply be the mechanical consequence of the increased synchronisation of output and income.

In addition, figure 5.1 also shows that the dispersion of consumption growth is always significantly higher than the dispersion of output growth, indicating that the opposite pattern tends to prevail for correlations. (This

---

[4] We use repeatedly the concept of dispersions to support the results obtained with simple correlations. Cross-sectional dispersions are meant to be the cross-sectional counterpart to correlations, and to provide the same underlying information. Our problem stems from the highly changing nature of the relationships we are focusing on, and from the limited size of the post-euro sample of observations. If returns are highly correlated, we expect that, more often than not, they will move together on the upside or on the downside. If they do, the instantaneous cross-sectional variance of these returns will be low. Conversely, lower correlations mean that returns often diverge, a fact translating into a high level of dispersion. Dispersions and correlations are thus inversely related. While correlations require a minimum sample length to be estimated with some precision, no such requirement is needed for dispersions, although the measure will be more imprecise if the number of returns entering in the variance measure is too small. Cross-sectional dispersions were first used in the context of equity returns by Solnik and Roulet (2000). As the dispersions are very noisy, we typically smooth them with Hodrick–Prescott (HP) filters to get a better idea of the underlying trends.

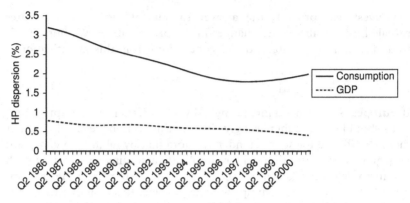

Figure 5.1. Consumption and GDP dispersions in the euro-zone, 1986–2000.
Source: Datastream.

result is in accord with those obtained by Flotho, 2002.) This, of course, suggests that risk-sharing opportunities are far from being fully exploited, since optimal international risk-sharing would imply the opposite inequality: consumption correlations exceeding income correlations. Complementary evidence is provided by Adam et al. (2002), who reject the hypothesis that consumption growth rates are unaffected by idiosyncratic changes in GDP growth rates, as would be the case under perfect risk-sharing among members of the euro area. Taking the opposite point of view, working on the basis of GDP rather than consumption data, Kalemli-Ozcan et al. (2005) paint a rosier picture, concluding that, for the first time in the latter part of the 1990s, non-negligible insurance through international capital income flows could be measured in Europe, and noting that 'in this respect Europe is beginning to converge towards the United States'.

Figure 5.2 offers a benchmark by providing the same type of evidence for the non-European members of the Organisation for Economic Co-operation and Development (OECD). The decrease in consumption dispersion is even more spectacular, with consumption and GDP dispersions being almost coincident since the early 1990s. Finally, figure 5.3 compares the consumption dispersions of euro-area countries and the other European countries, respectively. Overall, these data are, quite surprisingly, evidence of a rather smaller degree of consumption synchronisation inside the euro area than elsewhere in Europe, or outside Europe. While this may be a reflection of differing macroeconomic realities, and measurement problems could be an issue, it is nevertheless difficult to find in the data presented in this section any reassuring evidence on the degree of international risk-sharing within the euro area.

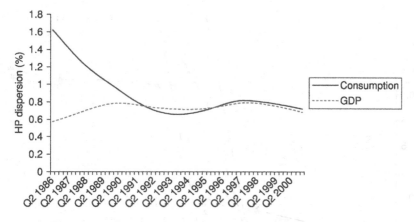

Figure 5.2. Consumption and GDP dispersions in the non-European OECD, 1986–2000.
Source: Datastream.

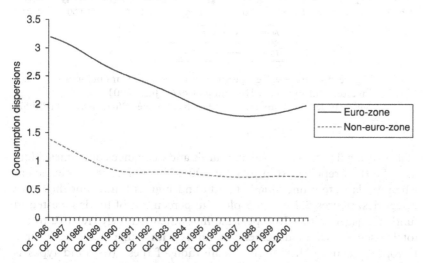

Figure 5.3. Consumption dispersions in the euro-zone and in non-euro-zone Europe, 1986–2000.
Source: Datastream.

3.   A look at portfolio composition

What direct evidence do we have that European investors are increasingly diversifying on an international basis? Figures 5.4 to 5.8 are excerpted from Adam et al. (2002). They provide some answers from the perspective of investment funds – money-market, bond and equity – and

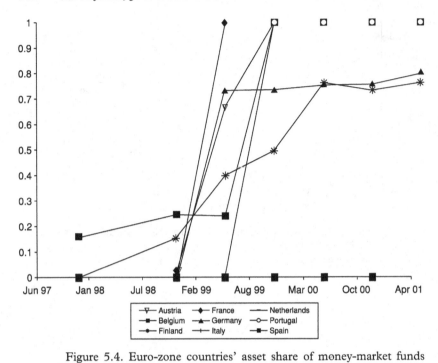

Figure 5.4. Euro-zone countries' asset share of money-market funds invested Europe-wide, December 1997 – June 2001.
Source: Fédération Européenne des Fonds et Sociétés d'Investissement (FEFSI).

of institutional investors – pension funds and insurance companies. Note that the data reported stop in June 2001. The evidence is spectacular when it relates to money-market and bond-market funds. For these two categories, figures 5.4 and 5.5 plot the percentage of funds invested in funds managed with a Europe-wide investment strategy (relative to the total assets under management in funds with either a domestic or a European focus). The internationalisation of these two fund types is seen to have made very significant progress during the first months of 1999 (except for the case of Spanish bond funds). The evidence is less overwhelming when one turns to equity funds. Although, from our perspective the main message of increasing international diversification is not contradicted (in most countries the trend is clearly upward), there are exceptions (Greece) or examples of progress followed by retrenchment (France, figure 5.6; Austria, figure 5.7; Italy and Spain, figure 5.8) in addition to the fact that the *levels* of internationalisation are not always as high as one might expect.

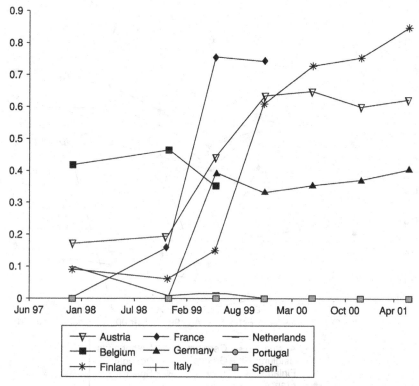

Figure 5.5. Euro-zone countries' asset share of bond funds invested Europe-wide, December 1997 – June 2001.
Source: FEFSI.

Further evidence is provided by Galati and Tsatsaronis (2001). They make specific observations on international portfolio flows originating from Germany, noting the significant acceleration in German investors' purchases of euro-area securities ahead of the introduction of the new currency, in 1998, and the intensification of these purchases, in 1999 and 2000. The same source reports detailed aggregate portfolio data for Italian mutual funds showing the decreasing allocations to Italian bonds and equities and the rise in the allocations to euro-area securities. The share of euro-area bonds in the overall bond portfolio increased from 8 per cent in 1995 to 23 per cent at the end of 2000. Galati and Tsatsaronis also report that, while the share of euro-area equities has followed a largely parallel path after 1998, Italian investors have looked outside the euro area for the primary source of diversification for their equity portfolios. Investments in industrialised economies outside the

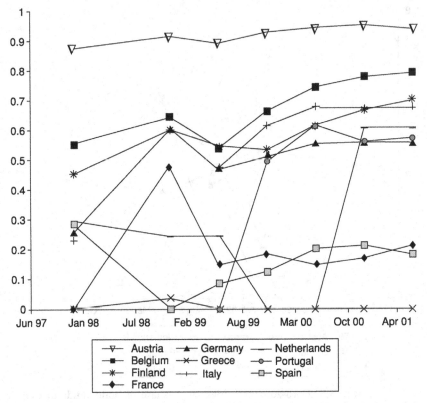

Figure 5.6. Euro-zone countries' asset share of equity funds invested Europe-wide, December 1997 – June 2001.
Source: FEFSI.

single-currency area have filled up the room freed by a declining equity allocation, and accounted for nearly half of the equity portfolio of these funds by the end of 2000. Finally, some additional information gathered from the 2002 report of the Federation of European Securities Exchanges (FESE: see FESE, 2002) is reported on figure 5.9. It displays the shares of national equity markets held by non-residents. In some sense, this graph is a direct answer to the question 'who owns Europe?' It indicates a rather stable situation, with a slight upward trend in the degree of foreign ownership, in particular in the cases of the United Kingdom and France.

This evidence relates mostly to institutional investors. We are not surprised on this front to see some effect from the relaxation of currency-matching rules. In the end, however, what we are interested in is

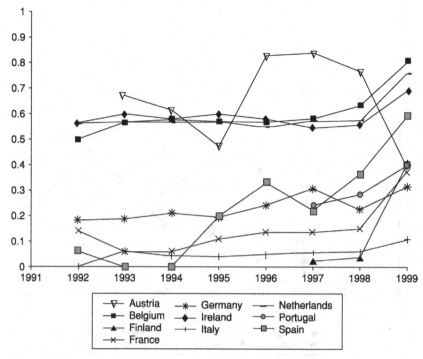

Figure 5.7. Pension funds: foreign equities as a percentage of total equities invested in euro-zone countries, 1992–1999.
Source: InterSec Research Corporation.

the net positions of individual investors, and in this respect we have very little direct observation. It is conceivable that the latter are not undergoing changes proportional to those described at the institutional level. This would be the result of offsetting changes made by individuals in their choices among investment funds. We believe this is unlikely. However, the scarcity of data on individual portfolio holdings permits neither ruling out this possibility nor inferring the hypothesis that the recorded changes at the institutional level are of no material consequences for the degree of diversification of individual European investors.

4.   The CAPM view

In this section and the next we look for evidence suggesting that changes in the behaviour of European investors and of investors investing in European markets have led to changes in the pricing of European assets. We first specifically focus on the return on short-term (risk-free)

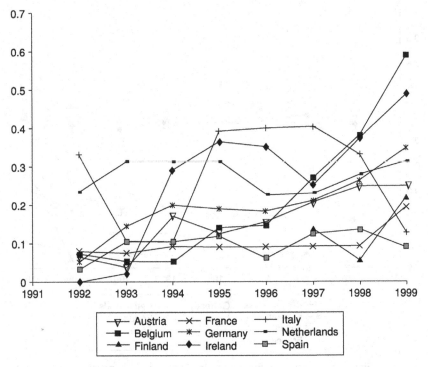

Figure 5.8. Insurance companies: foreign equities as a percentage of total equities invested in euro-zone countries, 1992–1999.
Source: InterSec Research Corporation.

government bonds and on the equity premium paid to stockholders, thus paralleling the standard decomposition of equity return into a risk-free rate and an equity premium.

4.1   *Changes recorded in the government bond markets of the euro area*

In this section we summarise the evidence gathered by Adjaouté and Danthine (2003; from now on AD) for the government bond markets of the euro area, and complement this evidence with observations that can be made on rates paid on euro-currency deposits. We gauge whether the recent evolution of these markets is in line with what would be expected if European investors were increasingly thinking in terms of a single government bond market and investing accordingly. Obviously, this line of reasoning has no direct implications for corporate ownership. It does, however, provide useful indications on the diversification process, while also permitting us to talk meaningfully about the equity premium in the next subsection.

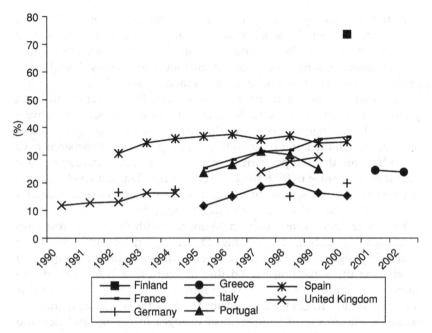

Figure 5.9. The proportion of equity shares of a country held by non-resident investors (individual and institutional investors), 1990–2002. *Source:* FESE.

The main observation here is that, when the home bias dominates and national fixed-income markets are segmented, the prices and returns of the corresponding securities are disconnected. The demand and supply of savings are matched country by country and the risk appetite largely depends on local circumstances. Since pricing differences are not arbitraged away (there is no way to trade on the basis of relative capital abundance and relative willingness to take risk), local capital-market conditions determine the interest rates on the national risk-free asset. Thus, an increase in international investing should be characterised by a convergence of interest rate levels as well as an increasing similarity in the time-series properties of the returns on the closest proxy to the risk-free asset.

While, even under segmentation, one does not necessarily expect interest rate correlations to be zero because contagion effects cannot be excluded (an Enron could have effects on the appraisal of the risk of financial assets in the neighbouring country even in the absence of capital mobility), one clearly anticipates correlations between risk-free bonds to increase with integration. One further expects that the return on the single risk-free asset of a larger economic area will be less volatile than the risk-free rates of the constituent elements of this large entity under segmentation. This is because the large-area risk-free rate should be less sensitive to idiosyncratic local market conditions than under segmentation. In other words, the specific local conditions should offset one another via the usual diversification mechanism.

AD provide evidence in line with this description. Government bond yields of the euro area have undergone an impressive process of convergence in levels (figure 5.10), and they display an increasing degree of correlation. On the latter point, figure 5.11 reports that dispersions have fallen by more than 90 per cent from an average of 2.28 in the pre-euro period to an average of 0.16 since the euro. From January 1999 onwards the various government bond yields in the euro area have exhibited a closely similar behaviour, as theoretically expected.

Finally, table 5.1 shows that, in conformity with theory, interest rates in Europe have become less volatile. The change in volatility is valid and statistically significant for each and every country in the sample – a striking result, suggesting indeed that the euro-area bond markets respond to a smaller extent to idiosyncratic local circumstances and that inter-market arbitrages tend to distribute across the whole area, and thus stabilise, the effects of sudden local changes in supply and demand conditions.

At first sight, this range of evidence provides spectacular support for the notion that the behaviour of European investors has changed

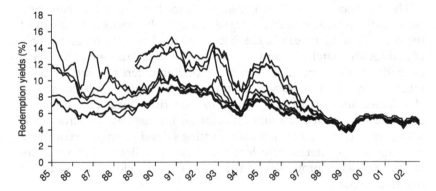

Figure 5.10. The convergence of euro-zone government bond redemption yields, 1985–2002.

Note: The redemption yield used for each country represents the average yield on benchmark bonds within maturity sectors. That is, within each maturity sector, sample bonds are selected based on their tradability and interest to international investors, and a weighted average redemption yield is computed on all selected bonds across the maturity spectrum.

Source: Datastream.

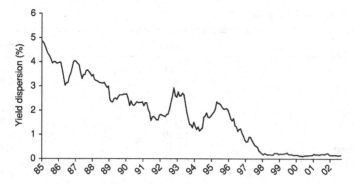

Figure 5.11. The redemption yield dispersion of euro-zone government bonds, 1985–2002.
Source: Datastream.

Table 5.1. *The volatility of government bond redemption yields*

	Pre-euro	Post-euro	Var. ratio stat	P-values
Austria	1.211	0.481	6.780	0
Belgium	1.809	0.535	3.759	0
Finland	3.094	0.517	1.206	0
France	1.797	0.474	2.994	0
Germany	1.162	0.409	5.318	0
Ireland	2.224	0.456	1.807	0
Italy	2.944	0.433	0.929	0
Netherlands	1.241	0.414	4.786	0
Portugal	2.842	0.507	1.366	0
Spain	3.117	0.492	1.070	0

Note: The pre-euro period goes from January 1985 to December 1998, and the post-euro period from January 1999 to August 2002.
Source: Datastream.

materially. AD, however, observe that these results could be the almost mechanical outcome of the convergence of inflation rates in the euro area without any change in investors' behaviour. Moreover, they present some evidence leading them to conclude that most of the convergence in nominal yields is in fact attributable to the convergence of inflation rates. Specifically, they compute *ex post* real yields by deducting the observed inflation rates from the nominal redemption yields, to show (i) that the result of lower volatilities is confirmed, but (ii) that the result of decreasing dispersion is not: no obvious time pattern is discernible, contrary to what was the case for the dispersion of nominal yields. The corresponding results are displayed in table 5.2 and figure 5.12.

Table 5.2. *The volatility of real yields*

	Pre-euro	Post-euro
Austria	0.911	0.741
Belgium	1.316	0.569
France	0.952	0.492
Germany	1.217	0.735
Ireland	1.669	1.445
Italy	1.599	0.400
Netherlands	1.229	1.103
Portugal	2.025	1.029
Spain	1.689	0.478

Source: Datastream.

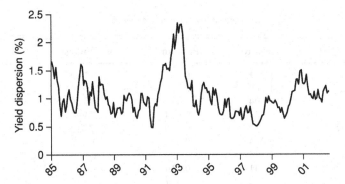

Figure 5.12. Monthly real yield dispersion, 1985–2001.
Source: Datastream.

These results can be viewed in two ways. On the one hand they do suggest that the convergence of yields may well be a macroeconomic phenomenon with little implication for the way that Europeans attempt to diversify. On the other hand, the evidence on real returns implies that the convergence of nominal yields has gone further than the convergence of inflation. And this is rather indicative of a financial phenomenon going beyond the needs of investors acting in semi-segmented markets.

As to the decrease in yield volatility, be it nominal or real, again, this result may be due to macroeconomic phenomena – monetary policy in particular – or, indeed, to an increase in the intensity with which investors arbitrage away idiosyncratic influences on national debt markets. To check whether the hypothesis of an internationalisation of the outlook of European investors has some element of truth, we take a look at the one-month euro-currency market. This is an interbank market that has been characterised by a strong international and integrated outlook since its inception. One would not expect the introduction of the euro to have significantly decreased the volatility of the rates paid on this market.

Figure 5.13 displays the evolution of euro-currency interest rates for euro-zone countries from January 1985 to June 2002. Figure 5.14 does

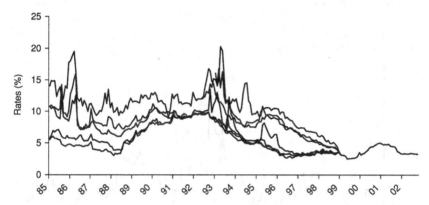

Figure 5.13. Nominal one-month euro-currency interest rates for euro-zone countries, 1985–2002.
Source: Datastream.

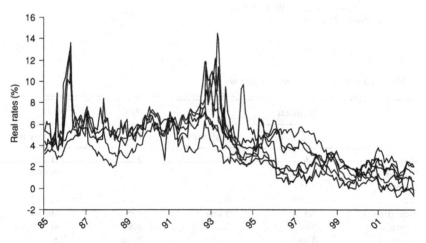

Figure 5.14. Real one-month euro-currency interest rates for euro-zone countries, 1985–2001.
Source: Datastream.

the same for real (deflated) euro-currency rates. And figure 5.15 displays the dispersion of real euro-currency rates. Finally, table 5.3 reports the volatility data for the same series. At all these levels of observation, the outcome appears similar to what was obtained for the yields on government bonds. This lends support to the view that the recorded evolution is indeed more likely to be the product of macroeconomic and monetary events than the consequence of a change in the investment behaviour of European investors.

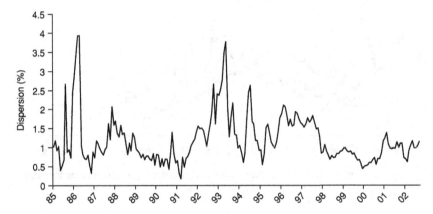

Figure 5.15. The dispersion of real euro-currency interest rates in euro-zone countries, 1985–2002.
Source: Datastream.

Table 5.3. *The volatility of euro-currency rates*

	Nominal		Real	
	Pre-euro	Post-euro	Pre-euro	Post-euro
Belgium	2.526	0.769	2.072	0.543
France	2.800	0.769	2.187	0.664
Germany	2.176	0.769	1.318	0.457
Italy	2.798	0.769	1.698	0.497
Netherlands	2.114	0.769	2.012	0.763
Portugal	3.617	0.769	2.510	0.568
Spain	3.194	0.769	2.305	0.484

Source: Datastream.

4.2   Equity risk premia

We now turn to an examination of the excess returns on equity viewed as indicative of equity premia. The CAPM suggests that, *ceteris paribus*, a more international outlook among investors of the euro area – that is, a lower home bias – would be expected to decrease the equity premium. This can be demonstrated using the simple reasoning of Stulz (1999). Assume a simple situation where all individuals display constant relative risk aversion. The price per unit of risk is constant and identical in initially segmented markets or in the whole integrated area. Let us denote it by P. In the case of full segmentation, local investors hold undiversified portfolios (from the viewpoint of the global economy). Their reference market portfolio is limited to national firms. The appropriate measure of risk for the local-country portfolio then is its standard deviation. That is, under segmentation the risk premium on a given security i will be $\sigma_i^2 P$, where σ_i^2 is the variance and σ_i is the standard deviation of the returns on asset i. In a single financial market, investors hold internationally diversified portfolios. The proper measure of risk for the local-country portfolio is not its standard deviation but its beta with the world portfolio. The same asset in an integrated market will therefore yield a risk premium of $\beta_i P = \rho_i \sigma_i \sigma_m P$, where β_i is the beta of country i market portfolio with respect to the world portfolio. β_i is a function of its covariance with the market portfolio, which can also be written in terms of the correlation coefficient between the market portfolio and the return on asset i, ρ_i. From this little exercise one obtains the result that, if the following condition is satisfied,

$$\frac{\sigma_i}{\sigma_m} > \rho_i$$

and thus, in particular if $\sigma_i > \sigma_m$, then the risk premium in an integrated market will necessarily be smaller than in segmented markets. But, as shown by AD, this inequality is satisfied for every country of the euro area. Figure 5.16 makes the point in the case of Germany.

Let us now turn to the direct evidence of equity premia. We compute the excess returns as the monthly total return on national equity indices over the one-month euro-currency return for the corresponding country. Figures 5.17 and 5.18 display the HP-filtered equity returns and equity excess returns respectively for the euro-zone countries. Two observations stand out. First, there is a clear convergence in both returns and excess returns up to the mid-1990s, a little-known fact that we find striking, but the evolution is less clear thereafter. Second, the strong market conditions at the end of the 1990s and the beginning of the new

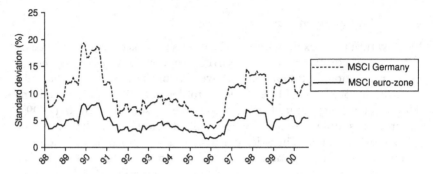

Figure 5.16. Twelve-month trailing standard deviation, December 1988–July 2001.

Note: The data come from the monthly Morgan Stanley Capital International (MSCI) price index series (inclusive of dividends) for each of the countries and the euro-zone area for December 1987 to July 2001. The first twelve monthly returns are used to compute the first standard deviation, and the window is moved each time by dropping one observation and adding a new one to obtain a time series of 152 standard deviations.

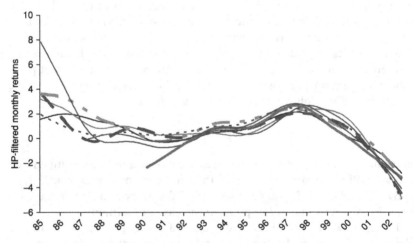

Figure 5.17. Euro-zone countries' filtered equity returns, 1985–2002.
Source: Datastream and own calculations.

century are clearly discernible, and the question of whether they have an overriding influence on the observations cannot be avoided. We then proceed to measure the dispersion of equity excess returns. The HP-filtered series is presented in figure 5.19. We find it particularly

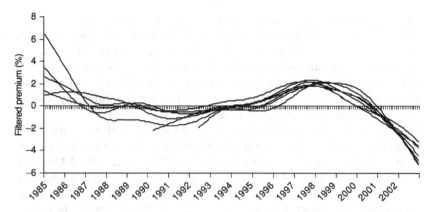

Figure 5.18. Euro-zone countries' filtered equity premia, 1985–2002.
Source: Datastream.

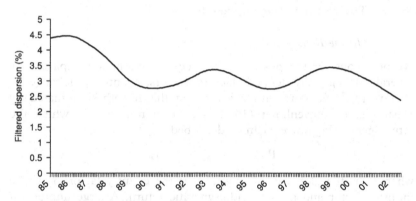

Figure 5.19. The filtered dispersion of equity premia in euro-zone
countries, 1985–2002.
Source: Datastream.

remarkable. It indeed suggests that the convergence of excess returns is
being pursued with a dispersion level falling below the 2.5 per cent mark
at the end of 2002 for the first time since the beginning of our sample
(1985). Here is some evidence in favour of the hypothesis that Europeans (and non-resident investors in the euro area) are increasingly
seizing the opportunities offered by the euro and financial integration.
Of course, this is not the only possible explanation for the observed
phenomenon. For one thing, *ex post* excess returns may be a poor
measure of the equity premium – a problem that is especially acute when
they fall into negative territory, as they have towards the end of our

sample. Moreover, measured excess returns appear to be very volatile, implying that we would need a longer observation period before being able to rule out special circumstances. Finally, another possible explanation is that the fundamentals underlying the priced assets are getting increasingly similar. The complementary data on total returns presented in the next section, to the extent that they are not fully congruent, constitute prima facie evidence against the latter explanation.

We note that, in accord with the evidence provided in figure 5.19, Hardouvelis et al. (2001) find that, within EU sectors, the cost of equity capital has fallen by between 0.5 per cent and 3 per cent in the 1990s and that there is evidence of convergence in the cost of capital for similar sectors across countries (stocks in the same sector tend to have the same cost across countries). Convergence across different sectors, however, appears to be slow.

5.   The multi-factor approach

5.1   *Heston–Rouwenhorst*

We now consider the possibility that equity returns are impacted by several (orthogonally defined) factors: sectors, countries, global (euro area/world).[5] We start with a version of this hypothesis initiated by Heston and Rouwenhorst (1994; HR from now on) in which the return-generating process can be described as,

$$R_{it} = \alpha_t + \gamma_{kt} + \delta_{jt} + \epsilon_{it}$$

where α_t is the global component, γ_{kt} is the country factor, δ_{jt} is the industry factor and ϵ_{it} is the idiosyncratic return. A large number of papers have investigated the issue of the relative importance of country and industry factors by first estimating this dummy variable model. In a second stage, the relative influence of both factors is determined by comparing either the relative variances or the mean average deviations (MADs) of country/industry effects. Until recently the literature was nearly unanimous in finding that country factors dominated industry factors; this finding was robust across different data sets. Significant papers include those by Beckers et al. (1996), Griffin and Karolyi (1998) and Rouwenhorst (1999). Rouwenhorst, for instance, analyses the returns of all 952 European stocks included in the MSCI indices of twelve European countries. His data set ends in August 1998. With an

---

[5] Kuo and Satchell (2001) and Hamelink et al. (2001) assume that returns are impacted by yet another factor, namely style.

eye on the potential impact of economic and monetary integration on the results of the variance decomposition, he concludes that the superiority of country effects has been effective at least since 1982, and that it has continued during the 1993–98 period 'despite the convergence of interest rates and the harmonization of fiscal and monetary policies following the Maastricht Treaty'.

The unanimity appears to have broken down recently, however, and papers using very recent data sets have detected an increase in the global industry effects. Arnold (2001) extends Rouwenhorst's study, using data up to 1999, and finds that, in the year following the introduction of the euro, industry factors have dominated country factors. Baca et al. (2000) find that industry and country effects have converged, while Cavaglia et al. (2000) also document the fact that industry factors have assumed a greater prominence than country factors since 1997. On the contrary, Isakov and Sonney (2004) confirm the dominance of the country effects for the period 1997–2000 with a sample including twenty developed countries, but they detect a shift in the last part of their sample. As shown in figure 5.20, allowing for time variations in the decomposition, they confirm that industry factors are growing in importance and that they have explained a larger fraction of the variance of returns since March 2000.

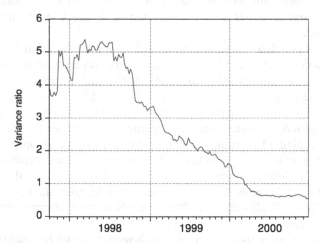

Figure 5.20. The evolution over time of the relative country/industry influences.

Note: This graph represents the evolution of the ratio of the variance of country effects to industry effects. Variances have been estimated over thirty-six-week intervals.

Source: Isakov and Sonney (2004).

5.2   Country and sector indices approach

The results obtained with the HR approach are not always convergent, however. Thus, Galati and Tsatsaronis (2001) arrive at slightly different conclusions. They look at the companies in the FTSE Eurotop300 index, completing their assessment with a time-series analysis of the weighted factor averages. They find that industry factors became more important than country factors for the first time a few months prior to the formal arrival of the euro. Contrary to most other researchers, however, they also find that the dominance of country factors was insignificant after the beginning of 1996, and even as early as 1992. These results are in sharp contrast with those of Rouwenhorst (1999), among others. A possible reconciliation arises from the observation that Galati and Tatsaronis concentrate their analysis on very large capitalisations. Such stocks have been found to be less sensitive to country factors than stocks with smaller capitalisations by Isakov and Sonney (2004), for example. It remains the case, however, that the results obtained with the HR approach appear to be quite sensitive to the data used, the definition of sectors and the period of analysis. Table 5.4 in Isakov and Sonney (2004), for example, shows that the ratio of the fraction of return variances explained by country and industries varies in a ratio of 2 to 11.5! Moreover, the HR methodology suffers from other drawbacks, implying that it needs to be completed with the use of alternative approaches.

The first problem associated with the HR approach is that it imposes the restriction that a firm belongs to a country and an industry, and that it cannot be sensitive to other countries/industries. This implies that, in a set-up where the asset manager is constrained to choose between a country or a sector dimension, whenever the fraction of the total variance explained by country factors becomes smaller than the fraction of variance explained by industry factors the first step of an optimal asset allocation should be done at the level of sector or industry indices (and conversely). However, Adjaouté and Danthine (2003) show that, if the assumption of factor orthogonality does not hold, then the optimal first step in the asset allocation in fact depends on the sensitivities to the different factors.

The assumption that factors are orthogonal is highly disputable in the face of the trend towards multinational firms and the reality that many firms have outputs or inputs connected with multiple industries. This difficulty is evident in the task of industry classification standard providers, as highlighted in MSCI–S&P joint GICS (Global Industry Classification Standard) publications. The classification of companies into given sectors proves increasingly difficult when there are many business segments contributing to turnover or operating income – the criteria used to typify companies. Assigning a country to a company has become equally tricky, with the country of origin or the country where the company is actually headquartered often having very little to do with the geographical areas that effectively influence the business of the company.

This view receives further support from the observation that, if the restricted HR model were true, the covariance of stock returns would show non-zero terms only for stocks in the same sector or belonging to the same country. This is far from being the case. We illustrate this point with the correlation matrix that we use in the next section and that corresponds to a higher level of disaggregation (we identify 77 country-sectors within the euro-zone, the unit being a sector in a country). This matrix includes 2,926 (77 × 76/2) independent correlations, out of which only 41 (68) are less than 0.1 in absolute value during the first (second) part of the sample!

A second problem associated with the HR approach is that it assumes that all stocks from the same country/industry have the same sensitivity to the country/industry factors. This assumption is clearly inconsistent with the most basic asset pricing model. A recent paper by Brooks and Del Negro (2002b) provides clear evidence against this assumption. These authors argue that there are reasons to believe that the exposure to a country factor may vary across firms in the same country, as some are more international than others. They go on to test this hypothesis, and unambiguously reject the constraints that the coefficients to own-country factors are all unity.

For this variety of reasons, it is of interest to complete the data analysis with an alternative methodology consistent with an unrestricted model simply stating that a security can be subjected to multiple sources of uncertainty owing to its multinational character (more than one country) and/or because it is a conglomerate operating in more than one sector (or, more generally, because its performance depends on the price of inputs originating in other industries than its own). Here we analyse the cross-sectional dispersion of country returns and global sector returns, respectively. The global correlation/dispersion is particularly useful in that it can be generated as a time series for the available frequency of return data. It reports on instantaneous relations involving no time averaging, and thus allows for a more thorough investigation of the evolution of the diversification opportunities in the euro-zone. The time series of raw country return and global sector return dispersions are highly time-varying while also following some cycles. The more

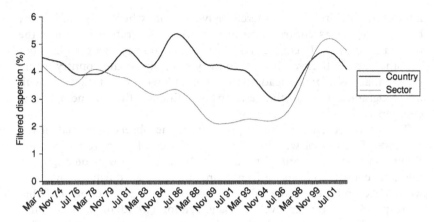

Figure 5.21. Filtered country and global euro-zone sector dispersions, 1973–2001.
Source: Datastream.

interesting cyclical pattern appears clearly if one filters the series to extract their slowly moving components. The result is displayed in figure 5.21 where the two series are shown together.

This analysis is revealing. Both country and sector dispersions have displayed a downward trend until the autumn of 1996, an evolution that Adjaouté and Danthine (2004) credit for the widespread view that correlations among country indices were increasing in Europe due to European integration and that diversification opportunities were indeed being hampered. But these dispersions have trended upward since reaching their most recent peaks around the end of 2000. By then the dispersion levels were at an all-time high for sectors, and had almost matched their highest point of the mid-1980s for country indices. Thus, in contradiction to the often expressed view, the post-euro period has been very favourable for diversification within the euro area, whether on a geographical or on a sectoral basis.

Viewed from this angle, the superiority of a country-based asset allocation was clear for most of the period (in conformity with Rouwenhorst, 1999). But there appears to be a reversal in this ranking taking place in early 1999.[6] This reversal can be associated with the reversal of the variance inequality in the HR context uncovered by different authors. This result is also consistent with the finding that euro-area business

---

[6] The exact dating of the reversal is likely to depend on the specific filtering or data-smoothing method.

cycles have become more synchronised, so that the orthogonal portions of the euro-area country factors are showing increasingly smaller variances. Yet the variability of the relationships and the fact that reversals have occurred in the past (this was the case from around 1977 to 1979) suggest that caution must be exercised before definitively linking this reversal to permanent structural changes. This is also the case because the difference between the two series is small by historical standards. In the end, the convergent results obtained by the two approaches followed in this subsection, HR and global dispersions, provide support for the assessment that industry effects have indeed been the dominant determinant of returns in the most recent time period.

5.3   Is it Europe-specific and does it relate to fundamentals or to integration?

At this stage one may wonder whether the growing importance of sectors relative to countries is specific to the euro area, thus being plausibly associated with greater economic and financial integration, and whether it is likely to be permanent. Alternatively, one may speculate that it could be a more universal phenomenon and/or that the recent stock market bubble could have played a role in this observation.

Brooks and Del Negro (2002a) provide interesting evidence in these regards. First, they observe that the correlation of the US equity market with other developed equity markets has moved from a low level of 0.4 in the 1980s to almost 0.9 in the late 1990s. They argue that this may be due to a decline in home bias, so that the marginal investor in German stocks is not necessarily German, and as a result country-specific investor sentiment now plays a minor role. Alternatively, the general rise in the co-movement of equity markets may be a manifestation of firms becoming more diversified internationally, and therefore increasingly exposed to the global business cycle, causing stock markets to move together more. Finally, there is the possibility that the rise in the co-movement of stock markets is a temporary phenomenon associated with the recent stock market boom and bust.

Brooks and Del Negro use a sample of companies representing three geographic regions: in MSCI's terminology, the Americas, the Far East and Europe. They estimate the standard dummy variables for the HR model and use the MADs of country and sector factors to assess the relative importance of each shock. The empirical evidence for the whole sample seems to suggest that industry factors have outgrown country factors in the late 1990s, in conformity with what we reported for the euro area. However, when US stocks and companies in the telecommunication, media, biotechnology and information technology (TMBT) sector are excluded from the sample, the evidence of industry factors dominating country factors disappears. The absence of evidence beyond TMBT sectors and the United States is interpreted by the authors as an indication that the recent dominance of industry effects over country effects is a *temporary* phenomenon associated with the stock market bubble. At the regional level, however, they report that the European evidence is *not* affected by the removal of TMBT sectors. Isakov and Sonney (2004) provide a converging assessment. Even when TMBT sectors are excluded from the sample, the recent superiority of sectors holds true in Europe.

To summarise, in general the estimation of the relative importance of countries and sectors is sensitive to the inclusion or exclusion of specific countries (the United States in particular) or sectors (especially TMBT). The fact that the evidence is more robust in the case of the euro area supports the hypothesis that something more fundamental is at work in that region. It remains to be seen, however, whether this more fundamental evolution is indicative of a movement towards better portfolio diversification or whether it is the result of macroeconomic changes associated with monetary unification and/or economic integration.

6.   Can the multi-factor perspective rationalise the shift in asset allocation paradigm?

The lack of data on the outcome of individual investors' investment decisions (section 3) makes it of interest to discuss the process by which individuals allocate their assets. Indeed, many observers would argue that it is at this level that the major change in the European equity scene has been registered. The large majority of investors intermediate their portfolio investments through commercial banks or independent asset managers. The most common practice among portfolio managers is to follow a top-down approach to asset selection. Traditionally, the first step of the top-down approach consisted in deciding on a country allocation grid, effectively placing first priority on an adequate geographical diversification of portfolios. The second step consisted in selecting the best securities in accord with this allocation – that is, within each national market, to the extent permitted by the grid. This practice has often been placed in the context of the discussion of our last section on the relative importance of country versus industry or sector factors in explaining the cross-section of international returns. The standard position arguing that country factors were dominant supported the geographical slant of the top-down approach. Everywhere, the argument is now made that the country orientation of the top-down approach should give way, within the euro area at least, to an industry or sector orientation. According to this view, the first step of the portfolio optimisation should be undertaken at the industry level. For many observers, this shift in the asset allocation paradigm is the hallmark of the euro for the asset management industry.

The change in asset allocation strategy is not a minor change. It is viewed as implying that the teams of analysts, until now organised along country lines, are to be reorganised along industry lines. This in turn is meant to imply that the sought-after competencies become the ability to analyse the prospects of an industry and of specific firms within that industry, as opposed to the prospects of a country, in particular its macroeconomic outlook. Because it is not a minor change, it is legitimate for us to ask whether we can make sense of this change and whether it has implications for the subject of our inquiry, portfolio diversification in Europe.

To place the change in asset allocation paradigm in perspective, we follow AD in disaggregating the data one step further. This is because, while the factor analysis has a tendency to rationalise asset allocation strategies in terms of country or industry indices, it is not clear that one can understand *either* strategy relative to the alternative of proceeding to a full optimisation across countries and sectors alike. To illustrate, why limit oneself to ten country indices or ten global sector indices when one could equally well use the full 10×10 matrix of what we will label 'country-sector' indices?

In fact, not all sectors are available in all countries, or only for a very short time period. We thus use a sample of seventy-seven country-sectors. Table 5.4 collects the evidence on the 77×77 correlation matrix, pre- and post-convergence. The displayed summary statistics are interesting, because they do not support the view that country-sector correlations have moved in either direction: the average pre-convergence

Table 5.4. *Country-sector index correlation statistics*

	Pre-convergence	Post-convergence
Minimum	−0.112	−0.064
Maximum	0.910	0.842
Average	0.407	0.406
Median	0.400	0.409

Source: Datastream.

correlation is 0.407, compared to 0.406 during the post-convergence period. We take this to mean that what is at work is not operative at company levels but is something affecting the appropriateness (for diversification purposes) of the specific portfolio weights characterising either country or sector indices.

To check further the time-series properties of the country-sector indices, we next turn to the dispersion measures, again meant to reflect instantaneous correlations. Figure 5.22 superposes on the series of figure 5.21 the filtered dispersion for the country-sectors indices. The result is illuminating. First, country-sector indices display the same sort of cycles as observed for the country or the sector indices. Second, at the disaggregated level of country-sectors, the most recent period is confirmed as a favourable period for diversification opportunities. Finally, and most importantly, it emerges clearly that the diversification possibilities are always better at the country-sector level than at either more aggregated level: country-sector portfolios have consistently been *less* correlated than country portfolios or global sector portfolios and the advent of the single currency had no impact on this reality.

This is a puzzling result, which may shed some light on the industry. Indeed, the lesson of figure 5.22 is that, if easily available diversification opportunities were appropriately exploited, the advent of the euro should not have been a significant event for the industry. Put differently, while the structural changes presented in section 5 are of interest to outside observers, as they may tell us something about the changes in return structures following the introduction of the euro or other

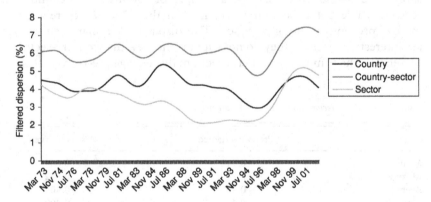

Figure 5.22. Filtered country, global and country-sector euro-zone sector dispersions, 1973–2001.
Source: Datastream.

measures of financial integration, they should not have led to any changes in paradigm. It was best to take asset allocation decisions at the country-sector level before the euro, and it remains so after the euro.

One may try to understand these observations in terms of cost. Thus, confronted with this evidence, AD argue that a two-step allocation is costlier than a one-step strategy. Small players could possibly afford only one step. The findings of the previous section suggest that the changes that have taken place imply the one step should now be industry. That is, the marginal diversification gain of adding an extra layer of optimisation is smaller when the first step is industry and the extra layer is country than when the first step is country and the extra layer is industry. But this reasoning is far from fully convincing. While the costs in question may possibly be understood when placed in the larger context of the costs of doing active portfolio management in a multi-industry international setting, they are hard to rationalise in the context of passive strategies.

Another possible reaction is that the discussion has been circumscribed to the matrix of return variances and covariances – that is, to a measure of diversification opportunities. In practice, one is equally interested in expected returns, and there is always the possibility that a shortfall in diversification possibilities is compensated for by gains on the expected returns front. But AD show that it is not the case. This can be understood from the fact that the set of *ex post* returns attainable with country or sector indices is also attainable with country-sector indices. Effectively, they show that the Sharpe ratios of both tangent and minimum-variance portfolios were much larger when optimising at the level of the country-sectors rather than with either of the more aggregated approaches.

Our second question is whether the change in the asset allocation paradigm is a good thing or a bad thing for diversification. Given our lack of understanding of the motivation for the change, this question is effectively unanswerable. One may argue that the new sectoral approach to asset allocation is a strong antidote to the home bias. This is because global sector indices are, by definition, impervious to national considerations, and the reliance on these indices at the first stage of the asset allocation process will automatically force investors towards a more international outlook. But one could as well argue that, on the contrary, once the optimal sector allocation has been defined, it will be natural for investors to try to fill in the grid with home stocks belonging to the required industries – something that will be possible in a majority of cases. Of course, doing so systematically would lead to further divergence from an optimal geographical diversification. In addition, the process may very well be further complicated if sector/industry indices are geographically concentrated.

All in all, there are clear indications that the step-by-step, top-down asset allocation process commonly adopted forgoes major diversification gains, and there is no guarantee that the current paradigm change will affect this reality. We cannot dispel our suspicion that the evidence displayed in this section in fact constitutes an indictment of current asset allocation practices. With recent events serving as a reminder that equity markets and their practitioners are not immune from fads and herding behaviour, one may wonder whether the most common asset allocation practices and the observed recent changes in these practices are not another manifestation of similar tendencies.

7.   Conclusion: on the state of portfolio diversification in Europe

Where do we stand in regard to the question raised in this chapter? Are we ready to conclude that the average European investor is now better diversified than in the recent past? We have certainly accumulated some modest evidence of favourable changes. This evidence relates mostly to the behaviour of institutional investors, who almost certainly have, to some extent, seized the opportunities opened up by the disappearance of relevant currency-matching restrictions within the euro area. We have also proposed new, albeit fragile, evidence suggesting that the equity risk premia, across European stock markets, are converging. This accords with *ex ante* reasoning on the effect of European integration and with complementary evidence that the cost of capital has decreased in Europe. There is also robust evidence that the structure of equity returns has changed, in Europe specifically. In particular, the country factors now appear to be dominated by the factors associated with industry or sector, and this finding is more robust – across databases and methodologies – than it is elsewhere. This latter result may, however, be simply the result of macroeconomic and monetary integration, and at this stage we cannot make strong inferences on the degree of portfolio diversification from these observations.

On the negative side, the relationships between national consumption patterns within the euro area do not reveal as strong a degree of international risk-sharing as one would expect from an area that is economically and financially integrated. In fact, they compare unfavourably with similar observations made in other regions of the world. Futhermore, we have not been able to dispel the suspicion that the most popular asset allocation process among European practitioners is seriously flawed. In particular our data do not permit the rationalisation of the observed change in the asset allocation paradigm often identified as the trademark impact of the euro on the industry.

At the end of this inquiry on the status of portfolio diversification in Europe, we are clearly standing in front of a glass that is half full – or half empty! Unfortunately, we have to reach our conclusion in the absence of a 'smoking gun' revealing, without ambiguity, that decisive progress is being made. But some advances are registered nevertheless. While leaving the reader free to choose his or her own appreciation of the uncovered reality, we cannot conceal our bewilderment at finding ourselves incapable of justifying the most important change associated with the euro by practitioners. This leaves us with the suspicion that Europeans continue to be seriously undiversified.

REFERENCES

Adam, K., T. Jappelli, A. Menichini, M. Padula and M. Pagano (2002), *Study to Analyse, Compare and Apply Alternative Indicators and Monitoring Methodologies to Measure the Evolution of Capital Market Integration in the European Union*, European Commission, Internal Market Directorate General, Brussels.

Adjaouté, K. and J.-P. Danthine (2003), 'European financial integration and equity returns: a theory-based assessment', in: V. Gaspar, P. Hartmann and O. Sleijpen (eds.) *The Transformation of the European Financial System*, European Central Bank, Frankfurt.

(2004), 'Portfolio diversification: alive and well in Euroland', *Applied Financial Economics*, 14, 1225–31.

Arnold, I. (2001), 'Country and industry effects in Euroland's equity markets', in: J. Choi and J. Wrase (eds.) *European Monetary Union and Capital Markets*, Vol. II, Elsevier, Amsterdam, 137–55.

Baca, S. P., B. L. Garbe and R. A. Weiss (2000), 'The rise of sector effects in major equity markets', *Financial Analysts Journal*, 56 (5), 34–40.

Beckers, S., G. Connor and R. Curds (1996), 'National versus global influences on equity returns', *Financial Analysts Journal*, 52, 31–9.

BIS Study Group on Fixed Income Markets (2001), *The Changing Shape of Fixed Income Markets*, Working Papers no. 104, Monetary and Economic Department, Bank for International settlements, Basel.

Brooks, R., and M. Del Negro (2002a), *The Rise in Comovement across National Stock Markets: Market Integration or Global Bubble?*, Working Paper no. 02/147, International Monetary Fund, New York.

(2002b), *International Diversification Strategies*, Working Paper no. 2002–23, Federal Reserve Bank of Atlanta.

Cavaglia, S., C. Brightman and M. Aked (2000), 'The increasing importance of industry factors', *Financial Analysts Journal* 56 (5), 41–54.

De Santis, G., B. Gérard, and P. Hillion (1999), 'The European single currency and world equity markets', in: J. P. Dermine and P. Hillion (eds.) *European Capital Markets with a Single Currency*, Oxford University Press, Oxford, chap. 7.

Federation of European Securities Exchanges (2002), *Share Ownership Structure in Europe*, mimeo, Economic and Statistics Subcommittee, Brussels.

Flotho, T. D. (2002), *A Note on Consumption Correlations and European Financial Integration*, Working Note no. 115.2002, Fondazione Eni Enrico Mattei, Milan.

Galati, G., and K. Tsatsaronis (2001), *The Impact of the Euro on Europe's Financial Markets*, Working Paper no. 100, Monetary and Economic Department, Bank for International Settlements, Basel.

Griffin, J. M., and A. G. Karolyi (1998), 'Another look at the role of the industrial structure of markets for international diversification strategies', *Journal of Financial Economics*, 50, 351–73.

Guiso, L., M. Haliassos and T. Jappelli (2003), 'Household stockholding in Europe: where do we stand and where do we go?', *Economic Policy*, 18, 117–64.

Hamelink, F., H. Harasty and P. Hillion (2001), *Country, Sector or Style: What Matters most when Constructing Global Equity Portfolios? An Empirical Investigation from 1990–2001*, Research Paper no. 35, International Center for Financial Asset Management and Engineering, University of Geneva.

Hardouvelis, G., D. Malliaropulos and R. Priestley (2001), *The Impact of Globalization on the Equity Cost of Capital*, working paper, Banque de France, Paris.

Heston, S., and K. Rouwenhorst (1994), 'Does industrial structure explain the benefits of industrial diversification?', *Journal of Financial Economics*, 36 (1), 3–27.

Isakov, D., and F. Sonney (2004), 'Are practitioners right? On the relative importance of industrial factors in international stock returns', *Swiss Journal of Economics and Statistics*, 140 (3), 355–79.

Kalemli-Ozcan, S., B. E. Sorensen and O. Yosha (2005), 'Asymmetric shocks and risk-sharing in a monetary union: updated evidence and policy implications for Europe', in: H. Huizinga and L. Jonung (eds.) *The Internationalisation of Asset Ownership in Europe*, Cambridge University Press, Cambridge, chap. 6.

Kuo, W., and S. E. Satchell (2001), 'Global equity styles and industry effects: the preeminence of value relative to size', *Journal of International Financial Markets, Institutions and Money*, 11, 1–28.

Massaro, R., and E. Laakari (2002), *The European and Euro-Zone Financial Structure – Rapid Changes in Recent Years*, Statistics in Focus series, Economy and Finance, no. 18, Eurostat, Brussels.

Rouwenhorst, K. G. (1999), 'European equity markets and the EMU', *Financial Analysts Journal*, 55 (3), 57–64.

Solnik, B., and J. Roulet (2000), 'Dispersion as cross-sectional correlation', *Financial Analysts Journal*, 56 (1), 54–61.

Stulz, R. (1999), 'Globalization of equity markets and the cost of capital', *Journal of Applied Corporate Finance*, Fall, 8–25.

6 Asymmetric shocks and risk-sharing in a monetary union: updated evidence and policy implications for Europe

Sebnem Kalemli-Ozcan, Bent Sørensen and Oved Yosha

1. Introduction

Assessing the economic consequences of financial integration is high on the agenda of economists and policy-makers around the world and, in particular, within the European Union, where financial integration is expected to increase rapidly following trade integration and the advent of the euro.

For the countries in the euro area, a major concern is that adverse shocks to the economies of individual members of the currency union can no longer be blunted by monetary policy if such shocks hit only a single country or a few countries. For example, if France happens to be in a recession while the rest of the euro area is booming, the European Central Bank will not be able to lower the interest rate in order to stimulate the French economy. Such shocks are denoted as *idiosyncratic* (or state-specific) shocks, and if idiosyncratic shocks are prevalent the economies are said to exhibit *asymmetry* of gross domestic product. In the face of significant GDP asymmetry, monetary union may lead to a loss of welfare due to the lack of independent monetary policy, unless mechanisms for achieving international income insurance and consumption-smoothing ('risk-sharing') are in place.[1]

Mechanisms for sharing risk internationally include central fiscal institutions as well as market institutions. Fiscal institutions provide inter-country income insurance via a tax–transfer system that, typically, lowers taxes in – and increases transfers (for individuals) and grants (for

We thank Philipp Hartman, Lars Jonung, Max Watson and participants at the DG ECFIN workshop 'Who will Own Europe? The Internationalisation of Asset Ownership in the EU Today and in the Future' for useful comments. The work presented in this chapter builds on many years of collaboration with Oved Yosha. Tragically, he died from cancer on 7 August 2003.
[1] In the long run, high GDP asymmetry may even, in the absence of international risk-sharing, destabilise the monetary union by generating incentives for secession in order to regain monetary independence.

governments) to – countries that suffer an economic setback. Market institutions include developed capital markets through which the members of a union can share risk by smoothing their income via the cross-ownership of productive assets (portfolio diversification). Alternatively, consumers may smooth their consumption (given their income) by adjusting their savings rate – i.e. adjusting the size of their asset portfolio in response to shocks.

In this chapter we will focus on income-smoothing using methods developed by Asdrubali et al. (1996), who examine risk-sharing among the states that make up the United States (a successful monetary union). For the period 1964 to 1990, they find that 39 per cent of idiosyncratic (state-specific) shocks to the per capita GDP of individual states are smoothed on average through inter-state ownership patterns – i.e. through capital income flows across state borders. Their methods are based on measuring how closely personal income (adjusted for federal transfers and contributions) follows state-level GDP – the details are spelled out in the next section.[2] They further find that the amount of insurance through inter-state capital income flows has been rising over time, and we will examine if this trend is still continuing.

Using similar methods, Sørensen and Yosha (1998) explore risk-sharing patterns among EU and OECD countries during the period 1966 to 1990, finding that factor income flows do not smooth gross national product across countries. These results suggest that EU capital markets have been less integrated than US capital markets, at least until a decade ago.

We update some of the above empirical results through to the end of the 1990s, focusing on income insurance from factor income flows. Two major findings emerge. First, the amount of insurance through inter-state capital income flows in the United States has been rising further. Second, in the latter part of the 1990s there is non-negligible insurance through international capital income flows in the European Union – about 10 per cent of idiosyncratic shocks to the GDP of individual countries are smoothed on average through this channel. In this respect, the European Union is beginning to converge towards the United States. This result is one of the first that actually corroborates empirically that unified Europe is becoming more similar to the union of US states in terms of integration at the macroeconomic level![3]

---

[2] They also find that 13 per cent of shocks are smoothed by the federal tax–transfer and grant system, and 23 per cent via saving or borrowing and lending, with 25 per cent of shocks not being smoothed at all. Therefore, although perfect insurance is not achieved, there is considerable risk-sharing among US states.

[3] A closely related literature, originating with Feldstein and Horioka (1980), finds a high correlation between aggregate investment and aggregate saving for most OECD

The process of economic and monetary integration itself may affect the symmetry of GDP fluctuations, and it is of interest to explore this issue in the European context. Kalemli-Ozcan et al. (2003a) demonstrate empirically that inter-country income insurance (which may itself be a result of economic integration) induces higher specialisation in production.[4] The simple intuition for this result is that, as long as ownership is diversified, countries or regions can be very specialised, with potentially high GDP volatility, while still having low volatility of income.

Kalemli-Ozcan et al. (2001) also establish empirically that higher specialisation in production translates into more asymmetry in GDP fluctuations. This result may not be surprising, but, nonetheless, it seems not to have been verified previously. Together, these findings substantiate an effect of income insurance on industrial specialisation that, other things being equal, results in less symmetric output fluctuations.

We update the empirical analysis of specialisation and GDP asymmetry, asking specifically whether specialisation and GDP asymmetry have risen in the European Union as a result of better risk-sharing. We find that country-level specialisation in the Union increased during the 1990s; however, GDP asymmetry declined in the 1990s relative to the 1980s. At least for this sample period, the effect of specialisation on asymmetry was overwhelmed by other forces which we do not attempt to identify in the present article.

Asymmetry in *output* (GDP) may not be important for the members of the Union if there is substantial risk-sharing between members of the union. Rather, the asymmetry in income and in consumption are, arguably, the relevant indicators of potential losses of welfare. Kalemli-Ozcan et al. (2003b) demonstrate that the asymmetry in *personal income* across US states is substantially lower than the asymmetry in *output* corroborating the empirical relevance of this observation. In this chapter we update the calculations for US states and further estimate the level of GNP asymmetry for the European Union. We find that, for the US states, asymmetry in income remains much lower than asymmetry in GDP. Surprisingly, for EU countries, GNP is *more* asymmetric than GDP, in spite of positive risk-sharing in the 1990s. We conjecture that a further rise in risk-sharing in the Union will reverse this result similarly to what we find for the US states benchmark.

---

countries and argues that such correlation is an indicator of a lack of financial integration. Giannone and Lenza (2003) find that investment–saving correlations became lower in the 1990s – a finding that is consistent with our results.

[4] 'Specialisation' here refers to specialisation *relative* to other countries (or states) within a group.

Overall, our results are encouraging in relation to concerns about the welfare effects of asymmetric shocks in the European Union, because they indicate that the *income* (and hence also the consumption) of EU members is slowly becoming buffered against country-specific shocks to GDP. While this increase in risk-sharing may encourage more industrial specialisation and, thereby, more asymmetry in output (other things being equal), this need not lead to more asymmetry in income (and consumption) across countries. Indeed, for the United States the asymmetry in state-level income is much lower than the asymmetry in state-level output. This last pattern is, however, not yet observed for the EU members. We have argued previously that risk-sharing may be particularly important for countries in the euro area, and we conjecture – no empirical evidence is yet available – that the formation of a monetary union itself will facilitate further risk-sharing, for instance, by increasing the international diversification of mutual funds through removing the costs of currency hedging and through greater transparency.

In the next section we give a fuller discussion of the existing empirical literature. In section 3 we present the updated empirical analysis, and in section 4 we discuss implications for policy in Europe.

2.   Literature review

2.1   *US states as a benchmark for the European Union*

There is by now a fairly substantial literature studying US states, and sometimes also regions within other countries, as examples of successful currency unions that can fruitfully be used as a benchmark for the countries in the European Union and, in particular, the euro area. Among the first papers in this tradition were those by Eichengreen (1990) and De Grauwe and Vanhaverbeke (1993), who contrast regional and national data on macroeconomic variables such as employment and output growth rates, labour mobility and the real exchange rate.[5] A recent volume that continues this tradition, and provides many more references, is edited by Hess and van Wincoop (2000). A particularly influential early paper, which aims to measure the amount of risk-sharing provided to US states by the US federal government through

---

[5] The literature initiated by Eichengreen (1990), Sala-i-Martin and Sachs (1992) and others was inspired by Mundell's (1961) classic analysis of optimum currency areas. Alesina and Barro (2002) provide a modern analysis of currency unions. They focus on the volume of trade within a currency union, assessing how trade costs affect the desirability of a union, and on the fact that joining a currency union can commit a country to monetary stability.

taxes and federal transfers to individuals, is that of Sala-i-Martin and Sachs (1992), who estimate that a $1 drop in the income of a state would be compensated for by an increase in transfers minus taxes of more than 60 cents. Their (very large) estimate of risk-sharing through federal government fiscal policy has been disputed by, *inter alios*, von Hagen (1992), who finds a significant but much lower level of risk-sharing from the federal government.[6]

2.2   Testing for full risk-sharing

The characterisation of full risk-sharing has been known for many decades since the seminal work of Arrow and Debreu. Yet the empirical implications of full risk-sharing, also known as perfect or efficient risk-sharing, were not investigated until recently. A good place to start is Cochrane (1991) and Mace (1991), who point out that, if idiosyncratic risk is fully shared among a group of consumers, then a consumer's consumption should be affected only by aggregate fluctuations and not by any idiosyncratic shock that hits the consumer, such as job loss, sickness or a change in the consumer's income. These authors test this proposition using micro-data (person or household data) from the United States.[7] Many similar tests have been carried out since, with the overall conclusion that the data do not support the full risk-sharing hypothesis. Obstfeld (1994b) carries over this logic to the country level, testing for full risk-sharing among G7 countries, and he also rejects the hypothesis. His line of research was refined by several authors. Important contributions come from Canova and Ravn (1996), who also reject full risk-sharing, and Lewis (1996).

2.3   Channels of risk-sharing

Asdrubali et al. (1996) shift the focus from *testing* for full risk-sharing to *measuring* the amount of risk-sharing that is achieved through various channels. The first channel consists of income insurance through an

---

[6] These authors were concerned with estimating the amount of income insurance provided by the US federal government to US states as a benchmark for the income insurance role that might be required from a future central fiscal authority in the European Union. We endorse von Hagen's estimate, which is close to the number obtained by Asdrubali et al. (1996). For further work on income insurance through fiscal policy, see Gavin and Perotti (1997), Fatas and Mihov (2001), Sørensen et al. (2001) and Buettner (2002). See also Atkeson and Bayoumi (1993) and Goodhart and Smith (1993).

[7] Townsend (1994) tests the full risk-sharing proposition using micro-data from villages in India.

inter-regionally or internationally diversified investment portfolio. The citizens or the government of a country can invest in stock markets overseas, or, more generally, can own claims to output produced in other countries. For example, if mutual funds or pension funds in one country invest internationally, the income of the citizens in that country includes factor income from abroad and will partly co-move with the output in other countries. If financial intermediaries in one country lend to firms in other countries, the flow of interest payments smooths the income of citizens in the lending country. If risk is not fully shared through factor income flows, there is scope for further income-smoothing through taxes and transfers by a supranational government (e.g. the US federal government).

The channel is the one identified first by Sala-i-Martin and Sachs (1992), except that Asdrubali et al. measure all risk-sharing in relation to shocks to *output* since shocks to income – used by Sala-i-Martin and Sachs – already reflect risk-sharing from the cross-ownership of assets. If risk is still not fully shared, there is scope for further consumption-smoothing through saving behaviour. (Such consumption-smoothing through saving is governed to a large extent by intertemporal consider-ations.)[8] Finally, some fraction of shocks may not be smoothed at all. If this fraction is statistically significant, this constitutes a rejection of full risk-sharing with an interpretation similar to the tests popularised by Mace (1991).

The method developed by Asdrubali et al. (1996) has recently been extended by Mélitz and Zumer (1999), who allow for risk-sharing to depend on such country-specific (or state-specific, depending on the case) features such as demographics, size and wealth. They apply the method to US states, obtaining results that are quite similar to those

---

[8] According to models of forward-looking consumer behaviour, if shocks to GDP are highly persistent, and not smoothed through international factor income flows and/or through taxes and transfers, individuals will optimally choose to engage in very little consumption-smoothing through saving. If the shocks to GDP are transitory, and not smoothed through international factor income flows, individuals will optimally choose to engage in much consumption-smoothing through saving. Baxter and Crucini's (1995) insight is relevant here. If, for some reason, there is no income insurance through factor income flows but agents can trade in a risk-less bond, then – if shocks to GDP are transitory – full risk-sharing will be closely approximated. That is, when shocks to GDP are transitory, a risk-less bond (i.e. the credit market) is a close substitute for income insurance (i.e. for capital markets). In contrast, if shocks to GDP are highly persistent, consumption-smoothing through trade in a risk-less bond will not approximate the full risk-sharing allocation – namely, the credit market will not closely mimic the role of capital markets: shocks that were not insured *ex ante* on capital markets will, by the logic of the permanent income model of consumption, not be smoothed *ex post* on credit markets.

obtained by Asdrubali et al. (1996), as well as to other federations and countries for which regional data are available (for instance, Canada and France). In all countries there are non-negligible amounts of risk-sharing via the various channels, but full risk-sharing is rejected.

Another important extension was suggested recently by Becker and Hoffmann (2002), who focus on the dynamic aspects of risk-sharing. In particular, they estimate the permanent and transitory components of a three-dimensional model involving country-level GDP, GNP and consumption. Their results indicate that permanent shocks are insured (*ex ante*), while transitory shocks are mainly smoothed (*ex post*) via saving behaviour. We believe that this is a promising line of research.

2.4 Consumption correlations and international real business cycle models

Closely related is the international real business cycle literature, most notably Backus et al. (1992), and more recently Baxter and Crucini (1995) and Stockman and Tesar (1995). These authors develop two-country general equilibrium models with complete financial markets. A central prediction of these models is that consumption correlations across countries should be high. These authors have taken this prediction to international macroeconomic data, finding that inter-country consumption correlations are nowhere close to unity. In fact, these consumption correlations are not higher than country GDP correlations, as we would expect if there were only partial international risk-sharing – a phenomenon that has become known as the 'international consumption correlation puzzle'.[9]

2.5 Welfare gains from risk-sharing

Another closely related literature calculates welfare gains from (international) risk-sharing. Testing for full risk-sharing and measuring the amount of risk that is shared through various channels is of interest only if such welfare gains are non-negligible. Research by Cole and Obstfeld (1991) found that these gains are small, but it soon became clear – see Obstfeld (1994c) and van Wincoop (1994) – that this result is due to their assumption that shocks to GDP are transitory. If shocks are

---

[9] Stockman and Tesar (1995) suggest country-specific taste shocks as an explanation of the puzzle. Sørensen and Yosha (1998) show that the low consumption correlations are consistent with taste shocks, although it cannot be ruled out that the low consumption correlations simply reflect noise (e.g. measurement error) in the consumption data.

permanent (or highly persistent) then the gains from insuring them are quite meaningful. Van Wincoop (1994) estimates that under the more realistic assumption of permanent shocks (more precisely: assuming that country-level GDP is well described by a random walk) the gain from perfect risk-sharing would be equivalent to a permanent increase in consumption of about 2 to 3 per cent. Obstfeld (1994c) provides a closed-form solution for the welfare gains due to a reduction in consumption variability in a partial equilibrium setting under the assumption that agents have constant relative risk aversion (CRRA) utility functions. Van Wincoop computes welfare gains from risk-sharing in a general equilibrium model – also assuming CRRA utility, as well as more general types of utility functions – relying on approximation techniques. More precisely, van Wincoop calculates non-exploited gains from risk-sharing using consumption data, measuring how many *further* gains from risk-sharing can be achieved by moving from the observed consumption allocation (in the data) to the perfect risk-sharing consumption allocation.

2.6   Risk-sharing and home bias

The finding of low international risk-sharing is fully consistent with the well-known 'home bias puzzle', documented by French and Poterba (1991) and Tesar and Werner (1995). In a world with full information, no moral hazard, no trading cost and the same degree of risk aversion across agents, all agents should (according to basic theory) hold an identical 'world' portfolio of assets. It is, however, observed that, for example, the British hold the vast majority of their assets in the form of UK equities and Americans hold the vast majority of their assets in the form of US equities – an observation that is referred to as 'home bias'.[10]

Sørensen et al. (2002) provide direct empirical evidence that these phenomena are indeed related: on average, risk-sharing from the international cross-ownership of assets, as measured by the smoothing of GNP, is higher in countries that hold a higher amount of foreign equity relative to GDP.[11] The lack of risk-sharing across countries, and its relation to home bias, motivated Shiller (1993) to propose the issuance of assets with returns that are directly linked to the growth of GDP in

[10] Coval and Moskowitz (1999) even find 'home bias at home'. They find that US institutional investors, while holding assets from all over the United States, still hold a more than proportional amount of assets issued in their own geographical region. (For a similar result, see Huberman, 2001.) However, this home bias is much less severe than the home bias found in international data.

[11] See Lane and Milesi-Ferretti (2001) for data on international asset holdings.

various countries. International macro-risk could then be alleviated via trade in such country-specific GDP-linked securities (by each country going short in the securities linked to its own GDP).

2.7   Economic integration, industrial specialisation and the asymmetry of economic fluctuations

Much of the debate on the desirability of economic integration centres on the degree of synchronisation (symmetry) in macroeconomic fluctuations across countries. It has been noted that the process of economic integration itself will affect the symmetry of macroeconomic fluctuations. Frankel and Rose (1998) argue that the removal of trade barriers will entail more correlated business cycles, since a higher level of trade will allow demand shocks to spread more easily across national borders. Further, they mention that economic integration will render policy shocks more correlated, and that knowledge and technology spillovers will increase (see also Coe and Helpman, 1995). These factors should also contribute to fluctuations becoming more symmetric following economic integration. Krugman (1993), on the other hand, claims that lower barriers to trade will induce countries to specialise more, rendering output fluctuations *less* symmetric.[12] We illustrate these various effects in figure 6.1, adapted from Kalemli-Ozcan et al. (2001).[13]

In the remainder of this chapter we focus on updating our previous work on specialisation and asymmetry, rather than attempting to provide a balanced view of the literature; in particular, we say little about the important issue of the effect of lower trade barriers.

2.8   Theoretical literature on risk-sharing and industrial specialisation

With uninsured production risk, the higher variance of GDP resulting from specialised output may entail a welfare loss that outweighs the benefits. The argument was first formulated by Brainard and Cooper (1968), Kemp and Liviatan (1973) and Ruffin (1974). In response, Helpman and Razin (1978) show that, if production risk can be insured through trade in assets, the benefits of specialisation will resurface.[14]

---

[12] Krugman corroborates his argument with the observation that US states are more specialised in production than European countries.

[13] Imbs (2003) contributes to this debate by estimating a three-equation system with three endogenous variables: pairwise GDP correlations, bilateral trade and industrial specialisation. His results are generally in line with previous research.

[14] Further work on this topic includes Anderson (1981), Grossman and Razin (1985) and Helpman (1988). See also Heathcote and Perri (2001) for models along these lines.

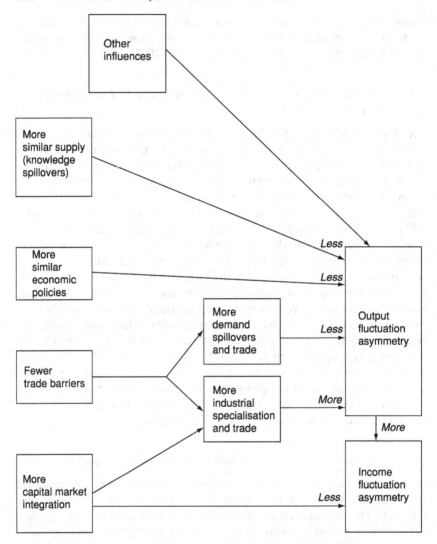

Figure 6.1. A stylised depiction of the effects of economic integration on fluctuation asymmetry.

This work has consequences for the theory of economic growth. Obstfeld (1994a) constructs a model in which countries choose between investing in risky projects with high average returns or in safe projects with low average returns. International asset trade allows them to hold a diversified portfolio and to shift investment towards high-return projects. Acemoglu and Zilibotti (1997) stress that developing countries have fewer opportunities to diversify production and tend to specialise in safe technologies. Insurance permits them to take risks that – with some probability – will translate into an economic take-off. In Greenwood and Jovanovic (1990), financial intermediaries pool risks and achieve higher and safer returns on investment. In Saint-Paul (1992), the basic trade-off is between the gains from specialisation due to comparative advantage in production and a lower variance of output, while Feeney (1999) develops the idea that, in the presence of learning by doing in production, specialisation entails higher growth during a transition period.

2.9   Empirical evidence on risk-sharing and specialisation

Kalemli-Ozcan et al. (2003a) demonstrate empirically that more insurance among regions (countries) is associated with higher industrial specialisation in these regions (countries). They estimate a cross-sectional regression using about 150 regional-level observations, and, to guard against the potential endogeneity (reverse causality) of the amount of inter-regional risk-sharing achieved, they use investor protection indices – suggested by La Porta et al. (1998) – as instruments.[15]

It is worth noting that Kim (1995) finds that specialisation in the United States (at the state level) has *decreased* continuously since the 1930s (after increasing in the late nineteenth century). Asdrubali et al. (1996) find that risk-sharing among US states has increased over time, which, together with the results of Kalemli-Ozcan et al. (2003a), would seem to predict an *increase* in specialisation. Our interpretation is that the effects we identify are only part of the picture, and that there are long-run technological changes that reduce the gains from specialisation for a given level of risk-sharing.[16] This process is probably on-going in the United States as well as in the European Union, although we expect it to be counteracted in the European Union during the next decade or two as financial markets continue to integrate.[17] Our work does not allow us to predict which effect will dominate in the short run,

---

[15] Ramey and Ramey (1995) note that, in the presence of *aggregate* uninsured risk, countries will take fewer additional risks. Therefore, the volatility of aggregate output may affect the regional specialisation within a federation of regions. To control for this, Kalemli-Ozcan et al. (2003a) calculate the volatility of group-wide GDP for each group of regions (countries) and include it as a control variable in the regression.

[16] Kim (1995) suggests that technological advances have made production less dependent on local resources, and that factors of production have become more mobile.

[17] The increase in specialisation in the United States in the late nineteenth century fits this picture, as the regional US capital markets were becoming integrated during that time; see Davis (1965).

although we suspect that the effect of financial integration may dominate for a while due to stronger international financial integration and reduction in home bias.[18]

2.10   *Economic integration and the asymmetry of output fluctuations*

Academic research on the asymmetry of shocks to regions and nations dates back at least to Cohen and Wyplosz (1989) and Weber (1991), who study country-level output growth rate correlations for European countries, and to Stockman (1988), who distinguishes between country-specific and industry-specific shocks. The latter paper inspired numerous studies, such as those by Kollman (1995), Fatas (1997) and Hess and Shin (1998). Bayoumi and Eichengreen (1993) focus on demand versus supply shocks and use a vector autoregression procedure to study them, whereas De Grauwe and Vanhaverbeke (1993) distinguish between region-specific and country-specific shocks. Massmann and Mitchell (2003) reconsider this literature and find that euro-zone business cycles became more correlated in the late 1990s, after a period of divergence in the early 1990s following German unification and the European currency crisis.

Industrial specialisation will probably have implications for the amount of asymmetry of macroeconomic shocks. If industry-specific shocks are important then greater specialisation should increase the asymmetry of shocks. Kalemli-Ozcan et al. (2001) deal with this question empirically, studying a cross-section of US states and a cross-section of EU and OECD countries.[19] They point out that the welfare gain from moving from financial autarky to full risk sharing, where the value of output is fully pooled through financial cross-ownership, can be used as a measure of asymmetry. The intuition is that the greater the asymmetry in GDP fluctuations within a group of countries (or regions) the larger the benefit from smoothing these fluctuations through risk-sharing within the group.

These authors derive a simple *closed-form* expression for the gains from risk-sharing under the assumption of CRRA utility.[20] The advantage of

---

[18] Imbs and Wacziarg (2003) provide evidence that industrial specialisation declines with GDP in the early stages of development and increases with GDP in the later stages of development. They do not relate their finding to risk-sharing or risk-taking.

[19] Kalemli-Ozcan et al. (2001) provide a simple model that helps clarify the role of industry-specific shocks versus other types of shock.

[20] Kim, Kim and Levin (2000), using a different approach, obtain analytical solutions for gains from risk-sharing allowing for quite general dynamics, although their set-up is restricted to a two-country framework, which makes it less applicable for actual empirical calculations.

this measure is that – subject to the simplifications needed to get analytical solutions – it can be interpreted as a measure of the disutility that such asymmetry will inflict on the average person.[21] They find that greater industrial specialisation does indeed lead to lower synchronisation of GDP fluctuations (i.e. more asymmetry). They stress, though, that more asymmetry need not be detrimental to the welfare of the residents of an economic or monetary union, because – in the presence of risk-sharing – income is partly insured from GDP fluctuation, and *income* (or GNP) fluctuations need not, therefore, be more asymmetric. In addition, although not the focus here, consumption may further be buffered from income fluctuations.

3.   Measuring risk-sharing, specialisation and fluctuation asymmetry

3.1   Risk-sharing

We construct a measure of the amount of risk-sharing obtained through the cross-ownership of financial assets. The measure takes the value 1 if there is perfect risk-sharing from cross-ownership – i.e. if the GNP of a typical country does not move with country-specific movements in its GDP – and the measure takes the value 0 if GNP moves one-to-one with GDP – the situation with no risk-sharing.

Consider the following set of cross-sectional regressions (one regression for each year t) for a group of countries indexed by sub-script i:

$$\Delta \log \text{GNP}_{it} - \Delta \log \text{GNP}_t = \text{constant} \\ + \beta_{K,t}(\Delta \log \text{GDP}_{it} - \Delta \log \text{GDP}_t) + \epsilon_{it} \qquad (1)$$

where GNP_{it} and GDP_{it} are country i's year t real per capita GNP and GDP, respectively, and GNP_t and GDP_t are the year t average real per capita GNP and GDP for the group.[22] The coefficient $\beta_{K,t}$ measures the average co-movement of the countries' idiosyncratic GNP growth with their idiosyncratic GDP growth in year t – i.e. the co-movement of GNP and GDP growth rates when aggregate growth rates have been

---

[21] Kalemli-Ozcan et al. (2001) also use simple measures of asymmetry based on pair-wise GDP correlations, obtaining similar results.

[22] 'Real' GDP (GNP) refers to GDP (GNP) divided by the consumer price index (CPI) of country i. We use the CPI, rather than a GDP deflator, because the relevant measure for risk-sharing is the value of GDP (GNP) in terms of consumption goods. The GDP deflator is typically quite similar to the CPI, although large differences in our sample can be found for countries (or states) in which proceeds from oil extraction constitute a large fraction of GDP.

subtracted. The smaller the co-movement the more GNP is buffered against GDP fluctuations. If income-smoothing is perfect then idiosyncratic GNP does not co-move with idiosyncratic GDP at all. In fact, for each country GNP growth equals the group's GNP growth. Therefore, $\beta_{K,t}$ takes the value 0 simply because the left-hand side of equation (1) is always 0.

Since GNP equals GDP plus net factor income flows, this regression provides a measure of the extent to which net factor income flows provide income insurance – the lower $\beta_{K,t}$ is the higher income insurance is within the group in year t.[23] We use $1 - \beta_{K,t}$ as a measure of risk-sharing through international factor income flows. If no country-specific risk is hedged in international capital markets we would expect to find $\beta_{K,t} = 1$ because, for each country in the group, GNP would then equal GDP and our risk-sharing measure, $1 - \beta_{K,t}$, would be 0.

Figure 6.2 displays a smoothed graph of the series $1 - \beta_{K,t}$ against time. The $\beta_{K,t}$ values are estimated year by year for a sample of EU member states (the fifteen then members excluding Luxembourg and Spain) and the values at neighbouring time periods are smoothed (using a normal kernel smoother) in order to focus on the trend movements in the series. Surprisingly, the estimated risk-sharing is negative in the early 1990s; in those years a decrease in GDP was typically associated with an even larger decrease in GNP! In order to examine if this was due to the banking crisis in Finland and Sweden during these years, or to the impact of the Soviet break-up on Finnish foreign trade, we also display a line leaving out those two countries. Clearly, the Scandinavian banking crisis explains much of the negative risk-sharing in those years. We do not know exactly why, but the large negative shocks to GDP that those countries suffered in that period were accompanied by even larger negative shocks to the countries' GNP. At the time, the degree of financial integration in the European Union was not large enough to compensate for this effect, resulting in negative average risk-sharing in the Union.

The main fact revealed by figure 6.2 is that by the end of the 1990s international financial integration in the European Union finally reached a level where GNP fluctuations are somewhat decoupled from GDP fluctuations. The increase in risk-sharing from factor income flows is quite dramatic, and seems much too steep to be driven by sample variation.

---

[23] See Asdrubali et al. (1996), Sørensen and Yosha (1998) and Mélitz and Zumer (1999).

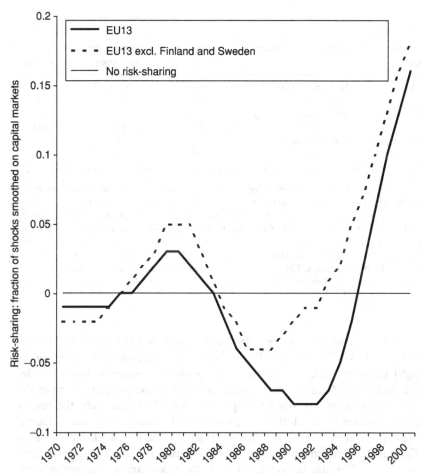

Figure 6.2. Risk-sharing in the European Union, 1970–2000.
Note: The solid line represents the average level of risk-sharing between the EU13 countries: Austria, Belgium, Denmark, Finland, France, Germany, Greece, Ireland, Italy, the Netherlands, Portugal, Sweden and the United Kingdom. The dashed line represents the average level of risk-sharing between EU13 countries without Finland and Sweden.

Alternatively, we estimate the amount of risk-sharing over several years using the panel data regression (which pools the regressions over all the years in the sample)

$$\Delta \log \text{GNP}_{it} - \Delta \log \text{GNP}_t = \text{constant} \atop + \beta_\kappa \left(\Delta \log \text{GDP}_{it} - \Delta \log \text{GDP}_t \right) + \epsilon_{it} \tag{2}$$

Table 6.1. *Risk-sharing in the European Union through international factor income flows,*
1972–2000

Sample		1973–1982	1983–1992	1993–2000
EU8	Risk-sharing $(1 - \beta_\kappa)$	4	2	11
	t-statistics	(2)	(1)	(3)
EU14	Risk-sharing $(1 - \beta_\kappa)$	0	−7	6
	t-statistics	(0)	(4)	(2)
Euro area	Risk-sharing $(1 - \beta_\kappa)$	2	−8	9
	t-statistics	(2)	(4)	(4)

Note: $1 - \beta_\kappa$ measures income insurance among the countries of the risk sharing group and is obtained from the panel regression $\Delta \log \text{GNP}_{it} - \Delta \log \text{GNP}_t = \text{constant} + \beta_\kappa (\Delta \log \text{GDP}_{it} - \Delta \log \text{GDP}_t) + \epsilon_{it}$, where $\Delta \log \text{GDP}$ and $\Delta \log \text{GNP}$ are growth rates of per capita GDP and GNP; t-statistics in parentheses. The entry for risk-sharing $(1 - \beta_\kappa)$ is the percentage of a country-specific shock to output (GDP) that is not reflected in GNP. The EU8 countries are Belgium, Denmark, France, Germany, Ireland, Italy, the Netherlands and the United Kingdom. The EU14 countries are the EU8 plus Austria, Finland, Greece, Portugal, Spain and Sweden. The euro area is the EU14 minus Denmark, Sweden and the United Kingdom.

In table 6.1, we show the results for the periods 1973 to 1982, 1983 to 1992 and 1993 to 2000.[24] We estimate the regressions for a group of eight long-time EU countries;[25] this group of countries may have developed closer financial integration during our sample periods than the more recent entrants to the European Union.[26] Alternatively, the results are also given for the full set of pre-2004 EU members (minus Luxembourg) and for the current euro area (again, leaving out Luxembourg). The results confirm the increase in risk-sharing in the 1990s displayed in figure 6.2. For the period 1973 to 1982 risk-sharing was basically nil among the EU countries (borderline positive for the smaller group), while risk-sharing was significantly negative for the larger group, as discussed previously. For the period 1993 to 2000, risk-sharing was positive and clearly statistically significant in all three groups of countries. The amount of risk-sharing was higher in the smaller group of long-time EU members for all sub-periods, although not strongly so

[24] The regression is similar to the one estimated by Asdrubali et al. (1996). They include time-fixed effects (a dummy variable for each year) rather than subtracting aggregate growth, but this makes little difference to the results, so we choose the slightly more transparent form here.
[25] Luxembourg is left out because it is small and atypical.
[26] Sørensen and Yosha (1998) consider risk-sharing among this group of EU countries. The results here will differ slightly for identical time periods due to revisions to the national accounts.

Table 6.2. *Risk-sharing in US states through capital markets, 1964–1998*

	1964–1970	1971–1980	1981–1990	1991–1998
Risk sharing $(1 - \beta_\kappa)$	29	42	48	55
t-statistics	(7)	(8)	(10)	(14)

Note: $\Delta \log y_{it} - \Delta \log y_t = $ constant $+ \beta_\kappa (\Delta \log \text{GDP}_{it} - \Delta \log \text{GDP}_t) + \epsilon_{it}$, where $\Delta \log \text{GDP}$ and $\Delta \log y$ are growth rates of per capita GDP and personal income; t-statistics in parentheses. The entry for risk-sharing $(1 - \beta_\kappa)$ is the percentage of a state-specific shock to output (to state-level GDP) that is not reflected in state income (more precisely, 'state income' as constructed in Asdrubali et al., 1996). The difference between GDP and state income includes inter-state factor income flows, depreciation and corporate saving.

except for the 1983 to 1992 period. It is likely that mutual financial integration and risk-sharing will increase more rapidly for the countries that have adopted the euro, but it will be some years in the future before this trend will be discernible by our statistical methods.

In table 6.2 we display the results for risk-sharing among the US states. The numbers have a slightly different interpretation from the numbers for risk-sharing through international factor income flows among countries because GNP numbers are not available at the state level. Instead, numbers for income are used; appendix 1 displays the relation between GDP, GNP and personal income in the national accounts.[27] In order to compare the OECD and the European Union more closely to the United States, Sørensen and Yosha (1998) also examine risk-sharing between OECD countries and EU countries based on personal income, and find that about 10 to 15 per cent of GDP shocks are smoothed, so one may want to subtract this order of magnitude from the US estimates of risk-sharing in order to get a rough comparison with the estimates for the European Union. Sørensen and Yosha find that the difference between the results obtained using GNP and the results obtained using personal income is mainly due to income-smoothing through corporate savings.

[27] More precisely, we use updated measures of 'state income' as constructed for 1963 to 1990 in Asdrubali et al. (1996). State income consists of personal income after subtracting all federal transfers and allocating all non-personal federal taxes to income (attempting to approximate what personal income would be without any federal taxes and transfers). Further, the income of state governments that is not derived from personal taxes – such as corporate and severance taxes – is available to the residents of states via the state governments and is also included in state income. We consider GNP the better 'income' measure to use, although the main patterns of risk-sharing can be expected to be quite similar. The difference between GDP and GNP in the national accounts is mainly due to cross-border flows of dividends and interest, while personal income for given GDP is also affected by, for example, patterns of corporate saving and capital depreciation.

In any event, the results of table 6.2 are consistent with the amount of risk-sharing increasing decade by decade, as found by Asdrubali et al. using data from 1963 to 1990 (some of the results for that sample differ slightly from those presented in Asdrubali et al. 1996, due to revisions of the state-level GDP data). Clearly, the trend identified by those earlier authors was continuing through the 1990s, with – according to the highly significant point estimate – more than half the variation of state-specific GDP shocks being smoothed through cross-state income flows in the 1990s.

As an alternative measure of risk-sharing, we calculate (for the EU sample) simple correlations of country-level GDP and GNP with Union-wide GDP and GNP, respectively, as popularised by Backus et al. (1992). (For brevity, we do not tabulate the details.) We find that the correlation of country-level GNP with Union-wide GNP increased in the late 1990s. This is the result that would be expected if international risk-sharing is increasing, and it is, therefore, consistent with the results presented above. This demonstrates that our results are not sensitive to the exact choice of empirical methods applied.

3.2   Specialisation

We here explain how the index of specialisation used by Kalemli-Ozcan et al. (2003a) is calculated, and update their results using the most recent data.

We calculate the specialisation index for sectors at the one-digit and two-digit manufacturing International Standard Industrial Classification (ISIC) levels. The one-digit sectors are manufacturing, agriculture, government and so forth. The detailed sector definitions for the one-digit and two-digit manufacturing sectors are listed in appendix 2.[28] The degree of specialisation at the one-digit level is likely to be more important for the overall diversification of shocks to the economy. However, we may get a clearer picture by looking at the manufacturing sub-sectors, which respond mainly to market forces. The level of output in one-digit sectors such as agriculture and mining is determined primarily by endowments of fertile soil and extractable minerals, or the activities of agricultural lobbyists. The size of the government (one-digit) sector is primarily determined by social and political factors.

The specialisation index for manufacturing is computed (for each country) for the relevant sample years as follows. Let GDP_i^s denote the

---

[28] The sectors used correspond to those used by Kalemli-Ozcan et al. (2003a). In the first draft of this chapter we presented figures based on slightly more disaggregated two-digit manufacturing sectors, but some of those sectors were very tiny and this made the results somewhat fragile.

GDP of manufacturing sub-sector s in country i, and GDP_i^M the total manufacturing GDP of this country. We measure the distance between the vector of sector shares in country i, $\text{GDP}_i^s / \text{GDP}_i^M$, and the vector of average sector shares in the European Union countries other than i

$$
\text{SPEC}_i = \sum_{s=1}^{S} \left(\frac{\text{GDP}_i^s}{\text{GDP}_i^M} - \frac{1}{\mathcal{J}-1} \sum_{i \neq j} \frac{\text{GDP}_j^s}{\text{GDP}_j^M} \right)^2 \tag{3}
$$

where S is the number of sectors and $\mathcal{J}$ is the number of countries considered (the subset of the European Union for which we have been able to find the relevant data). Notice that SPEC_i measures how the composition of manufacturing in country i differs from the composition of manufacturing in the other countries of the Union. The index of one-digit specialisation is computed similarly, using total country-level GDP rather than manufacturing GDP and one-digit sectors rather than manu-facturing sub-sectors. We calculate similar indices for the fifty US states for the same sub-period.

Figures 6.3 and 6.4 display the average specialisation index for the EU countries and the US states, for one-digit sectors and two-digit manu-facturing sectors, respectively, for the period 1991 to 1999. (We have data only for a few countries prior to 1991. Belgium and the Netherlands are omitted since our data source includes data for these countries only from 1995 onwards.)

The figures show that the US states are much more specialised than the EU countries. This result is not surprising, given that US states are smaller on average than EU countries.[29] We focus on the time trends of the indices. The more interesting results are found in figure 6.3, for the one-digit level: for the United States, specialisation has declined, extending the trend found by Kim (1995). Importantly, this trend is *not* found for the EU countries, where the degree of specialisation has increased significantly at the one-digit level. Our interpretation is that the downward trend found for the United States reflects the long-run technological factors identified by Kim, but that this trend has (at least temporarily) been reversed in the European Union due to financial market integration.[30]

---

[29] A larger region is likely to be less specialised, due to the greater heterogeneity of the population and of within-region geophysical characteristics, such as climate, landscape and natural resources. Furthermore, in larger regions scale economies in production are more likely to be exhausted for some industries.

[30] This may also be the result of lower trade barriers (see Krugman, 1993), but since barriers to trade within the European Union have been low for some time now one might conjecture that the rise in financial integration in the late 1990s, as documented above, could have played an important role in the recent rise in country-level specialisation.

A

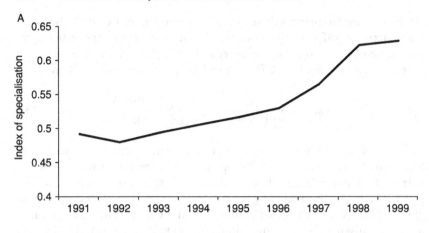

B

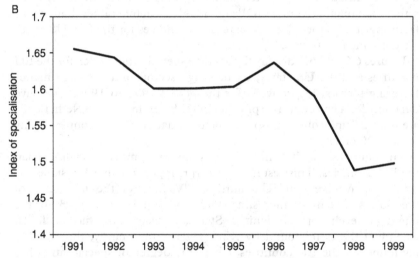

Figure 6.3. Average specialisation in the European Union and the United States at the one-digit ISIC level, 1991–1999.

Note: In the upper panel the solid line represents the average level of specialisation in Austria, Denmark, Finland, France, Germany, Ireland, Italy and the United Kingdom. In the bottom panel it represents the average level of specialisation in all fifty US states.

For the two-digit manufacturing sectors we see – for the European Union and the US states alike – an increase followed by a decline. An inspection (not in the figure) of the two-digit specialisation pattern reveals that this pattern (in the EU case) is mainly driven by Ireland, which displayed very high growth during the 1990s, partly due to large

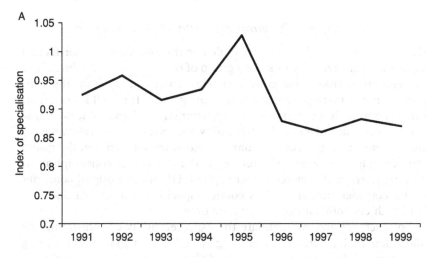

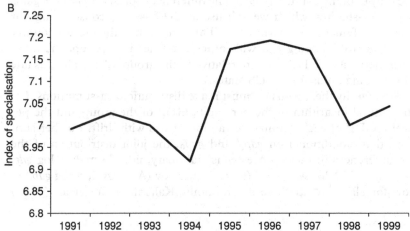

Figure 6.4. Average specialisation in the European Union and the United States at the two-digit ISIC level, 1991–1999.
Note: In the upper panel the solid line represents the average level of specialisation in Austria, Denmark, Finland, France, Germany, Ireland, Italy and the United Kingdom. In the bottom panel it represents the average level of specialisation in all fifty US states.

inflows of foreign direct investment. Nonetheless, the weak overall trends at the two-digit level seem to be slightly downward for the EU countries, and may be slightly upward for the US states – contrary to the finding for the one-digit level. However, the two-digit trends are clearly not significant.

3.3   Asymmetry of GDP versus asymmetry of GNP and income

Our measure of GDP asymmetry builds on the following counter-factual thought experiment.[31] Consider a group of countries each inhabited by a representative risk-averse consumer who derives utility from the consumption of a homogeneous non-storable good.[32] It is well known that, under commonly used assumptions (symmetric information, no transaction costs, and identical CRRA utility and rate of time preference (δ) for all countries), perfect risk-sharing among the countries in the group implies that $c_t^i = k^i \, gdp_t$.[33] Here c_t^i is the per capita consumption in country i, gdp_t is the aggregate per capita GDP of the group of countries under consideration and k^i is a country-specific constant that does not vary with economic outcomes or over time.

For each country we compare the expected utility of consuming the allocation under perfect risk-sharing ($k^i \, gdp_t$) with that of consuming the output of the country (gdp_t^i). The difference represents *potential* gains from risk-sharing, which we will use as the basis for constructing our measure of fluctuation asymmetry. The logic is that, the more a country can gain from sharing risk with other countries in a group, the more asymmetric its GDP shocks are relative to the group. (An analogous line of reasoning holds for the US states.)

To quantify these gains we must make distributional assumptions. Let the natural logarithm of the per capita GDP of the group and the per capita GDP of each country be random walks with drift. Further suppose that, conditional on gdp_0^i and gdp_0, the joint distribution of the log-differences of these processes is stationary, iid, Normal: $\Delta \log gdp_t \sim N(\mu, \sigma^2)$, $\Delta \log gdp_t^i \sim N(\mu^i, \sigma_i^2)$, and cov ($\Delta \log gsp_t^i$, $\Delta \log gdp_t$) = cov^i for all t.[34] With these assumptions, Kalemli-Ozcan et al. (2001)

---

[31] See Kalemli-Ozcan et al. (2001).

[32] In macro-theoretic parlance, this group constitutes a 'stochastic endowment economy', in the sense that the GDP of these countries is regarded by consumers as exogenous and stochastic.

[33] The CRRA utility function, which includes the logarithmic utility function as a special case, is commonly used in macroeconomics and is generally considered as having good properties. The critical assumption here is that all countries or states are assumed to have the same attitude towards risk. If one region were less tolerant of risk than others it would be optimal for it to invest in international assets that would help lower the variance of consumption below that of 'world' (EU or total US) output in return for a lower average level of consumption. Note that we here abstract from investment, depreciation, etc. and simply assume that world consumption equals world output; our regressions are not affected by this short cut, which is made to simplify the discussion.

[34] This assumption involves an approximation, since the aggregate GDP cannot, in general, be strictly log-normally distributed if each country's GDP is log-normally distributed.

derive closed-form solutions for the potential gains from risk-sharing assuming identical CRRA utility functions for all countries. We will here use the solution for log-utility, which yields simple and intuitive expressions.[35]

The potential gains from risk-sharing are expressed in terms of consumption certainty equivalence. We do so by calculating the permanent percentage increase in the level of consumption that would generate an equivalent increase in expected utility. More precisely, the gain in utility (of moving from autarky to perfect risk-sharing) equals the gain in utility that would be achieved by increasing consumption permanently from gdp_{i0} to $gdp_{i0}^{\star} (1 + G_i)$. G_i is our country-by-country measure of fluctuations asymmetry and, for log-utility, is given by the expression

$$G_i = \frac{1}{\delta}\left(\frac{1}{2}\sigma^2 + \frac{1}{2}\sigma_i^2 + \text{cov}^i\right) \tag{4}$$

The intuition for this formula is straightforward. First, the gain from sharing risk is higher for countries with a lower covariance between $\Delta \log gdp_t^i$ and $\Delta \log gdp_t$. The interpretation is that countries with 'countercyclical' output, provide insurance to other countries by stabilising aggregate output, and such countries are compensated accordingly in the risk-sharing agreement. Second, the higher the variance of country i's GDP, other things being equal the more it will benefit from sharing risk with other countries. Third, the higher the variance of the aggregate gross product of the group, keeping the variance of country i's GDP constant, the more other countries will be willing to 'pay' country i for joining the risk-sharing arrangement.

In the empirical implementation, the parameters σ^2, σ_i^2 and cov^i are estimated using country-level (or state-level) and aggregate GDP data. δ is the discount rate and we use a value of 2 per cent. Because our measure is based on the utility that a country would obtain from consuming the value of its GDP we use, as our output measure, nominal GDP deflated by the CPI.[36]

We calculate the asymmetry measure for EU countries and for US states for the 1980s and the 1990s. We also calculate the measure using GNP data rather than GDP data. Note that, if risk-sharing from factor income flows is perfect, such that the GNP of all countries (states) shows

---

[35] The empirical results are not very different for general CRRA utility.
[36] We stress the logic of deflating by the CPI rather than by a GDP deflator. Since our measure is utility-based, we want measured output to reflect consumption in autarky (with countries consuming the *value* of their GDP). Thus, we want to translate GDP to the amount of consumption that it can buy. This is obtained by deflating using the CPI.

identical growth, the GNP-based measure of asymmetry will be zero, as no further gains from risk-sharing are possible.

We show the results in table 6.3. For both US states and European countries the level of GDP asymmetry has declined dramatically from the 1980s to the 1990s. It seems that country-level and regional-level business cycles have become less asymmetric. We cannot tell what lies behind this observation; whether it is a 'structural' more permanent pattern, or whether it is the result of the types of shocks driving GDP variation in the 1980s versus the 1990s (the early 1980s saw much turmoil in financial markets). If we were to venture a guess, we would opine that the decline in asymmetry in the 1990s is due to the different types of shocks hitting the economies in these two sub-periods.

For the US states, high risk-sharing is reflected in a much lower asymmetry of income than of state-level GDP. Surprisingly, for the EU countries GNP is *more* asymmetric than GDP. Recall that GNP equals GDP plus net factor income (mainly profits, dividends and interest) from other countries. If net factor income flows from other countries are as volatile as the GDP of those countries (as in the textbook case where countries directly trade rights to country-level output), then GNP asymmetry *must* be lower than GDP asymmetry as long as these factor income flows from abroad are not perfectly correlated with domestic GDP and therefore smooth GNP (and income). The empirical finding

Table 6.3. *Asymmetry in GDP versus asymmetry in GNP and income in the United States and the European Union, 1983–2000*

Sample		1983–1991	1991–1999
United States	Asymmetry (GDP)	2.99	0.89
	Asymmetry (income)	0.82	0.42
Sample		1983–1991	1991–2000
EU14	Asymmetry (GDP)	1.23	0.61
	Asymmetry (GNP)	1.49	0.79

Note: The asymmetry measure is calculated as the average over the countries or states in the group. The value for country (state) i is $10^2 * \frac{1}{\delta}(\frac{1}{2}\sigma^2 + \frac{1}{2}\sigma_i^2 - cov^i)$, where $\sigma_i^2 =$ var $(\Delta \log GDP^i)$, $\sigma^2 =$ var $(\Delta \log GDP)$, $cov^i = cov (\Delta \log GDP^i, \Delta \log GDP)$ and $\delta = 0.02$ GDP is the GDP of the relevant aggregate. The entry for asymmetry is interpreted as the welfare gain that a state/country would obtain from fully diversifying any state-/country-specific variance in output/GNP/personal income expressed in terms of the percentage permanent increase in GDP that would result in the same utility gain. The EU14 countries are Austria, Belgium, Denmark, Finland, France, Germany, Greece, Ireland, Italy, the Netherlands, Portugal, Spain, Sweden and the United Kingdom.

that GNP asymmetry is higher than GDP asymmetry implies that the volatility of net factor income flows from abroad is higher than the volatility of GDP in the countries of origin. We speculate that this happens due to the high (some would say 'excessive') volatility of financial returns and due to these returns not providing a hedge against domestic GDP fluctuations (i.e. foreign asset holdings are not acquired mainly for hedging domestic output risk and, thus, do not provide returns that are negatively correlated with the output of the home economy). As long as a substantial fraction of the foreign asset holdings in EU countries takes the form of assets traded on foreign stock and bond exchanges, rather than foreign direct investment, it may be the case that the asset income from such international investments boosts the variance of GNP in each country, rather than stabilising it. As financial integration deepens, and more foreign investments take the form of direct investment in productive assets, it is likely that the degree of GNP asymmetry will decline and fall below that of GDP asymmetry, as is the case in the United States.

4.   Implications for Europe

To start with one point that seems to have been somewhat ignored in the literature: asymmetry in output shocks is not likely to create strains in a currency union unless it creates high asymmetry in *income* and consumption.[37] Asymmetry in output is obviously a determinant of income asymmetry, but this asymmetry is directly mitigated if inter-country risk-sharing is significant. Our measure of risk-sharing has the simple interpretation of measuring the percentage of country-specific shocks to output (in percentage growth terms) that is passed on to income. In the United States, we find that less than 50 per cent of output shocks are reflected in income shocks (which are further smoothed through federal taxes and transfers). We expect countries in the European Union to reach similar levels of risk-sharing, and our results indicate that this process is currently gaining momentum.[38] It is worth noting that the

---

[37] Supranational governments can smooth disposable income, but (according to Asdrubali et al., 1996), even in the United States, where the federal government is quite big, this channel is less important than income-smoothing on capital markets. Asymmetry in consumption fluctuations is, in our view, generally less reliable empirically, because variation often seems to be caused by taste shocks, making measures of consumption asymmetry suspect for evaluating welfare gains from risk-sharing.

[38] The US results are not directly comparable, since they also include within-state income-smoothing through corporate earnings retention (dividend pay-out) patterns.

degree of risk-sharing in the United States is still increasing, in spite of having already reached a high level.

The impact of trade on asymmetry, stressed by Krugman (1993), has received much attention. Other things being equal, lower trade barriers should lead to more inter-industry trade and greater industrial specialisation, which, in turn, should result in greater GDP asymmetry. Frankel and Rose (1998) argue that demand spillovers and (in particular) more intra-industry trade might dominate this effect and could render GDP asymmetry smaller, not larger. They show empirically that this effect does indeed dominate in the data. Their work does not take into account the direct effect of risk-sharing on specialisation documented by Kalemli-Ozcan et al. (2003a) and the resulting effect on asymmetry documented by Kalemli-Ozcan et al. (2001) and Imbs (2003).

The current chapter does not update the analysis in these earlier papers but, rather, looks at the time-series patterns. These seem highly consistent with these earlier results, that risk-sharing in the European Union has been increasing, and so has industrial specialisation. We speculate that risk-sharing plays an important causal role, because trade barriers have been low within the Union for a long period of time and the effect of lower trade barriers may, therefore, partly have played itself out. More empirical work will be needed to test this conjecture.

Surprisingly, output asymmetry has declined steeply over the last two decades. We cannot tell which of the channels we identify in figure 6.4 is the cause of this result. It may be due to more coordinated policy as countries adjusted their fiscal policy in order to meet the Maastricht criteria, but a similar result was found for US states, so the finding may be simply due to the different nature of the shocks to the world economy in the 1990s (inflation being conquered in the 1990s, the 'new economy', etc.).

We find higher asymmetry in GNP than in GDP among EU countries. As has already been mentioned, one component of net factor income flows is returns from international equity investment. An active literature has documented the fact that developed country stock and bond market returns have been highly correlated recently, diminishing the stabilising impact of diversification; see, for example, Goetzman et al. (2002) and Mauro et al. (2002). It may be that these findings from financial markets have the same roots as our findings of declining GDP asymmetry, although we leave empirical corroboration of this conjecture for future research. This does not rule out GNP asymmetry being higher than GDP asymmetry if international investments take place mainly through equity traded on stock markets, because stock market volatility typically far exceeds the volatility of GDP. Our expectation is that, as financial integration progresses further and cross-border investments become further diversified, the variance of factor income flows will decline and GNP will become less asymmetric than GDP. This conjecture is, of course, strongly influenced by the observation that risk-sharing among US states has led to sharply lower asymmetry in income relative to the asymmetry in state-level GDP.

All in all, we expect to see risk-sharing between EU countries increase further. This should lead to more specialisation, and we expect the resulting increase in the asymmetry in GDP fluctuations to have small welfare costs as better risk-sharing lowers the asymmetry in *income* (and GNP) fluctuations.

EU governments can help promote inter-country risk-sharing by removing barriers to international flows of credit (for example, by being more supportive of cross-border mergers of financial institutions). They can further provide risk-sharing by strengthening funds that provide insurance against economic calamities that may affect whole countries. However, in light of the findings for the United States, the bulk of risk-sharing within the European Union can be expected to come from further private capital market integration. EU governments can help this process by removing any remaining barriers affecting the ability of mutual funds and, in particular, pension funds to diversify internationally.

Appendix 1: Relation between GDP and GNP of (for example) the United States

	US GDP (gross value of production physically *in* the United States)
+	Income from US-owned direct investment in other countries
−	Income of foreign-owned direct investment in the United States
+	Income from US-owned portfolio investment in other countries
−	Income of foreign-owned portfolio investment in the United States
+	Income from US-government investment in other countries
−	Income of foreign investment in United States government assets
+	Wage and salary earned in other countries by residents of the United States
−	Wage and salary earned in the United States by residents of other countries
=	US GNP (gross value of production *owned* by US residents)
+	Subsidies – indirect business taxes
−	Corporate saving
−	Net interest
+	Personal interest income

Table (cont.)

−	Contributions for social insurance
+	Government transfers to persons

=	Personal income

Notes: (i) Residents of the United States contribute to US GNP whether they are citizens of the United States or not and, while the number of foreign citizens in the United States is large, the total wage and salary of foreign residents in the United States is fairly small (less than 4 per cent of total US income payments to foreign countries in 2002).

(ii) Government investments abroad are mainly official currency reserves, while government liabilities are mainly treasury securities.

(iii) This table is a simplified version, which leaves out some minor components. See, for example, the National Income and Product Accounts published by the US Bureau of Economic Analysis (BEA) for further details. Numbers for international income receipts and payments can be found at www.census.gov/prod/2002pubs/01statab/foreign.pdf, table 1281.

Appendix 2: Data

Data for US states are collected from various sources (state-level GDP data are from the BEA), as documented in Asdrubali et al. (1996). National accounts data for the European Union are from the OECD's National Accounts, Volume I, revision 2002. To calculate the specialisation index we use data from the OECD's National Accounts, Volume II, revision 2002, in current prices. Ten one-digit ISIC sectors and nine manufacturing GDP two-digit ISIC sectors are shown below.

One-digit ISIC sectors

1 Agriculture, fishing, hunting and forestry
2 Mining and quarrying
3 Construction
4 Manufacturing
5 Electricity, gas and water supply
6 Transport, storage and communication
7 Wholesale and retail trade
8 Finance, insurance and real estate
9 Services
10 Government

Two-digit manufacturing ISIC sectors

1 Food, beverages and tobacco
2 Textile, wearing apparel and leather industries

3 Wood and wood products, including furniture
4 Paper and paper products, printing and publishing
5 Chemicals and chemical petroleum, coal, rubber and plastic products
6 Non-metallic mineral products, except products of petroleum and coal
7 Basic metal industries
8 Fabricated metal products, machinery and equipment
9 Other manufactured products

REFERENCES

Acemoglu, D., and F. Zilibotti (1997), 'Was Prometheus unbound by chance? Risk, diversification, and growth', *Journal of Political Economy*, 105, 709–51.

Alesina, A., and R. Barro (2002), 'Currency Unions', *Quarterly Journal of Economics*, 117, 409–36.

Anderson, J. E. (1981), 'The Heckscher–Ohlin and Travis–Vanek theorems under uncertainty', *Journal of International Economics*, 11, 239–47.

Asdrubali, P., B. E. Sørensen and O. Yosha (1996), 'Channels of interstate risk sharing: United States 1963–90', *Quarterly Journal of Economics*, 111, 1081–110.

Atkeson, A., and T. Bayoumi (1993), 'Do private capital markets insure regional risk? Evidence from the United States and Europe', *Open Economies Review*, 4, 303–24.

Backus, D., P. Kehoe and F. Kydland (1992), 'International real business cycles', *Journal of Political Economy*, 100, 745–75.

Baxter, M., and M. Crucini (1995), 'Business cycles and the asset structure of foreign trade', *International Economic Review*, 36, 821–54.

Bayoumi, T., and B. Eichengreen (1993), 'Shocking aspects of European monetary integration', in: F. Torres and F. Giavazzi (eds.) *Adjustment and Growth in the European Monetary Union*, Cambridge University Press, New York, 73–109.

Becker, S. O., and M. Hoffmann (2002), *International Risk-Sharing in the Short Run and in the Long Run*, mimeo, University of Munich and University of Dortmund.

Brainard, W., and R. Cooper (1968), 'Uncertainty and diversification of international trade', *Food Research Institute Studies in Agricultural Economics, Trade, and Development*, 8, 257–85.

Buettner, T. (2002), 'Fiscal federalism and interstate risk sharing: empirical evidence from Germany', *Economics Letters*, 74, 195–202.

Canova, F., and M. Ravn (1996), 'International consumption risk sharing', *International Economic Review*, 37, 573–601.

Cochrane, J. (1991), 'A simple test of consumption insurance', *Journal of Political Economy*, 99, 957–76.

Coe, D., and E. Helpman (1995), 'International R&D spill-overs', *European Economic Review*, 39, 859–87.

Cohen, D., and C. Wyplosz (1989), 'The European Monetary Union: an agnostic evaluation', in: R. Bryant, D. Currie, J. Frenkel, P. Masson and R. Portes (eds.) *Macroeconomic Policies in an Interdependent World*, Brookings, Washington, DC, 311–37.

Cole, H., and M. Obstfeld (1991), 'Commodity trade and international risk sharing: how much do financial markets matter?', *Journal of Monetary Economics*, 28, 3–24.

Coval, J., and T. Moskowitz (1999), 'Home bias at home: local equity preference in domestic portfolios', *Journal of Finance*, 54, 2045–74.

Davis, L. (1965), 'The investment market, 1870–1914: the evolution of a national market', *Journal of Economic History*, 25, 355–99.

De Grauwe, P., and W. Vanhaverbeke (1993), 'Is Europe an optimum currency area? Evidence from regional data', in: P. Masson and M. Taylor (eds.) *Policy Issues in the Operation of Currency Unions*, Cambridge University Press, New York, 111–29.

Eichengreen, B. (1990), 'One money for Europe? Lessons from the US currency union', *Economic Policy*, 10, 117–87.

Fatas, A. (1997), 'EMU: countries or regions? Lessons from the EMS experience', *European Economic Review*, 41, 743–51.

Fatas, A., and I. Mihov (2001), 'Government size and automatic stabilizers: international and intranational evidence', *Journal of International Economics*, 55, 3–28.

Feeney, J. (1999), 'International risk sharing, learning by doing, and growth', *Journal of Development Economics*, 58, 297–318.

Feldstein, M., and C. Horioka (1980), 'Domestic savings and international capital flows', *Economic Journal*, 90, 314–29.

Frankel, J., and A. Rose (1998), 'The endogeneity of the optimum currency area criterion', *Economic Journal*, 108, 1009–25.

French, K., and J. Poterba (1991), 'Investor diversification and international equity markets', *American Economic Review: Papers and Proceedings*, 81, 222–6.

Gavin, M., and R. Perotti (1997), 'Fiscal policy in Latin America', in *NBER Macroeconomics Annual 1997*, National Bureau of Economic Research, Cambridge, MA, 11–61.

Giannone, D., and M. Lenza (2003), *The Feldstein-Horioka Fact*, mimeo, European Center for Advanced Research in Economics and Statistics, Free University of Brussels.

Goetzman, W., L. Li and K. G. Rouwenhorst (2002), *Long-Term Global Market Correlations*, mimeo, Yale University, New Haven, CT.

Goodhart, C., and S. Smith (1993), 'Stabilization', *European Economy*, Reports and Studies no. 5, 419–55.

Greenwood, J., and B. Jovanovic (1990), 'Financial development, growth, and the distribution of income', *Journal of Political Economy*, 98, 1076–107.

Grossman, G., and A. Razin (1985), 'International capital movements under uncertainty', *Journal of Political Economy*, 92, 286–306.

Heathcote, J., and F. Perri (2001), *Financial Globalization and Real Regionalization*, mimeo, Duke University, Durham, NC, and Leonard N. Stern School of Business, New York University.

Helpman, E. (1988), 'Trade patterns under uncertainty with country specific shocks', *Econometrica*, 56, 645–59.

Helpman, E., and A. Razin (1978), *A Theory of International Trade under Uncertainty*, Academic Press, New York.

Hess, G. D., and K. Shin (1998), 'Intranational business cycles in the United States', *Journal of International Economics*, 44, 289–313.

Hess, G. D., and E. van Wincoop (eds.) (2000), *Intranational and International Macroeconomics*, Cambridge University Press, New York.

Huberman, G. (2001), 'Familiarity breeds investment', *Review of Financial Studies*, 14, 659–80.

Imbs, J. (2003), *Trade, Finance, Specialization and Synchronization*, mimeo, London Business School.

Imbs, J., and R. Wacziarg (2003), 'Stages of diversification', *American Economic Review*, 93, 63–86.

Kalemli-Ozcan, S., B. E. Sørensen and O. Yosha (2001), 'Regional integration, industrial specialization and the asymmetry of shocks across regions', *Journal of International Economics*, 55, 107–37.

(2003a), 'Risk sharing and industrial specialization: regional and international evidence', *American Economic Review*, 93, 903–16.

(2003b), 'Regional integration, industrial specialization and the asymmetry of shocks across regions', reprinted from the *Journal of International Economics*, with extensions, in: E. Helpman and E. Sadka (eds.) *Contemporary Economic Policy: Essays in Honor of Assaf Razin*, Cambridge University Press, New York, 121–56.

Kemp, M., and N. Liviatan (1973), 'Production and trade patterns under uncertainty', *The Economic Record*, 49, 215–27.

Kim, J., S. Kim and A. Levin (2000), *Patience, Persistence and Welfare Costs of Incomplete Markets in Open Economies*, mimeo, University of Virginia.

Kim, S. (1995), 'Expansion of markets and the geographic distribution of economic activities: the trends in U. S. regional manufacturing structure 1860–1987', *Quarterly Journal of Economics*, 110, 881–908.

Kollman, R. (1995), 'The correlations of productivity growth across regions and industries in the United States', *Economics Letters*, 47, 437–43.

Krugman, P. (1993), 'Lesson of Massachusetts for EMU', in: F. Giavazzi and F. Torres (eds.) *The Transition to Economic and Monetary Union in Europe*, Cambridge University Press, New York, 241–69.

Lane, P., and G. M. Milesi-Ferretti (2001), 'The external wealth of nations: measures of foreign assets and liabilities for industrial and developing countries', *Journal of International Economics*, 55, 263–94.

La Porta, R., F. Lopez-de-Silanes, A. Shleifer and R. W. Vishny (1998), 'Law and finance', *Journal of Political Economy*, 106, 1113–55.

Lewis, K. (1996), 'What can explain the apparent lack of international consumption risk sharing?', *Journal of Political Economy*, 104, 267–97.

Mace, B. (1991), 'Full insurance in the presence of aggregate uncertainty', *Journal of Political Economy*, 99, 928–56.

Massmann, M., and J. Mitchell (2003), *Reconsidering the Evidence: Are Eurozone Business Cycles Converging?*, mimeo, University of Bonn, University of Oxford and National Institute of Economic and Social Research, London.

Mauro, P., N. Sussman and Y. Yafeh (2002), 'Emerging market spreads: then versus now', *Quarterly Journal of Economics*, 117, 695–733.

Mélitz, J., and F. Zumer (1999), 'Interregional and international risk sharing and lessons for EMU', *Carnegie–Rochester Conference Series on Public Policy*, 51, 149–88.

Mundell, R. (1961), 'A theory of optimum currency areas', *American Economic Review*, 51, 657–65.

Obstfeld, M. (1994a), 'Risk-taking, global diversification, and growth', *American Economic Review*, 84, 1310–29.

(1994b), 'Are industrial-country consumption risks globally diversified?', in: L. Leiderman and A. Razin (eds.) *Capital Mobility: The Impact on Consumption, Investment, and Growth*, Cambridge University Press, New York, 11–44.

(1994c), 'Evaluating risky consumption paths: the role of intertemporal substitutability', *European Economic Review*, 38, 1471–86.

Ramey, G., and V. Ramey (1995), 'Cross-country evidence of the link between volatility and growth', *American Economic Review*, 85, 1138–51.

Ruffin, R. (1974), 'Comparative advantage under uncertainty', *Journal of International Economics*, 4, 261–73.

Saint-Paul, G. (1992), 'Technological choice, financial markets and economic development', *European Economic Review*, 36, 763–81.

Sala-i-Martin, X., and J. Sachs (1992), 'Fiscal federalism and optimum currency areas: evidence for Europe from the United States', in: M. Canzoneri, P. Masson and V. Grilli (eds.) *Establishing a Central Bank: Issues in Europe and Lessons from the US*, Cambridge University Press, Cambridge, 195–219.

Shiller, R. (1993), *Macro Markets: Creating Institutions for Managing Society's Largest Economic Risks*, Oxford University Press, Oxford.

Sørensen, B. E., and O. Yosha (1998), 'International risk sharing and European Monetary Unification', *Journal of International Economics*, 45, 211–38.

Sørensen, B. E., Y. T. Wu and O. Yosha (2001), 'Output fluctuations and fiscal policy: US state and local governments 1978–1994', *European Economic Review*, 45, 1271–310.

(2002), *Home Bias and International Risk Sharing: Twin Puzzles Separated at Birth*, mimeo, University of Houston, Binghamton University, Binghamton, NY, and Tel Aviv University.

Stockman, A. C. (1988), 'Sectoral and national aggregate disturbances to industrial output in seven European countries', *Journal of Monetary Economics*, 21, 387–409.

Stockman, A. C., and L. Tesar (1995), 'Tastes and technology in a two-country model of the business cycle: explaining international comovements', *American Economic Review*, 85, 168–83.

Tesar, L., and I. Werner (1995), 'Home bias and high turnover', *Journal of International Money and Finance*, 14, 467–92.

Townsend, R. (1994), 'Risk and insurance in village India', *Econometrica*, 62, 539–91.

van Wincoop, E. (1994), 'Welfare gains from international risk sharing', *Journal of Monetary Economics*, 34, 175–200.

von Hagen, J. (1992), 'Fiscal arrangements in a monetary union: evidence from the U. S.', in: D. Fair and C. de Boissieu (eds.) *Fiscal Policy, Taxation, and the Financial System in an Increasingly Integrated Europe*, Kluwer, Boston, 337–59.

Weber, A. (1991), 'EMU and asymmetries and adjustment problems in EMS – some empirical evidence', *European Economy*, 1, 187–207.

Part III

Country studies

7 The Swedish model of corporate ownership and control in transition

Magnus Henrekson and Ulf Jakobsson

1. Introduction

In the 'Swedish ownership model' the controlling ownership in firms is typically concentrated in one or two owners. Often, but not always, these owners are Swedish families. The Swedish ownership model thus resembles the predominant corporate governance model on the European continent. Sweden differs from most countries in Continental Europe in a couple of respects, however. First, the entire ownership on the stock exchange is dominated by a few controlling owners. Second, Swedish controlling ownership is based on a smaller capital base than it is in other Continental European countries.

Sweden appears to have found a model combining strong owners and an egalitarian wealth policy. But, as we shall see, the large gap between the ownership of capital and control creates considerable problems for the Swedish model. In the long run, this might mean that it is phased out in order to be partly or entirely replaced by other models of corporate governance. The weak supply of capital makes the Swedish model both politically and financially unstable.

The purpose of this chapter is to analyse the development of the Swedish corporate ownership and control model in the post-war period and how it has been shaped by political decisions, mainly within the areas of taxation and corporate law. The main focus of our analysis is on listed firms.

1.1 Framework and outline

We distinguish between different categories of owners: families, private institutional owners, public or semi-public institutional owners and

We thank Christina Håkanson for her excellent research assistance and Lars Jonung and Peter Högfeldt for their constructive comments and suggestions. Magnus Henrekson gratefully acknowledges financial support from Sven Hagströmers och Mats Qvibergs Stiftelse.

foreign owners. The last group of owners can be subdivided into the same categories as domestic owners. Generally, we treat them as one group, however.

One owner or a couple of owners can have ownership dominance – that is, a dominant influence in the firm. Moreover, a single agent may have an influence in several firms due to ownership dominance. In that case, we may speak of a high concentration of ownership control. Controlling a firm is based on the control of a large part of the votes of the outstanding shares of the firm. It is common for shares to have differential voting rights. Thus, the influence in a given firm needs not be proportional to the capital invested. Pyramid ownership also works in this direction.

The major part of our analysis deals with the post-war period. Since the end of World War II ownership related to cash-flow rights has undergone dramatic changes, while the ownership control structure at the stock exchange has remained surprisingly constant. However, the sharp increase in foreign ownership has resulted in the disappearance of several large independent firms from the Swedish stock exchange. A number of firms have either become wholly owned subsidiaries of foreign multinationals or merged with a foreign competitor. The new, larger firm has subsequently become domiciled elsewhere and delisted from the Stockholm Stock Exchange.

At the beginning of the post-war period ownership in Swedish listed firms was mainly private. There was strong ownership dominance across all firms. Ownership was concentrated in a small number of families and groupings. This concentration reflected not just the considerable concentration of large private fortunes but the fact that there were different mechanisms separating control from the number of shares owned. These mechanisms consisted of differences in voting rights between different shares, pyramiding and cross-ownership.

These mechanisms were also used in other countries, but, over time, their importance became greater in Sweden than in other industrialised countries. Therefore, we may talk about a typical Swedish ownership model, with a concentrated ownership based on a small equity base. In the period studied, the gap between the distribution of ownership rights and the distribution of control rights has widened. Since the capital share among controlling owners has continually been decreasing, the supply of capital has increasingly come from other sources. Loan financing played an important part until the mid-1980s. Subsequently, the stock exchange has become more important as a source of financing.

The type of legislation in a country affects the kinds of management and financing allowed. The empirical literature in this area has largely concentrated on the relation between 'corporate law' and 'corporate governance'. Seminal studies in this tradition are those of La Porta et al. (1998, 1999), based on a cross-sectional analysis of a large number of countries. A general result is that the legal framework is of crucial importance for the system of corporate governance in a country and for the financing of the activities of the firm.

One problem with their results is that they give no explanations for the considerable changes over time in many countries in the variables to be explained. An example from Sweden is the trend in stock market capitalisation as a percentage of GDP. This variable plays a crucial role in the analysis of La Porta et al. As shown in figure 7.1, it has undergone considerable changes over time, despite the fact that the explanatory variables used by La Porta et al. have changed only to a limited extent. They focus on the legal origin as the ultimate explanation of the system of corporate governance for a particular country. Since the legal origin is taken as exogenous and time-invariant, this approach obviously cannot be used to explain large changes over time in the system of corporate governance.

There is a growing literature where the regulations that shape the design and operations of corporations and securities markets are seen as the outcome of a political process in each country. Here, changes in the political environment pave the way for changes in corporate regulations. See Pagano and Volpin (2001) for a review. Still, the main

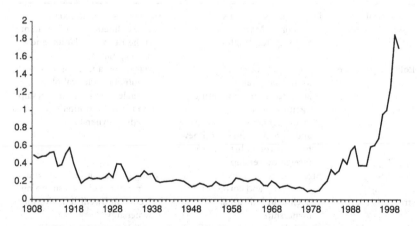

Figure 7.1. Stock market capitalisation on the Stockholm Stock Exchange relative to GDP, 1908–2000.
Source: Data received directly from Daniel Waldenström and Statistics Sweden.

210   *M. Henrekson and U. Jakobsson*

focus here is on corporate law and regulations, even if these laws and regulations are explained within a new political economy framework.

We argue, with Sweden as a point of reference, that the development of ownership structures and systems for corporate governance can be explained by several factors, of which corporate law is just one. As a result, we want to widen the analysis. The factors stressed here are:

- taxation policy;
- financial market regulations;
- the channelling of savings in the economy;
- labour market policy; and
- corporate law.

As illustrated in table 7.1, the policy on the ownership of firms in Sweden can be divided into two periods, with the proposal for wage-earners' funds constituting a natural end point for the first period, which was characterised by a long-term socialist vision. In the second period this vision disappeared from the political agenda. Instead, the policy stance has been largely 'market liberal', but the taxation policy has discriminated against Swedish individual ownership.

Table 7.1. *A stylised outline of ownership policy and structure in Sweden during the post-war period*

	Phase I (1945–1985)	Phase II (1985–)
Ideological superstructure	Long-run vision of a socialist economy; Marx, Schumpeter, Wigforss	Ambiguous combination of market liberalism, adjustment to the European Union and anti-capitalism
Policy in practice	Aimed at discouraging individual wealth accumulation, stimulating institutional ownership, favouring large companies, and impeding small and new firms. Strong obstacles to foreign ownership	Deregulation and greater market orientation, removal of obstacles to foreign ownership and fiscal discrimination against Swedish ownership
Resulting ownership structure	Strong increase in institutional ownership and corresponding decline in individual ownership	Strong increase in international ownership and corresponding decline in Swedish institutional ownership
Corporate control	'Swedish ownership model'	'Swedish ownership model'

In this chapter, we provide a detailed analysis of the policy and its effects on the various aspects of ownership structure mentioned above. In many cases we draw on previous studies, while in other instances we have to rely on more scattered evidence and economic reasoning. A summary of our analysis is presented in table 7.2. This table may also serve as an overview of the contents of the remainder of this chapter.

The next section provides a survey of the development of the ownership of firms since the end of the nineteenth century. Then the policy and its effects during the period 1945 to 1985 are described. The ensuing section analyses the turning point, or the transition to the second period. Then we present developments after the turning point.

While there have been considerable changes in a number of the variables studied here, we have already established that the Swedish model of corporate ownership and control has remained strikingly invariant during the whole period. One conclusion of our analysis is, however, that the Swedish ownership model is not stable. The other major changes that have taken place with regard to ownership have undermined the Swedish ownership and control model. We argue that the model is not sustainable in a longer-term perspective. We conclude by discussing likely ownership and control models in the future.

The major problem for the continued existence of the Swedish ownership model is the increasing gap between the value of ownership wealth and the exercise of ownership control in Swedish firms. The first great threat to the model was in the shape of a 1970s programme for nationalising Swedish business. The present threat to the model instead comes from the 'market'.[1]

In today's deregulated and globalised capital markets, it is no longer possible to base a dynamic and expansive ownership role on the thin capital base that constituted the basis for individual ownership and control in Sweden in the past.

2.   Historical background

Beginning in the late 1860s the Swedish economy embarked on a long period of modernisation and sustained economic growth. This was greatly facilitated by a number of economic reforms in the mid-1860s, notably the granting to all Swedish men and women of the freedom to start a business, and the liberalisation of foreign trade. In 1870 the

---

[1] Another threat that emerged early in 2003 is the discussion within the European Union to abolish differential voting rights as part of a new merger and takeover directive for the single market.

Table 7.2. Effects of policy design on ownership, firm structure and financing in the business sector in the post-war period, phase I (1945–1985) and phase II (1985–)

Firm-related variables	Form of ownership										Firms		Financing					
	Individual ownership		Institutional ownership		Foreign owner-ship		Ownership dominance		Ownership concentration		Large firms versus small firms		Stock exchange		Loans		Retained earnings	
Policy area	I	II	I	II	I	II	I	II	I	II	I	II	I	II	I	II	I	II
Tax policy	−	−	++	+		++	+	0	+	0	++	+	−	0	++	0	+	0
Regulation of financial markets	−	0	++	0	−	0	++	0	++	0	++	0	−	+	+−	0	0	0
Channelling of savings	−	0	++	+		0	+	0	+	0	+	0	−	++	++	0	+	0
Labour market policy	0	0	0	0	0	0	0	0	0	0	+	+	0	0	0	0	0	0
Corporate law	+	+				0	++	++	+	+	0	0	−	−	0	0	0	0

+ (−) = positive (negative) effect; ++ (−−) = strongly positive (negative) effect; + − = counteracting effects; 0 = neutral effect.

Swedish productivity level was the second lowest in Europe, but from 1870 to 1913 Sweden experienced the highest rate of productivity growth of all countries for which comparable data are available (Maddison, 1982). A number of highly innovative entrepreneurs, such as Gustaf de Laval, Alfred Nobel and L.-M. Ericsson, were active during these years. In the period before World War I a number of new industries and important firms were created. In fact, thirty-five of the fifty largest Swedish firms in terms of sales in 2000 were established before 1914 (NUTEK and ALMI, 2001).

Foreigners had been banned from owning Swedish real estate and mines since the nineteenth century. Restrictions for foreign owners were further extended in 1916, when new legislation was passed that prevented foreign owners from having more than 20 per cent of the voting rights in Swedish corporations owning natural resources. This law mainly hit firms in mining, forestry, pulp and paper, and iron and steel (Glete, 1981).[2] In 1934 legislation was passed that outlawed earlier methods to circumvent the restrictions on foreign ownership by means of using a Swedish citizen as a 'dummy'.

Furthermore, the same year a new bank law prohibited banks from buying new stock, and existing portfolios had to be sold. Four years' grace was allowed to save the banks from incurring losses. The major banks solved this problem by creating new holding companies, constructed as closed-end investment funds, the main assets of which were the stocks previously held by the banks. Ownership of the investment companies was distributed on a pro rata basis to the owners of the respective banks.[3] Since these investment companies were, and still are, organised as pyramid holding companies with dual-class shares they immediately became important instruments for corporate control.

At the beginning of the post-war period corporate control was highly concentrated. This is clearly documented by Lindgren (1953) in a study based on the 1945 Swedish census. He shows that 6 to 7 per cent of shareholders controlled 65 to 70 per cent of the stock market value. In no less than 60 per cent of the large firms (with more than 500 employees), a single individual represented the majority of the votes at the shareholders' general meeting. In more than 90 per cent of these firms,

---

[2] In 1934 the law was made more restrictive so that foreign owners could not own more than 20 per cent of the capital either.

[3] Stockholms Enskilda Bank (controlled by the Wallenberg family) started two such companies, Investor (originally founded in 1916 as an equity issuing company) and Providentia; Svenska Handelsbanken started Industrivärden; and Skandinaviska Banken formed Custos.

three or fewer owners had a controlling majority. The concentration of control was almost as high in public companies. Here, a single individual had the majority of the votes in 53 per cent of the cases. In 85 per cent of the regularly quoted firms the two largest owners represented more than 50 per cent of the votes.

At the end of the 1940s households were still the dominant owner category, and also when it came to cash-flow rights. According to calculations by Spånt (1975), households in terms of final ownership held 75 per cent of all Swedish listed shares. Shortly after the onset of the World War II foreign exchange controls were introduced. These controls entailed a number of measures that restricted the foreign ownership of Swedish firms and property. In practice, this legislation ruled out a substantial foreign ownership share in Swedish industry. The purpose of this legislation was openly protectionist – i.e. to ascertain that 'Swedish firms remain controlled by Swedish interests' (Swedish government, 1986, p. 143).

In 1938 a number of important changes in the tax code were introduced. Income tax rates were increased, all investments could be written off instantaneously, and dividends were hit by double taxation for individual owners but not for institutional owners. These changes benefited incumbent firms and institutional owners (Montgomery, 1946).

3.   The Swedish corporate control model and its role in the corporatist model

3.1   Ideological background

The Social Democrats have dominated the political scene and the policy discussion from the early 1930s until the present day. It is, furthermore, apparent that the most important Social Democratic thinkers have seen the large industrial corporation as the major unit of production.

Ernst Wigforss, Minister of Finance from 1925 to 1926 and 1932 to 1949, and probably the most influential of all Social Democratic ideologues, was clear on this point (Wigforss, 1956). He argued that the then clear tendency in capitalist societies – that economies of scale favoured large firms (Schumpeter, 1942; Galbraith, 1956) – would facilitate the collectivisation or socialisation of the productive capital stock, which was seen as the ultimate goal of the labour movement. He also maintain that, in the long run, the large industrial corporations had to be converted into 'social enterprises without owners'. In this perspective, a strong concentration of ownership could be seen as a natural –

and even desirable – intermediate station on the road towards the ultimate goal.[4]

In the medium term a more pragmatic strategy was adopted by the ruling Social Democrats. State ownership of industry was limited and the government, trade unions and bank-related business groups came to constitute an explicit, tripartite negotiating culture, which was the main characteristic of the Swedish social democratic corporatist model. This model presupposed the existence of a fairly small number of owners or ownership groups, together constituting an identifiable industrial elite, which acknowledged and accepted that the Social Democrats would use their political power to implement far-reaching welfare reforms, while the labour movement would abstain from socialising the industrial sector. It would have been very difficult to develop this culture of compromise and negotiations between different elites (Steinmo, 2003; Katzenstein, 1985) without the predominance of a few large firms and even fewer ownership groups (Reiter, 2003).

3.2   Reinforcing policies

A key policy instrument in promoting the social democratic model was *taxation*. A number of channels were used. First, until the late 1970s taxable wealth amounted to 100 per cent of the net worth of unlisted companies and 100 per cent of the market value of listed companies. The tax rate has typically been 1.5 per cent of taxable wealth. In practice, these rules resulted in very high real rates of wealth taxation on individually owned corporate assets in the 1970s and 1980s. The wealth tax was not deductible at the company level, so the funds required to pay the wealth tax were first subjected to the mandatory payroll tax and the relevant marginal income tax rate.[5] Second, dividends were subject to taxation both at the corporate and individual level, which normally gave rise to a total tax rate on the order of 90 per cent (Norrman and McLure, 1997). Third, high inheritance and gift taxes made it extremely expensive to transfer ownership from one generation to the next (Du Rietz, 2002).[6] A sell-out was often the only feasible alternative for the next generation.

---

[4] This point is developed at greater length in Henrekson and Jakobsson (2001).

[5] Typically, 7 kronor had to be withdrawn from the firm for every krona paid in wealth tax in the early 1980s.

[6] In the late 1970s every krona to be paid in inheritance tax entailed a payment of a total of roughly 10 kronor in taxes, if the heirs had to withdraw the necessary funds from their firm.

On the other hand, capital gains taxation was designed so that it became exceptionally advantageous for individual owners to sell their firms. Until 1976 the taxation of long-term (more than five years) realised capital gains on shares and the sale of partnerships was negligible. Between 1976 and 1990 60 per cent of nominal capital gains were exempt from taxation for assets held more than two years.

To get a full understanding of how corporate taxation can be expected to affect corporate ownership and financing, one needs to calculate how real rates of taxation are influenced by how a venture is owned and financed. Table 7.3 lists effective marginal tax rates for different combinations of ownership and sources of finance. Three categories of owners and sources of finance are identified, and the effective marginal tax rate has been calculated assuming a pre-tax real rate of return of

Table 7.3. *Effective marginal tax rates for different combinations of owners and sources of finance (10 per cent real pre-tax rate of return at actual inflation rates), 1960, 1970, 1980 and 1985*

	Debt	New share issues	Retained earnings
1960			
Households	27.2	92.7	48.2
Tax-exempt institutions	−32.2	31.4	31.2
Insurance companies	−21.7	41.6	34.0
1970			
Households	51.3	122.1	57.1
Tax-exempt institutions	−64.8	15.9	32.7
Insurance companies	−45.1	42.4	41.2
1980			
Households	58.2	136.6	51.9
Tax-exempt institutions	−83.4	−11.6	11.2
Insurance companies	−54.9	38.4	28.7
1985			
Households	46.6	112.1	64.0
Tax-exempt institutions	−46.8	6.8	28.7
Insurance companies	−26.5	32.2	36.3

Note: All calculations are based on the actual asset composition in manufacturing. The following inflation rates have been used: 1960: 3 per cent; 1970: 7 per cent; 1980: 9.4 per cent; and 1985: 5 per cent. The calculations conform to the general framework developed by King and Fullerton (1984). The average holding period is assumed to be ten years. A negative tax rate implies that the rate of return after tax is greater than before tax. For instance, a tax rate of −83 per cent for a debt-financed investment owned by a tax-exempt institution in 1980 tells us that a real rate of return of 10 per cent before tax becomes 18.3 per cent after tax.
Source: Södersten (1984).

10 per cent. A negative number means that the real rate of return is greater after than before tax.

Table 7.3 highlights four important aspects of the Swedish tax system during the post-war period through to the 1980s. First, debt financing consistently received the most favourable treatment and new share issues the least. Second, retained earnings were consistently taxed at lower rates than newly issued equity, which favoured incumbent firms relative to entrants. Third, the taxation of households as owners was much higher than for other categories, and their rate of taxation increased during the 1960s and 1970s, whereas the reverse occurred for insurance companies and tax-exempt institutions.[7] From some point in the 1960s until the 1991 tax reform, more than 100 per cent of the real rate of return was taxed away for a household buying a newly issued share. Fourth, tax-exempt institutions benefit from a large tax advantage relative to the other two categories of owners, and this advantage increased strongly during the 1960s and 1970s.

A high aggregate saving and investment rate was an essential part of Swedish economic policy during the first decades of the post-war period (Bergström, 1982). This goal was reached by running large surpluses in the public sector and by having a highly regulated credit market. Throughout the post-war period until the mid-1980s, Swedish capital market policy was aimed at low interest rates for favoured sectors of the economy. The credit volume to the industrial sector was generally subjected to quantitative restrictions and the rate of interest was also regulated, which resulted in a situation of virtually continuous credit rationing. This set of regulations clearly favoured credit access by larger, older, well-established firms and by genuinely capital-intensive firms with ready sources of collateral (see Jonung, 1994). Moreover, having firmly established links to banks was a clear advantage, and the two major ownership spheres (the Wallenberg group and Industrivärden) were both closely tied to a large bank.

The mandatory national pension system (ATP) instituted in 1960 transformed the public sector into the most important supplier of credit. Large surpluses were accumulated in the national pension funds, the so-called 'AP' funds. In the early 1970s the AP funds accounted for 35 per cent of total credit supply (Pontusson, 1992). The decision to accumulate savings to such a great extent in the AP funds led to a massive further

---

[7] By definition, tax-exempt institutions pay no tax on interest receipts, dividends or capital gains. This category includes charities, scientific and cultural foundations, foundations for employee recreation set up by companies, pension funds for supplementary occupational pension schemes and the national pension funds (the 'AP' funds).

Table 7.4. *Household net saving as a percentage of disposable income in Sweden, the OECD and OECD Europe, 1960–1989*

	1960–1969	1970–1979	1980–1989
Sweden	6.1	4.0	1.1
OECD	9.7	12.1	11.2
OECD Europe	12.0	13.6	11.6

Source: OECD (1982, 1997).

institutionalisation of savings, which can be expected to have benefited large, well-established firms with a good credit rating that could operate on a high debt/equity ratio.[8] The AP fund system also benefited incumbents through the so-called 'lending back' system (*återlån*), based on the rule that employers were allowed to borrow up to half the amount they had paid into the fund during the previous year. The potential for using this credit channel was therefore proportional to the wage bill of the firm. This type of lending was abolished in 1987.

The structure of the Swedish tax and pension system reduced incentives for individual wealth accumulation in general, not only in the form of corporate assets. As shown in table 7.4, Swedish household saving was exceptionally low by international comparison through the 1980s. Since the availability of equity financing is a critical factor for both start-ups and the expansion of incumbent firms' equity (Blanchflower and Oswald, 1998; Lindh and Ohlsson, 1996; Holtz-Eakin et al., 1994), this can be expected to contribute to a low prevalence of start-ups and high-growth firms.

Labour market legislation was changed in a number of respects in the first half of the 1970s, aiming to giving labour direct influence on corporate decision-making. Prime examples are union representation on corporate boards of directors and the Codetermination Act of 1976 (see Pontusson, 1992). Moreover, the Employment Security Act (LAS) of 1974 gives employees extensive protection against dismissal. The only legal grounds for dismissal are gross misconduct and redundancies. In the latter case, LAS stipulates a 'last in, first out' principle.

Strict employment security provisions and formalised labour influence on managerial decisions are likely to be more harmful for small and potentially fast-growing employers than for large, well-established firms.

[8] The gradual introduction of mandatory supplementary pension schemes can be expected to have the same effect.

The road from small to large for a fast-growing firm – a 'gazelle' (Birch and Medoff, 1994) – is far from straight, since the activities of new firms, in particular, are subject to genuine uncertainty (Davis et al., 1996; Brown and Medoff, 1989). If, under such circumstances, rules are imposed that reduce the firms' leeway to rapid adjustment, one should expect both a lower willingness to expand in general and fewer firms, despite a good product or a viable idea, growing from small to large in a short period of time.[9]

As documented in many studies – see, for example, Edin and Topel (1997) and Davis and Henrekson (2000) – the Swedish *wage negotiation system* produced a very narrow wage dispersion and high relative wages for low-productivity workers. At the same time, numerous studies show that the wage level increases with the size, age and capital intensity of the firm (e.g. Brown and Medoff, 1989). By implication, the Swedish wage negotiation system has in many cases raised labour costs above a free-market outcome in small, new and labour-intensive firms, and analogously lowered labour costs in large incumbent firms. This fact can be expected to lower the likelihood that small firms become large firms that eventually pay higher wages (Audretsch, 2002).

3.3   Resulting ownership and control structure

Before the 1990/91 tax reform the combined effect of taxation on capital gains, wealth, profits and dividends forcibly discouraged individuals from owning firms, and from wealth accumulation in general. Moreover, the tax system encouraged debt financing, which can be expected to benefit large capital-intensive firms with close ties to specific financial institutions. We have also pointed to some other policies that are likely to be conducive to a development towards large-firm dominance and few and financially weak owners. Do observed outcomes square with these expectations?

Figure 7.2 demonstrates that the expected change in ownership structure actually took place: during the post-war period the household ownership share of listed stock fell sharply from 75 per cent in 1950 to 18 per cent in 1990, while the institutional share rose commensurately.

The fact that the tax code enhanced the accumulation of retained earnings in firms implied that existing corporate wealth owned by households was locked into incumbent firms.[10] According to traditional

---

[9] Davis and Henrekson (2000) discuss these issues more fully.

[10] Deferred tax payments ('hidden reserves') were typically as large as total equity in listed companies in the 1980s (Josefsson, 1988).

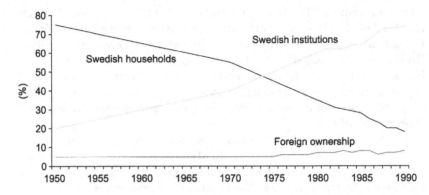

Figure 7.2. The distribution of the ownership of Swedish listed shares as a percentage of market capitalisation, 1950–1990.
Source: Spånt (1975), Norrman and McLure (1997) and data received directly from Statistics Sweden and OM Stockholm Stock Exchange.

financial theory in the Modigliani–Miller tradition, such within-firm saving should be translated into household wealth through appreciated stock market values. In practice, matters did not turn out this way. Until the early 1980s stock market values were extremely depressed,[11] which in most cases implied that the net worth of Swedish companies greatly exceeded their stock market value. Södersten (1984) calculates that Tobin's q (the stock market value of the firms divided by their replacement value) was approximately unity in 1960, and that it fell to 60 per cent in 1970 and further to 30 per cent in 1980. When Tobin's q is below unity there is no incentive to finance investment through new share issues, since it implies wealth destruction. At the same time, there are strong incentives to use internally generated funds to finance investments in incumbent firms, when taxation is high on funds withdrawn from existing firms. As shown in figure 7.3, new equity issues (including initial public offerings – IPOs) fell to negligible levels during the post-war period up to the mid-1980s. Another indication of low market values is given by the price/earnings (P/E) ratios for large Swedish companies. The P/E ratios for firms such as Ericsson, Electrolux and Volvo were typically between 2 and 4 in the 1970s.

---

[11] David and Mach (2004) report that stock market capitalisation was equivalent to only 3 per cent of GDP in Sweden in 1975, compared to 12 per cent for Germany, 30 per cent for Switzerland and 48 per cent for the United States. The figure reported for Sweden in figure 7.2 is higher, which might be due to the use of data from different sources.

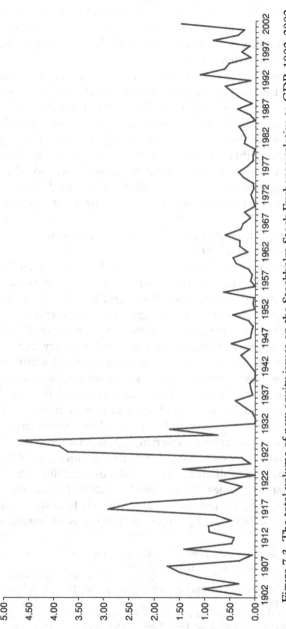

Figure 7.3. The total volume of new equity issues on the Stockholm Stock Exchange relative to GDP, 1902–2002.

Note: The data are the sum of new issues by already listed firms and IPOs.

Source: Own calculations, based on data from Althaimer (1988), *Annual Reports* from the OM Stockholm Stock Exchange and Statistics Sweden.

The combined effect of the tax code and credit market regulations also provided strong incentives to transfer the ownership of closely held firms to institutionally owned investment companies closely connected to a bank. Credit availability was crucial, since debt financing was so heavily subsidised by the tax system.[12]

These tendencies were also reflected in the development of the industry structure and the size distribution of firms. First, the industry distribution of employment and output tilted towards industries that were characterised by large firms and establishments and a compressed wage distribution (Davis and Henrekson, 1997, 2005). Second, there is plenty of evidence indicating that the relative importance of large firms became greater in Sweden than in any other country. Henrekson and Johansson (1999) provide an evaluation of the available evidence.[13] The mirror image of this fact is that the rate of self-employment became low. Between the early 1970s and 1990 Sweden exhibited the lowest ratio of non-agricultural self-employment to civilian employment among all OECD countries (OECD, 1992).

As expected, given the legal impediments, the foreign ownership share also remained low: the foreign ownership share of listed stock never exceeded 8 per cent throughout the 1980s, and less than 5 per cent of private sector employees worked in foreign-owned companies.

Hence, it is clear that the expected development of ownership, financing structure, the size distribution of firms and industry distribution took place. However, the disincentives to private wealth accumulation and the household ownership of corporate stock did not result in a control deficit or an increased tendency to managerial control (Berle and Means, 1932). The widely cited government commission report *Ownership and Influence in Private Industry* (Swedish government, 1967) identified seventeen important ownership groups/families in 1963.[14] Within the next few years ownership concentration increased considerably and by 1967 the Wallenberg family alone controlled ten of the twenty-five largest companies (Glete, 1994, p. 289). Individual wealth was still modest by current standards. Total privately held wealth among the members of the Wallenberg family in 1963 was estimated to be

---

[12] From the mid-1960s to the mid-1980s the debt/equity ratio in listed firms increased from slightly more than unity to four (Josefsson, 1988).

[13] The share of employees in the private sector working in firms with at least 500 employees increased from 27 per cent in 1964 (Swedish government, 1967) to 47 per cent in 1993 (NUTEK, 1995).

[14] The then leader of the Communist Party, C.-H. Hermansson, had already coined the expression 'the fifteen families' in his 1962 book *Monopol och storfinans* (*Monopoly and Big Business*). According to him these fifteen families controlled Swedish industry. The government commission also identified fifteen families and two bank-connected groups.

SEK 125 million (Swedish government 1967), which corresponded to 0.14 per cent of GDP. This can be compared to the estimated wealth of the Kamprad and Rausing families, the founders of IKEA and TetraPak. Their respective wealth was equivalent to some 8 per cent of Swedish GDP in 2001.[15]

Control was upheld and even reinforced through a number of capital-saving control devices, notably dual-class shares, pyramiding and cross-ownership. At any rate, in the late 1960s the Swedish corporatist model reached its apogee, and at the time a handful of ownership groups, represented by identifiable individuals, had crystallised. In fact, concentrated ownership control was a necessary condition for the model to function (see Reiter, 2003).

3.4   The first attack on the model: the wage-earner funds proposal

By the late 1960s there was, therefore, an unusual concentration of ownership control and domination by large firms in Swedish industry. Schumpeter (1942) asserts that, in an economy increasingly dominated by giant corporations and devoid of entrepreneurs, capitalism has no constituency. Instead, capitalism will have to confront increasing hostility. Eventually, a democratic and peaceful transformation of the economy to socialism will take place. It was indeed the case that popular support for capitalism was extremely low in Sweden by the mid- to late 1970s.[16]

Consistent with Schumpeter's thesis, the labour movement was strongly radicalised in the early 1970s. This was reflected in two ways: open demands for the socialisation of control rights in enterprises and a quest for increased influence by pressing for legislation in labour's favour (Stephens, 1979). During the 1970s the blue-collar workers' trade union, the Swedish Trade Union Confederation (the LO), was very successful in inducing the government to take a number of legislative measures aiming at giving labour direct influence on corporate

---

[15] These families left Sweden in the 1970s. Kamprad and one branch of the Rausing family are residents of Switzerland. In 2002 they were ranked first and second in terms of individual wealth in Switzerland. The individual wealth of today's richest family in Sweden, the Persson family (founders and controlling owner of H&M), was equivalent to roughly 2 per cent of GDP in 2002. Special legislation passed in the mid-1990s has exempted this and other super-rich families from wealth taxation on their stockholdings.

[16] In 1978 only 30 per cent of the respondents in a poll believed that it was important to encourage entrepreneurship and firm formation and only 37 per cent of the respondents believed that business leaders/entrepreneurs were most efficient in running a firm; see Henrekson and Jakobsson (2001).

decision-making.[17] The radicalisation of the labour movement in the early 1970s also entailed explicit demands for increased collective ownership.[18]

These demands were voiced on a grand scale at the 1976 LO congress, where Rudolf Meidner and his colleagues presented a plan for an inexorable transfer of ownership from private hands to collective 'wage-earner funds' – (see Meidner, 1978). This can be interpreted as a concrete plan for implementing Wigforss's original vision of converting the large corporations into 'social enterprises without owners'.

The wage-earner fund scheme entailed a gradual transfer of ownership of all firms with more than fifty employees to wage-earners as a collective group. The firms should be obliged to issue new shares to the wage-earner funds corresponding to a value of 20 per cent of the profits. Thus, the transfer of ownership would be more rapid the more profitable the firm. Incidentally, assuming a rate of profit of 10 per cent, it would take thirty-five years for the wage-earner funds to obtain a majority equity share in the individual company. The wage-earner equity thus acquired was intended to remain within the firm as working capital. The voting rights and other ownership prerogatives were to be exercised by the trade unions (including representatives of other interests in society).[19]

Understandably, the wage-earner fund proposals met with unprecedented opposition from capital owners.[20] Moreover, the original Meidner proposal never gained full acceptance within the Social Democratic Party, and subsequent joint proposals from the LO and the Social Democratic Party were less radical than the original plan. Politically, any proposals were blocked from being carried out until the Social Democrats were returned to power in 1982. At this stage public opinion had shifted against wage-earner funds, but under pressure from the LO the government introduced a considerably watered down version

[17] In addition, labour strengthened its relative position during this period, with legislation on job security, substantially increased powers for the local trade union safety officer, extended rights for elected trade union officials to get paid time off work for trade union activities, etc.

[18] This also became the ideological line of the Social Democratic Party. When the then party leader Olof Palme presented the new party platform in 1975, he explained that the Swedish labour movement was moving to the third stage of its long struggle to transform capitalist society. The first two stages were political democracy and co-determination, and the third stage was economic democracy.

[19] It is interesting to note that this form of socialisation was in line with Schumpeter's (1942) prediction of 'laborism' as the last stage of capitalism.

[20] The wage-earner funds were probably important also in that they provided the igniting spark that mobilised Swedish industrialists in defence of private ownership and entrepreneurship; see Blyth (2001) for a discussion.

in 1984. These funds were abolished in 1992 by the non-socialist government that had come to power in the election of the previous year.

A fundamental consequence of the wage-earner fund battle was a dismantling of the controversy on the ownership issue. There were no more serious demands for a collectivisation of corporate control and ownership. On the other hand, the tax system was not reformed in order to facilitate the emergence of new, individually held corporate wealth.

4. A new regulatory environment

During the 1970s the major industrial countries witnessed a renaissance of the liberal market economy. Somewhat belatedly relative to the leading countries, Sweden embarked on a comprehensive reform track. First, the capital markets were reformed in a number of steps. This is outlined in table 7.5. Without going into details, we note that domestic credit markets were fully deregulated by 1986 and the deregulation of capital markets, including restrictions on foreign ownership, was completed in 1993.

Table 7.5. *Major steps in the deregulation of Swedish capital markets*

Permission for corporations and municipalities to borrow abroad	1974
Deregulation of banks' deposit rates	1978
Deregulation of interest rates on corporate bonds	1980
Deregulation of lending rates by insurance companies	1980
Banks granted permission to issue certificates of deposit	1980
Liquidity ratios for banks abolished	1983
Deregulation of banks' lending rates	1985
Loan ceiling on bank lending lifted	1985
Marginal placement ratios for banks and insurance companies abolished	1986
Relaxation of foreign exchange controls on stock transactions	1986–88
Remaining foreign exchange controls lifted	1989
Removal or annulment of:	
regulation for establishment of foreign banks' branches	1990
regulation for foreign acquisition of shares in Swedish commercial banks, broker firms and finance companies	1990
regulation for establishment of financial institutions other than banks	1991
restrictions on foreign acquisition of Swedish companies	1992
trade permit requirement for foreigners	1992
restrictions in the articles of associations regarding foreigners' right to acquire shares in Swedish companies	1993
Payments Services Act	1993

Source: Reiter (2003), Henrekson (1992) and Jonung (1994).

Table 7.6. *Effective marginal tax rates for different combinations of owners and sources of finance (10 per cent real pre-tax rate of return at actual inflation rates), 1980, 1994 and 2001*

	Debt	New share issues	Retained earnings
1991			
Households	31.7	61.8	54.2
Tax-exempt institutions	−9.4	4.0	18.7
Insurance companies	14.4	33.3	31.6
1994			
Households	32.0/27.0[a]	28.3/18.3[a]	36.5/26.5[a]
Tax-exempt institutions	−14.9	21.8	21.8
Insurance companies	0.7	32.3	33.8
2001			
Households	29.7/24.7[a]	61.0/51.0[a]	44.1/34.1[a]
Tax exempt institutions	−1.4	23.6	23.6
Insurance companies	19.6	47.2	44.7

Note: [a]Excluding wealth tax; the wealth tax on unlisted shares was abolished in 1992. The calculations conform to the general framework developed in King and Fullerton (1984). The average holding period is assumed to be ten years.
Source: Calculations provided by Jan Södersten; see Södersten (1993)and Braunerhjelm (2003).

The earlier tax-favouring of debt financing presupposed strictly regulated capital markets. However, the tax system remained virtually unchanged while capital markets were deregulated, creating an asset price bubble in the latter half of the 1980s (Jonung, 1994; Norrman and McLure, 1997). There were a series of reforms to the tax system between 1985 and 1994; most important were the reforms of 1990/91,[21] when the distortions in tax bands across different owners and sources of finance were to a large extent evened out. Since 1995 the differences in tax bands have increased once again, largely following the previous pattern; see table 7.6.

The new system represented a significant step towards neutrality among Swedish owners. However, the tax burden on Swedish individual ownership remained heavier than the tax burden on individual ownership in most other countries.

Table 7.7 reports a representative tax calculation for different owners using the 2002 tax code. The fact that individuals are disfavoured relative to institutions is once again evident. This also applies relative to foreign institutions. Moreover, it is clear from table 7.8 that a large

---

[21] Agell et al. (1998) provide a detailed examination of the 1990/91 tax reform.

Table 7.7. *The taxation of dividends for different owner categories according to the 2002 tax code – investment of SEK 10,000 and 10 per cent return paid as a dividend*

	Swedish household	Swedish pension fund	Swedish foundation	Foreign investment fund
Corporate tax (SEK)	280	280	280	280
Income tax (SEK)	216	90	0	0
Wealth tax (SEK)	120	0	0	0
Net return (SEK)	384	630	720	720
Tax rate (%)	62	37	28	28

Note: The household is assumed to pay full wealth tax (on 80 per cent of the market value) on its shareholdings. An individual foreign owner has the same tax burden as a foreign investment fund in those countries where there is no wealth tax on shareholdings and where dividends are taxed at the firm level only.

number of countries have a lower level of taxation of shareholdings for individuals than Sweden. Hence, the combined effect of foreign and Swedish taxation is a favouring of all kinds of foreign ownership relative to Swedish individual ownership.

Some deregulatory measures were also taken in the labour market, and several previously regulated product markets have been deregulated, such as telecommunications (1993), electricity (1996), domestic airlines (1992), the financial sector (1993) and postal services (1993). In addition, EU membership in 1995 and the generally increased integration of product and capital markets have contributed to the erosion of the old corporatist model.

5.   Ownership and control through the late 1990s

We noted in section 2 that the Swedish corporatist model reached its apogee in the late 1960s, when industry was dominated by a small number of identifiable actors and agreements could be struck between elites. Although one outcome of the wage-earner fund battle was a broad acceptance of private ownership in the industrial sector, policies with respect to taxation, savings and labour legislation continued – albeit to a lesser extent than previously – to promote a move towards institutionalised ownership, the increased predominance of large capital-intensive firms and higher debt/equity ratios.

However, the concentration of control rights continued to increase in firms listed on the Stockholm Stock Exchange until the late 1990s. The

Table 7.8. *Some important aspects of the taxation of shareholders in selected industrialised countries, 2000*

No taxation of dividends at the owner level	No wealth tax	Low wealth tax/large exemptions and/or low/no taxation of dividends	No capital gains tax on long-term holdings	Capital gains tax > 0 but ≤ 20% on long-term holdings
Finland	Australia[a]	Finland	Austria	Ireland
France	Austria	France	Belgium	Italy
Germany	Belgium	Luxembourg	Denmark	Japan
Greece	Canada	Portugal	Germany	Luxembourg[d]
Italy	Denmark	Spain	Greece	Norway
Luxembourg	Germany	Switzerland	Luxembourg	Poland
New Zealand[a]	Greece		Mexico	Spain
Norway	Ireland		Netherlands	United States
Spain	Italy		Poland	
United Kingdom	Japan		Portugal	
	Netherlands[b]		South Korea[a]	
	New Zealand		United Kingdom[c]	
	Poland			
	Portugal			
	United Kingdom			
	United States			

[a]Pertains to 1999.
[b]Effective as of 2001.
[c]Large exemption.
[d]50 per cent of the income tax rate – i.e. a maximum rate of 23 per cent.
Note: The definition of 'long-term holdings' varies between three months and five years. In some instances the situation refers to a representative case.
Source: The Federation of Swedish Industries, Institutet för Utländsk Rätt and the *European Tax Handbook* (published by KPMG).

most important control mechanisms used dual-class shares, pyramiding and cross- or circular ownership. The use of dual-class shares to ensure concentrated control increased strongly after the mid-1960s – see table 7.9. During the quarter-century from 1968 to 1992 the percentage of listed companies using dual-class shares increased from 32 to 87 per cent.

The most important means for wielding control of the largest firms have been (and in many cases still are) closed-end investment funds organised as pyramid holding companies. These investment companies

Table 7.9. *The percentage of listed companies on the Stockholm Stock Exchange with dual-class shares, selected years 1968–1998*

Year	Share	Number of firms	Year	Share	Number of firms
1968	32	146	1986	74	217
1972	36	134	1992	87	202
1977	44	130	1998	63	304
1981	54	128			

Source: Bergström and Rydqvist (1990), Isaksson and Skog (1994) and Agnblad et al. (2001).

enjoy a privileged tax status. Capital gains and dividends on their holdings are tax-exempt. The only tax levied is a flat tax on the net worth of total holdings at year's end.[22] This is currently 1.5 per cent, but new legislation in 2003 has made investment companies wholly tax-exempt as long as the voting rights in their respective holdings exceed 10 per cent. The most important of these investment companies were started as a result of legislation in 1934 that prohibited banks from owning stock. As shown by Petersson (2001), a second wave of new investment companies were formed in the first half of the 1960s. They all had close ties to specific banks, and in a detailed analysis of six of them Petersson documents a total of 111 acquisitions of mostly medium-sized family-owned firms in the 1962–1989 period. In some cases large firms were acquired: nineteen of the acquisitions were firms with more than 500 employees. In 1971 there were as many as nineteen investment companies listed on the stock exchange (Lindgren, 1994b). This development was inevitable given the extent to which the tax system penalised individual ownership of firms. During this period a great many entrepreneurs sold their firms to investment companies or to other large firms and emigrated.[23]

The deregulation of domestic capital markets in the 1980s (see table 7.5) provided ample opportunities for new actors on the ownership market; the unique position of bank-connected ownership groups was quickly undermined. The requisite capital could be mobilised for (sometimes hostile) takeovers, asset-stripping, etc. During the 1980s there was also an explosion of takeover activity. In the 1950s there was roughly one

[22] This tax can be avoided in full if the investment company pays dividends to its owner that are at least as large as the sum of the dividends received and the flat tax.
[23] Lindkvist (1990) finds that 30,000 Swedes who emigrated in the 1965–1989 period were granted permission by the Swedish central bank to export capital from Sweden.

corporate takeover per year in the Swedish stock market. This increased to an annual average of three in the 1960s, and four in the 1970s (Isaksson and Skog, 1994). In the period 1980 to 1992 there were 253 takeover bids among firms where both the bidder and the target were listed on the Stockholm Stock Exchange, and 212 of those bids were successful (Agnblad et al., 2001).

In order to fend off these new threats, cross-holding arrangements emerged. Cross-holdings hardly existed in the 1970s, but they rapidly gained in importance during the 1980s: by 1988 there were twenty-six cases among listed companies of cross- or circular ownership where the companies involved held at least 2 per cent of each other's voting rights (Isaksson and Skog, 1994).

The use of dual-class shares, pyramiding and the numerous takeovers led to a substantial increase in the concentration of ownership control; the average voting power of the largest single owner in listed companies increased by roughly 15 percentage points between the late 1970s and 1991. In the 165 firms with voting right differentials of 1 to 10 in 1991, the largest owner on average held a voting share of 53 per cent (Isaksson and Skog, 1994).[24]

Following the removal of all foreign exchange controls and all barriers to foreign ownership of Swedish firms and real estate, a number of changes ensued. First, the foreign ownership share of listed shares began to increase rapidly. As shown in figure 7.4, the foreign ownership share went from 7 per cent in 1989, when foreign exchange controls were lifted, to 40 per cent ten years later. Domestic institutions lowered their share almost as much. The foreign ownership share decreased somewhat in 2001–2002 following the sharp drop in the valuation of firms in the information technology (IT) sector.

Even more importantly, as shown in figure 7.5, the number of employees in wholly foreign-owned companies (in most cases wholly-owned subsidiaries or branches of foreign multinationals) has grown rapidly in Sweden over the last two decades. In 1980 approximately 113,000 Swedes were employed in foreign firms. By 2001 this figure had risen to 520,000, and more than one out of five employees in the business sector (21 per cent) worked for a foreign firm (ITPS, 2002).[25]

---

[24] The capital ownership share averaged 35 per cent.

[25] The trend is similar in all industrialised countries, but it is much more pronounced in Sweden. From the mid-1990s inward FDI has been very large in Sweden, both in an absolute sense and compared to other countries. On average, it corresponded to 55 per cent of total gross investment. This figure may be compared to a corresponding level of 31 per cent in Ireland, the country that is usually mentioned in this context (UNCTAD, 1999; OECD, 1992).

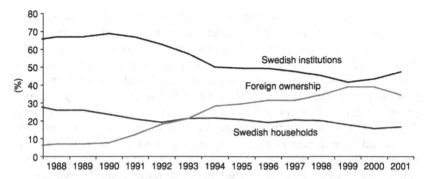

Figure 7.4. The distribution of the ownership of Swedish listed shares as a percentage of market capitalisation, 1988–2001.
Source: Data received directly from Statistics Sweden and OM Stockholm Stock Exchange.

Figure 7.5. Employees in foreign-owned firms in Sweden and their share of all employees in the Swedish private sector, 1980–2001.
Source: Strandell (2000) and ITPS (2002).

Until the late 1980s foreigners established themselves in Sweden mainly by making greenfield investments. But, after ASEA merged with Brown Boveri in 1987, to become a Swiss-based company, many – often very large – Swedish firms have been acquired by foreign owners.[26]

---

[26] The predominance of foreign ownership is particularly evident in the pharmaceutical industry, with an ownership share of 86 percent in 2001.

Foreign owners have thus strengthened their control of the Swedish corporate sector considerably through the acquisition of Swedish firms. In terms of total activity, most of this increase concerns the acquisition of firms listed on the Stockholm Stock Exchange and controlled by Swedish owners.[27] Nevertheless, the control of listed firms became even more concentrated, at least until the late 1990s. Agnblad et al. (2001) provide a detailed analysis of the control situation among the 304 listed firms in late 1998. At that point, the largest shareholder on average controlled 38 per cent of the voting rights, in 34 per cent of the firms the controlling owner had more than 50 per cent of the votes, and 82 per cent of the firms had a well-defined owner with more than 25 per cent of the votes, which in practice implied operational control of the firm. Hence, the typical firm had *one* clearly identifiable controlling owner. In most cases the controlling owner was a family or a single individual (in 62 per cent of all listed firms).

IPO activity also gradually became very intense in Sweden, beginning in the early 1980s. Holmén and Högfeldt (2004) report 352 new listings on the Stockholm Stock Exchange between 1979 and 1997. The number of new listings in the years 1998 to 2001 was thirty-five, fifty-four, sixty-two and twenty-four, respectively. Hence, there was a virtual explosion of IPOs in the late 1990s. This activity came to an almost complete standstill after the bursting of the IT bubble, and in 2002 the number of IPOs was just ten. Among the 352 IPOs examined by Holmén and Högfeldt, 69 per cent of the firms were family- or individually controlled. The private owners in control normally retained all shares with high voting power (A-shares), and on average they kept 68.5 per cent of the voting rights after the IPO. If the firm remained intact after five years and if it had not suffered severe financial problems, the original owners still possessed two-thirds of the votes five years after the IPO. If sold, control blocks were always sold wholesale in a block transfer, or at the time of takeover, in order to protect control rents (Bebchuk et al., 2000).

Among the largest firms, investment companies organised as pyramid holding companies become important vehicles for control. Following the profound changes in the tax system in the early 1990s most of the investment companies were gradually dismantled. However, two of them, Investor AB and Industrivärden, gradually strengthened their control even further. Investor is privately controlled by the Wallenberg family and Industrivärden is institutionally controlled by a management

---

[27] Henrekson and Jakobsson (2002) document that about thirty listed companies were sold to foreign owners following the ASEA–Brown Boweri deal in 1987 until the end of 2000.

team closely tied to Handelsbanken. Agnblad et al. (2001) report that, in 1998, Investor – i.e. the Wallenberg sphere – controlled fourteen large listed firms with a market value comprising 42 per cent of the total market capitalisation at the Stockholm Stock Exchange. With an ownership share of 19.4 per cent (41.3 per cent of the votes) the Wallenberg foundations had total control of Investor. Investor's share of the total market capitalisation was, in turn, 4.6 per cent. Hence, the Wallenberg foundation's ownership of approximately 1 per cent of the total market value of the stock exchange was sufficient to control 42 per cent of the total market value (see figure 7.6).

Similarly, the Handelsbanken sphere, through Industrivärden, controlled eleven listed companies, which constituted 12 per cent of the total market capitalisation. Jointly, the two ownership spheres thus

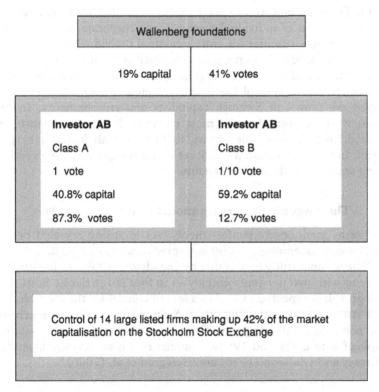

Figure 7.6. The Wallenberg control of Swedish firms through Investor AB, 1999.
Source: Investor AB (1999).

controlled 54 per cent of the total market value, using two closed-end funds with a combined market value of 6.2 per cent of the stock exchange.

In summary, in the late 1990s the Stockholm Stock Exchange was characterised by an extreme separation of ownership and control. In particular, it is evident that the Wallenberg family is much more proficient than other well-established families in taking advantage of the ownership vacuum brought about by the far-reaching institutionalisation of ownership during the post-war period (Lindgren, 1994a). Moreover, it is evident that founders of firms that go public with few exceptions manage to retain full control of their firms, and, consequently, that external investors have been willing to acquire sizeable ownership rights without demanding any influence. This extreme division of ownership and control is explained by the contradictory ways that tax policies and corporate laws have treated owners of individual wealth. The main objective of tax policies in this area has been to curtail the accumulation of individual wealth, while corporate laws have provided ample opportunities for entrepreneurial individuals or families to base the control of a firm on a relatively small amount of capital.

The structure of incentives has gone against private wealth formation while concentrated control has been promoted. These incentives have affected the norms of Swedish capitalists and entrepreneurs. In this section we have seen that the most powerful Swedish capitalists are prepared, to a considerable extent, to forgo wealth in order to gain control. In the next section we shall see that this pattern is also prevalent among smaller Swedish entrepreneurs.

6.   The Swedish ownership model at the crossroads

The norms mentioned manifest themselves in strong revealed preferences for control among Swedish entrepreneurs/business owners in general. The seminal study here is that by Davidsson (1989). In his study of 400 firms with two to twenty employees in four industries he finds that, when growth is expected to lead to a loss of control for the founder, this has a strong growth-deterring effect. Wiklund et al. (2003) reach the same result in a follow-up on this study where they look at a larger sample of firms in the mid-1990s.[28] Similar results are reached in studies by Cressy and Olofsson (1996) and Berggren et al. (2000).

---

[28] Saemundson (1999) looks specifically at university spin-offs, where he finds a similar pattern. These firms are often unwilling to grow if that results in a loss of control and independence.

In a similar vein, Holmén and Högfeldt (2004) find that family-owned firms with large growth potential tend to be undercapitalised relative to comparable firms with a different control structure. As a result, the family-controlled firms invest less than the comparable firms, since the equity requirements would reduce the family's control of the firm.[29]

This revealed preference for control relative to growth is quite consistent with an institutional environment that makes it very risky to aim at rapid growth, and, moreover, with a regulatory package penalising individual wealth accumulation, the opportunity cost for forgoing growth is lowered.

There are many indications that the observed 'control culture' is detrimental to growth and economic dynamism in the corporate sector. It is illuminating to compare this culture with the one that seems to be dominating in successful clusters in the US economy. A typical feature of US venture capitalism is that the entrepreneur who has started up a firm is bought out by the venture capitalist at an early stage of the life cycle of a firm.[30] While the entrepreneur loses control he or she often gets very wealthy through the buy-out and the selling of his/her remaining stock when both the venture capitalist and the entrepreneur exit in an IPO (Gompers and Lerner, 2001). The entrepreneur as well as the venture capitalist typically use their acquired wealth to invest in new projects. Obviously, this is a model that could be expected to be more conducive to start-ups and new firm growth than the Swedish model, where the entrepreneur often clings to the control of his start-up throughout his entrepreneurial career.

Empirical observations clearly confirm this expectation. Not a single one of the fifty largest firms in Sweden in 2000 was founded after 1969 (figure 7.7). This may be compared to the very different situation in the United States in recent decades, where new and fast-growing firms are generating not just most of the jobs but also the new industries (Audretsch and Thurik, 2000). In 2002 roughly 60 per cent of the fifty largest firms in the United States had been founded later than 1970.

Let us now turn to the current and likely development of the control structure in the large-firm sector. The Wallenbergs are currently waning in importance. In 1998 Investor AB controlled fourteen large listed firms (Agnblad et al., 2001). In late 2002 Investor retained a voting share exceeding 20 per cent in just seven listed firms (Ericsson, Saab,

---

[29] This is consistent with the findings by Morck et al. (2000) on Canadian data. They find that firms where control has been inherited grow more slowly than comparable firms with a dispersed ownership structure.

[30] Empirical evidence of this process is given by Hellman and Puri (2002).

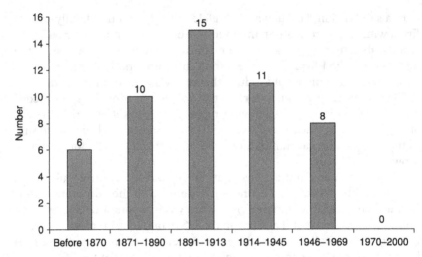

Figure 7.7. The period of establishment of Sweden's fifty largest private corporations by turnover, 2000.
Source: NUTEK and ALMI (2001).

WM-Data, Atlas Copco, Electrolux, Gambro and SEB), and they had a voting share of 15 per cent in Scania and 17 per cent in OM. Except for Investor and Industrivärden (and to a lesser extent Kinnevik), the numerous investment companies have either vanished completely through asset-stripping or been downsized through share redemption schemes or a transfer of the shares in individual companies directly to the shareholders of the investment company on a pro rata basis. As a result, investment companies are losing in importance as control vehicles on the Swedish stock market.

The main reasons for this development have to do with the growth and the internationalisation of the stock market. In this environment investment companies do not have the capacity to expand or the flexibility that is needed in order to keep their position. There are several reasons for this. First, the shares of investment companies trade at a significant discount relative to the net portfolio value of their assets. This is no recent phenomenon. As shown in figure 7.8, Investor has always traded at a discount relative to the net value of its assets. At times this discount has been as high as 40 per cent. As long as the investment companies trade at a discount, they cannot issue new equity; given that the overall stock market is growing, it is therefore virtually impossible for them to expand their resources in tandem with the growth of the aggregate market.

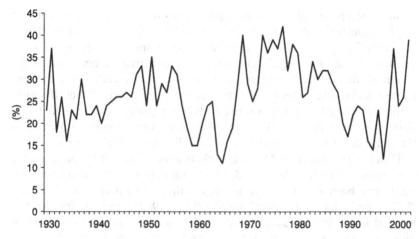

Figure 7.8. The discount on Investor AB's share price relative to its net asset value, 1930–2002.
Source: Lindgren (1994b) and Investor AB (2003).

Second, their control is often based on historical holdings of A-shares with great voting power. A-shares in other firms are often hard to come by, and when barred from the issuance of new equity, the best an investment company can do is to retain control of its historical holdings. Third, investment companies are not fully tax-exempt; a flat tax of 1.5 per cent of its net asset value at the end of the year is levied. This tax can be avoided if the investment company pays large dividends to its share-holders, but that weakens its potential for retaining control even more.[31] Fourth, the companies controlled by means of a high voting share and small capital share have suffered from low valuation. In two spectacular cases (Electrolux and SKF) this has already forced Investor to reduce voluntarily the voting rights of the A-shares from 1,000 to 10 (Reiter, 2003). Following prolonged and heated discussion, Ericsson was the last remaining to reduce its voting share differential from 1:1,000 to 1:10.[32]

In many cases, and in the case of the Wallenberg family in particular, the power is tied to share holdings by a family foundation at the top of the pyramid. The family foundations are tax-exempt, but, as a prerequis-ite for tax exemption, family foundations are obligated to donate 80 per cent of their dividend income to charity. This not only diminishes their

[31] Effective from 2003 this tax can be largely avoided, since it is not levied on holdings where the investment company's voting share is at least 10 per cent.
[32] In the case of Electrolux this measure reduced the voting share of the Wallenberg sphere from 94 to 25 per cent.

financial strength, but it is also suspiciously similar to a tax – except that the foundation is able to determine how the 'tax' will be used. Thus, although family foundations are fully tax-exempt, they are as a consequence of the same legislation financially constrained and can hardly generate the means to expand as rapidly as the overall stock market. Furthermore, the system generates incentive problems. When dynastic ambitions cease to serve as a sufficiently strong incentive, family foundations will no longer be able to maintain their competence as owners to the same degree as those who can freely dispose of their returns.

That the globalisation of asset markets generally tends to penalise the owners of firms with a large wedge between control rights and cash-flow rights has been observed by, amongst others, Giannetti and Simonov (2005) and Denis and McConnell (2003). When the playing field is levelled across investors and sources of finance, the tax incentives for low dividends and financing through retained earnings go down. This spurs the valuation of firms, and it once again becomes attractive to finance expansion by issuing new equity. The choice for the old owners now becomes very difficult: they either have to refrain from rapid expansion, thereby forgoing business opportunities and/or risking a takeover bid, or they have to dilute their ownership share and control rights.

7.   The future ownership model: obstacles and challenges

From the analysis in the previous two sections it is clear that the traditional Swedish ownership and control model is currently under attack. First, a progressively larger share of savings is being channelled to institutions, as a result of a number of factors: a larger proportion of the pension system is funded and voluntary pensions saving schemes are greatly favoured by the tax system. Second, the central government has stopped selling out its stockholding and has emerged as the largest owner on the Stockholm Stock Exchange, with more than 5.6 per cent of total holdings (as at December 2002).[33] Third, investment companies cannot raise capital through equity issues, and hence they are doomed to decrease in relative importance over time. Fourth, institutional investors become increasingly unwilling to accept dual-class shares, thereby putting pressure on listed firms to reduce the differential between cash-flow and control rights.

In table 7.10 we list the total assets of state and corporatist pension funds as of mid-2002. It is clear that their assets are very large relative to the total stock market; their total assets exceed 50 per cent of the total

---

[33] Sundin and Sundqvist (2003).

Table 7.10. *Assets and domestic stock market investments by state and corporatist pension funds, 2002*

Fund	Investments on the Swedish stock market	Total assets
AFA Försäkring[a]	16.2	145.5
Alecta[a]	42.7	296.3
AMF Pension[a]	29.9	184.9[b]
AMF Pension fonder[a]	5.0	
Andra AP-fonden[a]	16.7	126.4
Banco Fonder	4.6	
Fjärde AP-fonden[a]	21.1	122.7
Första AP-fonden[a]	12.3	126.6
HQ Fonder	3.8	
KP Pension och försäkring[a]	3.7	38.5
Länsförsäkringar fonder	5.1	
Nordea fonder	26.1	
Robur fonder	50.5	
SEB fonder	26.9	
SEB-SPP Trygg försäkring	13.0	
SHB fonder	22.0	
Skandia	24.5	
Skandia Carlson fonder	7.7	
Tredje AP-fondena	16.8	129.7
Total domestic funds	348.6	
Total stock market capitalisation	1,648.0	
Ownership share of domestic funds (%)	21.2	
Total assets, state and corporatist funds[c]		1,170.6
Investment capacity of state and corporatist funds as a share of total stock market capitalisation (%)[c]		> 70

[a]Denotes a state or corporatist pension fund.
[b]Group.
[c]As at 30 June 2002.
Note: All data, unless otherwise specified, are in billions of Kronor as at 30 December 2002.
Source: Sundin and Sundqvist (2003, p. 32), annual financial reports.

market capitalisation of the Stockholm Stock Exchange, and, given the all-encompassing pensions saving schemes, these funds are bound to increase in importance as a source of finance relative to other sources.

So, what is the likely future for the Swedish ownership and control model under current circumstances? It is hard to see that any *one* model will supersede the traditional control model. Instead a number of new ownership models are likely to gain in importance at the expense of the old model.

(1) *Foreign ownership.* In this case Swedish firms become subsidiaries to foreign-owned firms, typically large multinationals.

(2) *Dispersed ownership.* In this case the firm may have both Swedish and foreign owners, with no owners exercising overall control. This is likely to lead to management control.

(3) *Corporatist or state pension funds as control owners.* This is a likely model in a number of cases in the future, since these funds, together with the government, are the largest owners on the stock exchange.

(4) *An entrepreneur backed by corporatist funds or the government.* This model is a highly likely variant of model number (3). In particular, in a time of crisis for a particular firm it is easy to conceive of situations in which government and corporatist money lines up with trusted individual investors or a private group.

One of the problems with the decline of the old model is that the emerging 'pension-fund capitalism' presupposes that the tax system makes room for tax-efficient performance contracts that induce entrepreneurs, portfolio managers and venture capitalists to behave as if they invested their own private money. However, the use of stock options to encourage and reward entrepreneurial behaviour among employees is highly penalised by the tax system, since gains on options are taxed as wage income when the stock options are tied to employment. Thus, they are subjected both to mandatory social security (33 per cent) and the marginal tax rate. Since the marginal tax rate is roughly 57 per cent, this entails a total tax rate of 68 per cent in 2002).[34]

In practice, therefore, stock options cannot be used as a means to reward entrepreneurial behaviour among wealth-constrained individuals. Neither can they be used efficiently to reward venture capitalists or portfolio managers who invest in venture capital firms. Venture capital firms can play a crucial role in the development of a small entrepreneurial venture, by converting high-risk opportunities to a more

---

[34] This stands in stark contrast to the United States, where an employee who accepts stock options can defer the tax liability to the time when the stocks are sold rather than when the options are exercised. In general, there are (i) no tax consequences to the employee upon the grant or the exercise of the option; (ii) the employee is taxed at capital gains rates when the stock acquired upon the exercise of the option is sold after a specified holding period; and (iii) there is no deduction available to the employer. This change in the law shifted the tax risk in the options back to the government, and thus accomplished two things: it increased the potential profit from the stock options, and it allowed budget-constrained individuals to sell stocks whenever they chose to do so (Misher, 1984).

acceptable risk level through portfolio diversification and by adding key competencies that the firm may be lacking. This is achieved by means of developing arrangements that align the incentives of the three agents – investors, venture capitalists and entrepreneurs (Zider, 1998; Gompers and Lerner, 2001; Kaplan and Strömberg, 2001). However, the above-described tax schedules apply to this industry as well, which means that a venture capital industry domiciled in Sweden cannot use high-powered incentives to reward investment managers.[35]

8.   Conclusions

We have documented the fact that corporate control in Sweden has been highly concentrated; even among listed companies most firms have been controlled by a single individual or a single family. At the same time, economic policies have been working against private wealth accumulation. The concentrated control has been made possible by a growing disparity between control rights and cash-flow rights for the dominant owners. A number of devices have been used to achieve this, the most important of which have been dual-class shares and pyramiding, with tax-favoured closed-end investment funds as the prime control vehicle.

Thus, the Swedish corporatist model shows a number of similarities with corporatist models on the European continent, but there are also traits that are unique for Sweden. First, the concentration of corporate control in Sweden became higher than in other European countries. Second, the equity on which the control is based is thinner in Sweden than in other corporatist European economies (Agnblad et al., 2001). This latter trait makes the Swedish model of control especially vulnerable to the threats posed by globalisation and the increasing dominance of pension funds on global stock markets.

A major threat to the Swedish model emerged in the late 1970s, when the proposals to introduce wage-earner funds gained considerable popular support. According to the most far-reaching proposals this would have led to a complete – albeit gradual – trade union takeover of the entire Swedish business sector, excepting the very smallest firms. With hindsight, the ideological battle that ensued marked the end point of the socialist vision that had been so important in Swedish politics for decades. Following the dismantling of the wage-earner funds, numerous market-oriented policy reforms have been implemented and demands for the socialisation of the private sector have been removed from the Social Democrats' political agenda.

---

[35] See Henrekson and Rosenberg (2001) for a fuller exposition of this issue.

In the long run the new, more market liberal order has undermined the traditional Swedish corporate control model. Paradoxically, this may lead to a situation where a large part of the control of the private sector becomes collectivised. Since the mid-1980s politically or trade-union-governed funds have grown rapidly. Their financial resources are becoming very large relative to other ownership groups. Moreover, the total international openness of the market for corporate control makes it increasingly difficult for traditional control owners to retain their control based on a tenuous capital base. The loss of control will, for the most part, take either of two forms: the sale of entire firms, mostly to foreign owners, and the voluntary reduction of control rights as a response to pressure from minority investors who are increasingly unwilling to accept large differentials between control and cash-flow rights.

To sum up, we have shown that the traditional Swedish ownership and control model is about to lose its dominant position and that a number of different control paths are likely to emerge. None of them is without its problems. The current quandary is not unique for Sweden, however. Similar problems characterise most of Continental Europe. A major challenge for the near future is to find new ways of ascertaining the existence of actors who can successfully assume the ownership role in the corporate sector.

REFERENCES

Agell, J., P. Englund and J. Södersten (1998), *Incentives and Redistribution in the Welfare State. The Swedish Tax Reform*, Macmillan, London.
Agnblad, J., E. Berglöf, P. Högfeldt and H. Svancar (2001), 'Ownership and control in Sweden: strong owners, weak minorities, and social control', in: F. Barca and M. Becht (eds.) *The Control of Corporate Europe*, Oxford University Press, Oxford, 228–58.
Althaimer, H. (1988), 'Börsen och företagens nyemissioner', in: I. Hägg (ed.) *Stockholms Fondbörs. Riskkapitalmarknad i omvandling*, SNS Förlag, Stockholm, 39–56.
Audretsch, D. B. (2002), 'The dynamic role of small firms: evidence from the US', *Small Business Economics*, 18 (1), 13–40.
Audretsch, D. B., and A. R. Thurik (2000), 'Capitalism and democracy in the 21st century: from the managed to the entrepreneurial economy', *Journal of Evolutionary Economics*, 10 (1), 17–34.
Bebchuk, L. A., R. Kraakman and G. Triantis (2000), 'Stock pyramids, cross-ownership, and dual-class equity: The creation and agency costs of separating control from ownership rights', in: *Concentrated Corporated Ownership 2000*, NBER Conference Report Series, University of Chicago Press, Chicago and London, 295–315.
Berggren, B., G. Lindström and C. Olofsson (2000), 'Control aversion and the search for external financing', *Small Business Economics*, 15 (3), 233–42.

Bergström, C., and K. Rydqvist (1990), 'Ownership of equity in dual-class firms', *Journal of Banking and Finance*, 14 (2), 255–69.

Bergström, V. (1982), *Studies in Swedish Post-War Industrial Investments*, dissertation, Department of Economics, Uppsala University.

Berle, A. A., and G. C. Means (1932), *The Modern Corporation and Private Property*, Macmillan, New York.

Birch, D. L., and J. Medoff (1994), 'Gazelles', in: L. C. Solmon and A. R Levenson (eds.) *Labor Markets, Employment Policy and Job Creation*, Westview Press, Boulder, CO, and London, 159–65.

Blanchflower, D. G., and A. J. Oswald (1998), 'What makes an entrepreneur?', *Journal of Labor Economics*, 16 (1), 26–60.

Blyth, M. (2001), 'The transformation of the Swedish model', *World Politics*, 54 (1), 1–26.

Braunerhjelm, P. (2003), *Annual Report from the SNS policy Group, kluster.se* SNS Förlag, Stockholm.

Brown, C., and J. Medoff (1989), 'The employer size wage effect', *Journal of Political Economy*, 97 (5), 1027–59.

Cressy, R., and C. Olofsson (1996), 'Financial conditions for SMEs in Sweden', in: R. Cressy, B. Gabdemo and C. Olofsson (eds.) *Financing SMEs – A Comparative Perspective*, NUTEK Förlag, Stockholm, 7–12.

David, T., and A. Mach (2004), 'The specificity of corporate governance in small states: Institutionalisation and questioning of ownership restrictions in Switzerland and Sweden', in: R. Aguilera and M. Federowicz (eds.) *Corporate Governance in a Changing Economic and Political Environment: Trajectories of Institutional Change on the European Continent*, Palgrave, London, 220–46.

Davidsson, P. (1989), 'Entrepreneurship – and after? A study of growth willingness in small firms', *Journal of Business Venturing*, 4 (3), 211–26.

Davis, S. J., J. Haltiwanger and S. Schuh (1996), *Job Creation and Destruction*, MIT Press, Cambridge, MA.

Davis, S. J., and M. Henrekson (1997), 'Industrial policy, employer size and economic performance in Sweden', in: R. B. Freeman, R. Topel and B. Swedenborg (eds.) *The Welfare State in Transition*, University of Chicago Press, Chicago, 353–97.

(2005), 'Wage-setting institutions as industrial policy', *Labour Economics*, 12 (3), 345–77.

Denis, D. K., and J. J. McConnell (2003), 'International corporate governance', *Journal of Financial and Quantitative Analysis*, 27 (1), 1–35.

Du Rietz, G. (2002), 'Kapitalskatterna och den kreativa förstörelsen', in: D. Johansson and N. Karlsson (eds.) *Den svenska tillväxtskolan: om den ekonomiska utvecklingens kreativa förstörelse*. Ratio, Stockholm, 249–75.

Edin, P.-A., and R. Topel (1997), 'Wage policy and restructuring – the Swedish labor market since 1960', in: R. B. Freeman, R. Topel and B. Swedenborg (eds.) *The Welfare State in Transition*, University of Chicago Press, Chicago, 155–201.

Galbraith, J. K. (1956), *American Capitalism: The Concept of Countervailing Power*, Houghton Mifflin, Boston.

Giannetti, M., and A. Simonov (2005), 'Which investors fear expropriation? Evidence from investors' stock picking', *Journal of Finance*, forthcoming.

Glete, J. (1981), *Kreugerkoncernen och krisen på den svenska aktiemarknaden*, Stockholm Studies in History no. 28, Almqvist and Wiksell, Stockholm.

(1994), *Nätverk i näringslivet*, SNS Förlag, Stockholm.

Gompers, P. A., and J. Lerner (2001), *The Money of Invention: How Venture Capital Creates New Wealth*, Harvard University Press, Cambridge, MA.

Hellmann, T., and M. Puri (2002), 'Venture capital and the professionalization of start-up firms: empirical evidence', *Journal of Finance*, 57 (1), 169–97.

Henrekson, M. (1992), 'Sweden: monetary and financial system', in: P. Newman, M. Milgate and J. Eatwell (eds.) *The New Palgrave Dictionary of Money and Finance*, MacMillan, London and New York, 622–4.

Henrekson, M., and U. Jakobsson (2001), 'Where Schumpeter was nearly right – the Swedish model and *Capitalism, Socialism and Democracy*', *Journal of Evolutionary Economics*, 11 (3), 331–58.

(2002), 'Ägarpolitik och ägarstruktur i efterkrigstidens Sverige', in: L. Jonung (ed.) *Vem skall äga Sverige*, SNS Förlag, Stockholm, 22–64.

Henrekson, M., and D. Johansson (1999), 'Institutional effects on the evolution of the size distribution of firms', *Small Business Economics*, 12 (1), 11–23.

Henrekson, M., and N. Rosenberg (2001), 'Designing efficient institutions for science-based entrepreneurship: lessons from the US and Sweden', *Journal of Technology Transfer*, 26 (2), 207–31.

Hermansson, C.-H. (1962), *Monopol och storfinans*. Arbetarkulturs förlag, Stockholm.

Holmén, M., and P. Högfeldt (2004), 'A law and finance analysis of initial public offerings', *Journal of Financial Intermediation*, 13 (3), 324–58.

Holtz-Eakin, D., D. Joulfaian and H. S. Rosen (1994), 'Sticking it out: entrepreneurial survival and liquidity constraints', *Journal of Political Economy*, 102 (1), 53–75.

Institute for Growth Policy Studies (ITPS) (2002), *Foreign-owned Enterprises 2001*, S2002:007, Stockholm.

Investor AB (2003), *Annual Report*.

Isaksson, M., and R. Skog (1994), 'Corporate governance in Swedish listed companies', in: T. Baums, R. M. Buxbaum and K. J. Hopt (eds.) *Institutional Investors and Corporate Governance*, Walter de Gruyter, Berlin and New York.

Jonung, L. (1994), 'The rise and fall of credit controls: the case of Sweden, 1939–89', in: M. D. Bordo and F. Capie (eds.) *Monetary Regimes in Transition*, Cambridge University Press, Cambridge, 346–70.

Josefsson, M. (1988), 'Börsbolagen 1987 – en jämförelse med tidigare år', *Skandinaviska Enskilda Banken Quarterly Review*, 17 (4), 76–91.

Kaplan, S. N., and P. Strömberg (2001), 'Venture capitalists as principals: contracting, screening, and monitoring', *American Economic Review*, 91 (2), 426–30.

Katzenstein, P. (1985), *Small States in World Markets*, Cornell University Press, Ithaca, NY.

King, M. A., and D. Fullerton (eds.) (1984), *The Taxation of Income from Capital: A Comparative Study of the United States, the United Kingdom, Sweden and West Germany*, University of Chicago Press, Chicago.

La Porta, R., F. Lopez-de-Silanes and A. Shleifer (1999), 'Corporate ownership around the world', *Journal of Finance*, 54 (3), 471–517.

La Porta, R., F. Lopez-de-Silanes, A. Shleifer and R. W. Vishny (1998), 'Law and finance', *Journal of Political Economy*, 106 (5), 1113–55.

Lindgren, G. (1953), 'Shareholders and shareholder participation in the larger companies' meetings in Sweden', *Weltwirtschaftliches Archiv*, 71 (2), 281–98.

Lindgren, H. (1994a), 'The comparative advantages of business groups: some Swedish evidence', in: M. Dritsas and T. Gourvish (eds.) *European Enterprise: Strategies of Adaptation and Renewal in the Twentieth Century*, Trochalia Publications, Athens, 69–84.

(1994b), *Aktivt ägande: investor under växlande konjunkturer*, Institute for Research in Economic History, Stockholm.

Lindh, T., and H. Ohlsson (1996), 'Self-employment and windfall gains: evidence from the Swedish lottery', *Economic Journal*, 106, 1515–26.

Lindkvist, H. (1990), *Kapitalemigration*, dissertation. Stockholm School of Economics.

Maddison, A. (1982), *Phases of Capitalist Development*, Oxford University Press, Oxford.

Meidner, R. (1978), *Employee Investment Funds: An Approach to Collective Capital Formation*, Allen and Unwin, London.

Misher, N. (1984), 'Tax consequences of exercising an incentive stock option with stock of the granting corporation', *The Tax Executive*, July, 357–63.

Montgomery, A. (1946), *Svensk ekonomisk historia mot internationell bakgrund 1913–1939*, Kooperativa förbundets bokförlag, Stockholm.

Morck, R. K., D. A. Stangeland and B. Yeung (2000), 'Inherited wealth, corporate control, and economic growth: the Canadian disease?', in: R. K. Morck (ed.) *Concentrated Corporate Ownership*, University of Chicago Press, Chicago, 319–69.

Norrman, E., and C. E. McLure (1997), 'Tax policy in Sweden', in: R. B. Freeman, R. Topel and B. Swedenborg (eds.) *The Welfare State in Transition*, University of Chicago Press, Chicago, 109–53.

NUTEK (1995), *Småföretagen i Sverige 1995*, NUTEK Förlag, Stockholm.

NUTEK and ALMI (2001), *Tre näringspolitiska utmaningar – allianser för hållbar tillväxt*, NUTEK Förlag, Stockholm.

Organisation for Economic Co-operation and Development (1982), *Historical Statistics 1960–1980*, Paris.

(1997), *Historical Statistics 1960–1995*, Paris.

(1992), *Employment Outlook*, July, Paris.

Pagano, M., and P. Volpin (2001), 'The political economy of finance', *Oxford Review of Economic Policy*, 17 (4), 502–19.

Petersson, T. (2001), 'Promoting entrepreneurship: bank-connected investment development companies in Sweden 1962–1990', in: M. Henrekson, M.

Larsson and H. Sjögren (eds.) *Entrepreneurship in Business and Research: Essays in Honour of Håkan Lindgren*, Institute for Research in Economic History, Stockholm, 113–38.

Pontusson, J. (1992), *The Limits of Social Democracy: Investment Politics in Sweden*, Cornell University Press, Ithaca, NY.

Reiter, J. (2003), 'Changing the microfoundations of corporatism: the impact of financial globalisation on Swedish corporate ownership', *New Political Economy*, 8 (1), 103–26.

Saemundsson, R. J. (1999), *New Technology-Based Firms Growing into Medium-Sized Firms*, licentiate dissertation, Department of Industrial Economics, Chalmers University of Technology, Gothenburg.

Schumpeter, J. A. (1942), *Capitalism, Socialism and Democracy*, George Allen and Unwin, New York.

Södersten, J. (1984), 'Sweden', in: M. A. King and D. Fullerton (eds.) *The Taxation of Income from Capital: A Comparative Study of the United States, the United Kingdom, Sweden and West Germany*, University of Chicago Press, Chicago, 87–148.

(1993), 'Sweden', in: D. W. Jorgenson and R. Landau (eds.) *Tax Reform and the Cost of Capital: An International Comparison*, Brookings, Washington DC, 270–99.

Spånt, R. (1975), *Förmögenhetsfördelningen i Sverige*, Prisma, Stockholm.

Steinmo, S. (2003), 'Bucking the trend? Social democracy in a global economy: the Swedish case up close', *New Political Economy*, 8 (1), 31–48.

Stephens, J. D. (1979), *The Transition from Capitalism to Socialism*, Macmillan, London and New York.

Strandell, A.-C. (2000), 'Utlandsägda företag', in: *Svenskt näringsliv och näringspolitik 2000*, NUTEK förlag, Stockholm, 38–69.

Sundin, A., and S. I. Sundqvist (2003), *Ägarna och makten*, SIS Ägarservice, Stockholm.

Swedish government (1967), *Ägande och inflytande inom det privata näringslivet*, Koncentrationsutredningen, Allmänna Förlaget, Stockholm.

Swedish government (1986), *Aktiers röstvärde*, Betänkande av röstvärdeskommittén, SOU 1986:23, Liber, Stockholm.

United Nations Conference on Trade and Development (1999), *World Investment Report 1999*, United Nations, New York and Geneva.

Wigforss, E. (1956), *Efter välfärdsstaten*, Tidens förlag, Stockholm.

Wiklund, J., P. Davidsson and F. Delmar (2003), 'What do they think and feel about growth? An expectancy-value approach to small business managers' attitudes toward growth', *Entrepreneurship Theory and Practice*, 27 (3), 247–70.

Zider, B. (1998), 'How venture capital works', *Harvard Business Review*, November–December, 131–9.

8 Foreign ownership in Finland: boosting firm performance and changing corporate governance

Pekka Ylä-Anttila, Jyrki Ali-Yrkkö and Martti Nyberg

1. Introduction

During the past ten to fifteen years foreign ownership in Finnish listed companies has increased rapidly and a large number of Finnish firms have been acquired by or merged with foreign firms. The share of the foreign ownership in the Helsinki Stock Exchange has increased dramatically since the early 1990s with foreigners holding some 70 per cent of Finnish market capitalisation by the end of the decade (figure 8.1).

As a result, the Helsinki Stock Exchange has become one of the most internationalised stock exchanges in the world. Parallel to increasing portfolio investment by foreigners, inward direct investment has grown too, although at a much slower pace. The change in ownership structure that has occurred in Finland has perhaps been more profound than that experienced in any other European country.[1]

The reasons for Finland's rapid internationalisation are obvious. Around the mid-1990s major Finnish firms and the economy at large were recovering from the most severe recession in the country's history, and the economy was growing rapidly. The country and its firms were attractive investment targets. At the same time, financial market liberalisation, which had begun in the 1980s, was completed with the lifting of the remaining restrictions on capital movements. Foreign ownership of shares in Finland was fully deregulated in 1993, when Finland became a member of the European Economic Area (EEA) as a step towards membership in the European Union and European Monetary Union a couple of years later. Furthermore, many Finnish firms – with Nokia in the forefront – were entering new growth industries such as ICT

We would like to thank Anthony de Carvalho, Lars Jonung, Maarit Lindström, Mika Pajarinen, Pentti Vartia and two anonymous referees for their helpful comments.
[1] In Sweden the ownership changes have been significant too. See Jonung (2002).

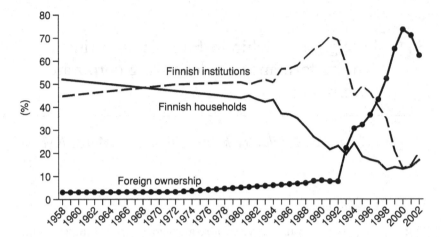

Figure 8.1. The distribution of the ownership of Finnish listed firms as a percentage of market capitalisation, 1958–2002.
Source: Ali-Yrkkö and Ylä-Anttila (2003).

(information and communication technology) making them attractive to overseas investors.

The globalisation of business is a two-way street. As figure 8.2 shows, the outflow of direct investment has exceeded the inflow by far. Portfolio investment by Finnish citizens and institutions has, instead, remained relatively modest. The globalisation of Finnish firms has taken place mainly through mergers and acquisitions (M&As), with an outcome of mixed Finnish and foreign ownership in many cases.[2] Hence, outward FDI has also contributed to the increasing share of foreign ownership.

These drastic changes in ownership structure and huge fluctuations in capital flows have raised both concerns and lively debate among top executives, researchers and policy-makers as well as the public. What are the consequences of increasing foreign ownership? What does it mean when a large part of the business sector is being controlled from abroad? Are foreign owners different from domestic ones? Do they have different goals? Do foreign-controlled firms behave differently? Is there even a risk of the direct transfer of income, jobs or domestically generated knowledge?

Contrary to the fears expressed in public debate, there is a growing body of international evidence that foreign-owned firms perform better than their domestically owned counterparts.[3] Differences in performance are found across industries and countries, and also at the plant level

[2] See Mannio et al. (2003).
[3] For a review, see Jungnickel (2002). For the Finnish case, see Ylä-Anttila (2000).

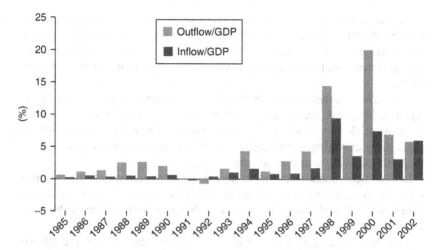

Figure 8.2. Inward and outward foreign direct investment as a percentage of GDP, 1985–2002.
Source: The Bank of Finland and the Research Institute of the Finnish Economy.

(Pfaffermayr and Bellak, 2002). Studies of performance differences usually concern financial performance or growth and productivity performance. It is a widely held view that FDI and foreign-owned firms are beneficial for local economies. As such, there is a race among countries and regions to attract foreign firms, with some countries developing different types of incentives for foreign firms, such as direct subsidies, tax relief or special services to help influence their location decisions.[4]

Why do foreign-owned firms perform better? Although the evidence that foreign-owned firms perform better financially and in terms of growth is unchallenged, relatively little is known about the causes and consequences of it. Ownership structure is a wider issue than merely its impact on performance. For a small Nordic country, it is about how the capital market model is changing and how it affects various kinds of social institutions.

The model of corporate governance in Finland has been in transition over the past decade, with the traditional Continental European system (the stakeholder framework) giving way to the Anglo-American system. This shift has undoubtedly increased efficiency within the business sector, but it is not yet clear what kind of impact it has had on, for

---

[4] For more about the race, and its causes and consequences, see Oxelheim and Ghauri (2004).

example, the economy's long-run growth performance or the national system of innovation. Some studies maintain that variations in national systems of corporate governance explain national patterns in foreign trade and technological specialisation (see Tylecote and Conesa, 1999).

Innovation activities and the location of corporate head offices have recently been the focus of Finnish public debate: both are crucial for promoting domestic value creation. The globalisation of business is potentially changing the attractiveness of smaller countries as a location for both innovation and head office activities.

In the next section we look at the transformation of the Finnish financial system and give a short historical review of Finnish economic developments, including the exceptionally severe depression of the early 1990s.

The third section summarises inward FDI and the role of foreign firms in the economy. To that end, we review the typical characteristics of foreign companies in Finland from the early 1800s to the present. This is followed by an overview of outward FDI and the internationalisation of Finnish corporations, in section 4.

In section 5 we analyse the relative performance of foreign-owned and domestically owned firms in Finland, finding that foreign-owned companies do indeed perform better than their Finnish-owned counterparts. We also look at how the globalisation of business affects corporate governance and firms' goals. Are there differences in goals and governance? Are companies' announced goals and actual financial performance in line with each other? The largest Finnish companies have adopted the maximisation of shareholder value as a major goal during the 1990s, the change coinciding with increases in foreign ownership. On the other hand, there seem to be significant differences between the objectives of foreign-owned and Finnish-owned companies.

Section 6 briefly discusses decisions concerning the location of corporate headquarters – an issue that has raised a lot of public discussion in many smaller countries. Finally, section 7 concludes.

2.   The Finnish economy in transition

Following the financial liberalisation of the 1980s, Finland experienced a major banking crisis and a collapse of its fixed exchange rate regime in the early 1990s. In addition, its economy underwent the most serious recession seen by any industrialised country since the Great Depression of the 1930s (see, for example, Kiander and Vartia, 1996, and Honkapohja and Koskela, 1999).

Table 8.1. *The Finnish economy, 1980–2000*

Average	Real GDP growth (%)	GDP per capita[a]	Inflation (%)
1980–1985	3.3	9,199	9.1
1986–1990	3.3	15,061	4.9
1991–1995	−0.6	20,263	2.2
1996–2000	5.1	26,754	1.6
Average	Export intensity (% of GDP)	Bankruptcies[b]	TFP relative to the United States[c]
1980–1985	30.9	120	73
1986–1990	20.5	235	75
1991–1995	25.5	509	85
1996–2000	32.7	284	95

[a]Millions of euros, current prices.
[b]Average number per month.
[c]Total factor productivity of Finnish manufacturing, United States = 100.
Source: Maliranta (2001).

Table 8.1 shows some key indicators of the Finnish economy, which reflect structural changes and cyclical developments.[5] The economy posted rapid growth in real GDP during the 1980s. In many ways, the recession that followed was exceptional, as Kiander and Vartia (1996) and Honkapohja and Koskela (1999) point out. Real GDP had never declined (on an annual basis) during the post-war period until the economic crisis of the early 1990s, when it dropped by over 10 per cent. Among the factors that contributed to the crisis were a major downturn in the forest-based industries, disruption in trade with the East due to the collapse of the Soviet Union, a speculative bubble in the domestic securities and real estate markets, uncontrolled credit expansion and mismanaged financial liberalisation, which eventually led to a credit crunch and excessive private sector (households and enterprises alike) indebtedness (Kiander and Vartia, 1996).

The recovery was pronounced, however, and the economy enjoyed strong growth through the rest of the 1990s. Over the same period the structure of Finnish industry shifted from an emphasis on metal, engineering and paper manufacturing towards knowledge-based industries,

[5] Besides the indicators shown in table 8.1, the unemployment rate closely follows movements in the Finnish economy. The unemployment rate remained at low levels in the 1980s, but in the crisis of the early 1990s it exploded and rose to almost 20 per cent.

such as ICT. As a result, the driver of economic growth has moved from traditional factors of production to innovation. By the end of the 1990s R&D intensity (R&D expenditure in relation to GDP) had grown well above 3 per cent – i.e. to one of the highest in the world.[6]

While the pulp and paper industry was by far the most important industrial sector until the early 1980s, today the ICT sector is the most significant. In a decade Finland went from being one of the least ICT-specialised countries to becoming the single most specialised one. Currently the Finnish ICT sector, with Nokia as its locomotive, consists of some 6,000 firms, accounting for some 10 per cent of the country's GDP and about a quarter of total exports (Koski et al., 2002).

This period also saw a reorganisation of Finnish financial markets. In the 1980s the Finnish financial system still had a house bank structure, like the financial systems in Japan and Germany. By the end of the millennium the financial system had changed, with relationship-based debt playing a diminished role as a form of financing, and the stock market gaining in influence.

Restructuring the financial market was integral to increasing the significance of high-technology industries and R&D investment. The role of small and medium-sized enterprises (SMEs) was also seen as important, for both long-term economic growth and stabilising the economy after the crises of the early 1990s. Both of these changes created demand for new forms of financing and for foreign capital.[7]

When the economic environment improved in the mid-1990s, stock market developments that had commenced in the late 1980s re-emerged. In the 1990s equity issuance on the stock market by non-financial firms increased, clearly outpacing that of financial institutions. IPO activity restarted immediately once economic conditions had improved. New companies were successfully listed on the Helsinki Stock Exchange. As Hyytinen and Pajarinen (2001) report, the venture capital market also grew.

The share of foreign investment in Finnish stocks began to rise in 1993, and rose very quickly during the latter part of the 1990s. Foreign investors comprise mainly institutional investors, such as mutual and pension funds, and the most important country of origin is the United States. By the beginning of 2000 about two-thirds of the shares on the Helsinki Stock Exchange, as measured by market capitalisation, were foreign-owned. Notably, more than 90 per cent of Nokia's shares are

---

[6] See Rouvinen and Ylä-Anttila (2003) for a more detailed description.
[7] For a detailed description, see Hyytinen and Pajarinen (2003). See also Hyytinen et al. (2003).

owned by foreign investors. Nonetheless, Nokia is regarded as a very Finnish company, since the company's head office is in Finland, its top management is made up of Finns and most of its strategic activities, such as R&D, take place in Finland.

3.   Foreign firms and entrepreneurs in Finland

Foreign investors, firms and entrepreneurs are not a new phenomenon in Finnish economic history. Foreign entrepreneurs have played an important role in Finland's industrialisation process, and also as importers of foreign know-how. In the late 1800s and early 1900s European entrepreneurs and artisans were highly mobile, seeking opportunities to apply their skills. In Finland the food and woodworking industries, as well as trade and commerce, benefited greatly from foreign entrepreneurs and expertise. Many industrial companies still in existence today were established by immigrant entrepreneurs. They brought their expertise to the country, but relatively little capital.

On the whole, however, the impact of foreign entrepreneurs and direct investment on the Finnish economy remained low compared to the situation in many other small industrial countries during the period before World War I. Foreign investment activity was also insignificant in the decades following independence (1917) and World War II. This had to do with the economic nationalism typical of a young country, and related reservations regarding foreign capital, but also with Finland's small size and remote geographic location as a market area.

Direct foreign investment in Finland did not surge during the decades that followed World War II, even though elsewhere in the world enterprises were experiencing a strong internationalisation trend. After the war, foreigners saw Finland as politically uncertain. Strict currency and import regulations did not make investments any more attractive. As a result, in the late 1950s inward FDI remained at the same low level that it had been at before World War II.

Finnish attitudes towards foreign companies became more positive during the 1960s. Simultaneously, social conditions were stabilising, as indicated by a decrease in the risk premia of foreign currency loans (Hjerppe and Ahvenainen, 1986). However, the law restricting foreign ownership remained in effect.

Throughout the 1960s inward direct investment was equivalent to around 0.2 per cent of GDP. The modest volume of investment reflected the fact that the majority of the foreign businesses established in Finland were marketing and sales companies, operating on small amounts of capital.

254 P. Ylä-Anttila, J. Ali-Yrkkö and M. Nyberg

The typical pattern with the newly established or acquired enterprises was that a foreign, frequently multinational, parent company was the sole owner of the subsidiary. Joint ventures that also had Finnish partners were less common; they were established mostly when the law restricting foreign ownership posed limits on operating a business. The strategy of most businesses was to enter the growing Finnish market and compete there. Some enterprises exported their products further, to Soviet markets, among others. A high percentage of the businesses that engaged in exporting imported the raw materials or semi-finished products they needed for production.

In the 1960s and 1970s foreign companies became tempted by Finland's low labour costs relative to most other Western competitor countries. Some of these investors included Swedish garment companies and metal and electronics industries, which set up assembly factories. The companies that came to Finland merely for the sake of the low cost of labour left the country again very quickly in the late 1970s and early 1980s, when the relative cost of labour began to rise.

Direct foreign investment began to increase in the 1980s, although, in relation to GDP, the investments were still fairly small. The targets for investment were increasingly buying and selling companies, especially small businesses with specialist know-how (Lovio, 1992). The most significant example of FDI in Finland in the 1980s was the deal between what was then Kymi-Strömberg and the Swedish ASEA, in which ASEA (later ABB) purchased Kymi-Strömberg's entire electrical operations unit. This event was indicative of how Finnish attitudes towards foreign companies began to shift in line with the outward-directed internationalisation trend of Finnish industry itself.

The situation changed in the 1990s, as legislation restricting foreign ownership was repealed and measures were taken to attract foreign capital to Finland. A special agency (Invest in Finland), with the specific intention of attracting foreign firms, was established in 1992. Although attitudes towards foreign companies and ownership have changed very rapidly, questions and criticism have not disappeared entirely. Parliamentary discussions on repealing the law restricting foreign ownership in 1991–1992, and on the merger between the Swedish and Finnish paper companies Stora and Enso a couple of years later, are good examples of the rapidity of the change as well as of the critical attitudes that continue to exist.[8]

---

[8] See *Globalisation and the Finnish Political System* by Väyrynen (1999), who records and analyses closely the rather heated debate surrounding the topic.

The 1939 law that restricted foreign ownership was liberalised step by step during the 1980s and early 1990s and finally overturned in 1992, a few years before Finland joined the European Union. There was strident criticism towards this development, however, particularly with regard to the freeing of land ownership. According to a popular impression, foreigners were going to 'rush to buy land at cut-rate prices'. Such talk died down quickly, however. At present the discussion has broadened to encompass the theme of globalisation, which has in some ways been rendered into concrete terms by several cross-border M&As. Border-crossing M&As are an essential part of the ongoing wave of globalisation. They are resulting in a new kind of tension, between different management styles and corporate cultures, which could not have been foreseen a few decades ago.

The national strategic significance associated with ownership has diminished in a fundamental way since the 1980s. Ownership has become more international, and international investors usually place only one demand on management: shareholder value. It has been recognised in the public debate that from the national economy's viewpoint it is important where the companies are located, and where they invest – not who their owners are. For this reason, what matters is whether Finland is seen as an attractive location for businesses and people alike.

Finland became much more attractive to foreign investors in the course of the 1990s as the remaining restrictions on capital movements were dismantled and business sectors that had previously been protected in one way or another were opened to competition. EU and EMU membership indicated that the country was part of a common market with free movement of capital, labour and technology.

Indeed, cross-border inward investment has been quite high during the past ten years. In the 1990s the number of inward cross-border deals (M&As) in relation to GDP was the second highest in Finland among the EU countries (figure 8.3). However, with respect to the value of the deals in absolute terms, Finland is ranked much lower. Hence, we can conclude that Finnish transactions have been relatively small; in other words, the target companies are, to a large extent, SMEs (see Ali-Yrkkö, 2003).

Foreign direct investment began growing rapidly in the world economy in general in the mid-1980s. In addition to reflecting the liberalisation trend in international capital markets, this growth was associated with developments in information and communications technology and the related services. These developments made it possible for a geographically decentralised company to operate more effectively than before. In many sectors, competition turned global. In order to survive in this environment, many companies have chosen to specialise strongly

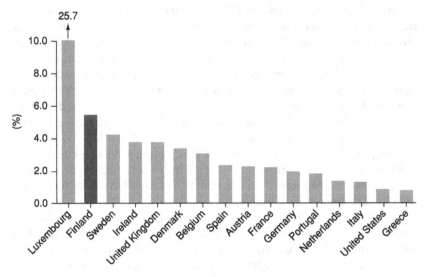

Figure 8.3. Countries as cross-border merger and acquisition targets, 1990–1999.
Note: Each observation is measured as the ratio of the sum of the number of inward cross-border deals during the period 1990 to 1999 to GDP at market prices in 1999 in millions of Euros.
Source: OECD (2001) and the authors' calculations.

and to grow their core businesses. Consequently, firms have increased direct investment in order to expand their markets.

The growth of direct investment in Finland has been partly, therefore, the product of an international trend. However, an important factor attracting additional FDI into Finland has been the emergence of numerous technology-intensive companies, especially in the ICT sector, where specialised know-how tends to draw foreign businesses. The motivation of foreign companies to locate to Finland is no longer to benefit from Finnish companies' firm-specific assets in the Finnish market but, rather, to benefit by making the know-how of these companies an integral part of their own operations.[9] Indeed, most of the Finnish companies that were acquired have benefited from the new ownership arrangement: as part of a multinational company, their technologies and products have found new, international, marketing and distribution channels. Financial resources have also increased notably in many cases (Pajarinen and Ylä-Anttila, 2001).

[9] See Pajarinen and Ylä-Anttila (1999).

Table 8.2. *The largest foreign subsidiaries engaged in industrial production in Finland, 2002*

Foreign parent company	Country	Finnish subsidiary	Sector of industry	Employees in Finland
ABB	Switzerland	ABB Finland	Electrical engineering	9,216
Kvaerner	Norway	Kvaerner Masa-Yards	Mechanical engineering	4,610
Flextronics	United States	Flextronics Holding Finland	Electrical engineering	1,710
Scottish & Newcastle	United Kingdom	Hartwall	Food and beverages	1,457
Pilkington	United Kingdom	Pilkington Finland	Chemical industry	1,400
Carlsberg	Denmark	Sinebrychoff	Food and beverages	1,190
Siemens	Germany	Siemens	Electrical engineering	1,097
Andritz	Austria	Andritz	Mechanical engineering	1,080
Aker Yards	Norway	Aker Finnyards	Mechanical engineering	1,010
Assa Abloy	Sweden	Abloy	Mechanical engineering	1,002

Source: ETLA's business database.

Direct foreign investment into Finland has also increased because big Finnish corporations have focused on their specific area of specialisation. Many operational units that had to be unloaded might not have found an appropriate or interested buyer in Finland at the time of sale. The large proportion of mergers and acquisitions among foreign companies' direct investments in Finland is reflected in table 8.2, which lists some of the largest subsidiaries of foreign MNEs that were engaged in industrial production in Finland in 2002. All (except for Siemens) were acquired by foreign companies and, with a few exceptions, were originally part of a larger Finnish group prior to being purchased.

4.   Outward FDI: the internationalisation of Finnish companies

In the late 1970s Finnish companies' international activities still consisted mostly of exporting from Finland. Today, large Finnish industrial corporations are highly internationalised, primarily because of FDI. Amongst the ten largest corporations, as much as 80 per cent of total revenues comes from foreign sales and over 60 per cent of production and personnel is located in foreign units (table 8.3).

Many of these companies have considerable foreign ownership, which is integral to their foreign operations and financing. Practically all of them could be characterised as Finnish multinationals rather than domestic companies, although all have group head offices still in Finland. However, the increased foreign ownership has affected management practices and governance structures in many ways.

In the 1980s and early 1990s Finnish companies usually became international in separate stages. Simple international operations gradually progressed into more complex ones. First, production units were established in the most important export markets, such as Sweden and Germany. Later, efforts were made to expand operations to other parts of Europe and North America. The pattern was clear: after several years of experience with exporting, companies moved on to more demanding forms of international operations, such as overseas production.

Today many companies begin targeting the world market at a very early stage. Companies in the high-tech industry in particular view the entire world as their potential market from the very start. As a result, foreign subsidiaries are already established during a company's product

Table 8.3. *Numbers of employees in large Finnish corporations, 1983 and 2002*

Company	[1983]		[2002]	
	Number of employees	Percentage abroad	Number of employees	Percentage abroad
Nokia	23,651	17.5	51,748	56.5
Stora-Enso	15,315	9.8	43,853	66.5
UPM-Kymmene	50,061	9.4	35,579	44.1
Metsälitto	7,891	7.5	30,247	67.4
Metso	15,371	12.8	28,489	62.9
Kone	13,137	66.2	35,864	87.0
Outokumpu	10,089	1.4	21,130	69.3
Huhtamäki	4,698	6.6	15,909	95.5
Fortum	7,076	21	13,118	43.3
Rautaruukki	7,712	1.6	12,804	41.9
Total	162,583	15.38	288,741	63.4

Source: Ali-Yrkkö and Ylä-Anttila (1997), updated in 2003.

development phase. Previously, research and development abroad was carried out only after the company had acquired international experience through other operations.

In the course of the last ten to fifteen years Finnish companies have internationalised into nearly all parts of the world, with Africa being perhaps the only exception. A majority of the investments of Finnish companies have gone to the EU region (mostly Sweden and Germany), followed by North America.

Growth in foreign investment activity by Finnish companies can also be seen in the location of their personnel, with a significant portion of the largest Finnish corporations' labour force working outside the country's borders. This trend has intensified drastically over the last fifteen years.

Summing up briefly, large Finnish corporations have experienced notable growth and other changes in recent years. Most of this growth has occurred abroad in response to the rapid expansion of international business operations, and all the signs suggest that this tendency will continue to grow in the future. It appears that companies want to operate close to their customers, helping to attract a growing share of investment away from Finland. Inevitably, the ownership of corporations will also become increasingly international, with a bearing on companies' systems of corporate governance.[10]

5.   Firm performance and goals: does foreign ownership matter?[11]

5.1   Background

In this section we take a look at the effects of the globalisation of business, ownership and corporate governance on firms' goals and performance. The globalisation of capital markets and ownership has triggered major changes in corporate governance towards the US model in most European countries, as discussed in the previous section (see, for example, Berglöf, 1997).

Empirical evidence on the effects of ownership structure and the nationality of ownership on firm's goals and performance is consistent with the view that ownership matters. Using data on European companies, Thomsen and Pedersen (2000) find that market-to-book value is higher in firms where the largest owner is a financial institution than in firms where the largest owner is a family, another firm or a government.

---

[10] See, for example, Pajarinen et al. (1998).
[11] This section draws heavily on Ali-Yrkkö and Ylä-Anttila (2003).

Table 8.4. *International differences in corporate governance*

	[Whose company is it?]		[Job security or dividends?]	
	All interest groups'	Shareholders'	Job security	Dividends
Japan	97%	3%	97%	3%
United States	24%	76%	10%	90%
United Kingdom	30%	71%	11%	89%
Germany	83%	17%	59%	41%
France	78%	22%	50%	50%

Note: The data are based on a survey made among business executives, reported originally in Institute of Fiscal and Monetary Policy (1996).

Interestingly, the nationality of the firm's owners has an impact on these relations. The results by Griffith (1999) concerning productivity differences between domestic and foreign-owned companies in the motor vehicle and parts industry support the view that foreign-owned firms have stronger financial performance. Chibber and Majumdar (1999) focus on the influence of foreign ownership on the financial performance of firms operating in India. According to their results, foreign-owned companies – i.e. subsidiaries of foreign firms – outperform domestic companies. Finally, raw data from Sweden[12] and Japan[13] suggest that, in terms of return on equity, foreign-owned companies outperform domestic companies.[14]

There is very little empirical evidence on the effects of foreign ownership on firm performance in Finland. Here we examine the effects of foreign ownership on the performance and goals of Finnish firms, and ask whether the internationalisation of ownership matters. Do foreign-owned companies perform better than or differently from Finnish-owned ones? Are there differences in goals and governance? Are the announced goals and actual financial performance in line with each other?

Table 8.4 illustrates the basic differences in the two types of corporate governance models – the Continental European/Japanese model and the Anglo-Saxon model. The message of table 8.4 is clear. In the United States and United Kingdom the shareholder perspective strongly

[12] See Statistics Sweden (1996) and Strandell (1997).
[13] See METI (2001).
[14] Jungnickel (2002) provides a good review of most recent studies.

dominates, while in Germany and Japan the stakeholder view seems to be prevalent.

The Nordic governance model has traditionally been akin to that in Germany/Continental Europe (and, to some extent, Japan). However, as a consequence of the rapid globalisation of capital markets and changes in corporate ownership, firms (and also governments) are facing a 'governance dilemma', namely whether to promote the adoption of the Anglo-Saxon model or to keep some of the features of the Continental European model.[15] Because the Anglo-Saxon corporate governance system emphasises return on capital and equity more than the Nordic and Continental European systems do, this difference in goal setting may have an effect on firm performance.

5.2   Ownership nationality: why might it matter?

5.2.1 The effects of competition   Differences in operating environment may cause differences in firm performance. Perhaps the most obvious sources of differences are the degree of competition and firms' exposure to international markets, which may vary greatly across countries and industries. Differences in the competitive environment are highlighted when restrictions on competition are removed in previously protected industries, precisely because the restrictions have often been in place to protect domestic companies from foreign competition.

Porter (1990) points to the importance of domestic competition in creating a competitive edge in international markets. Protected and non-competitive home markets lead to inefficiencies and uniformity in firm strategies. The management literature provides strong evidence showing that a competitive environment leads to more efficient decision-making structures and increases the incentives to monitor costs (see, for example, Caves, 1980). The economics literature offers fairly little empirical evidence on the effects of competition on firm performance. The existing evidence does point, however, in the same direction: deregulation and a higher level of competition are associated with productivity gains.[16]

5.2.2 The effects of ownership change   Lichtenberg (1992) has proposed that ownership change is caused by lapses in firms' efficiency. These lapses may be due to the incompatibility (or 'bad matching') between a plant (an asset) and the characteristics of an owner (i.e. a parent firm). This argument, which is the key hypothesis of Lichtenberg's

[15] See, for example, Holmström and Kaplan (2001) and Goergen (1998).
[16] For a review, see Allen and Gale (1999).

'matching theory', is based on three primary assumptions: (i) that some owners have a comparative advantage in owning certain plants; (ii) that the quality of the match is a decisive factor in the decision to maintain the ownership of the plant; and (iii) that the quality of the match can be measured by productivity performance.

The matching theory of plant turnover does not assume that there are good and bad owners, but that there are good and bad matches. This view has two major implications. First, a poor match, which is indicated by a low level of current productivity, may lead to a change of ownership. Second, a change of ownership will lead to an increase in plant productivity. The quality of each match is assumed to be randomly distributed. Thus, given that the quality of the first match was low, the expected value of a new match (from an identical distribution) is higher.

In practice, many acquisitions are preceded by a deterioration in the target firm's economic performance. This deterioration may act as a signal to an owner that he or she is operating the plant less efficiently than an alternative parent would. Because the liberalisation of capital movements and capital markets has increased the potential for better international matches, a growing number of cross-border mergers and acquisitions are likely to follow. The primary motive for these transactions may well be related to the opportunity of profiting from differences in firm performance across countries.

The international trade and business literature refers to firm-specific assets or advantages and their transferability within multinational enterprises. As Caves (1996), for example, argues, firm-specific assets exhibit external economies because they are intangible and have characteristics of public goods. Firm-specific assets can be transferred with low cost within – but not between – multinational companies. This would lead to higher than average performance by affiliates of MNEs, since other (domestic) firms do not have access to these assets. It is simply a matter that specific skills and resources developed by MNEs can be exploited by the MNE network but not outside it.

5.2.3 Finnish ownership and the globalisation of capital markets

The ownership of major Finnish companies was for long concentrated, with founding families, banks, other companies or the state typically wielding considerable control.[17] In the 1990s

---

[17] The number of listed companies was rather small, and banks served as a major source of finance for Finnish companies. These basic characteristics of the traditional system are described in more detail by Kasanen et al. (1996). Changes in institutional and legal settings in the 1990s are described by Hyytinen and Pajarinen (2003).

companies, their governance and their operations all changed remarkably. Cross-ownership diminished when banks and large industrial companies sold their shares of other companies. The privatisation of state-owned companies also proceeded rapidly during the past decade; in many cases, the buyer was a foreign firm or investor.

During the 1990s both inward foreign portfolio and direct investment grew rapidly (figures 8.1 and 8.4). At the same time Finnish firms increased their investment abroad – mainly in the form of M&As, which also increased foreign ownership and the significance of international capital market in firms' financing.

As a consequence of the globalisation of Finnish capital markets, a number of changes in corporate governance have taken place. First, the supervisory board, which used to be quite common in large Finnish companies, is rarely encountered today. Second, the board of directors no longer consists only of operating management. Third, a number of diversified companies have focused on their core competencies by selling off less strategic businesses. Fourth, as we will show below, companies have changed their targets. Shareholder value has become one of the key targets in most large companies. All these changes are consistent with the view that the nationality of ownership matters. How the increasing foreign ownership has affected the behaviour and performance of Finnish firms is considered in more detail in what follows.

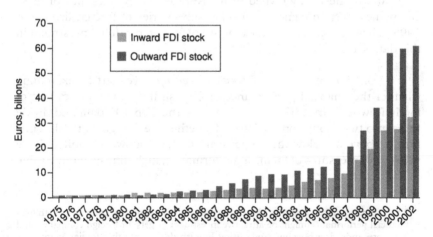

Figure 8.4. Stocks of inward and outward foreign direct investment in Finland in billions of euros at fixed 2002 prices, 1975–2002.
Source: Bank of Finland and ETLA.

5.2.4 Empirical analysis using firm-level data   Differences in corporate governance, the degree of competition, the ability to utilise the firm-specific assets of an MNE network, and lapses in the matching of resources suggest that the nationality of ownership might cause differences in firms' goal-setting and performance. In this section we examine whether firm-level data also support the existence of such differences. We examine, in particular, whether there are differences between foreign and Finnish-owned firms in terms of their goal-setting, investment rates and financial performance.[18]

We use two data sets on Finnish companies. The first data set ('Top 100') is derived from a database on the 100 largest Finnish corporations (ranked according to sales). The database covers the period from 1986 to 1998. However, due to mergers and restructuring we have comparable data over the whole period on only fifty corporations. The database includes information on firms' financial performance and corporate governance, detailing aspects such as the ownership structure, organisation, and what kinds of goals (shareholder value, growth, etc.) the companies have pursued.

The second data set ('Top 500') consists of financial statement data on the 500 largest companies in Finland over the same period. The data allow us to make financial performance analyses, but do not include information concerning firms' goal-setting or other measures of governance structures. As far as the ownership structure is concerned, a distinction can be made only between foreign-controlled (majority owned) firms and domestically owned firms. Approximately one-third of these companies were foreign-owned – i.e. subsidiaries of foreign firms – in 1998. There are no data on the amount of foreign portfolio investment in this data set.

5.2.5 Foreign versus domestic ownership   We start by examining whether the financial performance of Finnish firms differs from that of foreign-owned firms. To this end, we use the Top 100 data and divide firms into two groups on the basis of whether the foreign ownership in a firm is above or below the 20 per cent level. As shown in table 8.5, we use several measures of financial performance, including economic value

---

[18] The causality might, of course, also run in the other direction; i.e. companies with high financial performance might be attractive investment targets for foreign companies and investors. Indeed, a previous study using Finnish data shows that foreign companies tend to acquire firms with higher than average rates of return. It is of interest to note that the difference in the rate of return between domestically owned and foreign-owned companies seems to grow after the acquisition. See Ylä-Anttila and Ali-Yrkkö (1997).

Table 8.5. *Performance by ownership, using Top 100 data, 1997 and 1998*

	Foreign ownership <20% (n = 121)	Foreign ownership ≥20% (n = 78)	t-statistics	p-value
Return on investment	14%	17%	−1.687	0.09
Capital turnover rate[a]	3%	3%	0.057	0.96
Equity share	47%	42%	2.389	0.02
Investments/net sales	13%	8%	2.132	0.03
Operating income/net sales	7%	7%	0.501	0.62
EVA, millions of markka[b]	79	447	−2.092	0.04
EVA/capital invested	6%	9%	−1.647	0.10

[a] The ratio of net sales to capital invested.
[b] The EVA without Nokia is markka 221 million.
Note: The number of observations is 199, since the sample is based on the Top 100 in 1997, but the merger between IVO and Neste reduces the number to 99 in 1998. The t-statistics are used to test H0: mean (domestically owned) = mean (foreign-owned).

added (EVA). Unlike traditional measures of corporate profitability, EVA also takes into account the opportunity cost of equity capital.[19]

Many of the indicators of financial performance differ significantly between Finnish and foreign-owned companies. The biggest difference relates to EVA, which is on average much higher in foreign-owned firms. Even if we exclude the largest Finnish multinational firm – Nokia Corporation – from the sample, the EVA of foreign-owned firms remains two times higher than that of Finnish firms. Although the larger size of foreign-owned firms may explain the difference, this finding is not inconsistent with the view that foreign-owned companies yield more value added to their owners. The ratio of EVA to capital invested describes the efficiency of capital use. It too indicates that the foreign-owned firms outperform the Finnish ones. Moreover, it seems that foreign-owned firms have invested less and have a lower equity ratio than domestically owned companies. Due to the small sample size, however, differences should be considered tentative.

In order to overcome the small sample problem, we turn to the Top 500 data; table 8.6 displays the results. Because we lack data on foreign

[19] Unlike traditional measures of corporate profitability, such as net operating profit after tax, and net income, EVA looks at a firm's 'residual profitability', net of both the cost of debt capital and the cost of equity capital (Grant, 1997). It is computed as follows: EVA = net result *minus* (riskless rate of interest *plus* beta *times* risk premium) *times* equity share, where the riskless rate of interest is measured using the treasury bond (five year) yield in Finland (source: Bank of Finland); beta is measured using betas by industries (source: *Finnish Economic Weekly*, 1997); and the risk premium is assumed to be 4.5 per cent.

Table 8.6. *Performance by ownership, using Top 500 data 1986–1998*

	Finnish-owned			Foreign subsidiaries		
Year	EVA, millions of markka	EVA/capital invested	Return on investment	EVA, millions of markka	EVA/capital invested	Return on investment
1986	−27	−1%	8%	2	1%	11%
1987	10	2%	10%	16	7%	15%
1988	24	3%	11%	18	8%	17%
1989	11	1%	10%	12	6%	16%
1990	−24	−1%	8%	−1	0%	11%
1991	−71	−4%	6%	−3	−4%	8%
1992	−70	−3%	8%	−2	−3%	9%
1993	−32	0%	9%	1	2%	12%
1994	13	3%	12%	11	10%	20%
1995	36	4%	16%	23	12%	27%
1996	14	4%	17%	19	9%	24%
1997	37	5%	18%	24	11%	26%
1998	54	5%	17%	23	10%	24%
Total average	−4	1%	12%	12	6%	18%

Note: The number of observations is 5,121.

portfolio investment in these companies, the definition of foreign ownership changes from what we used above; i.e. we look at foreign multinationals' subsidiaries in Finland where foreign ownership is more than 50 per cent. We use only EVA, the ratio of EVA to capital invested and the conventional rate of return on investment as indicators of firm performance.

The message from the tables 8.5 and 8.6 is clear. Foreign-owned companies have performed much better than domestic ones. Indeed, foreign companies created slightly negative economic value added during the recession (1991 to 1993), but the EVA performance of Finnish-owned companies during the same period was highly negative. The ratio of EVA to capital invested, which is less driven by differences in firm size, has averaged 1 per cent in Finnish companies, while the same figure for foreign-owned companies is 6 per cent. The rate of return on capital invested in foreign companies is also higher than in Finnish-owned companies.

Table 8.7 reports the capital turnover rate, the ratio of investment to net sales and the number of companies. The conclusion appears to be that Finnish-owned companies need far more capital to generate the same sales or value added as foreign-owned companies.

Table 8.7. *Investment by ownership, using Top 500 data, 1986–1998*

Year	Finnish-owned			Foreign subsidiaries		
	Capital turnover rate	Investment/ net sales	Number of companies	Capital turnover rate	Investment/ net sales	Number of companies
1986	2.5	11%	190	2.8	7%	39
1987	2.5	10%	249	2.8	5%	50
1988	2.4	13%	292	3.1	5%	58
1989	2.5	11%	318	3.2	6%	74
1990	2.6	12%	360	4.3	6%	88
1991	2.8	8%	399	3.6	6%	91
1992	3.5	10%	339	3.1	5%	77
1993	3.6	8%	334	4.9	4%	88
1994	4.1	7%	299	7.9	4%	93
1995	3.5	8%	289	6.7	3%	110
1996	5.5	8%	297	7.2	4%	115
1997	3.8	9%	286	6.3	4%	117
1998	5.2	10%	333	7.1	5%	136
Total average	3.4	10%	3,985	5.3	5%	1,136

Note: The number of observations is 5,121.

The performance differences between domestic and foreign-owned companies are statistically significant.[20] The investment ratio of foreign-owned companies is lower than that of domestically owned companies. Finnish companies are also, on average, more capital-intensive than foreign-owned companies. This finding does not change significantly even if the capital-intensive forest industry is eliminated from the data. In a previous study on the financial performance of Finnish companies (Ali-Yrkkö and Ylä-Anttila, 1997), the industry differences between domestic and foreign companies were carefully controlled for. The result was that the industry differences did not explain the divergences in performance.

Why do these differences exist? Are Finns poor managers? Anecdotal evidence is not consistent with poor management. Case studies of firms that have been taken over by foreign firms show that the previous management has often been allowed to keep its position after the takeover. However, the performance of these firms has improved. These findings are consistent with the view that foreigners are more demanding owners than Finns – i.e. that more is squeezed out of the firm.

[20] For statistical tests, see Ali-Yrkkö and Ylä-Anttila (2003).

5.2.6 Goals and ownership   The annual reports of Finnish companies usually include a section describing their goals and targets. All companies state several goals. Figure 8.5 shows that profitability and its improvement were the main goals throughout the 1990s. Companies announced that they would either maintain profit performance at the same level as before or that they would try to improve it. Another goal, not shown in figure 8.5, is improving the debt/equity ratio. Since the sample is small, any conclusions based on it should be regarded as tentative.

Furthermore, figure 8.5 also shows that, during the recession of the 1990s, companies became less interested in growing their business. This finding is not surprising, because growth was not a realistic goal in the depths of the recession. In fact, most companies tried to keep their sales at the same level as before. The goal of customer orientation also declined during this period. It may be that many companies were forced to concentrate on improving their financial position, such as debt/equity ratios, at the expense of other goals.

During the 1990s firms increasingly began to stress their owners' role, announcing that they sought value added for their shareholders. By the end of the decade almost half of the large companies stated shareholder value as one of their key goals. Shareholder value is, of course, closely related to other targets, such as profitability and growth. However, stating it explicitly as one of the key goals sends a specific signal to

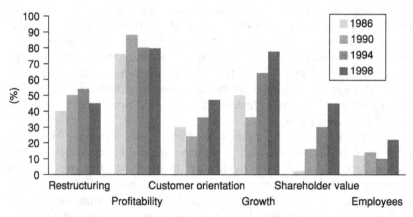

Figure 8.5. The goals of the largest Finnish companies on a percentage basis 1986, 1990, 1994 and 1998.

Note: The data are from the Top 100 data set and consist only of firms that mentioned their goals.

Table 8.8. *A comparison of firms' goals, using Top 100 data, 1997 and 1998*

	Foreign ownership <20%	Foreign ownership ≥20%	t-statistics	p-value
Restructuring	38	38	−0.353	0.720
Profitability	76	67	0.406	0.680
Customer orientation	49	63	−2.721	0.000
Growth	63	73	−2.313	0.010
Shareholder value	28	52	−3.990	0.000
Employees	38	29	−1.474	0.140

Source: The number of observations in 199, since the sample is based on the Top 100 in 1997, but the merger between IVO and Neste reduces the number to 99 in 1998. The t-statistics are used to test H0: mean (domestically owned) = mean (foreign-owned).

current and potential owners, and is at least an indication of how shareholder value became an increasingly common goal of Finnish firms in the 1990s.

Table 8.8 shows how goals differ between Finnish and foreign-owned companies. The results in the table suggest that foreign-owned companies are more orientated to their customers, growth and shareholder value than domestic companies. To summarise, these results support the hypothesis that foreign and domestic-owned companies have different goals.

Taken together, our data show that shareholder value has increasingly been adopted as a major goal in most large Finnish companies since the early 1990s. This trend coincided with a rise in foreign ownership in the Finnish business sector. Our empirical results suggest that ownership matters in goal-setting. There are significant differences between foreign-owned and domestically owned firms in terms of their announced objectives.

Furthermore, our comparisons suggest that foreign-owned companies have not invested as much as domestic companies. This partly explains why foreign-owned companies produce a higher rate of return on capital than domestically owned companies. The difference applies not only to companies that are majority-owned and controlled by foreigners (subsidiaries of foreign firms) but also to companies with lower (but still significant) foreign ownership. Consistent with earlier empirical evidence, our analysis also shows that foreign companies perform better than Finnish-owned companies.

The evidence of this section suggests that increases in foreign ownership have improved the efficiency of capital use. The results also imply that in less integrated and partly protected markets it was possible to pursue other goals at the expense of the rate of return on capital. In the future, the nationality of ownership (domestic versus foreign) in determining firm performance will probably diminish. Owners will pursue high rates of return irrespective of their nationality.

6.   The location of corporate headquarters

Does increasing foreign ownership affect the location of headquarters? Does the relocation of headquarters have any impact on economic growth in Finland? Does it affect government tax revenues?

In this section we discuss the factors affecting the location of Finnish firms' corporate headquarters. This has recently become the object of popular concern, since it is a strategic issue not only for firms but also for policy-makers.

Figure 8.6 shows how the proportion of Finnish firms with corporate headquarters abroad has grown throughout the 1990s. Table 8.9 lists the thirty-two largest Finnish companies that have relocated their corporate headquarters outside Finland. The headquarter relocation activity has, in almost all cases, taken place as a consequence of international mergers or acquisitions. Thus, the existing headquarters of a foreign company that acquires a Finnish firm most often determines the location of the

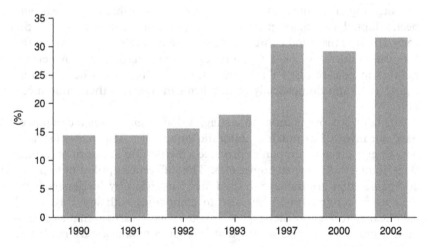

Figure 8.6. The percentage of Finland's 250 largest firms with corporate headquarters abroad, 1990–2002.
Source: Ali-Yrkkö and Ylä-Anttila (2002).

Table 8.9. *The largest Finnish firms that have relocated their corporate headquarters abroad*

Firm	Where to	Firm	Where to
Ahlströmin leijukerroskattilat	United States	Servi Systems	Denmark
Nokian Paperi	United States	Sinebrychoff	Denmark
Kyrel	United States	Cultor	Denmark
Metsä-Serla Chemicals	United States	Nokian Kaapeli	Netherlands
Ojala-yhtiöt	United States	Leaf	Netherlands
Timberjack	United States	Ahlström Pumps	Switzerland
Martis	United States	Nokia-Maillefer	Switzerland
Sonera	Sweden	Hartwall	United Kingdom
Enviset	Sweden, United States	Arctia (hotels)	United Kingdom
Salcomp	Sweden	LK Products	United Kingdom
Tamrock	Sweden	Asko Kodinkone	Italy
Assa-Abloy	Sweden	Andritz-Ahlström	Austria
STV	Sweden	Aker Finnyards	Norway
Leiras	Germany	Polarkesti	France
Marli	Germany	Transtech	Spain
Huolintakeskus	Germany	Lohja Rudus	Ireland

Source: Ali-Yrkkö and Ylä-Anttila (2002).

newly formed company. However, there are some cases in which the relocation decision has been made independently of the merger or acquisition. In these cases, the firms have been small or medium-sized and have typically operated in the high-tech industry. Some small IT companies, in particular, tend to locate their head offices abroad, just to be closer to their markets and sources of international venture capital funding (Ali-Yrkkö and Ylä-Anttila, 2002).

In 2002 the Confederation of Finnish Industry and Employers undertook a survey of factors affecting the location of headquarters. The results, presented in figure 8.7, indicate that Finland's history, social stability and data communication links favour locating headquarters there.

Clearly, the country's high income tax rate and heavy taxation of personal stock options, as well as concerns over promoting growth in affiliates, are factors favouring the relocation of headquarters abroad. There were clear differences in the responses depending on how globalised the firm in question was, with more globalised firms perceiving more advantages in locating their headquarters abroad.

In addition, factors affecting decisions on headquarter location vary across industries. In particular, firms in industries that need new capital

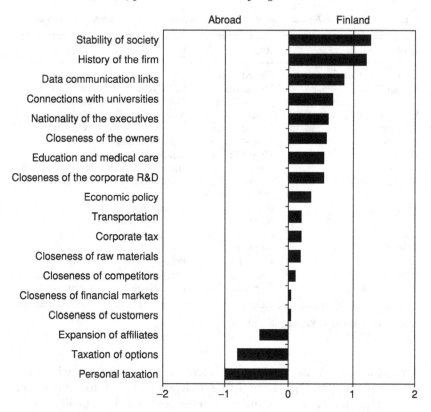

Figure 8.7. Factors favouring the location of headquarters in Finland and abroad.

Source: Confederation of Finnish Industry and Employers and Ali-Yrkkö and Ylä-Anttila (2002).

Note: Values scaled between −2 and 2. 2 is strongly in favour of locating in Finland, 1 is somewhat in favour of locating in Finland, 0 is neutral, −1 is somewhat in favour of locating abroad and −2 is strongly in favour of locating abroad.

may want to be located near the main financial markets, such as New York and London, where many analysts, investment banks, venture capital firms and other financial institutions operate (see Braunerhjelm, 2004). This may help them become better known among investors and therefore increase their ability to raise new capital.

Problems in recruiting personnel may also have an effect on the location of corporate headquarters. Large multinational firms, in particular, operating in a small country may find it difficult to persuade personnel to move to remote peripheral areas.

Even when large Finnish firms have headquarters in Finland, some operations take place elsewhere. For example operations related to finance and R&D are commonly undertaken both at home and in foreign affiliates' offices. Indeed, during the last five years the internationalisation of R&D has increased rapidly, bringing the share of Finnish industrial firms' R&D activity performed abroad up to around 40 per cent in recent years.

6.1   The importance of corporate headquarter location

The internationalisation of headquarters and their possible relocation to another country raises the question of what effect this has on the Finnish economy. Because the definition of headquarters is far from unambiguous, the consequences of relocation are considered from the viewpoint of the parent company's actual physical location and the location of headquarter operations and the company's top executives.

The location of the parent company determines where the company pays corporate taxes. If the parent company of such a group moves to another country, the country it leaves will forgo future corporate tax revenues from that firm. Relocation may also have an impact on the firm's image. The presence of a large MNE head office may be of great importance, especially in small countries. Undoubtedly, Nokia's success has generated huge positive external effects by enhancing Finland's reputation as a high-tech country.

As mentioned earlier, the relocation of Finnish corporate headquarters abroad has almost always resulted from a merger or an acquisition. This development will probably continue in the future. The location of corporate headquarters and the parent company is especially interesting when two equal firms merge. In this case, how heavily corporations are taxed may be an important factor influencing the decision.

Some of the largest Finnish firms could possibly relocate their headquarters abroad over the next few years without a merger or an acquisition. The globalisation of large firms already extends to sales, production, R&D and ownership. As a part of this globalisation trend and the decreasing importance of Finland as a factor and product market, some parent companies and top management may relocate abroad. The most likely host countries would be the United Kingdom and the Netherlands.

7.   Conclusions

There are both potential benefits from and drawbacks to increasing foreign ownership. In the case of Finland, growing inflows of both portfolio and direct investment have had a positive bearing on economic efficiency. The rate of return on capital has increased more rapidly in companies with high foreign ownership. The same applies to labour productivity. It is also evident that Finnish firms that have been acquired by foreign multinationals have benefited from their global distribution networks and management capabilities.

It is not clear, however, how foreign ownership has affected Finnish companies' R&D and accumulation of other intangible assets and hence their long-run growth prospects. Informal evidence seems to indicate, however, that even in this respect the impacts of foreign ownership have been positive.

Recent studies show that high technology in certain fields, such as in the ICT sector and the paper industry, tends to attract foreign investment. Assuming that the technology base cannot be constantly upgraded and cannot maintain its attractiveness indefinitely, there is a risk that the accumulated knowledge may flow out of the country when the MNEs relocate their assets to increase the overall performance of the corporation. There is a constant race among countries and regions to attract high-tech firms and plants. These firms are important not only for the purposes of technological infrastructure and taxation but also for social and economic systems as a whole.

Increasing foreign ownership and the globalisation of business have profoundly changed many national institutions. They have triggered major changes in corporate governance towards the US model. Firms with significant foreign ownership more often announce that shareholder value is their major objective, and generate higher economic value added to their owners than Finnish-owned firms. It remains to be seen how these changes will affect the country's technological specialisation in the future – whether they favour high-risk and high-tech activities, or whether they reduce long-term investment in R&D.

REFERENCES

Ali-Yrkkö, J. (2003), 'Patterns of Finnish merger and acquisition activity', in: A. Hyytinen and M. Pajarinen (eds.) *Financial Systems and Firm Performance: Theoretical and Empirical Perspectives*, Series B 200, Research Institute of the Finnish Economy, Taloustieto Oy, Helsinki.

Ali-Yrkkö, J., and P. Ylä-Anttila (1997), *Yritykset kansainvälistyvät: Katoavatko työpaikat? (Companies are Becoming more International: Are Jobs being*

Exported?), Series B 130, Research Institute of the Finnish Economy, Taloustieto Oy, Helsinki.

(2002), *Pääkonttorien sijainti, kansainvälistyminen ja verotus (The Location of Headquarters, Internationalisation of Business and Taxation)*, Discussion Paper no. 831, Research Institute of the Finnish Economy, Helsinki.

(2003), 'Globalization of business in a small country: does ownership matter?', in: A. Hyytinen and M. Pajarinen (eds.) *Financial Systems and Firm Performance: Theoretical and Empirical Perspectives*, Series B 200, Research Institute of the Finnish Economy, Taloustieto Oy, Helsinki, 249–68.

Allen, F., and D. Gale (1999), *Corporate Governance and Competition*, Wharton Financial Institutions Center, 99–28, The Wharton School, University of Pennsylvania.

Berglöf, E. (1997), 'Reforming corporate governance: redirecting the European agenda', *Economic Policy*, 12, 91–123.

Braunerhjelm, P. (2004), 'Heading for Headquarters? Why and how the location of headquarters matters among the EU countries', in: L. Oxelheim and P. Ghauri (eds.) *European Union and the Race for Foreign Direct Investment in Europe*, Elsevier, Oxford, 123–48.

Caves, R. (1980), 'Industrial organization, corporate strategy and structure', *Journal of Economic Literature*, 18, 64–92.

(1996), *Multinational Enterprise and Economic Analysis*, Cambridge University Press, Cambridge.

Chibber, P. K., and S. K. Majumdar (1999), 'Foreign ownership and profitability: property rights, control, and the performance of firms in Indian industry', *Journal of Law and Economics*, 42, 209–38.

Finnish Economic Weekly (Talouselämä) (1997), 20.

Goergen, M. (1998), *Corporate Governance and Financial Performance: A Study of German and UK Initial Public Offerings*, Edward Elgar, Cheltenham.

Grant, J. (1997), *Foundations of Economic Value Added*, Frank J. Fabozzi Associates, New Hope, PA.

Griffith, R. (1999), *Productivity and Foreign Ownership in UK Industry*, Working Paper no. WP99/11, Institute for Fiscal Studies, London.

Honkapohja, S., and E. Koskela (1999), 'The economic crisis of the 1990s in Finland', *Economic Policy*, 14, 400–36.

Hjerppe, R., and J. Ahvenainen (1986), 'Foreign enterprises and nationalistic control: the case of Finland since the end of the nineteenth century', in: A. Teichova, M. Levy-Leboyer and H. Nussbaum (eds.) *Multinational Enterprises in Historical Perspective*, Cambridge University Press, Cambridge, 286–98.

Holmström, B., and S. N. Kaplan (2001), 'Corporate governance and merger activity in the United States: making sense of the 1980s and 1990s', *Journal of Economic Perspectives*, 15 (2), 121–44.

Hyytinen, A., and M. Pajarinen (2001), *Financial Systems and Venture Capital in Nordic Countries: A Comparative Study*, Discussion Paper no. 774, Research Institute of the Economy, Helsinki.

(eds.) (2003), *Financial Systems and Firm Performance: Theoretical and Empirical Perspectives*, Series B 200, Research Institute of the Finnish Economy, Taloustieto Oy, Helsinki.

Hyytinen, A., P. Rouvinen, O. Toivanen and P. Ylä-Anttila (2003), 'Does financial development matter for innovation and economic growth? Implications for public policy', in: A. Hyytinen and M. Pajarinen (eds.) *Financial Systems and Firm Performance: Theoretical and Empirical Perspectives*, Series B 200, Research Institute of the Finnish Economy, Taloustieto Oy, Helsinki, 379–447.

Institute of Fiscal and Monetary Policy (1996), *Socio-Economic Systems of Japan, the United States, the United Kingdom, Germany and France*, Ministry of Finance, Tokyo.

Jonung, L. (ed.) (2002), *Vem skall äga Sverige? (Who Will Own Sweden?)*, SNS Förlag, Stockholm.

Jungnickel, R. (ed.) (2002), *Foreign-Owned Firms: Are They Different?*, Palgrave Macmillan, London.

Kasanen, E., J. Kinnunen and J. Niskanen (1996), 'Dividend-based earnings management: empirical evidence from Finland', *Journal of Accounting and Economics*, 22, 282–312.

Kiander, J., and P. Vartia (1996), 'The Great Depression of the 1990s in Finland', *Finnish Economic Papers*, 9, 72–88.

Koski, H., P. Rouvinen and P. Ylä-Anttila (2002), 'ICT clusters in Europe: the great central banana and small Nordic potato', *Information Economics and Policy*, 14, 145–65.

Lichtenberg, F. R. (1992), *Corporate Takeovers and Productivity*, MIT Press, Cambridge, MA.

Lovio, R. (1992), *The Influence of Foreign Companies on the Birth and Development of the Finnish Electronics Industry*, Discussion Paper no. 393, Research Institute of the Finnish Economy, Helsinki.

Maliranta, M. (2001), *Productivity Growth and Micro-level Restructuring: Finnish experiences during the turbulent decades*, Discussion Paper no. 757, Research Institute of the Finnish Economy, Helsinki.

Mannio, P., E. Vaara and P. Ylä-Anttila (eds.) (2003), *Our Path Abroad: Exploring Post-war Internationalization of Finnish Corporations*, Taloustieto Oy, Helsinki.

Ministry of Economy, Trade and Industry (2001), *Summary of the 2000 Survey of Foreign Affiliates' Business Activities*, www.meti.go.jp/english/statistics/downloadfiles/h2c201be.pdf.

Organisation for Economic Co-operation and Development (2001), *New Patterns of Industrial Globalisation: Cross-Border Mergers and Acquisitions and Strategic Alliances*, Paris.

Oxelheim, L., and P. Ghauri (eds.) (2004), *European Union and the Race for Foreign Direct Investment in Europe*, Elsevier, Oxford.

Pajarinen, M., P. Rouvinen and P. Ylä-Anttila (1998), *Small Country Strategies in Global Competition: Benchmarking the Finnish Case*, Series B 144, Research Institute of the Finnish Economy, Taloustieto Oy, Helsinki.

Pajarinen, M., and P. Ylä-Anttila (eds.) (1999), *Cross-Border R&D in a Small Country: The Case of Finland*, Taloustieto Oy, Helsinki.

(2001), *Maat kilpailevat investoinneista: teknologia vetää sijoituksia Suomeen (Countries Compete for Investment: Finnish Technology Attracts Foreign Firms)*,

Series B 173, Research Institute of the Finnish Economy, Taloustieto Oy, Helsinki.

Pfaffermayr, M., and C. Bellak (2002), 'Why foreign-owned firms are different: a conceptual framework and empirical evidence for Austria', in: R. Jungnickel (ed.) *Foreign-Owned Firms: Are They Different?*, Palgrave Macmillan, London, 13–57.

Porter, M. E. (1990), *The Competitive Advantage of Nations*, The Free Press, New York.

Rouvinen, P., and P. Ylä-Anttila (2003), 'Case study: little Finland's transformation to a wireless giant', in: S. Dutta, B. Lanvin and F. Paua (eds.) *The Global Information Technology Report 2003–2004*, Oxford University Press (for the World Economic Forum), New York, 87–108.

Statistics Sweden (1996), *Foreign-Owned Enterprises* (in Swedish), Report no. F18SM9701, Stockholm.

Strandell, A. (1997), 'Foreign-owned enterprises in Sweden', in: *Swedish Industry and Industrial Policy 1997*, NUTEK Publications, Stockholm.

Thomsen, S., and T. Pedersen (2000), 'Ownership structure and economic performance in the largest European companies', *Strategic Management Journal*, 21, 689–705.

Tylecote, A., and E. Conesa (1999), *Corporate Governance, Innovation Systems and Industrial Performance*, CRITEC Discussion Paper no. 18, Centre for Research in Innovation and Technological Change, University of Sheffield.

Väyrynen, R. (1999), *Globalisaatio ja Suomen poliittinen järjestelmä* (*Globalisation and the Finnish Political System*), Taloustieto Oy, Helsinki.

Ylä-Anttila, P. (2000), 'Globalization of business in a small country: implications for corporate governance and national systems of innovation', *Ekonomiska Samfundets Tidskrift*, 1, 5–20.

Ylä-Anttila, P., and J. Ali-Yrkkö (1997), 'Foreign owners set their sights higher than local ones', *Unitas*, 2, 14–19.

9   Attitudes to foreign direct investment in the United Kingdom

Forrest Capie, Geoffrey Wood and Frank Sensenbrenner

1.   Introduction

Foreign ownership of domestic firms is almost a non-issue in the United Kingdom. Almost, but not quite. Occasionally, there is concern over the purchase by foreigners of a well-known British firm. (This concern, incidentally, appears to be entirely oblivious of the fact that quite often these firms have, in British hands, fared rather badly.) Sometimes there is complaint about FDI in Britain; but the complaint is that there is not enough of it. 'Britain in Europe', an organisation that campaigns for British membership of EMU, has maintained that Britain's not using the euro will reduce foreign investment in Britain. 'Business for Sterling', an organisation that, as its name suggests, is opposed to British membership of EMU, maintains that failure to adopt the euro will have no such harmful effects. Note the use of the word 'harmful'. Foreign investment in Britain is usually seen as a good thing.

Documenting and explaining the British attitude is an important part of this study. We also, however, consider foreign investment in two industries in which it has attracted particular attention: motor car production and financial services.

The structure of the chapter is as follows. We first provide some historical background, setting UK investment in a long-run context. This context, we argue, is of importance in influencing UK attitudes. Then we turn to laying out some possible approaches to the analysis of inward investment and of attitudes to it, following this with some hypotheses based on them. In turn we follow this discussion with a review of previous work on inward investment into the United Kingdom; the work is interesting not just for the conclusions it reaches but for the questions it addresses. Next, having set out our data, and their very

This chapter has benefited greatly from the thorough and insightful comments of Dirk Heremans, its discussant at the EU conference at which it was first presented, and of Lars Jonung and George Vernon. We are also indebted to two anonymous referees.

substantial limitations, we consider how our hypotheses stand up in the face of them. Finally, we draw some conclusions.

2.   Historical overview

In the two or three hundred years prior to 1800 the prevailing political and economic philosophy was mercantilism. This meant different things to different people at different times and in different countries. But at its core was a concern with the centrality of the state and with state-building. It was generally believed that the best means of achieving that was by regulation. (For a recent discussion of these issues, see Engerman, 1994.) Regulation extended to most parts of the economy and had particular implications for international trade and payments. The result was that international trade was distorted and so were the accompanying capital movements.

Reaction against this system in the nineteenth century saw trade increase hugely and capital flows grow at the same time. The United Kingdom was the leading industrial and financial power then; it was the world's largest economy and the greatest trader. From the middle of the century it began exporting capital on an ever-increasing scale. The period 1870 to 1914 was one of extraordinary flows. Britain was consistently lending several per cent of its national income over these years, culminating in a rate of around 10 per cent of national income in the few years immediately prior to World War I.

These capital flows began by going to Europe, and then went further and further afield, to India, North America, Latin America, Australasia and elsewhere. The capital flowed into all parts of the infrastructure: ports, railroads, mining projects and countless other enterprises. By 1914 Britain was a creditor on a vast scale – indeed, on a scale never since equalled. That year Britain held approximately £4,000 million in foreign assets, mostly in the form of portfolio holdings but with a fair amount of direct investment. This was, roughly, equivalent to twice national income at that point. By comparison, Japan, the world's biggest creditor of the late twentieth century, held foreign assets approximately equal in value to its national income – half the size. Britain was responsible for almost half of all foreign lending in the late nineteenth and early twentieth centuries (see Alder, 1967; Obstfeld and Taylor, 1998; and Capie, 2002).

Such capital for development purposes was eagerly sought and willingly given. But there were always those who found fault, and a long-running criticism of the British economy is that it lent too much abroad and, in the process, starved British enterprise of needed funds. Keynes argued this in 1924 when he criticised the Colonial Act of 1900 for allowing certain British trusts to invest abroad when previously they had to invest in the United Kingdom. These arguments are reviewed and appraised in Best and Humphries (1986) and also in Pollard (1989). Keynes's arguments appeared in 'Foreign investment and national advantage', published in volume 35 of *Nation and Athenaeum* (p. 586).

In the inter-war years Britain's capacity to lend was damaged by its weak current account. Then World War II saw the introduction of exchange controls, which were to last until 1979. Furthermore, the Bretton Woods arrangement required and allowed capital controls, and the period from the end of the war until the 1970s was one of limited international capital movements. As exchange controls were lifted and floating exchange rates proliferated so capital began to flow again, and in the last two decades of the twentieth century these capital flows were greater than ever. It should be remarked, though, that, while in real absolute terms this is clearly the case, it is less easy to be so sure in terms of percentages of GDP. Obstfeld and Taylor's (1998) calculations for a limited number of countries suggest that the percentage shares were actually bigger in the nineteenth century; see also Capie, 2002.

The abolition of exchange controls in Britain in 1979 revived the opposition to capital flows, and the old arguments began to be heard again. There was by this time a clear political divide between the Conservative Party, which favoured open markets, and the Labour Party which was opposed. Indeed, Labour talked in 1980 of reintroducing controls at the next general election, which they believed they would win. In a pamphlet of the time (Labour Party, 1982) the argument was made that 'since the removal of exchange controls (1979) institutions have invested far too large a proportion of their funds abroad... The City's efforts have not therefore concentrated on the needs of the domestic economy' (p. 12). They proposed, then, to prevent and reverse such flows through the establishment of a National Investment Board, which, in turn, would direct assets into British industry. Pension funds and unit trusts were the main target and the idea was to cap the overseas content of their portfolios. The ambition was to repatriate substantial capital, which would then be channelled into British industry.

On the other side Britain has also attracted large amounts of foreign investment, and although still a net creditor there is substantial foreign ownership in Britain. We turn to an examination of the data below. It is worth remarking here that there has been little evidence in the United Kingdom of any public disquiet over the growing extent of foreign ownership. Similarly, in the United States in the nineteenth century, when there was quite extensive British ownership of assets, there appears to have been little concern – in spite of the antagonism that affected the two countries in the late eighteenth and early nineteenth centuries.

3.   Approach to analysis

When John Stuart Mill called his book on economics *The Principles of Political Economy* he was – and one can be absolutely sure that this was conscious – using words deriving from classical Greek to signify that he was dealing with the economy, the management of resources, of a nation rather than of a family. The modern usage of 'political economy', at least among economists, differs from that. Economists now try to analyse systematically the effect that policy has on the economy; and they do this not only in the once-traditional framework of neoclassical welfare economics, where politicians are viewed as benevolent – sometimes even omniscient – social planners, but, rather, in a framework where policy-makers are self-interested, responding to political incentives. They are treated, in other words, just like other economic actors, except that they respond to a different, or sometimes additional, set of incentives.

The approach has been fairly extensively applied to the analysis of macroeconomic policy-making. It is one of the ways (although far from the only way) by which it is argued that macroeconomic policy should be guided by rules rather than discretion; or that it should be delegated to some body not affected by the desire to win elections. A case for central bank 'independence' can be constructed by this means.[1]

The approach can also be applied elsewhere. It has been used to help understand why financial regulation often creates problems and stifles innovation. It can help understand why and when financial regulation will change. This it does by exposing which groups are benefiting from a particular regulatory framework, and what might change the balance of forces against them so that new groups can change the regulation in order to capture its benefits for themselves. Thirdly, it can explore how regulation can protect particular constituencies via its economic effects. The approach when thus applied sees laws and economic outcomes as jointly determined by politics.

Examples of such applications can be drawn from the study of banking, of corporate control and corporate governance, and of securities markets. Kroszner and Strachan (1999) analyse changes in banking regulation in the United States, showing how the timing of branching deregulation was determined by the relative strengths of the affected interest groups. Roe (2000) maintains that the differences in corporate

---

[1] See Capie et al. (1994) for a discussion of the various meanings of 'independence' in this context.

governance between the United States and Continental Europe reflect the 'social democratic' political framework of most of Continental Europe. Studies (see, for example, Holmström and Kaplan, 2001) have shown how workers and managers can unite to protect incumbents and to restrict the market for corporate control. Rajan and Zingales (2001) explain the erratic – advancing and retreating – development of securities markets. They suggest that incumbent firms seek to restrict such development as new entrants need access to capital markets, while incumbents already have a stream of profits. But, as free trade opens up goods markets, this not only diminishes the influence of the incumbents but increases the likelihood that they too will want access to new sources of capital. Hence is explained the common relationship between changes in financial market regulation and free trade.

Despite these examples, 'new political economy' explanations are hard to test. This is because they endogenise institutional factors that were previously taken as given, thus reducing the set of predictions the models can produce. Further, it can be hard to separate ideological from economic determinants of political choices. (Some, indeed, argue that ideology is ultimately economically determined.) Nevertheless, as the approach has proved fruitful in some areas related to the issues being examined here, we seek to apply it to the present issue.

4.   Hypotheses

The 'new political economy' or 'public choice' approach has found much more favour in the United States than it has in the United Kingdom. Economists and analysts in the former country are much more willing to accept, until shown otherwise by the evidence, that politicians and officials are guided by utility maximisation in their public decisions just as they are in their private ones. We would suggest that the reason for this lies in the different nature of the governmental institutions in the two countries.

Although this is changing a little under Britain's recent governments, the British civil service *at every level* has traditionally sought resolutely to be apolitical. It did try to carry out what elected politicians wished; but a part of its duty was to encourage caution, to think of an ill-defined but valuable concept of 'the national interest'. There are also institutions (the office of the Auditor General, for example) with the explicit role of supervising expenditure so that value for money is obtained, and also ensuring that taxpayers' funds are spent neither on party political purposes nor on ways designed to benefit a member or members of that party.

Although unlikely to be infallible these limitations have tended to constrain partisan – as opposed to political – actions. With that qualification in mind, can the 'new political economy' identify groups or parties that might be opposed to – or, alternatively, favour – inward investment into the United Kingdom? What conjectures can be offered?

One can consider the following groups as having an interest in foreign investment in Britain: the Conservative, Labour and Liberal Democratic Parties (the three main parties – in alphabetical order); trade unions; employers' organisations; local government; and companies that wish simply to sell themselves to the highest bidder. That partitions the polity for this purpose.[2]

Unfortunately, when one makes this division what emerges is that the groups have either internally conflicting interests in this matter or a clear-cut interest but little influence. To see this, consider the groups in the above order. First, the Conservative Party. The trouble with this party (in the present context) is that it has no consistent views on what might broadly be termed 'international economic policy'. The views have, of course, varied *within* the party – all political parties in Britain are implicit coalitions – and the views have varied over time. The Conservative Party was, for example, at one time the party of protection by 'imperial prefer-ence' (see appendix 1 for details on this). But at other times it was close to being a party of 'Manchester Liberals' (a nineteenth-century group that favoured free trade and light, if any, regulation of markets).

Within our data period that latter phase coincides, broadly speaking, with the period when Margaret Thatcher was Prime Minister; so one hypothesis we explore is that inward investment was likely to be unusually high in those years.

What of the Labour Party? Here, too, there has been some inconsist-ency. But, with socialist inclinations, it was for many years the party of state control, of regulation, of protection of workers. Quite often, how-ever, that did not differ in this respect much from the 'paternalistic' phase of the Conservative Party – a phase that characterised that party in particular in its early post-war years. We would expect the two parties to differ significantly in the 'Thatcher years', but not really at other times. Again, reflection suggests that trade unions and employers' or-ganisations would not differ a great deal; both, albeit perhaps for differ-ent reasons, would prefer local (i.e. domestic) ownership of industry. Management *may* be concerned solely with maximising the present

---

[2] Those wishing details on the development, structure and policy approaches of the main British political parties will find abundant information in Coxall and Robins (1998), Brivati and Heffernan (2000) and Bell (1998); and, for the workings of Parliament, Griffith and Ryle (1989).

value of the firm, in which case it would not bother about ownership. But managers may have other objectives – possibly even nationalistic ones. They could fear that subsidiaries will have less opportunity to carry out R&D. If workers feel less secure in their jobs, productivity may decline as the workers invest less, or cease to invest at all, in firm-specific capital; this would reflect badly on the management. Workers, or their representatives, wish to retain influence in the firm so as to form the decision-making process to their advantage. All these points suggest that influence matters. The costs of gaining and exerting such influence increase with distance from the strategic centre. But both groups would also prefer that firms continue to be active than that they close down. Unions would like it because it creates employment; employers' organisations because one firm's activities create business for other firms. (This last point emerges when we touch, below, on developments in the British motor industry.)

And, finally, in the interest groups we come to local authorities and firms that are up for sale. These groups have a clearly identifiable interest. Both want more inward investment, the latter for obvious and straightforward commercial reasons, the former because more employment brings prosperity (and popularity for incumbent politicians) and an expanded tax base. So the interest is clear; but so, too, is the lack of influence. There can be persuasion and lobbying from the groups, but that is all. Further, there is no reason to expect these motives or the power behind them to vary over time; so we do not expect much discernible influence on overseas investment from these bodies.

Summarising on interest groups, then, we would expect the Thatcher years to stand out with regard to inward investment; but no other 'interest group' influence is likely to be notable. Even if one accepts – as not all that many do – the usefulness of the political economy approach in the United Kingdom, it does not help one to identify groups with sharply contrasting views on foreign investment, and to make predictions accordingly.

This does not mean that we do not expect politics, broadly defined, to matter. Tax rates, for example, may well be important. But that is to go beyond the domain of 'pressure group politics'.

5.   Previous work[3]

A notable feature of previous work on foreign investment in the United Kingdom is how sparse and fragmentary this work is – in itself, perhaps,

[3] Bora (2003) provides a good overview of research in this area, looking in part at theory, but includes no studies of EU countries.

evidence of lack of concern. There are four major studies we consider, these being either books or government publications. They are Hood and Young (1983), Stopford and Dunning (1983), Stopford and Turner (1985) and Young et al. (1988).

Hood and Young (1983), the first of these (it was written largely by Hood and Young, with contributions by Reeves and Milner), focuses on investment by multinationals in what were then termed 'assisted areas' – that is to say, areas in which there was government encouragement to foreign investors. It is thus a source for information on a particular kind of foreign investment, although it does not give the total of foreign investment into the United Kingdom. There is a considerable amount of detail but not always the detail one would wish. We do not discuss this volume beyond referring to its data; but we would note that its line with regard to multinational investment, when it is critical, is critical that there has not been enough of what is – from the point of view of raising both employment and labour productivity – a good thing. Stopford and Dunning's work is a part of their study of multinationals; so it allows comparisons on inward investment in various countries, and of the kinds of activities the inward investment has been in. But that is as far as it takes us; we do not refer to it further. The volume by Stopford and Turner is mainly an analysis of the effects that multinationals have had on the British economy, but in its introductory chapter some data on the extent of overseas investment in the United Kingdom are presented. Finally, Young et al. provide a variety of snapshots of data. What general conclusions do these studies reach?

Stopford and Turner (1985), like Young et al., focus on multinational firms; but they are concerned more with the firms and less with the British economy. Their study addresses such topics as why firms become multinational, the role of US firms and the responses of British firms. There is, however, a broader perspective in three chapters: two look at the impact on the economy, one at political attitudes. Looking first at employment, they find that there is little evidence that foreign-controlled jobs are 'more unstable' than domestically controlled ones. When employment in a sector has declined, the decline has usually been more in domestic firms. They also very cogently observe (p. 167) the following: 'The removal of exchange controls in 1979 rekindled a debate that had been discussed for decades: is outward direct investment beneficial or damaging to the health of the economy? Precisely the same question is asked about inward investment. *Were clear answers available, the matter would have been settled long ago.*'

For example, in assessing the effects on trade, it has proved almost impossible to disentangle the effects of investment from those of openness. Even the Reddaway Report (1968) on British investment overseas made progress by *assuming* that, without investment, trade would have been lost to the United Kingdom. Subsequent work indicated that the two go together, but has had little success in establishing causation or answering counter-factuals.

What do they think the political implications were? They describe attitudes as being uncoordinated but broadly supportive. Even when there were restrictions on foreign ownership, they were less restrictive than elsewhere. There was concern about foreign ownership of major financial institutions. (We discuss in a separate section developments in the financial sector.) But inward investment was uncontroversial. An interesting item of evidence cited was referrals to the Monopolies and Mergers Commission: 2.2 per cent of acquisitions by foreign companies were referred to the Monopolies and Mergers Commission between 1978 and 1981, as opposed to 1.6 per cent of acquisitions by domestic companies.[4]

The aim of the study by Young et al. (1988) was 'to examine the impact of multinational companies on the British economy, and the British Government's policy responses'. The period covered was the late 1980s. The authors' starting point was the 'British economy's decline in relation to...its principal competitors'. Economists do not usually see economies as competing with one another. There is a variety of reasons for this. Most obviously, few economies have a central planner to focus the economy on a sole objective. Less obviously, but more fundamentally, by engaging in free trade in goods, services and assets, and allowing free movement of labour, countries achieve mutual benefits by specialising in production according to their resource endowments and skills, and consuming according to their tastes rather than being constrained in consumption by what they can produce. But, setting that aside, what questions did these authors ask, how did they seek for answers and what answers did they find? They see Britain's 'decline' as being due to the decline of its manufacturing industry, and to the extent that this has occurred seek to ask how inward investment (by 'foreign multinationals') could reverse this manufacturing decline.

---

[4] At first glance this might seem to reflect hostility, but in fact it resulted from the (usually) large size of multinational firms. This size is also important in another way, as it explains how there can simultaneously be greater fears of job insecurity over jobs at foreign firms and greater job security at these firms. The reconciliation is that jobs at foreign firms are less secure than jobs at domestic firms of the same size; but foreign firms are, in general, well above average size, and jobs at large firms are more secure than jobs at small ones.

Within this intellectual framework there has already been some previous work. One was by a House of Lords Select Committee on Overseas Trade (1985). This has expressed four main points.

(1) There would not be sufficient inward investment to 'sustain a permanent deficit in manufacturing'.
(2) 'Many British firms have much to learn from foreign practices in the drive to be competitive. . .'
(3) There is concern over the high import content of goods produced by foreign companies.
(4) Government should focus less on the 'job-creating aspects of foreign investment' and more on 'the level of manufacturing and value added'.

Further, possibly inconsistently with the Select Committee's desire for British companies to learn from foreign ones, governments are urged to be careful about encouraging the input of 'foreign R&D' as it may discourage the 'development of new technologies' by British firms.

The study by Young et al. essentially reflects these varied and sometimes conflicting concerns, and it shares the mercantilist viewpoint under which nations are seen as 'competing' in international trade.

The desire to import new technology was not, of course, confined to Britain. In the 1950s and 1960s multinational investment on these grounds was generally welcomed (Dunning, 1974). But, in the 1970s, concerns emerged over the ownership of raw materials and the dominance of multinationals in the high-technology sectors.

By the 1980s opinion seemed to have shifted back to a middle ground. Young et al. (1988) ascribe this change in part to the recession of the time leading to a political focus on reviving employment. Further, in the 1980s the United Kingdom was still a bigger overseas investor than a recipient of foreign investment – by a two-to-one ratio by value (Stopford and Dunning, 1983). Inward investment had been in decline as a share of total (i.e. worldwide) investment by multinationals. What characteristics did these multinational investors in Britain have? They were, unsurprisingly, important firms. They employed more workers on average than British firms did. They were more productive in terms of output per head (by between 17 per cent and 30 per cent) and they paid higher average wages (by some 15 per cent).

What impact did the foreign firms have? Despite concerns about poor UK technology, the technology transfer from investment was not great. The investment had a bias towards technology-intensive sectors, but that did not bring much transfer. There was encouragement to locate R&D in the United Kingdom. But the resulting pattern seemed to reflect worldwide trends – for example, the tendency of pharmaceutical firms to concentrate R&D in a few locations (which led to substantial pharmaceutical R&D in Britain) – rather than either UK efforts or the lack of them. Similarly, while in a few sectors multinationals seemed to become dominant, concentration was not greatly affected by their presence, and no evidence was advanced that competition was affected. No evidence of their having greater success than domestic firms at creating barriers to entry has emerged.[5] The employment effects were not notable, even in areas of high unemployment. But the impact of employment practices was more widespread. Those firms are credited with encouraging – if not introducing – reduced union power, more firm as opposed to industry wage bargaining, the decline of unionisation, more emphasis on communication with employees, and more stringent recruitment procedures.

In general, the effects of investment were seen as sometimes hard to measure, but in broad terms beneficial. It created employment, helped raise productivity, modernised work practices, and certainly did not reduce the R&D carried on in Britain. Interestingly, substantial productivity differences seemed to emerge: a recent study finds that investment in the United Kingdom by US firms has higher productivity than such investment by EU firms. Harris and Robinson (2002) suggest that this is due to the US firms importing US technology. Mayes (1996), in a volume examining various possible sources of productivity growth, also finds FDI to be modestly beneficial.

Detailed studies of foreign investment in deprived areas have confirmed the overall view that the impact was welcome, albeit small. Most studies of this investment have examined the effects of the incentives to come to these areas and create jobs. The verdict is downbeat. Firms came to secure market access, to diversify production locations, and at times when the exchange rate made the move look good. Once firms had decided to move to the United Kingdom, taxpayer-provided financial assistance was of some relevance to determining location; but, even then, the availability of the right kind and quality of labour was more important (Breck and Sharp, 1984). Interestingly, 1984 changes in subsidies (reducing them, and imposing a 'cost per job' limit) had no discernible effect – a point supported by our data for a later period. But, although foreign investment had a favourable effect on employment, productivity and overall prosperity in areas of high unemployment, the fear was expressed that the firms operated in 'an antiseptic work environs' (Young et al.). They did not interact with local firms. That concern was,

---

[5] Their effects on the balance of trade were thought to be 'favourable'.

however, based on a study of the electronics industry in Scotland; that may well have been a special case.

The conclusion of the study of the effect of investment in the United Kingdom by foreign multinationals is that it was, in every dimension, modest but beneficial.[6] It is not surprising, then, that both policy and attitude have been benign neglect, but to this we turn subsequently.

6.   Investment in the United Kingdom

Having reviewed this burst of work on FDI in the United Kingdom, which was focused on multinationals, we turn now to reviewing a long run of data and its interaction with political and economic factors. Once these data have been set out and discussed we turn to a series of special issues, including some unique to the United Kingdom, before drawing our conclusions.

We report at this point the various administrations elected since World War II, and the size of their overall majorities (table 9.1). Figure 9.1 shows the ratio of foreign investment to GDP between 1963 and 2002. One immediately notices the truly remarkable surge at the end of the period. This is not an error but, rather, a reflection of a particular aspect of the UK economy; this is discussed subsequently.[7] We then show various breakdowns of foreign investment. Figure 9.2 shows the breakdown between direct and portfolio investment, in constant prices, with total FDI separated into oil and non-oil, while Figure 9.3 shows the same breakdown figures in relation to GDP. Figure 9.4 shows the breakdown between FDI and portfolio investment, as a percentage of GDP.

Before discussing these data, two definitions are necessary, for direct and portfolio investment. The definitions below are quotations from the Office of National Statistics publication *UK Balance of Payments*, taken from the glossary to the 2002 edition.

Direct Investment – net investment by UK/foreign companies in their foreign/ UK branches, subsidiaries, or associated companies. A direct investment in a company means that the investor has a significant influence on the operations of the company. Investment covers not only acquisition of fixed assets, stock building and stock appreciation, but also other financial transactions such as additions to or payments of, working capital, other loans and trade credit, and acquisitions of securities. Estimates of investment flows allow for depreciation in

---

[6] A recent study by Goma and Gorg (2002) finds rather more mixed results than its predecessors.

[7] It may also, perhaps paradoxically, be a result of the introduction of the euro; for that reduced the portfolio-diversifying effect of EMU countries investing in other EMU countries.

Table 9.1. *General election dates, governments and majorities since 1945*

Election date	Party	Leader	Overall Majority
5 July 1945	Labour	Clement Attlee	146
23 February 1950	Labour	Clement Attlee	5
25 October 1951	Conservative	Winston Churchill, then Anthony Eden	54
26 May 1955	Conservative	Anthony Eden, then Harold Macmillan	60
8 October 1959	Conservative	Harold Macmillan, then Alec Douglas-Home	100
15 October 1964	Labour	Harold Wilson	5
31 March 1966	Labour	Harold Wilson	96
18 June 1970	Conservative	Edward Heath	30
28 February 1974	Labour	Harold Wilson	–
10 October 1974	Labour	Harold Wilson, then James Callaghan	4
3 May 1979	Conservative	Margaret Thatcher	43
9 June 1983	Conservative	Margaret Thatcher	143
11 June 1987	Conservative	Margaret Thatcher, then John Major	102
9 April 1992	Conservative	John Major	21
1 May 1997	Labour	Tony Blair	179
7 June 2001	Labour	Tony Blair	167
5 May 2005	Labour	Tony Blair	67

Source: www.psr.keele.ac.uk/area/uk/uktable.htm.

any undistributed profits. Funds raised by the subsidiary or associate company in the economy in which it operates are excluded as they are locally raised and not sourced from the parent company.

Portfolio Investment – investment in equity and debt securities issued by foreign registered companies, other than that classed as direct investment, and in equity and debt securities issued by foreign governments. A portfolio investment, unlike a direct investment, does not entitle the investor to any significant influence over the operations of the company or institution and represents less than 10% of the equity capital.

A second important matter is how to 'scale' the series. Very obviously, in a country such as the United Kingdom, which has had high and variable inflation in part of our data set, nominal values can be misleading. This would suggest deflation by a measure of the general price level; but this is not our preferred transformation of the series, for there seem to us to be two problems with it. First, is any one of the deflators appropriate when we are concerned primarily with investment goods? Second, are non-UK companies concerned with the real sterling value of

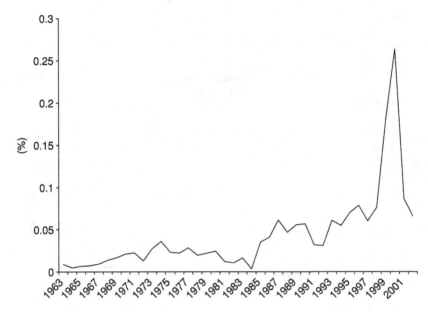

Figure 9.1. Total foreign investment as a percentage of GDP, 1963–2002.

their investment, or rather, perhaps, the real value of their investment in their home currency? Either is plausible. It seems to us that a more appropriate approach to scaling the variables is available. This is to deflate the nominal investment series by nominal GDP. This is, in our view, more appropriate because, insofar as the main focus of the study is attitudes to foreign investment, these are surely likely to be affected not by the 'real' value, however measured, of such investment, but rather its size relative to the economy – which can be proxied by a measure of national income. That is, therefore, the series on which we focus attention.

It might seem natural at this point to compare FDI in the United Kingdom with that in other countries. But we resist that temptation. We do so because the substantial problems of interpretation and reliability – and, indeed, meaning – that affect the UK data (and are discussed below) suggest that there will be similar problems affecting the data on this matter from other countries. Accordingly, making reliable comparisons is a major research project in itself, despite the sometimes cavalier way the data are used by polemicists in, for example, the UK debate over EMU membership.

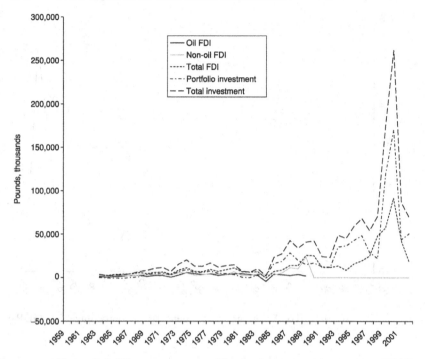

Figure 9.2. The components of foreign investment in constant (2002) terms, 1963–2002.

7.   The data discussed

We now briefly discuss the data, before turning to comment, interpretation, special cases and some slightly novel data.

The first thing to remark is how little there is to remark; the series 'bounce around', so to speak, and not very vigorously, until the mid-1980s. They then start to rise rapidly.

At this point it is necessary to refer to table 9.1, as the first, and most obvious, hypothesis is that hostile governments might have deterred foreign investment. As is clear, and most notably when one bears in mind our comment on the economic philosophy of the Thatcher governments, that does not seem to fit the facts at all. One might conjecture that multinationals waited to see if the changes her governments introduced lasted, and thus say the political hypothesis holds with a time lag. Maybe it does. But, until there are several changes in political climate, the hypothesis thus amended is not refutable, and is therefore of very

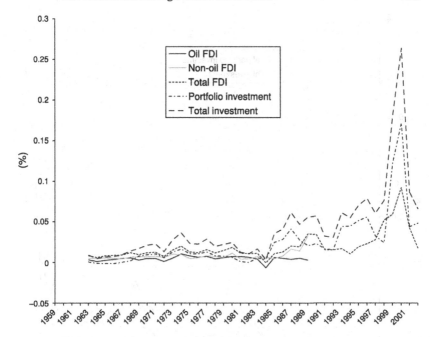

Figure 9.3. The components of foreign investment as a percentage of GDP, 1963–2002.

limited interest. The one change that Britain has experienced recently is not sufficient for any meaningful testing.

Moving on from that we come to 'economic' determinants. First, recollect that *restrictions* on financial support for inward investment were imposed shortly *before* the big surge in such investment. This certainly does not show that incentives do not matter; but it does say that other things matter more.

Does the exchange rate regime matter? It is the conventional wisdom that pegged, or even fixed, exchange rates encourage international trade, and also international investment. But, although that is the conventional wisdom, a good body of evidence is inconsistent with it. Bailey et al. (1986) find that it does not fit US data; Mills and Wood (1993, 1994) find it inconsistent with a long run of UK data; and Carse et al. (1980), by examining the microfoundations of trade, suggest reasons for exchange rate volatility not mattering a great deal. The work of Frankel and Rose (1997) seems inconsistent with that; but several authors have suggested that their results were a special case, produced by a wide variety of factors and not just exchange rate regime change.

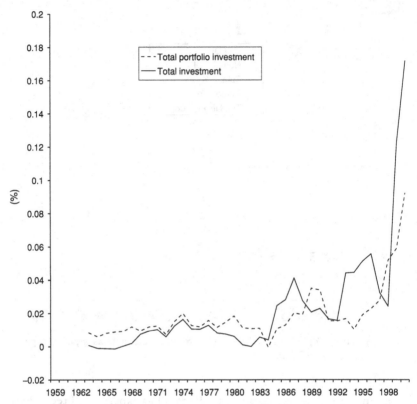

Figure 9.4. The components of foreign investment as a percentage of GDP, 1959–1999.

Two recent studies by the OECD (2002a, 2002) both support this interpretation of the work of Frankel and Rose. In the first, the focus is on Latin America. It is found that FDI has beneficial economic effects, and can be encouraged by improved economic governance. Exchange rate pegging, beyond the stability provided by a stable economic background, seems to make little contribution. Similar findings emerge in the second study, which looks at FDI experience in various transition economies.

How well does the conventional wisdom fit the present data set? A reasonable answer would be 'not at all'. Indeed, it surely is rejected by it. Inward investment rises after the abandoning of fixed exchange rates, and even further after Britain's departure from the Exchange Rate Mechanism (ERM) in September 1992. One could strain, and argue that foreign investors are forward-looking and, therefore, expecting EMU entry. But this would be hard to reconcile with the caution one must ascribe to them if their behaviour is to be consistent with the political regime. We turn again to EMU below.

Similarly, and unsurprisingly, neither short-term interest rates nor long-term rates seem to matter. Indeed, apparently perversely, the lower these rates are the more attractive Britain has been to foreign investment. This is discussed subsequently. It will emerge in subsequent discussion why we do not compare these British interest rates to rates overseas.

There is, however, a more complex hypothesis that can be advanced relating FDI to economic variables. This relates it not to fluctuations in any one series or set of series but, rather, to what might be termed the 'economic climate'.

Note that the lower level, and greater stability, of both long-term and short-term interest rates were associated with a move first towards, and then actually arriving at, an institutional framework that underpinned low and stable inflation; this is why we consider UK interest rates alone, without foreign comparisons, to be revealing. The move to a new monetary framework was started by Conservative Chancellor Norman Lamont, in a search for a monetary anchor after Britain left the ERM in 1992; and it was completed by Labour Chancellor Gordon Brown when he gave the Bank of England 'operational independence' to achieve an inflation target as his first action on taking office in 1997. That same period over which these changes took place coincided with a sustained boom in the real economy. Furthermore, and not apparent in the figures, there is some evidence of an upward change in the United Kingdom's trend growth rate in the early 1980s (see, for example, Mills and Wood, 1994). When we add to this the fact that unemployment fell steadily from Britain's leaving the ERM until the time of writing (early 2004), it seems reasonable to conclude that the economic climate in Britain became more stable, and not only stable but benignly so, from the early 1980s. This may well be seen as a contributing factor to the increase in FDI.

A further factor to note is the removal of exchange control restrictions. These were first suspended, by Mrs Thatcher's first Chancellor of the Exchequer (Sir Geoffrey Howe), and then abolished. This surely contributed to a feeling that Britain was becoming economically more liberal, more open to the world economy – that it was moving back to the kind of situation, described at the beginning of this chapter, that had prevailed when Britain was *the* major overseas investor. Of course, there was also, soon after that, a gradual relaxation in other countries' restrictions on their residents (whether individuals, companies or pension funds) investing overseas. This may also have contributed to the inflow.

Finally in this section, what was the impact of tax? Again, it is hard to see any. Of course, when companies are setting up, effective tax rates will vary from company to company. But the period in the first half of the 1970s, when individual marginal tax rates reached 98 per cent and companies were being taxed on nominal profits when inflation was high, with the effect that the companies were being steadily squeezed of capital, did not affect inflows.

The 'climate of opinion' explanation to which this overview tends is very relevant when considering attitudes to investment from overseas. But, before we reach these, there are two special industrial cases to consider, and some data on jobs to examine. It would, of course, be highly desirable before moving on to these to construct an index that combined objective variables so as to proxy the climate of opinion, a subjective one. One could do so on these data; but one could not test it, as the *changes* in the climate are few. A cross-country study of the role of 'climate of opinion' might be revealing, but the substantial measurement problems would become even greater. Nevertheless, it could well merit future work.

8.   Special cases

8.1   Motor cars

Britain was one of the countries in which motor car production was pioneered; and for some years, especially in the 1930s, mass-production as well as specialist production flourished. The industry then went into a long decline, initially relative and slow but later absolute and accelerating. The British government tempted Chrysler to Scotland; that factory did not prosper. The government promoted amalgamations among the traditional mass manufacturers. These did not prosper either, and nor did the specialist firms that were merged into the group. Nothing seemed to work: not industrial relations, not design, and not the cars themselves – or, at least, not very reliably.

There is now a thriving motor car industry in the United Kingdom once again, and it is largely due to foreign investment that this has come about. Reactions, however, were initially both curious and mixed. The curious aspect is that there should seem to be different attitudes to two different kinds of foreign investment. When Japanese companies arrived, either to set up their own factories (Toyota and Nissan) or originally in partnership with existing firms (Honda's chosen route), the reaction was a welcoming one. They seemed to be about to bring prosperity to areas of high unemployment; and, indeed, so they did. But that was not the only kind of foreign investment. Other manufacturers tried to save struggling British car manufacturers. This, curiously, seemed to arouse, not everywhere but certainly to an extent, a measure of hostility. The workforces were somewhat resistant; occasionally the press displayed a little chauvinism. But these companies ended up in foreign hands, with the exception of Rover; and the chauvinism has died down, just as the cars they produced, even under traditional British names, have been praised.

We do not go further into the details of the decline and recovery of motor car production in the United Kingdom, for that would take us beyond our brief (details and further references can be found in, for example, Owen, 1999). What is interesting about the episode from our point of view is that, first, it is the only example of any note where there have been objections to foreign investment, and, second, because when companies were asked why they moved to the United Kingdom, the 'favourable investment climate' was a key part of the answer (Owen, 1999).

8.2   The City

In 'the City', the conventional shorthand for the financial industry, there is occasional reference to 'Wimbledonisation'. By that is meant the phenomenon notable in regard to the famous tennis tournament played at Wimbledon in south-west London: that the facilities are provided in London but all the notable players come from overseas. The term has been used by many, and the original source is not known: but examples can be found in a *Guardian* article on 8 May 2002; in an article by Rolf Ackermann in the *Frankfurter Allgemeine Zeitung* on 1 February 2002; and, most notably, in a speech given by the Governor of the Bank of England to a City University (London) conference on 7 December 1999. It is well worth quoting from that speech as it demonstrates our key conclusion very clearly.

A few years ago Japanese bankers used to tease me by asking what I thought of the 'Wimbledonisation' of the City – meaning that this country organised the best competition in the world but the visitors carried off the prizes. I used to explain to them that it was activity – rather than nationality of ownership or even control – that mattered in terms of the City's contribution to the wider economy.

Following what was known as *Big Bang* in 1986, the traditional barriers between various types of firms broke down. Stockbrokers and stockjobbers (i.e. wholesalers) no longer had to be separate; banks and other financial institutions could own either or both; merchant banks (the traditional raisers of capital for industry) were open to be taken over; and discount houses, the market-makers in short-term government securities, were similarly available. Subsequently building societies,

Britain's traditional mutually owned mortgage providers, were allowed to 'demutualise' and diversify. By demutualising they became open to takeover. Banks, meanwhile, went into the business of mortgage lending. Foreign banks poured into London, taking over businesses, issuing credit cards, and so forth.

Britain, because of the Eurodollar market, had been an international financial centre for a good few years. It then became an even bigger international financial centre, with a large number of important foreign participants. This attracted comment (and the above-noted nickname): sometimes the nostalgic observation that it was a pity the British had lost their dominance, but absolutely no resistance or complaint. There were no objections at all to this wave of foreign investment. (The absence of something is hard to document; but a reading of the press for the years 1986 to 1990, for example, finds comment on the phenomenon and occasional nostalgia for the old days, but no serious complaints.)

Some reasons are not hard to find. The prices paid for companies, especially early in the process, could often be described as startling, bringing wealth to those who had before enjoyed simply solid prosperity. There is also a second part of the story. This relates to the curious earnings structure in the financial sector. The aspect of this that is relevant to the present discussion is the division between labour and capital. Employment conditions are very unusual. There is, generally, a (very substantial) basic pay, with the possibility of a bonus payment of several multiples of that should the firms and the individual do well in a year. There is also acceptance that job security is low. This has all combined to produce the result that a major part of the profits in good years goes to employees; and in bad years the losses are borne by the shareholders, who may see the workers lose their jobs but do not have the option of smoothing jobs and profits. As a good number of the employees are either British nationals or long-term British residents it is straightforward to see why 'Wimbledonisation' has attracted comment but few complaints.

9.   Employment and inward investment

It is natural to follow that discussion of employment conditions with a discussion of employment numbers.[8]

---

[8] We are grateful to Invest-UK for the data we discuss in this section. This is the source that is sometimes used when it is claimed that Britain is 'losing out' in terms of inward investment through not being in the euro-zone. Unfortunately, neither those who use this argument nor those who oppose it pay due heed to the limitations of the data. A crucial one is touched on below.

Table 9.2 shows job creation as a result of FDI. The years are financial years (from 1 April in one year to 31 March in the next).

Several definitional points need to be made, including an important qualification to the data to note first. As the figures include only those projects in which the Department of Trade and Industry's Invest-UK or its regional partners were involved or that came to their notice, the figures are, in other words, an estimate of the lower bound. Other definitional points to note are that 'new jobs' represent expansion or a new facility and 'safe jobs' represent takeovers of an existing firm. And, oddly, 'associated jobs' is the total of the two.

What light can the data shed? It has to be admitted that it is regrettable that the data are available only after the upturn in FDI, thus allowing no comparison with the earlier, pre-mid-1980s, period. But, within the period they cover, they show a steady, though much gentler, rise in projects than the spectacular rise shown in the headline figures for foreign investment over a longer period (see table 9.3). This apparent discrepancy is resolved below. The FDI shows constantly favourable employment effects, although the relationship between projects and jobs

Table 9.2. *Job creation as a result of FDI, 1985–2002*

Year	Number of projects	Total new jobs	Total safe jobs	Total associated jobs
1985/86	425	26,686	22,771	49,547
1986/87	359	19,430	13,521	32,951
1987/88	380	33,838	30,222	64,060
1988/89	356	26,862	16,071	42,933
1989/90	379	35,997	41,995	77,992
1990/91	365	23,756	60,900	84,656
1991/92	354	22,423	31,093	53,516
1992/93	332	17,821	43,359	61,180
1993/94	431	29,841	69,645	99,486
1994/95	455	38,351	53,757	92,108
1995/96	492	47,347	51,167	98,514
1996/97	497	46,400	51,939	98,339
1997/98	631	46,562	82,771	129,333
1998/99	669	45,157	75,523	120,680
1999/2000	800	54,365	81,587	135,592
2000/2001	881	71,178	52,359	123,537
2001/2002	835	35,127	24,062	59,189

Source: Invest-UK.

Table 9.3. *Foreign investment in the United Kingdom, 1959–2000*

Year	FDI	Portfolio	Total
1959	172		172
1960	190	43	233
1961	311	115	426
1962	187	61	248
1963	257	19	276
1964	200	−39	161
1965	288	−46	242
1966	335	−58	277
1967	370	11	381
1968	528	87	615
1969	448	354	802
1970	622	491	1,113
1971	732	603	1,335
1972	486	390	876
1973	1,126	927	2053
1974	1,778	1,450	3,228
1975	1,410	1,172	2,582
1976	1,537	1,352	2,889
1977	2,367	1,931	4,298
1978	1,991	1,399	3,390
1979	3,030	1,549	4,579
1980	4,355	1,431	5,786
1981	2,932	257	3,189
1982	3,027	−11	3,016
1983	3,386	1,701	5,087
1984	−181	1,288	1,107
1985	3,865	8,913	12,778
1986	4,987	10,911	15,898
1987	8,681	17,710	26,391
1988	9,218	13,220	22,438
1989	18,344	10,860	29,204
1990	19,132	12,880	32,012
1991	9,197	9,818	19,015
1992	9,416	9,579	18,995
1993	10,943	28,770	39,713
1994	7,099	30,680	37,779
1995	13,831	37,315	51,146
1996	17,562	42,985	60,547
1997	22,823	26,670	49,493
1998	45,054	20,926	65,980
1999	54,131	112,274	166,405
2000	88,622	165,045	253,707

Note: All figures are in millions of pounds.

is highly variable. Interestingly, the number of projects as well as the number of jobs created, continued to rise even as unemployment in the United Kingdom continued to fall; a pool of unemployed labour is not, on these figures, a prerequisite for inward investment. Again, rather, the data tell a story of a 'favourable climate' being important.

10.   The vast acceleration

Before summing up, and discussing the British attitude to inward investment, one point remains. What produced the vast acceleration to almost incredible levels from around 1995 onwards? (We reject measurement error, not on the untenable grounds that there is none but because there is no reason to believe it suddenly got worse.) Here we come to a different aspect of London's role as a financial centre. The details are given in appendix 2, so here it is possible to be brief, and essentially make the point by illustration.

When Vodafone took over Mannesmann, Vodafone paid not in cash but in shares, which were issued in London. The issuing and taking up of these shares produced a surge of investment in a British-registered company, and hence inward investment in the United Kingdom. In other words, the sudden surge reflects M&A activities occurring in London.

Of course, Britain was a major recipient of overseas investment even before this acceleration. It might be imagined that this resulted from the 'failure' of banks to finance British industry. But, although that charge has been often made, it is false. Capie and Collins (1992) demonstrate this in some detail; the basic point is that those who made the charge were confused, believing that because loans were repayable on demand they were short-term. They could be that – but usually they were not (see also Capie and Wood, 2001).

11.   Conclusions

Just as Britain was a major overseas investor at the end of the nineteenth century, so it has become a significant recipient of inward investment by the end of the twentieth century and the beginning of the twenty-first. Why has this happened? What have attitudes to it been? Is it thought to have impinged on or hampered domestic macroeconomic policy?

We have suggested that a 'climate' comprised of various factors has contributed. The abolition of exchange controls re-symbolised Britain's traditional acceptance of the benefits of economic openness. The liberalisation of the economy made Britain a better place to invest than it had been for some years. The emergence of a policy framework designed to impart economic stability also helped. What did *not* seem to matter very much, at least in the absence of these conditions, was the party in government, the exchange rate regime or the current state of the economy.

Our verdict on the reasons for the strong overseas investment in Britain thus is, therefore, very close to what Sir Geoffrey Owen (1999) advanced for Japanese investment in the British motor car industry: 'Britain benefited from the [globalisation] process because, thanks to Margaret Thatcher, it had become a more attractive location for investment.'[9]

Note the word 'benefited'. It was plainly Owen's view that there had been benefits. This seems to be the overall view; the policy earlier was described as one of benign neglect. In general, foreign investment was welcomed and given modest incentives. It was not seen either as important to secure or important to repel. One confirmation of this is provided by statistics on foreign ownership. Figures for the foreign ownership of British companies do in principle exist; every holding of 3 per cent in a company has to be notified to the stock exchange, as has every further 1 per cent purchased. But no running totals are published; it is thus impossible to say from day to day which British-registered companies are owned by British residents. Whether they are owned by British citizens (a somewhat different group from residents) is probably impossible in many cases to find out. Still further confirmation is provided by the complete absence from mainstream political discourse of the notion that 'multinationals' have somehow taken over, or impeded the actions of, national government.

What is the source of this attitude? In part, it is probably just the relaxed view of a major overseas investor: 'We invest there, so why shouldn't they invest here?' But there is more to it than that. The Anglo-Saxon system of corporate governance is different from that of most of Continental Europe – and different in a way that we consider crucial to explaining the attitude in the United Kingdom.

The United Kingdom has an 'outsider' corporate governance system, in contrast to the mostly 'insider' corporate governance systems on the European continent.

---

[9] This conclusion, that 'attitudes' matter, suggests that hostility (such as that manifested by the German government to Vodafone's takeover of Mannesmann, or the French government's promotion of 'national champions'), may also have implications for FDI.

These are the chief characteristics of the outsider system.

(i) The ownership of listed firms on the stock exchange is dispersed, often to a large extent among institutional investors.

(ii) Minority shareholders are strongly protected by:

- Disclosure requirements for equity stakes;
- a threshold of 30 per cent limiting voting rights for a single investor; above this threshold the investor must make a formal take over bid; and
- strict 'arm's-length' obligations for dealings by controlling shareholders.

Hence, managers are in control of the firm, sometimes due to their own shareholdings in the firm, but, much more importantly, thanks to the proxy votes they hold on behalf of institutional investors.

As a result, UK management is usually strongly entrenched, and it is not easy to acquire a controlling ownership stake. Ownership, being mostly spread over a number of minority stakes (and this, by implication, therefore also applies to foreign ownership), does not matter much for decision-making.

In contrast, the insider corporate governance system on the European continent has different characteristics.

(i) There is a high level of concentration of ownership.

(ii) There are fewer safeguards for minority shareholders.

(iii) There is not much separation between ownership and management in controlling the company.

Hence, on the Continent, foreign ownership may threaten the (national) autonomy of decision-making, shift the centre of decision-making and have some less desirable implications with respect to R&D. In the United Kingdom, by contrast, management remains firmly in control and foreign ownership may not have much impact upon the autonomy of decision-making. As a result, foreign ownership involves less danger for productivity, R&D, and so forth.

To summarise, the attitudes towards FDI and foreign ownership depend upon the effects; and these may be shaped by institutional factors such as the corporate governance system.

In support of this we would note that attitudes to investment from overseas are very similar in most countries that have the 'Anglo-Saxon' corporate governance system. US and UK attitudes are similar: benign neglect, apart from occasional concern over 'trophy assets' (which surprisingly, in *both* countries are often assets that are losing money in domestic hands). Other countries – such as Australia, Canada and New Zealand – are broadly similar but perhaps marginally less welcoming. This marginal difference may result simply from their being, economically at any rate, smaller: foreign ownership is more noticeable.[10]

Accordingly, we conclude that the attitude to foreign investment in the United Kingdom is indeed one of 'benign neglect', notwithstanding the very substantial volume of these inflows. This attitude is, we believe, partly that of a country that itself invests very substantially overseas, but is primarily the result of the UK corporate governance system. At least at present levels, no one much worries about 'who owns' British industry, so long as British residents have savings somewhere. Foreign ownership is a non-issue in Britain.

Appendix 1: Imperial preference

Imperial preference was a system of preferential trading arrangements among countries of the British Empire/Commonwealth. Different preferences were extended by different Empire countries from as early as the late nineteenth century. Joseph Chamberlain's tariff reform campaign from 1903 onwards advocated turning this into the core of the United Kingdom's trading policy. As Britain was an essentially free trade country British opportunities for offering preferences were limited, though it did grant easier access to the London capital markets to these countries. However, after 1932, when Britain adopted a general tariff of 10 per cent, the possibilities increased and were extended. The tariff was soon raised to 33.3 per cent. But it was on manufactured goods in the main, and the Empire countries were not (with just one or two exceptions) manufacturing countries. The impact of imperial preference on trade was not large but the principle greatly annoyed Britain's biggest trading partner, the United States. A condition of the Lend-Lease that the United States gave Britain in World War II was that Britain would remove imperial preference after the war. The preferences were indeed slowly phased out after the war.

---

[10] In his most helpful comments, our discussant Dirk Heremans suggested a fascinating extension of this argument as to the relevance of particular institutional corporate environments to attitudes to foreign investment. 'It raises also the issue of converging corporate governance structures in Europe, eventually towards the outsider model as a better way to preserve national interests through the separation of management and ownership.' Such developments would also generate data that would facilitate the (currently infeasible) testing of our hypothesis.

Appendix 2: The London market and inward investment

The London market has historically performed as a conduit for portfolio investment across the Atlantic. The City's role as a pre-eminent financial centre allowed Britain to perform as an intermediary in capital flows both westward across the Atlantic (in the nineteenth century) and, subsequently eastward. However, these financial flows have rarely settled in the United Kingdom. Yet, with the recent merger boom, exemplified by Vodafone's takeover of Mannesmann, investment *has* come to settle in the United Kingdom. As the consideration for Mannesmann was in share capital, share issuance led to an increased foreign participation in UK financial markets. Several other mergers were financed in this way, leading to a massive increase in both foreign direct investment and foreign portfolio investment over the past few years.

The most recent *UK Balance of Payments* shows that both categories have returned to their pre-1995 trends. Arguably, therefore, one might conclude that the scale of mergers between UK companies and foreign firms had increased. Furthermore, for an increase in foreign holdings in the United Kingdom, the mergers had to be initiated by UK companies. Therefore, the merger boom displays the increasing international presence of British firms, as opposed to foreign firms 'invading' the London market. As such, foreign ownership is an acceptable corollary to increased British presence abroad. In this sense, British firms have adopted a global scope, which is reflected in the increased foreign ownership of their share capital. Given the previous definitions of direct investment and foreign investment, any merger boom fuelled chiefly by equity capital will provide a similar increase in foreign ownership. Therefore, recent spikes in the foreign ownership of UK shares tend to reflect an active profile on the part of domestic firms, as opposed to foreign capital proactively seeking investment in the United Kingdom.

REFERENCE

Alder, B. J. H (ed.) (1967), *Capital Movements and Economic Development*, Macmillan, London.

Bailey, M. J., G. S. Tavlas and M. Ulan (1986), 'Exchange rate variability and trade performance: evidence for the Big Seven industrial countries', *Weltwirtschaftliches Archiv*, 122, 466–77.

Bell, S. (1998), *The Conservative Party since 1945*, Manchester University Press, Manchester.

Best, M., and J. Humphries (1986) 'The City and industrial decline' in: B. Elbaum and W. Lazonick (eds.) *The Decline of the British Economy*, Clarendon Press, Oxford, 223–39.

Bora, B. (ed.) (2003), *Foreign Direct Investment: Research Issues*, Routledge, London and New York.

Breck, M., and M. Sharp (1984), *Inward Investment: Policy Options for the UK*, Routledge, London.

Brivati, B., and R. Heffernan (eds.) (2000), *The Labour Party: A Centenary History*, Macmillan, London.

Capie, F. H. (2002), *Capital Controls: A 'Cure' Worse than the Problem?*, Research Monograph no. 56, Institute of Economic Affairs, London.

Capie, F. H., and M. Collins (1992), *Have the Banks Failed British Industry?* Institute of Economic Affairs, London.

Capie, F. H., T. C. Mills and G. E. Wood (1994), 'Central bank independence: an exploratory analysis of historical data', in: P.Siklos (ed.) *Varieties of Monetary Reform*, Kluwer Academic Publisher, London, 95–131.

Capie, F. H., and G. E. Wood (2001), 'What kind of stability helps industry?' in: F. McHugh and S. F. Frowen (eds.) *Financial Competition, Risk and Accountability: British and German Experience*, Palgrave, London, 58–69.

Carse, S., J. Williamson and G. E. Wood (1980), *Financing Procedures in UK Foreign Trade*, Cambridge University Press, Cambridge.

Coxall, W., and L. Robins (1998), *Contemporary British Politics*, Palgrave, London.

Dunning, J. H., (1974) 'The future of the multinational enterprise', *Lloyds Bank Review*, 113, 15 22.

Engerman, S. (1994) 'Mercantilism and overseas trade, 1700–1800', in: R. Floud and D. McCloskey (eds.) *The Economic History of Britain since 1700*, Cambridge University Press, Cambridge, 182–204.

Frankel, J., and A. Rose (1997) 'The endogeneity of the optimum currency area criteria', *Swedish Economic Policy Review*, 42, 487–512.

Goma, B., and H. Gorg (2002) *Foreign Ownership, Returns to Scale, and Productivity: Evidence from UK Manufacturing Establishments*, Discussion Paper no. 3503, Centre for Economic Policy Research, London.

Griffith, J. A. G., and M. Ryle (1989), *Parliament: Functions, Practice, Procedures*, Sweet and Maxwell, London.

Harris, R., and K. Robinson (2002), *Spillover from Foreign Ownership in the United Kingdom: Estimates for UK Manufacturing using the ARD*, paper presented to Royal Economic Society annual conference, 25–27 March.

Holmström, B., and S. N. Kaplan (2001) 'Corporate governance and merger activity in the United States: making sense of the 1980s and 1990s', *Journal of Economic Perspectives*, 15 (2), 121–44.

Hood, N., and S. Young (with A. Reeves and M. Milner) (1983) *Multinational Investment Strategies in the British Isles*, HMSO, London.

House of Lords (1985) *Report from a Select Committee on Overseas Trade: Session 1984–85*, HMSO, London.

Kroszner, R. S., and P. Strachan (1999), 'What drives regulation? Economics and politics of the relaxation of bank branching restrictions', *Quarterly Journal of Economics*, 114 (4), 1437–69.

Labour Party (1982), *Investing in Britain*, London.

Mayes, D. (ed.) (1996), *Sources of Productivity Growth*, Cambridge University Press, Cambridge.

Mills, T. C., and G. E. Wood (1994), 'Does the exchange rate regime matter?', *Federal Reserve Bank of St Louis Review*, 75 (4), 3–20.

(1993), 'Capital flows and the excess burden of the exchange rate regime', in: D. Sapsford (ed.) *The Economics of International Investment*, Edward Elgar, Chelterham, 147–74.

Obstfeld, M., and A. M. Taylor (1998), 'The great depression as a watershed: international capital mobility over the long run', in: M. Bordo, C. Goldin and E. N. White (eds.) *The Defining Moment: The Great Depression and the American Economy in the Twentieth Century*, University of Chicago Press, Chicago, 353–402.

Organisation for Economic Co-operation and Development (2002a), *Foreign Direct Investment for Development*, OECD, Paris.

(2002b), *New Horizons for Foreign Direct Investment*, OECD, Paris.

Owen, G. (1999), *From Empire to Europe: The Decline of and Revival of British Industry since the Second World War*, HarperCollins, London.

Pollard, S. (1989), *Britain's Prime and Britain's Decline*, Edward Arnold, London.

Rajan, R. G., and L. Zingales, (2001), 'Financial dependence and growth', *American Economic Review*, 88, 559–87.

Reddaway, W. B. (in collaboration with S. J. Potter and C. T. Taylor) (1968), *UK Direct Investment Overseas*, Vols. I and II, Cambridge University Press, Cambridge.

Roe, M. J. (2000), *Political Preconditions to Separating Ownership from Control: The Incompatibility of the American Public Firm with Social Democracy*, Working Paper no. 155, Center for Law and Economic Studies, Columbia Law School, NY.

Stopford, J. M., and L. Turner (1985), *Britain and the Multinationals*, John Wiley, Chichester.

Stopford, J. M., and J. H. Dunning, (1983), *Multinationals: Company Performance and Global Trends*, Macmillan, London.

Young, S., N. Hood and J. Hamil (1988), *Foreign Multinationals and the British Economy*, Croom Helm, London.

10 Foreign ownership and firm performance in Italy

Sergio Mariotti, Fabrizio Onida and Lucia Piscitello

1. Introduction

The increasing globalisation of markets and firms is mirrored in a wide variety of phenomena ranging from international trade to strategic alliances, joint ventures and foreign direct investment. The latter, in particular, has increased dramatically over the last few decades, both in relative and absolute terms, mainly due to a series of technological, economic and political changes, including the diffusion of ICT as well as liberalisation and privatisation processes.

Before falling dramatically in 2001 and 2002 due to the collapse of the speculative bubble, and following a decade of 13 per cent annual growth during the 1980s (to be compared to 5 per cent growth in GDP and 7 per cent in exports), world FDI flows almost reached $1.300 billion in 2000, a record 19 per cent of the world's gross product (UNCTAD, 2001). In 2001 sales of foreign subsidiaries (estimated at $18.517 billion) were far more than double the total volume of world exports of goods and non-factor services ($7.430 billion), and the gross output of foreign subsidiaries ($3.495 billion) was almost 11 per cent of world GDP ($31.900 billion) (UNCTAD, 2002).

The geographical pattern of world FDI has undergone significant changes in the post-war period. The falling share of the United States in the stock of outward FDI was matched by an increasing US role as an area of destination. Over the last two decades the location of the world FDI inward stock has shifted in favour of the United States (from 13 per cent to 19 per cent), Western Europe (from 36 per cent to 40 per cent) and Latin America (from 4.5 per cent to 6 per cent). In the most recent period Eastern Europe and Asia (China, above all) have played an increasingly important role as the location for greenfield investments.

Italy's position has been modest and shrinking over the last decade, from 3.1 per cent of the world inward stock in 1990 to 1.6 per cent in 2001. In the same period the share of the European Union as a whole has hovered around 39 per cent. The ratio of inward FDI to gross domestic product at the end of 2000 was 10.5 per cent for Italy, as against 17.1 per cent for the world average and 30.3 per cent for the European Union. The ratio of inward FDI to gross fixed capital formation was increasing worldwide in the last few years of the twentieth century. While Italy went from less than 2 per cent to 6.3 per cent in 2000, the European Union went from 6.5 per cent up to an exceptional 50.1 per cent. With regard to cumulative flows of inward and outward OECD investments between 1992 and 2001, Italy ranked twelfth as an investor ($97.7 billion), and fifteenth as a country of destination ($60.6 billion – less than half the level achieved by Mexico and Spain). In terms of the UNCTAD 'transnationality index of host economies' (measured as each country's share in world FDI inflows relative to its share in world GDP, employment and exports) Italy also ranks quite low, lagging behind most European countries as well as a number of large developing countries, such as Brazil, Indonesia, China, Mexico and South Korea (UNCTAD, 2002, p. 21). Within the world's top hundred non-financial MNEs ranked by foreign assets in 2000 (a group that generates about 15 per cent of world employment and 16 per cent of world turnover), Italy had only two (Fiat and Eni). The same figure held for Spain, Sweden and Canada, while Germany accounted for ten groups, France and the United Kingdom for thirteen, Japan for sixteen and the United States for twenty-four.

This chapter concentrates on the internationalisation of the Italian system (with reference to the inward side of the story) as of the beginning of 2002, and the recent historical trends. In particular, the aim of the study is twofold: to provide a detailed description of foreign ownership in Italy, and in comparison with other major industrialised countries; and to provide some further evidence on the controversial topic of the consequences of foreign ownership for local companies' labour productivity and employment.

The remainder of the chapter is organised as follows. Section 2 provides some evidence about foreign direct investment in Italy at the beginning of 2002, and also for the last fifteen years. Data are drawn from the Reprint database, developed at Politecnico di Milano and sponsored by ICE (the Italian Institute for Foreign Trade). Section 3 briefly reviews the empirical literature on the impact of FDI on the host country and the local economy. Section 4 focuses on the methodology and data employed in the empirical study. Specifically, the empirical analysis covers foreign M&As[1] in Italy during the 1990s, and the

---

[1] The focus is on M&As as they constitute the lion's share of the foreign initiatives and the most visible face of globalisation (as far as developed countries are concerned).

methodology employed relies on parametric tests (T tests on matching pairs) run on counter-factuals – i.e. comparing local firms that were the subject of foreign acquisition with firms that were not. Section 5 illustrates the empirical findings, while section 6 summarises.

2.   Foreign ownership in Italy in the 1986–2002 period

2.1   The Reprint database

In order to illustrate foreign direct investment in Italy, we rely on the Reprint database, developed by Politecnico di Milano since the late 1980s and sponsored by ICE.[2]

Reprint registers inward and outward Italian FDI since 1986, and it is updated every two years. Traditionally, data have been gathered only for manufacturing sectors, while the 1 January 2002 update included information on manufacturing, service and business-related service sectors. In particular, the following sectors have been included.

  (i) Mining and manufacturing – codes 11–37 (Ateco nomenclature).
 (ii) Public utilities (energy, gas and water) – Ateco codes 40–41.
(iii) Buildings – Ateco code 45.
 (iv) Wholesale trade – Ateco code 51.
  (v) Transport and logistics – Ateco codes 60–63 (excluding 63.3).
 (vi) Telecommunication services – Ateco code 64.2.
(vii) Software and IT services – Ateco code 72.
(viii) Other business services – Ateco codes 71, 73, 74.
 (ix) Service sectors, but only including business-related services, therefore excluding agriculture, real estate, retail trade, and social services.

It is also worth observing that, for the sake of data homogeneity, the financial sector (banking and insurance, financial services, financial holdings) has not been included, mainly due to its peculiar accounting rules. That having being said, one should notice that the sector of financial intermediation absorbed a very large share (39 per cent) of the stock of inward FDI in Italy at the end of the 1990s: a share much larger than in other major European countries (from a minimum of 5.3 per cent in Sweden to a maximum of 26.5 per cent in the United Kingdom at the end of 1998). By contrast, the share in the manufacturing sector was more or less in line with that in other European partners (Mariotti and Mutinelli, 2002).

[2] The database had traditionally been sponsored by CNEL (the National Council for Economy and Labour), while ICE started sponsoring it at the beginning of 2001.

2.2   The general picture

Reprint lists 5,421 Italian affiliates of foreign parent corporations at the beginning of 2002, with nearly 882,500 employees and a 2001 turnover of more than €324 billion (table 10.1).

The foreign share in the manufacturing sector is overwhelming, ranging from 42.8 per cent of firms to 69.5 per cent of employees. The second most important sector is wholesale trade, with a share of 34.4 per cent in terms of firms and 10.6 per cent in terms of employees.

The marked, long-standing preference of foreign investors for majority-owned firms in their Italian involvement is clearly shown in tables 10.2 and 10.3: 4,991 firms (92.1 per cent of the total), more than 744,000 employees (84.3 per cent), about €276 billion turnover and €56.2 billion gross output (85.1 per cent and 88.5 per cent, respectively) relate to majority-held interests.

The share of FDI in domestic employment is about 8.2 per cent (17.9 per cent in domestic employment in firms with twenty or more employees – see table 10.4), ranging from 12.8 per cent in manufacturing industry to 0.5 per cent in energy, water and gas. The share of foreign ownership in manufacturing employment is well below that in the other major European countries, the only exception being Germany, which exhibits a lower rate of foreign penetration partly because of the remarkable increase of domestic employment after reunification, while very few foreign investors were inclined to enter the former East Germany. Ireland, where about half of the total workforce in manufacturing belongs to foreign affiliates, is a well-known example of a country with favourable locational advantages, as well as having a successful 'invest in' public policy. In general, one may see countries such as Ireland, Spain and Portugal as relatively young members, with lower labour costs and a more energetic approach to the marketing of their own territorial attractiveness.

This confirms the low attractiveness of the Italian economic system already highlighted in UNCTAD (2000). Italy is a laggard, not only in relation to major developed countries and other countries similar in terms of comparative advantage, such as Spain (see Bugamelli, 2001); in fact, Italy is also behind countries such as Hong Kong, Mexico, Argentina, Singapore, Australia and Malaysia.

However, these conclusions are in line with the results of the standard 'gravity model' used to predict FDI flows based on the determinants of intra-industry trade, which typically show a depressing effect of the dummy variables associated with Italy (see, for example, CER, 1999).

Table 10.1. *Inward FDI in Italian industrial and service sectors, 2002*

	Firms		Employees		Turnover		Value added	
	Number	Percentage share	Number	Percentage share	Value (euros million)	Percentage share	Value (euros million)	Percentage share
Mining industry	13	0.2	1,512	0.2	366	0.1	133	0.2
Manufacturing industry	2,321	42.8	613,346	69.5	185,412	57.1	40,150	63.3
Construction	40	0.7	5,409	0.6	3,868	1.2	1,417	2.2
Energy, water and gas	56	1.0	6,745	0.7	1,681	0.5	434	0.7
Wholesale trade	1,863	34.4	93,369	10.6	92,856	28.6	8,764	13.8
Logistics and transport	264	4.9	39,296	4.5	11,035	3.4	2,180	3.4
Software and TLC services	389	7.2	79,385	9.0	19,606	6.1	7,271	11.5
Other business services	475	8.8	43,367	4.9	9,664	3.0	3,094	4.9
Total	5,421	100.0	882,429	100.0	324,488	100.0	63,444	100.0

Table 10.2. *Inward FDI in Italian industrial and service sectors: the sectoral composition of majority-owned operations, 2002*

	Firms		Employees		Turnover		Value added	
	Number	Percentage share	Number	Percentage share	Value (euros million)	Percentage share	Value (euros million)	Percentage share
Mining industry	13	0.3	1,512	0.2	366	0.1	133	0.2
Manufacturing industry	2,063	41.3	501,540	67.4	147,550	53.5	34,609	61.6
Construction	32	0.7	3,094	0.4	1,822	0.7	595	1.1
Energy, water and gas	46	0.9	5,985	0.8	1,425	0.5	346	0.6
Wholesale trade	1,791	35.9	90,626	12.2	90,240	32.7	8,580	15.3
Logistics and transport	240	4.8	35,484	4.8	10,163	3.7	2,009	3.6
Software and TLC services	360	7.2	64,336	8.6	15,547	5.6	6,904	12.3
Other business services	446	8.9	41,544	5.6	8,958	3.2	2,993	5.3
Total	4,991	100.0	744,121	100.0	276,071	100.0	56,168	100.0

Table 10.3. *Inward FDI in Italian industrial and service sectors: the percentage share of majority ownership control by sectors, 2002*

	Firms	Employees	Turnover	Value added
Mining industry	100.0	100.0	100.0	100.0
Manufacturing industry	88.9	81.8	79.6	86.2
Construction	80.0	57.2	47.1	42.0
Energy, water and gas	82.1	88.7	84.8	79.7
Wholesale trade	96.1	97.1	97.2	97.9
Logistics and transport	90.9	90.3	92.1	92.2
Software and TLC services	92.5	81.0	79.3	95.0
Other business services	93.9	95.8	92.7	96.7
Total	92.1	84.3	85.1	88.5

Table 10.4. *The percentage share of foreign affiliates in domestic employment, 2002*

	Total FDI		Majority ownership control	
	Total Employment[a]	Employment in larger firms[b]	Total Employment[a]	Employment in larger firms[b]
Mining industry	4.1	8.5	4.1	8.5
Manufacturing industry	12.8	21.5	10.5	17.6
Construction	3.7	3.8	2.1	2.2
Energy, water and gas	0.5	2.5	0.4	2.2
Wholesale trade	6.3	30.4	6.1	29.5
Transport and communications	5.4	7.7	3.2	4.5
Business services	5.6	18.1	5.2	16.7
Total	8.2	17.9	6.8	14.9

[a]Employees in foreign affiliates / total domestic employment.
[b]Employees in foreign affiliates / domestic employment in firms with twenty or more employees.

2.3   Trends in inward FDI in the manufacturing industry, 1986–2002

Our analysis of trends in foreign investment in Italy in the last decade focuses upon the manufacturing industry, since no time series is available for services.

Table 10.5 shows that there has been a gradual increase in inward FDI in Italian industry. In particular, the most remarkable increase in foreign

Table 10.5. *Majority investments held by foreign parent companies in Italian industrial enterprises, 1986–2002*

	Majority investments (a)		Total (b)		(a)/(b) (per cent)
	Number	Index	Number	Index	
Italian affiliates of foreign parent companies in manufacturing industry					
January 1986	1,180	100.0	1,375	100.0	85.8
January 1991	1,481	125.5	1,706	124.1	86.8
January 1996	1,667	141.3	1,902	138.3	87.6
January 2000	1,973	167.2	2,199	159.9	89.7
January 2001	2,036	172.5	2,285	166.2	89.1
January 2002	2,063	174.8	2,321	168.8	88.9
Employees of Italian affiliates in manufacturing industry					
January 1986	375,622	100.0	465,143	100.0	80.8
January 1991	421,702	112.3	514,193	110.5	82.0
January 1996	421,934	112.3	523,035	112.4	80.7
January 2000	486,995	129.7	559,181	120.2	87.1
January 2001	498,312	132.7	609,853	131.1	81.7
January 2002	501,540	133.5	613,346	131.9	81.8

investment started from the mid-1980s, probably due to the approach of the Single Market. Indeed, between 1986 and 2002 the number of Italian industrial affiliates of foreign parent companies rose from 1,375 to 2,321 (an increase of 68.8 per cent). The number of employees in the same period rose from 465,143 to 613,346 (an increase of 31.9 per cent). The faster increase in the number of affiliates, relative to the size of employment, reflects the marked orientation towards investment in smaller companies.

A breakdown of employment by the nationality of the investor, and by the broad sectoral classes defined by Pavitt (1984),[3] over the period 1986 to 2002 is shown in tables 10.6 and 10.7.

In particular, concerning the geographic composition (table 10.6), several points are worthy of note. At the beginning of 2002 three-fifths (60.9 per cent) of employees belonged to foreign affiliates of Western European MNEs, and more than one-third (33.8 per cent) to affiliates of North American parent companies, while the role of other countries is

---

[3] It may be worth reminding ourselves that Pavitt's taxonomy classifies industries as characterised either by (i) 'science-based' firms, (ii) 'production-intensive' firms or (iii) 'supplier-dominated' firms. The second group is further divided into the categories of 'scale-intensive' production and 'specialised suppliers'.

Table 10.6. *A breakdown of employees of Italian affiliates of foreign parent companies by their home country, 1986, 1996 and 2002*

	January 1986		January 1996		January 2002	
	Number	Percentage share	Number	Percentage share	Number	Percentage share
Western Europe	257,396	55.4	350,242	67.0	373,492	60.9
North America	200,156	43.0	138,544	26.5	207,249	33.8
Japan	2,444	0.5	13,302	2.5	19,696	3.2
Other countries	5,147	1.1	20,947	4.0	12,909	2.1
Total	465,143	100.0	523,035	100.0	613,346	100.0

Table 10.7. *A breakdown of employees of Italian affiliates of foreign parent companies by Pavitt's sectoral taxonomy, 1986, 1996 and 2002*

	January 1986		January 1996		January 2002	
	Number	Percentage share	Number	Percentage share	Number	Percentage share
Supplier-dominated sectors	30,866	6.7	30,057	5.7	36,055	5.9
Scale-intensive sectors	206,172	44.3	255,490	48.9	327,163	53.3
Specialised supplier sectors	86,156	18.5	101,458	19.4	110,699	18.1
Science-based sectors	146,644	31.5	136,030	26.0	139,429	22.7
Total	465,143	100.0	523,035	100.0	613,346	100.0

rather modest (the weight of Japan is 3.2 per cent out of the remaining 5.3 per cent). The share of US subsidiaries declined until the mid-1990s (from 43 per cent in 1986 to 26.5 per cent in 1996), and then recovered subsequently (33.8 per cent in 2002). A corresponding increase until the mid-1990s and a decrease thereafter was recorded in the share of Western European MNEs: in terms of employees, their share went up from 55.4 per cent in 1986 to 67 per cent in 1996, and then declined to 60.9 per cent in 2002). In the long run the Japanese presence has increased slightly, from just 0.5 per cent in 1986 to 3.2 per cent in 2002.

Looking at the sectoral breakdown (table 10.7), it is no wonder that more than half the employees in foreign affiliates at the beginning of

2002 belonged to scale-intensive sectors, as this is a reflection both of a high propensity worldwide to FDI in these industries and of the relevant size of the Italian domestic market. At the opposite end of the spectrum, one could also expect a relatively minor role (less than 25 per cent of the total) for specialised suppliers and supplier-dominated industries, both strongholds of Italian comparative advantages and characterised by a high fragmentation of output among smaller-sized companies. A distinguishing feature of Italian inward FDI, compared to most advanced countries, is the relatively small and declining share (from 31.5 per cent in the mid-1980s to 22.7 per cent in 2002) of high-tech (or science-based) sectors.

The regional distribution of inward FDI (table 10.8) is consistently skewed in favour of northern Italy (about four-fifths of the total in terms of employees), with a tendency for the north-eastern region to gain share (from 12.9 per cent in 1986 to 18.1 per cent in 2002) vis-à-vis the north-west, where the share declined from 65.1 per cent to 62.3 per cent in the same period. Central regions absorb 13.3 per cent and the remaining southern regions (including the islands of Sicily and Sardinia) a modest 6.3 per cent of the total.

Concerning the entry mode preferred by foreign firms in Italy (table 10.9), the trends look similar to those in most of the highly industrialised countries. Especially in the most recent years, the bulk of foreign initiatives consist of the acquisition of already existing local firms, while only a marginal share is undertaken as a greenfield operation. Greenfield investments comprised only about 14 per cent of the total number of initiatives over the period 1986 to 2001, and less than 4 per cent in terms of employees.

Table 10.8. *A breakdown of employees of Italian affiliates of foreign parent companies by region, 1986, 1996 and 2002*

	January 1986		January 1996		January 2002	
	Number	Percentage share	Number	Percentage share	Number	Percentage share
North-west	302,734	65.1	336,479	64.3	382,268	62.3
North-east	60,141	12.9	81,282	15.5	111,302	18.1
Central Italy	68,112	14.7	64,054	12.3	81,399	13.3
South, Sicily and Sardinia	34,156	7.3	41,220	7.9	38,377	6.3
Total	465,143	100.0	523,035	100.0	613,346	100.0

Table 10.9. *The incidence of greenfield investments as a percentage of new foreign initiatives, 1986–2001*

	All new initiatives (a)		Greenfield investments (b)		(b)/(a) (per cent)	
	Affiliates	Employees	Affiliates	Employees	Affiliates	Employees
1986	68	14,887	20	1,719	29.4	11.5
1987	117	41,591	8	297	6.8	0.7
1988	146	29,312	15	949	10.3	3.2
1989	213	53,617	23	1,125	10.8	2.1
1990	200	34,349	43	2,166	21.5	6.3
1991	107	18,632	11	1,807	10.3	9.7
1992	105	17,118	17	800	16.2	4.7
1993	119	33,203	17	946	14.3	2.8
1994	131	30,787	14	809	10.7	2.6
1995	131	44,457	23	1,169	17.6	2.6
1996	188	38,632	25	2,251	13.3	5.8
1997	128	17,194	16	1,007	12.5	5.9
1998	146	25,304	20	1,920	13.7	7.6
1999	151	32,613	30	1,519	19.9	4.7
2000	151	70,097	18	200	11.9	0.3
2001	79	14,565	8	262	10.1	1.8

3.   The effects of inward FDI on the host country's performance and local firms' productivity

The impact of inward investment on the host economy has raised considerable interest within the theoretical and empirical literature, owing to the increasing role played by MNEs as engines of growth and technology diffusion. Such interest is borne out by the increasing number of incentives and measures put forward by policy-makers to attract MNEs and stimulate inward FDI.[4] The issue has to do with various aspects of the balance of payments, capital stock and resources, the transfer of profits, profitability and – above all – labour productivity and employment. Empirical studies consistently reveal that the impact of inward investment on the host economy stems partly from the existence of performance gaps between foreign-owned and domestically owned firms across countries and industries, over time and also at the plant level. In particular, two specific concerns have been raised.

---

[4] Hanson (2001) and UNCTAD (2001) report that, during the 1990s, about 135 countries relaxed constraints regarding FDI, and that 94 per cent of the 1,035 changes worldwide in the laws governing FDI created a more favourable framework for it.

First, whether foreign-owned firms are more efficient than domestically owned ones (McGuckin et al., 1995; Doms and Jensen, 1998; Girma et al., 2000; McGuckin and Nguyen, 2001). Most of the literature acknowledges that, according to the dominant theories of the multinational firm, foreign MNEs enjoy ownership advantages that allow them to compete successfully in the host country, thus making them more efficient than their domestic counterparts (for a survey, see Görg and Strobl, 2001). The reasons for performance differences between foreign-owned and domestically owned firms are nicely summarised by OECD (1996): in general, they are 'due to the technological and organisational advantages of the firms, which have the resources to operate internationally, the advanced industries in which they operate, and their larger average size'.

The second concern is whether foreign direct investment engenders positive or negative externalities for domestic factors of production (Globerman et al., 1994; Blomström and Kokko, 1998; Görg and Greenaway, 2001; Lipsey, 2002) so as to influence domestic plant productivity (Aitken and Harrison, 1999) and the turnover of domestic firms (Görg and Strobl, 2000). On the one hand, positive externalities occur if the entry and expansion of relatively efficient foreign firms (i) trigger the diffusion of technology and a managerial culture to host-country firms through movements of highly skilled staff from MNEs and the so-called 'demonstration effect', and (ii) encourage domestically owned firms to achieve comparable levels of productivity by enhancing competition and the search for greater X-efficiency (the 'competition effect'). On the other hand, competition may also reduce productivity in domestic firms because MNEs divert demand from their domestic competitors. This is called the 'market stealing effect', and induces negative spillovers on domestic firms (see Haddad and Harrison, 1993, in the case of Morocco, and Aitken and Harrison, 1999, in the case of Venezuela).

Empirical studies dealing with these research issues investigate the impact of foreign direct investment on labour or total factor productivity at the industry level (Caves, 1974; Globerman, 1975; Davies and Lyons, 1991; Driffield, 1996, 1999).

Empirical studies dealing with these research issues also investigate the impact of a foreign presence on labour or total factor productivity at the industry level (Caves, 1974; Globerman, 1975; Driffield, 1999; Dimelis and Louri, 2002). The evidence supporting the hypothesis that foreign-owned firms should engender improvements in the labour productivity level of the target company has already been provided with reference to the Anglo-American context. Concerning the United States, Doms and Jensen (1998) show that the labour productivity of plants owned by purely domestic firms is lower than that of both foreign-owned plants and plants owned by US multinational companies. With reference to the United Kingdom, Davies and Lyons (1991), Driffield (1996) and Girma et al. (2000) find that foreign-owned firms record higher productivity than domestically owned firms. Griffith and Simpson (2001) confirm such a result, as they find that labour productivity, investment per employee and wages further increase over time. Likewise, in analysing firm productivity and efficiency in Belgium, De Backer and Sleuwaegen (2002) find that foreign firms are significantly more productive than domestic ones.

Conyon et al. (2002a) provide a systematic empirical analysis of the impact of foreign ownership on productivity in the United Kingdom for the period 1989 to 1994, finding that firms that are acquired by foreign companies exhibit an increase in labour productivity of some 13 per cent in the four-year period covering the year prior to ownership change and the three years following the event. Finally, Pfaffermayr and Bellak (2000) corroborate the evidence with reference to 524 Austrian manufacturing firms between 1997 and 2000.[5]

Consistent with this extensive literature, we argue that a foreign acquisition engenders in the target local company a medium-term performance that is not necessarily worse, and indeed may be better, than what it would be otherwise (i.e. with no ownership change). While some of the most popular views on the effect of M&As highlight the likely downsizing of the workforce, some considerations should be added when considering a foreign acquiring company. The latter may on the one hand be less constrained and sensitive to host-government imperatives and reactions, and social pressures (Globerman et al., 1994), and therefore act on the local workforce more freely; on the other hand, foreign acquiring firms enjoy superior ownership of firm-specific assets that can be transferred to their affiliates.

These countervailing effects lead us to state that, when a local company undergoes an ownership change, its performance (in terms of labour productivity and employment level) does not necessarily worsen, especially when the acquirer is a foreign company. Specifically, the hypotheses submitted for empirical investigation are as follows.

Hypothesis 1: foreign acquisitions cause changes in the labour productivity of the target companies that are not necessarily worse, and

---

[5] It is worth acknowledging that some opposing evidence has been provided, for example by Girma and Görg (2001), recording that the event of a foreign takeover reduces employment growth, particularly for unskilled labour.

indeed can be better, than those that would occur without any ownership change.

Hypothesis 2: foreign acquisitions cause changes in the employment level of the target companies that are not necessarily worse, and indeed can be better, than those that would occur without any ownership change.

Furthermore, we expect the hypotheses to be more accurate for smaller target firms. Indeed, when the target company is relatively small, it is less likely to present the duplications and the potential for overlapping redundancies that rationalisation would certainly entail. Moreover, takeovers addressed towards smaller target companies are often driven by the desire to constitute them as 'launching pads', which generally need both additional assets and complementary resources, thus resulting in productivity and employment level improvements. Empirical evidence for that has been already provided, for example by McGuckin and Nguyen (2001). Indeed, with reference to a wide sample of US establishments between 1977 and 1987, they find that changes in the employment level and labour productivity due to the ownership change is significantly positive for small and medium plants, while the effect is significantly smaller for large plants. Therefore, a further hypothesis can be formulated:

Hypothesis 3: ceteris paribus, hypotheses 1 and 2 hold especially when foreign acquisitions target smaller firms.

The literature suggests that different effects may arise according to the bidder's home country (this is mostly a case of the United States differing from the rest of the world). Davies and Lyons (1991) point out that international productivity differentials between parent country and host country do matter. Oulton (1998) emphasises an additional productivity advantage for US affiliates in the United Kingdom of 9–20 per cent, and similar results are provided by Conyon et al. (2002a). In contrast, Globerman et al. (1994) find no significant difference between parent countries. Therefore, our hypothesis is stated as follows.

Hypothesis 4: the acquirer's home country may influence differently the target company's performance (in terms of labour productivity and employment level).

With specific reference to the Italian case, we do not have any a priori expectations of the differences between US as opposed to non-US (i.e. mainly European) acquiring companies. On the one hand, US MNEs may impact on the local target firm's labour productivity and employment less positively than European companies because they are likely (i) to be set on establishing in Italy just a bridgehead, which does not normally require any sequential investment; (ii) to adopt a wait-and-see attitude, which involves a slower adaptive learning vis-à-vis the local environment; and (iii) to be less sensitive to the local labour pressures. On the other hand, it is worth observing that acquisitions undertaken by US companies (i) may require lighter restructuring than those undertaken by European MNEs (being already in the European market, duplications are indeed more likely in the latter case); (ii) are more likely to be interested in the European market as a whole rather than in the local national market, and therefore more likely to expand their local presence rapidly; and (iii) are more likely to target smaller local companies, which generally learn and grow more rapidly in the local market.

Finally, as the efficiency improvements recorded in foreign affiliates may be due not only to superior efficiency but also to their participation in the multinational network of the parent company, we expect the same effects (i.e. hypotheses 1, 2 and 3) to be found when the target firm is acquired by an Italian MNE. Doms and Jensen (1998) find that foreign-owned plants are superior to US-owned plants of non-multinational firms, even large firms, in both labour productivity and Total Factor Productivity, but that they are behind plants owned by US multinationals. Likewise, Pfaffermayr and Bellak (2000) find, with reference to a sample of manufacturing firms in Austria, that marked differences exist between domestically owned firms that are not multinationals and foreign-owned firms, while foreign and domestic multinationals differ only marginally. Specifically, controlling for the most important determinants, they find evidence that the productivity gap and the profitability gap are not explained by foreign ownership per se, but that belonging to or operating within an MNE network is an important factor contributing to the gaps.

Accordingly, our last hypothesis can be formulated as follows.

Hypothesis 5: hypotheses 1 to 3 should hold even when the acquisition is due to a domestic MNE.

4.   An empirical analysis of the Italian case: methodology and data

4.1   The methodology

This chapter aims to investigate the impact of foreign acquisition upon the local target company, namely whether the ownership change induces any significant variation in its labour productivity and employment level.

We purpose to evaluate the impact of the ownership change in the medium term, by investigating what would happen in the absence of such a change. In order to do this, we compare labour productivity and employment dynamics for firms that have experienced acquisitions with the same dynamics for firms that have not undergone any acquisition at all in the same period (which, therefore, constitute the control sample). Similar procedures, consisting of comparing 'like with like', have been applied to investigating the effects of domestic ownership changes on employment and wages, for example by Lichtenberg and Siegel (1987), Armington and Robb (1988) and Brown and Medoff (1988). In order to define 'similar' firms, we take into account the caveats highlighted by the recent empirical literature, of which three, in particular, stand out.

First, multinational entrants may be attracted to more productive and/or more profitable industries (e.g. Dunning, 1985), thus leading to a spurious observed relationship between ownership changes and the productivity levels of target firms in cross-sectional studies. Second, since establishments changing owners are normally smaller than those not changing owners, in the absence of any effect from ownership change on employment growth one would expect the former to exhibit higher employment growth (Lichtenberg and Siegel, 1992; McGuckin and Nguyen, 2001; Conyon et al., 2002a). Indeed, it is well known that there is a strong negative correlation between the initial size of firms and their subsequent growth rates (Hall, 1987). Third technological progress may also impact upon a firm's performance and productivity during the period of a takeover. Therefore, it is necessary to control for the effect of time in order to rule out idiosyncrasies in particular periods.

The methodology we employ tries to circumvent these three sources of bias. Operationally, we proceed in the following way:

$A_{ij}^{t_0}$ is a firm, belonging to the dimensional class i and to the industrial sector j, which has been acquired at time t_0;

$i = 1, 2, \ldots. 7$ are the dimensional classes (in terms of employees) as defined by the Italian National Institute for Statistics;[6]

$j = 1, \ldots. 59$ refer to the three-digit industrial classification Ateco 91;

$t_0 = 1993, 1994, 1995, 1996, 1997$.

To each firm $A_{ij}^{t_0}$ there has been associated a domestically owned firm (randomly selected from the set $[I_{ij}^{t_0}]$) that is 'similar' to the former.

Following the three aforementioned caveats, similarity has been defined in terms of (i) industry, (ii) dimensional features and (iii) interval period. Therefore, the main difference between the two samples of firms is that the former have undergone an acquisition while the latter have not experienced any ownership change in the period considered.

---

[6] The seven classes are these: 1–19; 20–49; 50–99; 100–199; 200–499; 500–999; ≥1,000 employees.

Then we calculate percentage changes in labour productivity (measured by value added per employee) and employment level (measured by the number of employees) in the medium term – i.e. in a T-year interval, with T = 2, 3, 4 after the acquisition (which occurred at t_0) – as follows:

$$LPROD_{T\_}A_{ij} = \{[LPROD_A ij^{t_0+T} - LPROD_A ij^{t_0}]/LPROD_A ij^{t_0}\} * 100$$

and

$$EMP_T A_{ij} = \{[EMP_A ij^{t_0+T} - EMP_A ij^{t_0}]/EMP_A ij^{t_0}\} * 100$$

These variables have been compared (through a paired t-test) to the analogous changes occurring in the control firms – i.e. the national firms (I_{ij}) that have not undergone any ownership change in the same time interval $t_0 - t_{0+T}$ but that present a (sectoral and dimensional) similar profile to firm A_{ij}:

$$LPROD_{T\_}I_{ij} = \{[LPROD_I ij^{t_0+T} - LPROD_I ij^{t_0}]/LPROD_I ij^{t_0}\} * 100$$

and

$$EMP_{T\_}I_{ij} = \{[EMP_I ij^{t_0+T} - EMP_I ij^{t_0}]/EMP_I ij^{t_0}\} * 100$$

The null hypothesis is

$$H_0 : [LPROD_{T\_}A_{ij} - PROD_{T\_}I_{ij}] \leq 0$$

Therefore, as rejecting the null hypothesis allows us to accept the alternative one (i.e. $[LPROD_{T\_}A_{ij} - LPROD_{T\_}I_{ij}] > 0$), we could in this case assert that the percentage change in labour productivity (and the employment level) for firms that have undergone an acquisition is higher than the change for their domestic counterparts that have not experienced any ownership change. It may not be out of place here to make it clear that, as the percentage changes may assume both positive and negative values, rejecting the null hypothesis implies that (i) when the labour productivity (and employment) change is positive, it increases more in firms that have undergone the ownership change, and (ii) when the change is negative, it decreases less for firms that have undergone the ownership change.

4.2   The data

This chapter considers acquisitions of domestic firms in the Italian manufacturing industry throughout the 1990s. Specifically, in order to disentangle the effects of ownership changes due to the foreign entry, we have tried to account for performance changes associated with a change in ownership per se (Brown and Medoff, 1988; Conyon et al., 2002b). To this end we employ a panel design that allows for firms subject to domestic acquisitions and those subject to no ownership changes to be used as controls. The firm-level data[7] used come from a unique database that was obtained by merging four data sources:

(i)   the Reprint database, for foreign acquisitions;
(ii) the database on M&As developed by the public stock corporation Nomisma, for domestic acquisitions. Specifically, Nomisma records more than 19,000 acquisitions undertaken by Italian companies from 1983 onwards;
(iii) the Central Balance Sheet Office, collecting the annual reports of all firms active in Italian manufacturing; and
(iv) the Aida database, recording financial and market data for more than 120,000 Italian firms from 1992 onwards.

Specifically, as our purpose is to investigate the medium-term impact (i.e. t_0+2, t_0+3 and t_0+4), we consider acquisitions that occurred in the five-year period from 1993 to 1997.

In order to isolate the effects of individual acquisitions, and partly to avoid the probable presence of measurement error problems, it was necessary to exclude those firms that suffered multiple acquisitions within the period analysed. Only acquisitions of the target company's majority ownership share have been considered. Additionally, since our aim is to study the effect of the change of ownership on labour productivity in the medium term, we screen the data for the availability of employment, wages and output for at least two years after the acquisition.

The final sample thus consists of 176 foreign and 121 domestic acquisitions, the yearly frequency distribution of which is illustrated in table 10.10. Accordingly, the control samples are constituted by 176 and 121 domestically owned firms that did not experience any ownership change in the period considered. Table 10.11 illustrates the average characteristics of Italian firms at the time of their acquisition (i.e. at t_0). It is worth observing that, although firms targeted by foreign bidders appear consistently smaller (both in terms of employment and value added) than those acquired by national companies, importantly, their labour productivity does not show significant differences.

[7] It is worth observing that, while most of the theoretical arguments refer to firm or company level, empirical analysis is often on the plant level. As plant-level analysis generally excludes spillovers between plants of the same company (an exception is that by Maliranta, 1997) and the advantages related to the MNE network, our analysis is run at the firm level.

Table 10.10. *The yearly frequency distribution of the acquisitions in the sample, 1993–1997*

	Domestic acquisitions		Foreign acquisitions	
	Number	Frequency (per cent)	Number	Frequency (per cent)
1993	11	9.09	17	9.66
1994	17	14.05	28	15.91
1995	28	23.14	28	15.91
1996	29	23.97	67	38.07
1997	36	29.75	36	20.45
Total	121	100.00	176	100.00

Table 10.11. *Descriptive statistics of the sample at* t_0

Acquirer company	Size (number of employees)	Value added (euros thousand)	Labour productivity (value added per employee)
Foreign			
Mean	132.00	6,052	54.30
Standard deviation	130.74	6,076	42.67
Min	5	−1,994	−12.01
Max	774	31,091	345.59
Domestic			
Mean	374.27	28,278	61.98
Standard deviation	1,428.95	149,478	84.45
Min	3	−3,862	−18.39
Max	11,806	1,419,826	811.67

5.   Empirical findings

Table 10.12 reports the results of paired t-tests for hypotheses 1 and 2 –
i.e. for the labour productivity and employment rate growth in the
medium term after the acquisition (t_0+2, t_0+3, t_0+4). They show that
the target company's labour productivity increases after the acquisition
by a foreign MNE; this increase is more than 50 per cent in the medium
term (t_0+2, t_0+3, t_0+4); additionally, it is never worse than the change
that occurred in 'similar' firms that did not undergo any ownership
change (the null hypothesis can be rejected at $p < 0.01$). Likewise, the
percentage change in the employment level goes from 21.5 per cent

Table 10.12. *Percentage changes in the target company's labour productivity and employment (paired t-test values)*

Foreign acquirer company	t_0+2	t_0+3	t_0+4
Observations	171	154	97
Labour productivity			
sample	58.1	65.2	54.9
Control sample	10.3	7.6	14.1
Paired *t*-test	$(2.660)^a$	$(3.321)^a$	$(3.209)^a$
Employment			
Sample	21.5	27.9	35.8
Control sample	6.7	10.7	13.4
Paired *t*-test	$(2.435)^a$	$(2.164)^b$	$(2.311)^b$
Domestic acquirer company	t_0+2	t_0+3	t_0+4
Observations	120	102	55
Labour productivity			
Sample	20.5	35.6	25.8
Control sample	9.4	18.6	7.2
Paired *t*-test	(1.055)	(1.097)	$(1.490)^c$
Employment			
Sample	13.6	16.3	17.9
Control sample	13.7	12.3	11.9
Paired *t*-test	(-0.210)	(0.557)	(0.607)

[a] H_0 can be rejected at $p < 0.01$.
[b] H_0 can be rejected at $p < 0.05$.
[c] H_0 can be rejected at $p < 0.10$.

(in t_0+2) to 35.8 per cent in t_0+4, and it is never worse than that recorded for the control sample firms (the null hypothesis can be rejected at least at $p < 0.05$).

The post-acquisition dynamics of the employment level suggests that the labour productivity improvement may have been brought about as a result of a more efficient use of labour rather than through downsizing. Specifically, according to the MNE theory, foreign firms have competitive advantages (ownership advantages) that make them more efficient than local indigenous companies. Controlling for the effects induced by domestic acquisition, we find evidence that the productivity increase is not explained by ownership change per se, but that ownership change due to the foreign entry is an important factor. Indeed, the average increase in the target's labour productivity after the domestic acquisition appears not to be significantly different from that recorded for non-acquired firms. Concerning the employment level, we could not reject the null hypothesis that changes in the employment level induced by domestic acquisitions in the target firms are lower than changes without acquisition.

When investigating the effects upon target companies according to their different dimensional classes, table 10.13 confirms our hypothesis 3 – i.e. hypotheses 1 and 2 hold especially for smaller firms (1–49

Table 10.13. *Post-ownership changes in labour productivity and employment by dimensional classes for foreign acquirer companies (paired t-test values)*

Foreign acquirer company	t_0+2	t_0+3	t_0+4
1–49			
Observations	52	45	29
Labour productivity			
Sample	40.6	52.8	21.1
Control sample	16.2	4.2	2.3
Paired t-test	(0.736)	(2.155)[a]	(1.318)[b]
Employment			
Sample	58.8	71.7	86.2
Control sample	8.9	11.5	19.3
Paired t-test	(2.815)[c]	(2.479)[c]	(2.596)[c]
50–249			
Observations	93	60	52
Labour productivity			
Sample	66.8	76.8	75.5
Control sample	7.3	7.6	22.5
Paired t-test	(2.327)[a]	(2.102)[a]	(2.527)[c]
Employment			
Sample	5.1	11.3	20.6
Control sample	6.5	15.9	11.3
Paired t-test	(−0.339)	(−0.739)	(1.112)
>249			
Observations	26	49	16
Labour productivity			
Sample	62.0	62.3	49.5
Control sample	8.9	10.7	8.1
Paired t-test	(1.458)[b]	(1.676)[a]	(1.624)[b]
Employment			
Sample	5.5	8.2	6.1
Control sample	3.0	3.5	9.7
Paired t-test	(0.483)	(0.807)	(0.997)

[a] H_0 can be rejected at $p < 0.05$.
[b] H_0 can be rejected at $p < 0.10$.
[c] H_0 can be rejected at $p < 0.01$.

employees). Indeed, when smaller firms are taken over by foreign companies their labour productivity does not decrease, and the effect on the employment level is even more significant as the null hypothesis can be rejected at $p < 0.01$. For the larger target companies, their labour productivity increase is more likely to stem from rationalisation and restructuring. As hypothesis 3 can be rejected when the acquisition is undertaken by domestic bidders (table 10.14), this confirms again that it is not the ownership change per se that matters but multinationality.

Table 10.14. *Post-ownership changes in labour productivity and employment by dimensional classes for domestic acquirer companies (paired t-test values)*

Domestic acquirer company	t_0+2	t_0+3	t_0+4
1–49			
Observations	25	22	11
Labour productivity			
Sample	−1.3	50.6	32.1
Control sample	−1.0	−13.5	−4.3
Paired t-test	(−0.270)	(1.804)[a]	(2.641)[a]
Employment			
Sample	40.4	49.3	67.5
Control sample	24.5	34.7	22.7
Paired t-test	(1.015)	(0.614)	(1.268)
50–249			
Observations	65	54	25
Labour productivity			
Sample	29.4	45.3	30.3
Control sample	13.9	34.3	3.2
Paired t-test	(0.850)	(0.454)	(1.124)
Employment			
Sample	9.0	9.7	7.9
Control sample	14.3	6.4	8.7
Paired t-test	(−0.579)	(0.377)	(−0.73)
>249			
Observations	30	26	19
Labour productivity			
Sample	19.5	2.8	16.2
Control sample	8.1	13.1	19.1
Paired t-test	(0.955)	(−0.691)	(−0.191)
Employment			
Sample	1.0	2.0	2.5
Control sample	3.3	5.6	10.0
Paired t-test	(−0.342)	(−0.453)	(−0.589)

[a]H_0 can be rejected at $p < 0.05$.

Table 10.15. *Post-ownership changes in labour productivity and employment by the acquirer company's country of origin (paired t-test values)*

Foreign acquirer company	t_0+2	t_0+3	t_0+4
EU acquisitions			
Observations	115	106	64
Labour productivity			
Sample	78.0	73.1	63.3
Control sample	11.9	8.7	18.3
Paired t-test	$(2.627)^a$	$(2.774)^a$	$(2.697)^a$
Employment			
Sample	23.6	32.9	39.4
Control sample	6.0	11.6	13.3
Paired t-test	$(2.513)^a$	$(1.918)^b$	$(2.476)^a$
US acquisitions			
Observations	48	41	29
Labour productivity			
Sample	33.2	50.8	51.7
Control sample	6.0	3.1	5.9
Paired t-test	$(2.345)^b$	$(2.071)^b$	$(2.570)^a$
Employment			
Sample	17.0	17.6	32.4
Control sample	9.9	11.4	17.6
Paired t-test	(0.524)	(0.752)	(0.648)

[a] H_0 can be rejected at $p < 0.01$.
[b] H_0 can be rejected at $p < 0.05$.

Consistent with other empirical studies (such as those by Globerman et al., 1994, Oulton, 1998, and Conyon et al., 2002a), we discriminate between acquisitions by firms from the United States and from the European Union.[8] The results for our hypothesis 4 are given in table 10.15. Specifically, an increase in productivity is observed for both US and EU acquisitions, although it is higher for the latter. The null hypothesis can be significantly rejected for both of them, thus meaning that they both induce improvements in labour productivity (as compared with firms that did not experience any ownership change). However, so far as the employment level is concerned, only European acquisitions seem to induce increases that are significantly higher than the control

---

[8] As with Conyon et al. (2002a), this tricotomisation of foreign acquisitions was essentially driven by the preponderance of EU and US acquirers. Unfortunately, the number of acquirers from Japan, the country most obviously associated with distinctively different work practices, was too small for meaningful analysis.

sample ones. The null hypothesis can indeed be rejected at least at $p < 0.05$. As mentioned in section 3, these results may be due to the fact that US MNEs are certainly less sensitive to the local labour pressures and also likely to set up just a bridgehead in Italy, which does not normally require any sequential investment and adopt a wait-and-see attitude, which involves a slower adaptive learning vis-à-vis the local environment.

6.   Summary and conclusions

After a prolonged post-war period of remarkable foreign ownership penetration, in the last two decades Italy has lost its leading position as a recipient of worldwide inward FDI. At the beginning of the new millennium Italy ranks about thirteenth regarding the stock, and twenty-first regarding flows, of inward FDI. The share of industrial employment belonging to foreign-owned companies (18 per cent) is much smaller than what we may observe in other major European countries, with the exception of Germany, which partly reflects the impact of reunification. Recent flows of inward FDI have been mainly directed towards smaller companies, as witnessed by the growth in the number of foreign affiliates (which is far higher than the growth in employment in the same foreign subsidiaries). Greenfield investment plays only a minor role, as in most developed areas of destination. The sectoral composition is characterised by a low and decreasing share of FDI in high-tech industries.

This chapter presents some results on the impact of foreign ownership on labour productivity and employment. To avoid the standard caveats concerning the interpretation of these comparisons, we have performed a series of paired t-tests between samples of companies that were subject to a change in ownership compared to an appropriate sample of companies that did not experience any change of ownership, controlling for firm size and sector.

Compared to firms that were not subject to any ownership change, companies targeted by foreign investors recorded an increase in both labour productivity and employment level a few years after the acquisition. This result holds especially if the target firm is a small firm and if the investor is a European MNE.

The major policy conclusion of our analysis, should one try to reach one from a study that by no means has an explicit policy orientation, is quite obvious: far from being a source of job-cutting strategies in the exclusive interests of foreign capital, foreign ownership is likely to bring long-lasting benefits to the recipient country in terms of job creation and competitiveness. Policies aimed at attracting foreign investors may therefore work in favour of both the quantity and the quality of the domestic labour force.

REFERENCES

Aitken, B. J., and A. E. Harrison (1999), 'Do domestic firms benefit from direct foreign investment? Evidence from Venezuela', *American Economic Review*, 89 (3), 605–18.

Armington, C., and A. Robb (1998), *Mergers and Acquisitions in the United States: 1990–1994*, Research Paper no. 98/15, *Center for Economic Studies*, US Bureau of the Census, Washington, DC.

Blomström, M., and A. Kokko (1998), 'Multinational corporations and spillovers', *Journal of Economic Surveys*, 12, 247–77.

Brown, G., and J. Medoff (1988), 'The impact of firm acquisition on labor', in A. J. Auerbach (ed.) *Corporate Takeovers: Causes and Consequences*, University of Chicago Press, London and Chicago, 9–25.

Bugamelli, M. (2001), *Il modello di specializzazione internazionale dell'area dell'euro e dei principali paesi europei: omogeneità e convergenza*, Temi di discussione no. 402, Banca d'Italia, Rome.

Caves, R. (1974), *Multinational Enterprise and Economic Analysis*, Cambridge University Press, Cambridge.

Centro Europa Ricerche (1999), *Le imprese, gli investimenti e le politiche pubbliche*, Rapporto VI, Rome.

Conyon, M. J., S. Girma, S. Thompson and P. W. Wright (2002a), 'The productivity and wage effect of foreign acquisition in the United Kingdom', *Journal of Industrial Economics*, 50, 85–102.

(2002b), 'The impact of mergers and acquisitions on company employment', *European Economic Review*, 46, 31–49.

Davies, S. W., and B. R. Lyons (1991), 'Characterising relative performance: the productivity advantage of foreign-owned firms in the UK', *Oxford Economic Papers*, 43, 584–95.

De Backer, K., and L. Sleuwaegen (2002), *Why are Foreign Firms more Productive than Domestic Firms?* paper presented at the 28th annual conference of the European Academy of International Business, 8–10 December, Athens.

Dimelis, S., and H. Louri (2002), 'Foreign ownership and production efficiency: a quantile regression analysis', *Oxford Economic Papers*, 54, 449–69.

Doms, M., and J. B. Jensen (1998), 'Comparing wages, skills, and productivity between domestically and foreign-owned manufacturing establishments in the United States', in: R. E. Baldwin, R. E. Lipsey and J. D. Richardson (eds.) *Geography and Ownership as Bases for Economic Accounting*, Studies in Income and Wealth no. 59, National Bureau of Economic Research, Cambridge, MA, 235–55.

Driffield, N. (1996), *Global Competition and the Labour Market*, Harwood, Reading.

(1999), 'Indirect employment effects of foreign direct investment into the UK', *Bulletin of Economic Research*, 51 (3), 207–21.

Dunning, J. H. (1985), 'The United Kingdom', in: J. M. Dunning (ed.) *Multinational Enterprises, Economic Structure and International Competitiveness*, John Wiley, Chichester, 13–56.

Girma, S., and H. Gorg (2001), *Blessing or Curse? Domestic Plant Survival and Employment Prospects after Foreign Acquisition*, Research Paper no. 2001/18, Leverhulme Centre for Research on Globalisation and Economic Policy, University of Nottingham.

Girma, S., D. Greenaway, K. Wakelin and N. Sousa (2000), 'Host country effects of FDI in the UK: recent evidence from firm-level data', in N. Pain (ed.) *Inward Investment, Technological Change and Growth: The Impact of Multinational Corporations on the UK Economy*, Palgrave, London, 104–21.

Globerman, S. (1975), 'Technological diffusion in the Canadian tool and dye industry', *Review of Economics and Statistics*, 57 (4), 428–44.

Globerman, S., J. C. Ries and I. Vertinsky (1994), 'The economic performance of foreign affiliates in Canada', *Canadian Journal of Economics*, 27 (1), 143–56.

Görg, H., and D. Greenaway (2001), *Foreign Direct Investment and Intra-Industry Spillovers: A Review of the Literature*, Research Paper no. 2001/37, Leverhulme Centre for Research on Globalisation and Economic Policy, University of Nottingham.

Görg, H., and E. Strobl (2000), *Multinational Companies and Indigenous Development: An Empirical Analysis*, Research Paper no. 2000/22, Leverhulme Centre for Research on Globalisation and Economic Policy, University of Nottingham.

(2001), 'Multinational companies and productivity spillovers: a meta-analysis', *Economic Journal*, 111, 723–39.

Griffith, R., and H. Simpson (2001), *Characteristics of Foreign-owned Firms in British Manufacturing*, Working Paper no. 10, Institute for Fiscal Studies, London.

Haddad, M., and A. E. Harrison (1993), 'Are there positive spillovers from direct foreign investment?', *Journal of Development Economics*, 42, 51–74.

Hall, B. H. (1987), 'The relationship between firm size and firm growth in the US manufacturing sector', *Journal of Industrial Economics*, 35, 583–606.

Hanson, G. H. (2001), *Should Countries promote Foreign Direct Investment?*, G-24 Discussion Paper no. 9, United Nations Conference on Trade and Development, New York and Geneva.

Lichtenberg, F. R., and D. Siegel (1987), 'Productivity and changes in ownership of manufacturing plants', *Brookings Papers on Economic Activity*, 3, 643–73.

(1992), 'Productivity and changes in ownership of manufacturing plants', in: F. R. Lichtenberg (ed.) *Corporate Takeovers and Productivity*, MIT Press, Cambridge, MA, 25–43.

Lipsey, R. E. (2002), *Home and Host Country Effects of Foreign Direct Investment*, paper presented at conference on Challenges to Globalisation, 24–25 May, Lidingo, Sweden.

Maliranta, M. (1997), *Plant Productivity in Finnish Manufacturing*, Discussion Paper no. 612, Research Institute of the Finnish Economy, Helsinki.

Mariotti, S., and M. Mutinelli (2002), *L'internazionalizzazione della produzione: un confronto tra Italia e principali Paesi industrializzati*, in: G. Galli and

L. Paganetto (eds.) *La competitività dell'Italia*, Vol. II, *Le imprese*, Il Sole 24 Ore, Milan.

McGuckin, R. H., and S. V. Nguyen (2001), 'The impact of ownership changes: a view from labour markets', *International Journal of Industrial Organisation*, 19, 739–62.

McGuckin, R. H., S. V. Nguyen and A. P. Reznek (1995), *The Impact of Ownership Change on Employment, Wages and Labour Productivity in US Manufacturing 1977–87*, Research paper no. 95–8, Center for Economic Studies, US Bureau of the Census, Washington, DC.

Organisation for Economic Co-operation and Development (1996), *Globalisation of Industry*, OECD, Paris.

Oulton, N. (1998), *Investment, Capital and Foreign Ownership in UK Manufacturing*, Discussion Paper no. 141, National Institute of Economic and Social Research, London.

Pavitt, K. (1984), 'Sectoral patterns of technical change: towards a taxonomy and a theory', *Research Policy*, 13 (6), 343–73.

Pfaffermayr, M., and C. Bellak (2000), *Why Foreign-owned Firms are Different: A Conceptual Framework and Empirical Evidence from Austria*, Discussion Paper no. 115, Hamburg Institute of International Economics, Hamburg.

United Nations Conference on Trace and Development (2000), *World Investment Report 2000: Cross-Border Mergers and Acquisitions and Development*, United Nations, New York and Geneva.

 (2001), *World Investment Report 2001: Promoting Linkages*, United Nations, New York and Geneva.

 (2002), *World Investment Report 2002: Transnational Corporations and Export Competitiveness*, United Nations, New York and Geneva.

Author index

335

Subject index

accounting standards 120, 122, 138
Aga 12
Aker Yards 257
ALMI (Swedish Business Development
    Agency) 213, 236
Amadeus database, evidence of FDI
    110–13, 120, 131, 135
Andritz 257
anti-director rights 120, 122, 138
anti-takeover statutes 51
AP Funds 217
ASEA 231, 254, 257
Assa Abloy 257
asset export taxation 4
asset holding 9, 125, 136–8
Atlas Copco 235

banking law 281
    in Sweden 213
banks, international 117
    tax payments 130
Belgium, golden shares 28–9
Benedetti, Carlo de 52
Big Bang 297
BIS Study Group on Fixed Income
    Markets 140
bond funds 146–7
break-through rule 7, 32–5, 54, 62–6
    ownership and control of target firm 36
Britain in Europe 278
British Airports Authority, UK special
    share 29
British Household Panel Survey 100
Brown Boveri 231
Brown, Gordon 295
Bureau of Economic Analysis (BEA) 81–4,
    86–8
Business for Sterling 278
business judgement rule 51

capital, export of 279–80
    exchange controls 280, 295

capital market integration 174
capital mobility
    extension to third countries 17–19
    and Maastricht 1, 7, 17
    and policy-making 4–6
    restrictions on 7
capital supply, in Sweden 207–8, 217
    categories of 207, 220
    foreign 212, 214, 230
    stock market trends 209, 220–2, 238
Carlsberg 257
cars, UK production 296–7
central bank independence 281, 295
Centro Europa Ricerche (CER) 311
Chamberlain, Joseph, tariff reform 304
Chrysler 296
City Code on Takeovers and Mergers 45,
    47–8, 52, 68
City of London, and foreign investment
    297–8, 301, 305
Codetermination Act 218
Colonial Act (1900) 280
Community air carriers 23
Community shipowners 23
company law in European Union,
    ownership and control structures 33
competition effect 261, 319
competition policy, in Maastricht
    Treaty 23
Confederation of Finnish Industry and
    Employers 271
Conservative Party (UK) 290
    and foreign investment 283–4
consumption correlations, and real
    business cycle theory 179
consumption smoothing 10
    through saving 178–9
control blocks, see shares
controlling minority shareholders 42
corporate assets
    dispersion of ownership 41–2
    private market for 38

Printed in the United States
By Bookmasters